ROBERT FROST

Bibliography

T. E. Lawrence: A Bibliography
Catalogue of the Library of the Late Siegfried Sassoon
George Orwell: An Annotated Bibliography of Criticism

Edited Collections

George Orwell: The Critical Heritage
Hemingway: The Critical Heritage
Robert Lowell: Interviews and Memoirs

Edited Original Essays

Wyndham Lewis *by Roy Campbell*
Wyndham Lewis: A Revaluation
D. H. Lawrence and Tradition
The Legacy of D. H. Lawrence
The Craft of Literary Biography
The Biographer's Art
T. E. Lawrence: Soldier, Writer, Legend
Graham Greene: A Revaluation

ROBERT FROST

A Biography

Jeffrey Meyers

A Peter Davison Book

A MARINER BOOK

HOUGHTON MIFFLIN COMPANY

BOSTON   NEW YORK

For information about permission to reproduce selections from
this book, write to Permissions, Houghton Mifflin Company,
215 Park Avenue South, New York, New York 10003.

For information about this and other Houghton Mifflin trade and reference
books and multimedia products, visit The Bookstore at Houghton Mifflin
on the World Wide Web at http://www.hmco.com/trade/.

Library of Congress Cataloging-in-Publication Data
Meyers, Jeffrey.
  Robert Frost : a biography / Jeffrey Meyers.
    p. cm.
  "A Peter Davison book."
  Includes bibliographical references and index.
  ISBN 0-395-72809-6
  ISBN 0-395-85603-5 (pbk.)
    1. Frost, Robert, 1874–1963 — Biography. 2. Poets,
American — 20th century — Biography.   I. Title.
PS3511.R94Z788   1996
811'.52 — dc20   95-45647
[B]   CIP

Printed in the United States of America

QUM 10 9 8 7 6 5 4 3 2 1

The author is grateful to Henry Holt and Company for permission to reprint the following:
Selected excerpts of Frost's poetry taken from *The Poetry of Robert Frost,* edited by Edward
Connery Lathem. Copyright © 1969 by Henry Holt and Co. Selected excerpts from various
letters written by Robert Frost taken from *Selected Letters of Robert Frost,* edited by Lawrance
Thompson. Copyright © 1964 by Lawrance Thompson and Henry Holt and Co., Copy-
right © 1992 by Janet Arnold Thompson. Selected excerpts from various letters from
Robert Frost to Louis Untermeyer taken from *The Letters of Robert Frost to Louis Untermeyer.*
Copyright © 1963 by Louis Untermeyer, © 1991 by Laurence S. Untermeyer. Selected quotations taken from *Selected Prose of Robert Frost,* edited by Hyde Cox and Edward Connery
Lathem. Copyright 1949, 1954, © 1966 by Henry Holt and Co., copyright 1946, © 1959 by
Robert Frost, copyright © 1956 by the Estate of Robert Frost. Selected quotations taken
from *Robert Frost Poetry & Prose,* edited by Edward Connery Lathem and Lawrance Thompson. Copyright © 1972 by Henry Holt and Co.

Contents

Illustrations

Isabelle Moodie Frost, 1876 *(Estate of Robert Lee Frost)*

William Prescott Frost, Jr., 1872 *(Harvard University Archives)*

Robert and Jeanie Frost, c. 1879 *(Estate of Robert Lee Frost)*

Jeanie Frost, c. 1900

Elinor White at the time of her marriage, December 1895 *(Estate of Robert Lee Frost)*

Robert Frost at the time of his marriage, December 1895 *(Dartmouth College Library)*

Lesley, Carol, Marjorie and Irma Frost, Plymouth, New Hampshire, 1911 *(Estate of Robert Lee Frost)*

John Bartlett, 1910

Sidney Cox in army uniform, c. 1917 *(Courtesy of William Evans)*

Louis Untermeyer, c. 1950 *(Lotte Jacobi)*

Frost in England, 1913 *(Dartmouth College Library)*

Ezra Pound, London, c. 1910 *(Bodleian Library)*

Edward Thomas in dejection, 1907 *(Courtesy of Myfanwy Thomas)*

The Frost family, New Hampshire, 1915. Elinor, Robert, Lesley, Irma, Marjorie, Carol *(Courtesy of the Herbert H. Lamson Library, Plymouth State College, Plymouth, New Hampshire)*

Frost, 1920s *(Courtesy of Peter Davison)*

Acknowledgments

Biography is a cooperative venture, and I am pleased to acknowledge the generous assistance I received while writing this book. My perceptive editor, Peter Davison, gave me valuable encouragement, aid and advice. Other friends were also extremely helpful. Phillip Knightley drove me to Frost's house in Gloucestershire and Ian Hamilton gave me copies of Lawrance Thompson's letters to Frost. Alfredo Bonadeo, Thomas Clayton, Quentin Curtis, Bill Daleski, Philip Gura, Barbara Hill, Katherine Powers and Jon Stallworthy sent useful information. Mary and Howard Berg, Jackson and Mary Bryer once again provided splendid hospitality while I was working in Boston and Washington.

For personal interviews I would like to thank: Richard Allen, Stanley Burnshaw, Armour Craig, Peter Davison, Denis Donoghue, Richard Eberhart, Lesley Lee Francis, Lillian LaBatt Frost and Nicholas Frost, Jack Hagstrom, Robin and David Hudnut, Edward Connery Lathem, William Meredith and Richard Harteis, Adrienne Rich, William Jay Smith, Anne Morrison Smyth, Ann Chalmers Watts, Richard and Charlee Wilbur; for telephone conversations: Daniel Aaron, Mary Johnston Colfelt, Harold Cone, Richard Emeny, Will Gahagen, Bessie Jones, Elena Levin, Geoffrey Moore, Myfanwy Thomas, Elinor Wilber.

For letters about Frost I am grateful to: Frederick Adams, Sir Isaiah Berlin, Joseph Brodsky, Gordon Brown, Richard Calhoun, John Cone, Hyde Cox, Alfred Edwards, Valerie Eliot, William Evans, David Foster, Doris Foster, Walker Gibson, Peter Gilbert, Allen Ginsberg, Donald Hall, Mark Harris, Anthony Hecht, Shalom Kahn, Justin Kaplan, Sandra Katz, X. J. Kennedy, Beatrice Lewis, James Merrill, Ray Mise, Helen Muir, Richard Poirier, Franklin Reeve, Louise Reichert, Alastair Reid, Helga Sandburg, Charles Schulz, Andrei Sergeev, Karl Shapiro, Donald

Sheehy, W. D. Snodgrass, Sir Stephen Spender, Janet Thompson, Diana Trilling, Stewart Udall and Douglas Wilson.

I read Frost's papers and was helped by the librarians at Amherst College, University of California, Berkeley, Dartmouth College, Harvard University, Jones Library in Amherst, National Archives and Stanford University. I also received copies of Frost's letters from Agnes Scott College, Boston University, Cambridge University, University of Chicago, Connecticut College, Hebrew University of Jerusalem, Huntington Library, Johns Hopkins University, King's College, Cambridge, Library of Congress, University of Michigan and Bentley Historical Library, Middlebury College, National University of Ireland, University of New Hampshire, New York Public Library, New York University, Oxford University, Plymouth State College, Princeton University, University of Reading, St. Lawrence University, State University of New York at Buffalo, University of Texas, Tufts University, University of Vermont, Wellesley College (and Alumnae Association), Wesleyan University and Yale University; and other information from various institutions: Bryn Mawr College Archives, Guggenheim Foundation (Thomas Tanselle), Israeli Embassy, Robert Frost Books, Syracuse University Press, U. S. Information Agency, U. S. State Department and *Xavier Review*. Hearing Frost read, toward the end of his life, at Michigan and Harvard, gave me firsthand knowledge of his extraordinary ability to command an audience.

As always, my wife, Valerie Meyers, scrutinized and improved each chapter and compiled the index.

I urge the interested reader to keep Frost's poems at hand while perusing this book. Permission to quote from Frost's unpublished letters and manuscripts and from *Interviews with Robert Frost* was kindly granted by Peter Gilbert, Executor of the Estate of Robert Frost.

Preface

Anyone interested in exploring the relationship between Robert Frost's poetry and life must confront the three-volume biography by Lawrance Thompson. The second volume was awarded the Pulitzer Prize in 1970 and the book was universally praised for its exhaustive detail — the record of Thompson's dedication to Frost. But it was also clear to every reader that the work expressed bitter resentment of its subject, distorted the meaning of the life and obscured our understanding of the poetry.

As a young man Thompson became fascinated by Frost's complex work and enigmatic personality. As Frost came to be revered as a wise and rugged cultural figure, Thompson's role as official biographer enhanced his academic career. Thompson gathered material for twenty-five years. But what began as an academic interest in an already elderly and never robust poet became a tense and uneasy relationship with a famous and cranky octogenarian. Frost evaded many of his biographer's questions and resented his dogged pursuit. Thompson, who often performed the duties of a servant, grew to dislike him intensely and took revenge in his biography. Thompson also competed with Frost by writing his life while he was living it. Because he participated in and even influenced the life he was recording, and became so emotionally caught up in the details of Frost's existence, Thompson had little sympathy for his subject. His book included a great deal of trivial information and merely presented his massive accumulation of facts instead of explaining what they meant. He knew too much and understood too little.

Despite its length and inclusiveness, Thompson's biography omitted a great deal of value and significance about Frost. Much of this material, more interesting than his published text, he relegated to the two thousand pages of "Notes on Robert Frost, 1939–1967" (now in the Univer-

sity of Virginia Library). On many occasions, Thompson did not challenge Frost's own accounts of his past history, which were either deliberately inaccurate or designed to obscure the facts. Many crucial aspects of
Frost's life were therefore left vague: his mother's dubious family background; the real (rather than ostensible) reasons why Frost left Dartmouth and why he went to the Dismal Swamp to commit suicide; his relations with his first English publisher. The strain of pretending that he
admired Frost erupted in his negative interpretation of many difficult
episodes in Frost's life, especially his relationship with his wife, Elinor,
and with his sickly and troubled children. The moralistic and judg-
mental Thompson blamed Frost for Elinor's death and for his son
Carol's suicide, though he was not responsible for these tragedies. He
also emphasized Frost's unremitting hostility toward other poets, to
whom Frost jokingly referred as his enemies. He minimized or ignored
Frost's important friendships with Pound, Eliot, Stevens, Ransom and
Robert Lowell, and did not give him credit for frequent acts of generosity and kindness to his younger contemporaries.

   In addition to these considerable defects, the heart of Thompson's biography was based on the lie—which Kathleen Morrison insisted upon,
and maintained in public and in private until she died in 1989—that
she was merely Frost's secretary and had remained the faithful wife of
Theodore Morrison. In the preface to his unpublished "Notes on Frost,"
Thompson wrote: "so long as Kathleen Morrison is alive, she will see to it
that the true significance of her influence on Frost is never made public.
But . . . [her] story will finally become public property whether she likes
it or not." Though Kay dominated the last quarter-century of Frost's life
and inspired his greatest love poems, Thompson's book did not even
mention her tumultuous love affair with Frost. He perpetuated the image of Frost as celibate widower, as a dignitary remote from all emotional
and moral entanglements. Kay's hold on Thompson was strong, since he
himself (like several other of Frost's friends) had had an affair with her.
Both struggled to control Frost during his lifetime and to influence his
reputation—as well as their own—after his death. Now, with the cooper-
ation of her daughter, Kay's involvement with Frost and her influence on
his poetry in *A Witness Tree* can finally be revealed and understood.

   In 1972 Robert Francis, a poet and a friend of Frost, observed that
Thompson's work "could provide a sort of anatomical foundation" for a
"book-length portrait of Frost," which would give "the whole man in all
his diversity and inconsistency . . . and emphasize his consistencies by dis-

covering and developing themes running through his life." Instead of trailing off at the end of his long career, Frost finished strongly. He received honorary degrees from both Oxford and Cambridge; he helped release Ezra Pound from an insane asylum; he went on officially sponsored trips to Brazil and Peru, Israel and Greece; he befriended John Kennedy and read poetry at his Inauguration; he lectured to vast audiences; he published his most successful book on his eighty-eighth birthday; he met Khrushchev in Russia.

Frost lived his life for and through poetry. Some of his most decisive actions—from the seduction of his future wife to his response to the death of his children—were prompted by his knowledge of poetry. His own poems are as densely allusive as Eliot's (though Frost's allusions are more cunning and covert) and he drew on English poetry, particularly Palgrave's *Golden Treasury,* as a fertile source throughout his career. Though Frost was *the* American poet of his day, he was influenced more by the English literary tradition and especially by the work of his kindred spirit, Thomas Hardy. The new discoveries about Frost's life have led to deeper understanding of his poetry and to new readings of "Into My Own," "Home Burial," "After Apple-Picking," "The Road Not Taken," "Nothing Gold Can Stay," "Stopping by Woods on a Snowy Evening," "Neither Out Far Nor In Deep," "Design," "The Silken Tent," "All Revelation," "The Most of It," "The Discovery of the Madeiras" and "Directive."

My interest in Frost goes back to poetry classes in high school, college and graduate school. Like most readers, I accepted the conventional view, mainly propagated by Thompson, that Frost was a mean old bastard and that his nature poetry was accomplished but superficial. But I was dissatisfied with Thompson's mass of facts, which I had never been able to finish, and was convinced that Frost, a handsome and vigorous man, must have had a sexual life after his wife's death. I thought Frost deserved a more concise, lively, balanced, honest and perceptive treatment.

As I studied the unpublished material, I came to admire Frost's wit, learning, conversational brilliance and personal generosity, and was impressed by his great moral courage when confronted with poverty, neglect and overwhelming personal tragedy. As I re-read the poetry, I was dazzled by its technical brilliance and sensual passion, its moral complexity and dark vision. I believe this biography offers a radically new view of Frost's character and an original interpretation of his poems. It attempts to see Frost whole, without suppressions and without rancor, so that his work appears in the context of his extraordinary private and public life. The Frost that emerges from this biography is neither the hayseed sage that he cultivated in his public persona nor the "monster in human form" portrayed by Thompson. He is, instead, a subtle and engaging, passionate and tragic figure.

I have written to keep the over curious out
of the secret places of my mind both
in my verse and in my letters.

ROBERT FROST

ROBERT FROST

1

San Francisco

1874–1885

I

Robert Frost's family came to America from Tiverton, Devon, in 1636, and embodied the colonial, military and Puritan traditions of New England. One ancestor was banished from Kittery, Maine, for intimacy with an Indian girl and not allowed to return until he had married an English wife. In the late seventeenth century a Charles Frost of Eliot, Maine, invited some Indians to a feast and when they had stacked their arms, he promptly killed them. A few of them escaped and, as Frost ambivalently wrote in his Whitmanesque poem "Genealogical" (1908), soon took their revenge. They waylaid Charles Frost one Sunday morning on his way home from church and killed him with great barbarity. Other eminent forebears served as commander of a Royal Navy frigate, as lieutenant in the Continental Army and as officer in the War of 1812.

Frost's father, William Prescott Frost, Jr., was the son of a farmer who became foreman in a textile mill. He was born in Kingston, New Hampshire (in the southeast corner of the state) on December 27, 1850. He took the classical course in Lawrence (Massachusetts) High School, sympathized with the rebellious South during the Civil War and tried, while still a teenager, to join the Confederate Army. Refused admission to West Point, he graduated with honors from Harvard in 1872. At college, Will reacted against his puritanical heritage and his domineering father, whom he hated. He rejected religion and behaved wildly, whored, gambled and drank. Will's blue eyes and blunt nose were framed by sideburns that curled round his face and joined his moustache. He was a good athlete, a strenuous walker and strong swimmer. He was also a dark and brooding man, like Heathcliff in his sullen silences.

Isabelle Moodie, Frost's mother, was born in Leith, the port of Edinburgh, on October 2, 1844. Her father, Thomas, was a captain who drowned at sea soon after she was born; her mother, Mary Gordon, "a hussy who ran away from the arduous duties of motherhood." Belle was brought up by her father's strict Presbyterian parents. The auburn-haired, high-colored girl, who spoke with a strong Scotch burr, was sent at the age of eleven to live with a prosperous uncle in Columbus, Ohio. It seems probable that her parents had never, in fact, been married and that "hussy" (a lewd woman) was a euphemism for prostitute. This would explain a great many puzzling but crucial aspects of Belle's life: why her mother had abandoned her, why she had been packed off to a distant relative before she could become aware of her dubious status and why she had no later contact with the family in Scotland. Her reluctance to marry and her fanatical piety also suggest a sense of shame about her illegitimate birth—a great stigma in the Victorian age. The Moodie family omitted her parents' names from their genealogy. Her husband's family, who must have been aware of her background, was extremely hostile to Belle. And Robert Frost was convinced that he himself had been conceived out of wedlock.

After finishing high school in Ohio, Belle joined its staff as an assistant instructor and taught math for seven years. In the fall of 1872 she accepted a position at Lewistown Academy, in central Pennsylvania, where she met Will Frost, the only other teacher in that small school. He taught the boys, she the girls—who were fascinated by her elaborate brooch and earrings, gold and jet with pearls. On February 1, 1873, five months after they met, Will formally proposed marriage in writing. Alluding to her Scottish background and her interest in poetry, he began his letter with a quatrain from "My Dear and Only Love" by James Graham, Marquis of Montrose. He mentioned and then discounted two potential problems—his lack of religious belief and the six-year difference in their ages (his own mother was seven years older than his father)—and ended with a convoluted but heartfelt wish: "I ask you now for that wealth of affection which it is yours to bestow on me, and I offer you in return a love than which, if more worthy, I am sure you can at least find none more devoted." On March 18, 1873, less than two months later and in the midst of the school year, they married in Lewistown.

The following June, as soon as the term was over, Will fulfilled his long-standing ambition to put a continent between himself and his oppressive family. He settled in San Francisco, a boom-town on a beautiful bay, where he planned to use journalism as a way into politics. On July

13, four days after arriving, he told Belle that he already had some articles published by the two leading newspapers and urged her to join him as soon as possible. He felt the "longing of a loving husband for the presence of his darling wife" and declared that "home is now to me the sweetest thing in life and home is anywhere in the wide world where you are."[1] Will became a reporter for the *Daily Evening Bulletin,* and, from 1875 until 1884, city editor and then business manager at the *Daily Evening Post.* Belle published a children's story and some Browningesque poetry; and reviewed books, including poems by Robert Herrick, for her husband's newspaper.

Belle hated cooking and despised the drudgery of housekeeping. When their home became too cluttered and dirty, Will would take pity on her and move to a family hotel, where she enjoyed the lively company and conversation. Then she would take pity on him and agree to move back to another house or flat. They were always on the move and had eight different addresses in eleven years, all of them north of Market and east of Van Ness. For three of these years they lived in the Abbotsford House, a great barn of a hotel, named after the palatial residence of Sir Walter Scott. Into this itinerant and erratic life Robert Frost was born, a year after his parents' marriage, in 1874.

Will had a passion for long-distance swimming and would terrify his young son by propelling himself far out into the Bay, disappearing in the choppy waves and then suddenly resurfacing on a distant buoy. His health deteriorated after he accepted the challenge of a six-day walking race. He beat the champion and then collapsed with exhaustion, which marked the beginning of his decline. He drank heavily, as he had done in college, and always kept a bottle of whiskey in the house. When drunk, he became enraged and broke up the furniture, and once grabbed a careless office boy and shook him out of a fourth-story window. When things went wrong, as they often did, he sometimes refused to speak to his wife and children for six weeks at a time. He was outraged when Belle used his hairbrush; he hurt her feelings with his voluble profanity and broke her heart by consorting with other women.

Belle had one happy year of marriage. But she was soon struck by the contrast between Will's idealistic proposals and sentimental effusions when he arrived in San Francisco and his brutish and violent behavior at home. Her intimate friend Blanche Rankin, who lived with the Frosts for six years, later told Robert: "Your father was not cruel to Belle, nor could I say he was good to her. As for showing affection for her, he was too selfish to be affectionate. . . . I would say Will's whole attitude toward life was one of irreverence—irreverence in everything but religion. In that he was indifferent." Frost later told his daughter: "Some people can't resist tragedy. My mother couldn't. Nothing could have saved her but my father's death. It was wretched, pitiful, wicked, but she was hopelessly committed to [him]." Belle disguised her husband's political fiascoes by telling a friend that he had met with little success, and loyally idealized his failures by exalting him as the champion of lost causes.

A confirmed believer in several religious sects, Belle escaped from a desperately unhappy marriage into the realms of religious mysticism and tried to live in a sphere of higher and holier harmonies. She was originally a Presbyterian, then a Unitarian and finally a Swedenborgian. The young Frost once tried to calm his mother's unease about Darwin's discoveries by explaining: "You seem to be troubled by all this evolution stuff. I don't see anything new in it. You always said God made man out of mud and this new theory says He made him out of *prepared* mud."[2]

The eighteenth-century Swedish scientist Emanuel Swedenborg claimed that he had personally received divine revelation from the Lord, who had explained to him alone the true sense of the Scriptures and had heralded the imminent Second Coming and Last Judgment. After conversing, by Divine Command, with the inhabitants of Heaven and Hell, he taught that the physical realm merely symbolized the higher reality of the spiritual world. Belle became completely dominated and clouded by these mystical doctrines. Most friends thought she was vague and dreamy. Blanche Rankin said she was "terribly queer" and Frost, later in life, frankly spoke of his mother's "incipient insanity."

II

During the 1870s, when the Frosts arrived, silver mining reached its height in San Francisco. In 1874 more than four thousand vessels visited the port and 62,000 immigrants, many of them Chinese, poured into the city. It was a cosmopolitan place, lawless and corrupt, with spittoons decorating the cramped wooden houses and vigilante committees on the dusty streets. Frost later remembered mobs horsewhipping editors, bullets rolling around in bureau drawers and a pair of pickled testicles on exhibit in his father's office. Bret Harte, Ambrose Bierce and Mark Twain lived in San Francisco in the 1860s; Trollope, Wilde and Kipling visited the city during the next two decades. In 1879 Robert Louis

Stevenson, after pursuing his future wife across the continent, settled on Bush Street. He described the heavy drinking and captured the rough-and-ready atmosphere of the town: "Everywhere the same tumble-down decay and sloppy progress, new things yet unmade, old things tottering to their fall; everywhere the same out-at-elbows, many-nationed loungers at dim, irregular grog-shops; everywhere the same sea-air and isleted sea-prospect."

In San Francisco Will became converted to the socialistic, single-tax ideas of Henry George, a huge man with a bald head and black beard, who was then writing *Progress and Poverty* (1879). In 1875 he joined George's crusading newspaper, the *Daily Evening Post.* George believed in

> free enterprise without private monopolism, free trade, equal opportunity, an economy of abundant production for all, a Christian state, an idealistic culture, an efficient government, a democracy uncorrupt and sensitive to the people's needs. . . .
>
> [His] office on the *Post* was a small room piled high with papers, magazines, and *Congressional Records,* and untidy with cigar ashes; he had a baize-covered sofa there, where he slept nights when he could not get away, or caught a cat nap as needed. . . . George drove himself incessantly and could be sharp with his associates. . . . His editorials arrived habitually late; his door was always open. . . . He tickled his associates by taking a shot of whiskey to buck himself for a temperance address.

Frost described his father as a patriotic Fourth-of-July American: a great celebrator of Independence Day, but too ambitious in politics and intransigent toward his political enemies. He was stricken by disease and depressed by failure before he had achieved his goals. He raised his son as a states' rights, free-trade Democrat and admired the idealistic Henry George, yet sold out to the blind, corrupt Democratic boss of San Francisco, Christopher Buckley. In *From Sea to Sea* (1899), Kipling explained how Buckley controlled the municipal votes: "The wise man is he who, keeping a liquor-saloon and judiciously dispensing drinks, knows how to retain within arm's reach a block of men who will vote for or against anything. . . . [San Francisco is] under the rule of a gentleman whose sight is impaired, and who requires a man to lead him about the streets. He is called officially 'Boss Buckley,' and unofficially the 'Blind White Devil.' " Frost bitterly told a friend that his father "soon became the willing slave of the blind boss, rushing to do his every bidding without question. He was always expecting to be named to some important post. The appointment never came. . . . My father stayed out in the cold without reward, a crushed man."[3]

Will Frost, trying to advance his political career, took an active part in three presidential campaigns. Frost remembered hearing his father talk at Democratic political meetings in a dry, harsh and reserved manner that completely failed to capture his audience. In 1876 Will backed the Democratic governor of New York, Samuel Tilden, who was defeated by Rutherford Hayes. At the Democratic state convention in San Francisco in April 1880 Will was selected as delegate to the national convention in Cincinnati, where the Union general Winfield Hancock was nominated for president. Young Rob took the ferry across the Bay and saw his father off at the train station in Oakland. But Hancock was defeated by James Garfield. In 1880 Will also wrote a campaign booklet for the hot-tempered, sharp-tongued Union general William Rosecrans, the hero of the battle of Chattanooga, who successfully ran for Congress in California. Two years later, at the Democratic state convention in San Jose, Rosecrans easily defeated Will Frost as congressional candidate for the first district by a vote of 75 to 23.

In 1884 Will finally seemed to break his losing streak. He backed the notable reformer Grover Cleveland, mayor of Buffalo and governor of New York, who opposed corruption, rejected the political machines that dominated American politics and was a staunch representative of integrity in government. Cleveland got on in politics, H. L. Mencken said, "not by knuckling to politicians, but by scorning and defying them. He didn't go around spouting McGuffy Reader slogans or wanting to be liked." Rob campaigned through the saloons with his father, who was chairman of the Democratic committee in San Francisco. When Cleveland won the election, the boy celebrated the victory by marching in a torchlight procession and riding on top of a fire engine.

Naturally expecting to profit from Cleveland's victory, Will ran for City Tax Collector in 1884, but lost the election. Crushed by defeat, he went on a drunken binge and did not come home for several days. He was particularly enraged by the Swedenborgian minister (his wife's idol), who had promised to support Will but (guided perhaps by angelic voices) voted for the rival candidate. Frost later described the same kind of bitter disillusionment with his father that Hemingway portrayed in "My Old Man." Frost's father was "ruthless in going after what he wanted but he always wanted things that were too small. His ends defeated his methods. He was beaten to start with. Money, political power. [Rob] used to worship him but he got over it when he learned how unscrupulous his father had been."[4]

III

Robert Frost—the quintessential New Englander—was born in San Francisco, midway between the Gold Rush and the Earthquake. He never discovered the exact place of his birth and, until late in life, was confused about the actual date. A contemporary of Chesterton, Churchill and Maugham, he was born on March 26, 1874. When the doctor arrived to deliver the baby, the ever volatile Will Frost pulled out a Colt pistol and threatened to kill the man if anything happened to his wife and child.

Frost was born nine years after the end of the Civil War, when Ulysses Grant was serving his second term as president. Will did not pass on his father's name, but called his son Robert Lee Frost, after the defeated Confederate general. Frost later praised Lee's admirable qualities while acknowledging his limitations and told a friend: "I am touched by Lee, so noble in character, so brilliant and punishing a smiter in the field, but so lost in the larger things of statesmanship and strategy." For most of his life, Frost believed that his parents had married hastily after his mother discovered that she was pregnant. To disguise this fact, he claimed he was born in 1875—a year later than his actual birth date. Though Frost, unlike his father, almost never used coarse language, he often made subtle but revealing sexual allusions in his letters and poems. Punning on the last word in a letter to his closest friend, the notoriously promiscuous Louis Untermeyer, Frost wrote a witty dialogue: "'And where were *you* born?' 'I was born out of wedlock, sir.' 'There's some very beautiful scenery in those parts.'" In "The Lovely Shall Be Choosers," a poem about his mother, he uses "joy" ironically and alludes to what he believed were the family secrets—her shameful pregnancy and hasty marriage:

> Be her first joy her wedding,
> That though a wedding,
> Is yet—well, something they know, he and she.
> And after that her next joy
> That though she grieves, her grief is secret:
> Those friends know nothing of her grief to make it shameful.[5]

At first Will was pleased with his new son. In November 1874, eight months after the baby was born, he fondly told his mother: "Bob is as beautiful as a little bear. He has commenced cutting his teeth, but the process does not appear to give him much trouble. This is an excellent climate for rearing infants." But as his own health deteriorated, his disappointments intensified and his drinking increased, he came to resent the burden of his family and began to torment, terrify and brutalize his son. He was a severe and humorless man, not especially fond of children, who almost never played with them but was an incorrigible tease and a strict disciplinarian. When Rob told a friend he was not allowed to have a jack-o'-lantern on Halloween, his father, infuriated by the criticism and complaint, slashed his son with a metal dog chain. But his behavior was also wildly inconsistent. When Rob was sent out to buy cigarettes and lost a precious dime on the way home, he feared for his life. But (after Rob had prayed with his mother) Will merely said "never mind" and let him off without harsh words or punishment.

To compensate for her husband's severity, Belle idolized, pampered and spoiled her son. He was so terrified of the dark that she allowed him to sleep in her room from the time his father died until the age of fifteen, and his cot remained set up in her bedroom until he went away to college. He described his nightmares and fear of the dark in "The Night Light," but attributed them to an older woman who prayed for the release of her terrors:

> She always had to burn a light
> Beside her attic bed at night.
> It gave bad dreams and broken sleep,
> But helped the Lord her soul to keep.[6]

By allowing her son to sleep in her room, Belle also satisfied her own emotional needs and, after she was widowed, kept him close to her. Despite his protracted dependence, Frost gained a certain psychological confidence. "A man who had been the indisputable favorite of his mother," wrote Freud, "keeps for life the feeling of a conqueror."

Belle drew Rob to her and strengthened their bond through reading and religion. She read Bible stories to him from his earliest years, until he had—like many Victorian authors—memorized great parts of the sacred book. Throughout his childhood she also read from works by serious nineteenth-century writers that children could also enjoy: Fenimore Cooper's *The Last of the Mohicans,* which recalled his unfortunate ancestor; Thomas Hughes' *Tom Brown's Schooldays*, a description of Rugby which appealed to the boy who never went to school until he was eleven; and Jules Verne's *The Mysterious Island*, about castaways' survival on a desert isle.

Belle provided a vital link to the British Isles, Scottish lyrics and English poetry. A member of the Caledonia Club in San Francisco, she was passionate about the dialect, folklore, heroes and history of Scotland. She emphasized her heritage by reading to Rob Walter Scott's *The Tale of a Grandfather* (1829), a history of Scotland to 1745; Jane Porter's extremely popular *The Scottish Chiefs* (1810), a fictionalized history of the medieval soldier and patriot William Wallace; and George MacDonald's enchanting children's stories, *At the Back of the North Wind* (1871) and *The Princess and the Goblin* (1872). Frost, who was named for Robert Burns as well as Robert Lee, heard his mother read aloud from the border ballads, Scott and Burns throughout his childhood. He alluded to Scott's poems in "Stopping by Woods," "Two Look at Two" and "On Being Chosen Poet of Vermont" (see Appendix I). He later identified with the charming farmer-poet and carefully examined Burns' manuscripts when he visited the rare books library at Buffalo.

Frost wrote a poem, "Maple," on the significance of names (mentioning the names of his own four children), and asked: "Where would the fairness be in giving me / A name to carry for life and never know / The secret of?" He named his eldest daughter after the heroine of Burns' "Bonnie Lesley":

> Thou art a queen, fair Lesley,
>   Thy subjects we, before thee:
> Thou art divine, fair Lesley,
>   The hearts o' men adore thee.

And he named his third daughter, Marjorie, after the mother of Robert the Bruce, who played a prominent role in *The Scottish Chiefs*. Frost adapted the title of Burns' "The Cotter's Saturday Night" for his own poem "An Old Man's Winter Night" and used the same tender, protective theme of Burns' "To a Mouse" ("Wee, sleekit, cow'rin', tim'rous beastie, / O, what a panic's in thy breastie!") in "The Exposed Nest." In this poem a ground nest full of young birds survives the passage of a hay-cutting machine, but is left unprotected and defenseless. Frost, who later became extremely well read, claimed that he had never read a book until his teens. But he learned—from hearing his mother read aloud to him—to value and delight in regional dialects (from both Scotland and New England) and to place primary emphasis in his own poetry on the actual *sound* of spoken words.

Following his mother's labyrinthine religious progression, Frost was baptized in the Presbyterian church, attended Unitarian Sunday school and finally worshipped with the Swedenborgians. "All this baptizing and church and Sunday school going may have had a bad effect on me," he told a friend. "I did so much of it when young that I never felt any call to continue it later in life." But he received one important legacy from his Swedenborgian training. He remembered that "as a boy living at the Abbotsford House, he often knelt in an armchair and, holding his hands over his ears, buried his face in the back of the chair to drown out the mystical voices calling to him." These supernatural voices did not reveal a secret truth or summon him to a higher destiny. He heard them but could not understand their meaning, and found them deeply disturbing. As an adult, Frost continued to hear the voices of unseen beings, who repeated everything he said with a slightly different inflection and seemed to mock his own thoughts. He was also fascinated by these voices and felt, if he could only decipher their message, that they might inspire his poetry.

Troubled by her husband's drinking and violence, Belle would urge Rob to use his will to hold himself in and control his feelings. He eventually developed his mother's strong will and emphasized the importance of this word in the title of his first book, *A Boy's Will*. In the spring of 1876, when her husband's wild behavior led to a major crisis in her marriage, Belle exerted her own will and left him. Pregnant and frightened, she took the two-year-old Rob across the country to visit the Frost family in Massachusetts. While in Lawrence, Belle gave birth on June 25 to her second child, Jeanie Florence. She stayed away from San Francisco for six months and did not return until Will agreed to have her high school friend Blanche Rankin live with them as her companion and supporter. Blanche remained with the Frosts for six years to help Belle care for the house and children, and to act as a buffer between the gentle wife and her increasingly embittered and irascible husband.

Rob's early schooling was extremely erratic. At the age of five he was sent to kindergarten at the "French, German and English Institute for Young Ladies" run by the Russian Madame Zeitska. "The kids were all picked up in a horse-drawn bus," Frost later recalled. "When night came the driver couldn't find our house, and we rode around a long time looking for it. I was badly frightened, thinking I would never see home again. So next morning I refused to go, and my private-school days were over."[7] Pleading severe stomach pains, Rob also refused to attend the first, second and third grades. His indulgent mother allowed him to stay away from school and taught him to read and write at home. He was so delicate as a child that the doctor said he would not live long. Though often incapacitated by illness during his youth and middle age, he became an astonishingly strong, healthy and vigorous old man.

Rob got a good deal of education in the streets and saloons of San Francisco. The alien Chinese were often the victims of his childish pranks. The boys would throw rocks at the doors of the Chinamen, who would then rush out with threatening knives. Frost wittily recalled that he "was raised in San Francisco, and with all the Chinese that are there I became an ancestor-worshiper." His early contact with poor Chinese immigrants engendered an irrational scorn for Oriental culture and a belief (expressed in "Kitty Hawk") that civilization has always progressed "West-Northwest" across Europe to America. In that poem he speaks of the East's long, stagnant meditation. Frost was never interested in sight-seeing or travel. In his caustic poem "An Importer," he satirizes tourists who seek cheap goods in the Orient, who hope to acquire wisdom in sacred rigmaroles and subterfuges for saving face, and again extols the superiority of Western culture.

In order to join the local gang of boys, Rob had to prove himself by stealing a valuable pair of wheels for the leader and then a pig, which he sold in Chinatown. He also had to prove his toughness in combat. Always fond of reminiscing about his past life, he told a friend how he had boasted "I could lick any two boys the size of one I named. The kids went out and brought in two boys. They didn't wait for me to jump 'em, but they jumped me first. I grabbed one around the neck and tried to gouge his eyes out. The other danced round and round and when he had a chance would rush in and scratch me. I was pretty well all in when we were separated, and I had to be taken home. Apparently nobody won the fight. My mother sent for a doctor who fixed up my scratches and gouged eyes. I suppose I was a little devil."[8]

Since Rob did not have to go to school and was freed from the drudgery of classes and study, he could sell newspapers on the streets, run errands for his father's newspaper and eat at the free-lunch counter in the saloons. Frost felt his father did not care for him, but liked to have him hang around the office. Though he allowed Rob to stay out of school, he was strict about his manners. He brutally whipped the boy for slight infractions, while Belle went down on her knees in the next room and prayed for mercy. Beaten by his father and spoiled by his mother, Rob was torn between Belle's idealism, religiosity and protectiveness and Will's volatility, drunkenness and cruelty.

Though he accepted his own punishments, he was bitter about the way his father treated his mother. In "The Lovely Shall Be Choosers," Frost's idealized portrait of Belle, a proud, beautiful and blameless woman is punished for her choice in marriage and destroyed by unaccustomed hardships. Though she once walked in brightness—an echo of Byron's "Hebrew Melodies"—invisible hands now press upon her and weigh her down. Her husband does not appreciate her fine qualities and love her for what she is. Having been brought up in comfort, she is unable to accommodate herself to their harsh way of life. Just as, in Herbert's "The Pulley," God gives man "a glass of blessings" but holds back Rest so that "weariness / May toss him to my breast," so in Frost's poem the lovely one is blessed with seven joys but unable to take pleasure in any of them.

IV

In 1882, when Rob was eight, his father finally realized that he had tuberculosis, an incurable disease, and became severely depressed. He had always planned to take time off to treat his illness and had thought of moving to Hawaii for his health. But, preoccupied with his career and his need to support a family, he never quite got around to it. Instead, he resorted to extreme remedies and took Rob with him to the slaughter-house, where he drank glass after glass of black blood that gushed directly from the slashed throat of a steer.

Though his father had never been demonstrative or affectionate, and had often beaten his son, an entirely different side of his character —tender, desperate, pathetic—emerged at the very end of his life. While stretched out on the sofa, the moribund father would ask Rob to lie down beside him to provide some human warmth and comfort. When he fell asleep the boy, fearful of disturbing him and unable to move, would feel Will's strained and heavy breath on his face.[9] Will, who took no precautions about spreading his infectious illness, endangered his son's life. Frost later said that his father "gave him" tuberculosis.

But Will was stoical about his impending death and gravely concerned about the welfare of his wife and children. On April 17, 1885, three weeks before his death, the thirty-four-year-old Will told his parents that he had lost control of his bowels and was doomed to die. He worried about the cost of his illness and suggested, since Belle would probably not be able to bring up the children on her own, that they be cared for by his parents: "The fact may as well be looked squarely in the face that consumption has an incurable hold upon me and that the end is not very far off. The only effort of the physician now is to prolong life by holding in check the diarrhea. . . . We do want money. We shall need some for funeral expenses and if I drag along for any length of time, which I don't think I shall, for incidental expenses connected with my illness. [And there] are the wife and children. . . . With the little ones on your hands, I don't think the mother would have any difficulty in caring for herself." On May 5, 1885, when the end came, Rob and Jeanie were sent out to play in the street. Soon afterwards a child told them: "There's crepe on your door," the signal of death in the house.

Will had warned his parents about his financial problems, but had speculated with his insurance money and left nothing when he died. For someone who had earned $1,250 a year when he began his career in journalism in 1873, a $20,000 benefit would have been a great fortune. Instead, when the funeral expenses and final bills were paid, Belle, with only eight dollars in the bank, was destitute. Will may have asked for burial in New England to encourage his family to go East and be cared for by his parents (who sent the rail fare) instead of remaining on their own in San Francisco. But Belle chose to keep the children with her, rather than hand them over to her in-laws, and by doing so had to endure the greatest hardship and poverty she had ever known.

When asked why he had left California, Frost claimed he had been carried out, when very young, kicking and screaming. The Frosts got on the wrong train on the first night out, during Rob's third trip across the continent, and he had a frightening "memory of being dragged out of an upper berth by a leg, and of huddling myself beside a railroad track in the darkness—pitch darkness. All our luggage was piled about us—a memory of something being very badly wrong." It was hard to enjoy the adventurous train ride with his father's corpse stored in the luggage compartment and the future so uncertain.

Though Frost wrote mostly about New England, he also composed five poems about California—all but one about his boyhood. "A Record Stride" is a playful, fanciful account (which alludes to the Latin *vagare*, to wander, in "extra-vagant wave") of a pair of old shoes, one of which has stepped into the Atlantic, the other into the Pacific. They symbolized

Frost's extensive experience of life at both ends of the continent. In "Auspex," Latin for one who watches birds for purposes of divination, a great eagle sweeps down on the little boy in the California Sierra, but (unlike the eagle in Chaucer's "House of Fame") does not pick him up. His parents claim he was rejected by Jove's royal bird because he would not make a suitable cup-bearer. But the self-confident little boy resents the implication that there is anything he cannot do. "At Woodward's Gardens" narrates how, at a popular San Francisco amusement park, a boy teased two caged monkeys by burning their noses with a lens that gathered solar rays. The monkeys were troubled and did not know what was irritating them, but were clever enough to snatch the glass out of the boy's hand, break the handle and binding, and hide it in the straw. The poem concludes with the ambiguous apothegm, "It's knowing what to do with things that counts." The boy knows how to use the glass to burn the monkeys, but the monkeys know how to trick the boy and destroy it. "A Peck of Gold" (rather than dirt) was inspired by the eruption in 1883 of a volcano on Krakatoa, an island between Sumatra and Java in the Dutch East Indies. The ash or dust was blown all the way across the Pacific, and even got into the food and drink, and Rob was told that some of this dust was really gold. While living at the Golden Gate they all had to adjust to the unpleasant reality and eat their peck of gold dust.

Frost's brilliant sonnet "Once by the Pacific"—the name of the tumultuous ocean is ironic—is much more serious and significant, and the force of the poem is personal as well as literary. It transforms Rob's childhood fear of being lost on the rough and rocky beach near the Cliff House, at the western edge of the city, into a universal terror:

> The sky must have clouded up, and night begun to come on. The sea seemed to rise up and threaten me. I got scared, imagining that my mother and father, who were somewhere about, had gone away and left me by myself in danger of my life. I was all alone with the ocean water rising higher and higher. I was fascinated and terrorized watching the sea; for it came to me that we were all doomed to be engulfed and swept away. Long years after I remembered the occasion vividly, the feeling which overwhelmed me, and wrote my poem, "Once by the Pacific."[10]

Frost's first eleven years in San Francisco left an indelible mark on his character. He admired and emulated his father's athletic prowess but feared his drink, violence and insanity, and remained bitter about Will's cruelty and failure. He rejected his mother's religion, but developed a keen awareness of her Scottish ancestry. He became abnormally attached to Belle, whose devotion he would idealize and seek in his wife and, later on, in his mistress. He was fascinated and tormented by strange inner voices, and learned to value the sound of the spoken word. Plagued by delicate health, he used invalidism to avoid unpleasant duties and, after staying out of school, became hostile to formal education. He developed a deep distrust of all political programs and parties, and was chauvinistic about the superiority of American culture. Hypersensitive to any slight or insult, he valued personal courage. But he suffered from a sense of vulnerability and deep insecurity that had been bred in him as a child.[11]

2

North of Boston

1885–1895

I

Lawrence, Massachusetts, where Rob's grandparents lived, was situated on the Merrimack River, twenty-five miles north of Boston. Its leading citizens, people of British origin, felt superior to the recent immigrants, who worked in the shoe and paper factories and in the mills that had made the place a world center for the manufacture of textiles. Cotton was king in Lawrence as well as in New Orleans. Both Rob's grandfather and his father had felt close to and sympathized with the Confederacy, which had supplied raw materials to their town. Yet when Rob arrived in industrialized Lawrence in 1885, there were no electric lights or telephones. There was nothing poetic about the blue-collar mill town, with its poor, run-down tenements in the working-class areas and the scattered churches and small shops of the obstinately provincial middle class. He disliked the Yankees, who seemed closed and narrow compared to the generous, big-hearted Californians, and could not get used to their stiff ways, nor to the dark skies and severe winters of the Northeast.

The cold, cheerless and depressing home of the grandparents, then in their sixties, epitomized everything he disliked about New England. There was a striking contrast between his grandmother's well-organized housewifery and Belle's domestic chaos, between his grandfather's careful and cautious way of life (he saved all rusty nails and bits of string) and Will's recklessness about his health and future. They never laughed and clearly resented the children, who seemed, despite their father's severity, to have been brought up badly. Rigidly set in their mode of life, they became intensely irritated when the children came into the house with muddy feet, let flies in through the open screen doors, wiped their dirty hands on pristine towels and ate greedily at table.

The grandparents disapproved of and looked down on Belle, a cultured woman who had grown up in genteel circumstances in Columbus, because of her dubious birth in Scotland. Though well aware of Will's dissolute habits at Harvard, they took no responsibility for his faults and irrationally blamed Belle for the failure and death of their only son. They felt no obligation to provide for the welfare of the widow and two young children, and did not use their influence to help her find a job in Lawrence. Motherless, orphaned in childhood, widowed after a miserable marriage and now penniless, Belle never remarried and withdrew into the consolations of mystical religion.

Despite her considerable teaching experience in Columbus and Lewistown, Belle had never attended a teachers' training college and was unable to earn a decent salary. There seemed to be many qualified teachers in New England and the only job she could get—after searching for six months—was in a small grade school in Salem, ten miles northwest of Lawrence, just over the New Hampshire border. She taught thirty children from the fifth to the eighth grade. Most of them did not go on to high school, ended their education at fourteen, and began to work in factories and farms. For the next seven years—in Salem, Methuen and Lawrence—she had to support herself and her children, while living in cramped rented rooms, on less than $400 a year. They moved to Salem in early 1886, and Rob and Jeanie began their formal education in their mother's fifth-grade class.

Rob had great difficulty adjusting to the strangeness of New England, to a regular school and to humiliating poverty. He seemed "different," a lazy and useless boy who could not even chop enough wood to keep the kitchen stove going. Despite his awkwardness, during his second year in Salem the twelve-year-old Rob fell in love with his best friend's sister, Sabra Peabody, and sent her some charming letters. When Sabra became jealous of another classmate, Rob assumed a man-of-the-world attitude and reassured her of his devotion: "I like you twice as much as I do her and always have thought more of you than any other girl I know of. . . . There are not many girls I like but when I like them I fall dead in love with them. . . . From your loveing, Rob."

Belle's appearance, according to one of her pupils, had dramatically deteriorated as years of struggle and hardship transformed her into a gaunt and haggard woman: "Her frame was angular, rather loosely knit, the type of figure we associate in a man with Lincoln. . . . [She had] the large, broad brow of the thinker; the eyes deep-set, somewhat cavernous, blue, with a humorous, kindly twinkle; a large, generous mouth. The

heavy graying hair was coiled at her neck, and always a stray lock de-
tached itself. There were eye glasses that never stayed put." During her
four years in Salem schools and three years in Methuen (on the northern
edge of Lawrence), Belle seems to have lost self-confidence. She was
known as a poor teacher who could not control the class, and who
favored the brighter and more ambitious students, particularly her own
two children. She was eventually forced to resign from Salem. After
being moved to four different schools, in the hope that she would
improve, she was also relieved of her teaching duties in Methuen. When
the Frosts moved back to Lawrence in February 1890 they had to live in
the slums near the freight yard. Later on, Frost's oldest daughter, writing
to her father, compared Belle to the impoverished widow of the poet
Vachel Lindsay, "a fine, intelligent, sensitive woman, needing the shel-
tered life and forced by circumstances into the economic struggle. She is
very much what I have pictured your mother as being. Every ounce of her
spiritual and physical strength is being drained to support those two
children."[1]

II

When Rob, following his father's footsteps, entered Lawrence High
School in the fall of 1888, his trousers were too short, he was shy and
awkward, and he was scorned by his fellow students as a country bump-
kin. He chose the classical curriculum, which would prepare him for
college and included Latin, Greek, ancient and European history, and
mathematics. At the end of the first year he received high marks in all
subjects, became head of his class (of thirty-two students) and maintained that position until graduation. He later paid tribute to his strict,
old-fashioned language teachers and told an interviewer: "Those ladies I
had in high school were the severest thing, no funny business. If you
translated enough wrong you could go two or three hundred below
zero"—a real permafrost. Though critical of their method, he was grateful to them for giving him a solid foundation in Classics. The Latin
instructor "taught Homer and Virgil for the grammar merely. She never
told us that this was great literature. I used to resent this. . . . [But] she
taught me at least to read the Latin poets in the original and I could
come to them later and discover their greatness for myself."

During his sophomore year Rob widened his interests through friendship with Carl Burell. A clumsy, lisping, peculiar young man, ten years older than Rob, he worked as a janitor and handyman but had returned to complete his high school education. Carl, self-taught and with unusual intellectual curiosity, lent Rob many books and was the first to awaken his lifelong interest in botany, astronomy and the crucial Victorian conflict (which tormented Rob's mother) between scientific discoveries and religious belief.

Rob now became interested, for the first time, in reading and writing poetry. When a teacher wrote on the blackboard William Collins' "How Sleep the Brave," which commemorated the soldiers who had fallen during the English victory against the Scots at Culloden, Rob was excited by its perfect rhythm and diction. He began to read Shelley, Keats, Poe and Arnold. And he was inspired by an incident in Book V, chapter 3, of Prescott's *Conquest of Mexico* (1843) that described the retreat of Cortez after the death of Montezuma and the slaughter of the Spaniards as they tried to escape from Tenochtitlán. Frost remembered writing his first poem, "La Noche Triste," in a Romantic mystical mood, as the natural elements swirled around and seemed to transfigure him, and he exulted in the thrill of poetic inspiration. "There was a wind and a darkness," he said, as when the Spirit of God moved upon the face of the waters. "I had never written a poem before, and as I walked, it appeared like a revelation, and I became so taken by it that I was late at my grandmother's." The long poem, consisting of a prologue and twenty-five quatrains, ends with two stirring stanzas:

> The flame shines brightest e'er goes out,
> Thus with the Aztec throne,
> On that dark night before the end,
> So o'er the fight it shone.

> The Montezumas are no more,
> Gone is their regal throne,
> And freemen live, and rule, and die,
> Where they have ruled alone.

Rob left this poem on the desk of Ernest Jewell, a senior and editor of the *High School Bulletin,* who published it on the front page in April 1890.

In his senior year Rob joined the football team as an end and became editor of the *Bulletin*. His classmates were so sluggish and indifferent that he had to write the entire triple-column, eight-page issue of December

1891 by himself. The one significant piece among the alumni news, school gossip, football reports, notes, clippings and jingles was "Petra and Its Surroundings," which described the ruins of an ancient city in modern Jordan. The essay may have been inspired by the famous opening lines of John Burgon's "Petra" (1845): "A rose-red city half as old as time."

During his final year of high school Rob courted a classmate, Elinor White, who was a year and a half older than he was. She had delicate features and a handsome profile, also loved poetry and published her verse in the school magazine. Her father had been a minister in the Universalist church (an eighteenth-century American denomination), which Rob's grandparents also attended, but had abandoned the pulpit to become a carpenter. The sweethearts had several other things in common. Both sets of parents were unhappily married and had come down in the world. Rob and Elinor each had a sister whose physical and psychological ailments had turned her into an invalid. Rob's stomach pains had prevented him from going to grade school; Elinor's "slow fever" had kept her out of high school for two years.

Rob and Elinor, the leading scholars in the classical and English sides of the school, were made co-valedictorians by the principal, who was delighted by their budding romance. Elinor, who would marry one of the most impressive talkers of his time, spoke on "Conversation as a Force in Life." Rob, whose lectures and speeches would always be spontaneous and informal, spoke on the awkwardly titled subject: "A Monument to After-Thought Unveiled." He argued that "the poet's insight is his after-thought. . . . The after-thought of one action is the forethought of the next."[2]

After graduation in the summer of 1892, Rob "fell dead in love" with Elinor. He conducted a passionate courtship that culminated in what Lawrance Thompson euphemistically called a Shelleyan rebellion against social convention. After "their own [secret] marriage ceremony" and exchange of wedding rings to seal their commitment, Rob persuaded the virginal Elinor to become his lover before they were actually married. The young man did not find the Shelleyan justification of free love in "Epipsychidion" (as Thompson suggested) but in "Love's Philosophy." Just as his father had courted an older woman with Montrose's love poem, so Rob read Shelley's poem aloud to convince Elinor that the commingling of the elements—rivers, winds, mountains, waves, sunlight and moonbeams—provided the natural and inevitable impetus for physical union:

The fountains mingle with the river
And the rivers with the ocean,
The winds of heaven mix for ever
With a sweet emotion;
Nothing in the world is single,
All things by a law divine
In one another's being mingle—
Why not I with thine?

See the mountains kiss high heaven
And the waves clasp one another;
No sister-flower would be forgiven
If it disdain'd its brother:
And the sunlight clasps the earth,
And the moonbeams kiss the sea—
What are all these kissings worth,
If thou kiss not me?

Frost later told Thompson that he had been "ruthless" with Elinor, that he had bent her to his will and forced her to submit to his passion. He also described her defloration in one of his most personal and revealing poems, "The Subverted Flower," which Elinor never allowed him to publish in her lifetime. In public lectures, after her death, he said that its real subject was "frigidity in women."[3] In this poem Frost portrays an intensely emotional scene between a young man and his girl. As she stands, with her shining hair let loose, in a field of goldenrod—outside the Edenic garden—he clasps her and urges her to respond to his feelings. But she resists his advances and sees him as a brute with a paw, a bark, a snout and a jagged muzzle, as a tiger at the bone or a demon of pursuit. As her heart fills with terror and his body with shame, her mother suddenly appears to interrupt his seduction. He runs away; and the girl, her mouth foaming with feral rage, spits out bitter words as her mother draws her home. He holds the tender-headed flower, subverted from its natural growth as the woman is from her sexual fulfillment, lashes it against his open palm and flings it away as her "frigidity" degrades him to a bestial state. "The Subverted Flower" re-creates, with astonishing sympathy and insight, Rob's "expense of spirit in a waste of shame" and Elinor's disgust at his "lust in action." It suggests that he paid dearly for his ruthlessness and her submission.

III

Frost passed almost all his entrance exams for Harvard. But his grandparents, who were paying his college expenses, did not want him to go there. They felt Harvard had ruined his father, and sent him to Dartmouth, which (then and now) had a reputation for heavy drinking. Frost won a scholarship that paid most of the tuition fee; his room in Wentworth Hall was $26 a year and board about $75. The prescribed courses for the first term of the freshman year were sixteen hours of Greek (Plato, Homer, Herodotus), Latin (Livy, Cicero, Horace) and mathematics (algebra, geometry, trigonometry). He was also required to attend daily college prayers and church services on Sunday.

He joined Theta Delta Chi fraternity, after a rich classmate paid his initiation fee, but was not an enthusiastic member. He preferred to take long solitary walks through the woods. When asked why he indulged in that strange practice, he evasively replied he had gone there to "gnaw bark." He formed only one close relationship, with the asthmatic and hunchbacked Preston Shirley, who, like Carl Burell, was physically disabled and extremely bookish. "He was my greatest and only very intellectual friend at Dartmouth in 1892," Frost recalled. "Though a frail boy and always a sufferer from ailments, he was the life of the place in many ways, full of old family and Dartmouth traditions."

The tradition that Frost enjoyed the most, and in which Shirley could not participate, was the rough, drunken, almost constant fighting between the freshman and sophomore classes. "Much of what I enjoyed at Dartmouth," Frost told a friend, "was acting like an Indian in a college founded for Indians. I mean I liked the rushes a good deal, especially the one in which our class got the salting [initiation] and afterwards fought it out with the sophomores across pews and everything (it was in the Old Chapel) with old cushions and even footstools for weapons. . . ."

Frost enjoyed the rough-house, but was disappointed with the "low ebb" of academic life at Dartmouth. Though the college was small, he never got to know any members of the faculty. The star pupil at Lawrence High School was bored with his classes and disillusioned with the conformist attitude of his classmates. They absorbed and repeated what their teachers had said in order to pass the exams, but had no intellectual curiosity or independent thought. He chafed against the rigid requirements (though he wanted to study Classics) and later explained: "I could not then live in a college or university atmosphere, because of the restraint. I could not do things because they had to be done. I suppose I have been guided in my life so far by instinct to protect what I was or wanted to be." College seemed to stifle rather than stimulate his imaginative faculty and, he wrote in his Introduction to *Dartmouth Verse, 1925*, had been "conducted with the almost express purpose of keeping him busy with something else till the danger of his ever creating anything is past." By January 1893, just before his first midyear exams, when the competition was intense and he was under great pressure to excel, he had lost focus and direction, and became completely disaffected. "I didn't seem to have any sense of what I was doing," he recalled. "I didn't think it was serious at all. . . . I sort of lost my interest."[4]

Frost maintained that he had impulsively decided to leave, after less than one semester, without even notifying the school authorities. His excuse was that his genteel mother had particular difficulty controlling the big, unruly boys in the Methuen school, and needed him to take over her troublesome class. Just before leaving he sat up all night with Preston Shirley, fooling around, saying farewell and eating a whole box of Turkish fig paste provided by Shirley's mother.

Frost bought a supply of rattan canes in the Methuen hardware store and quickly restored discipline by beating the boys. They deeply resented him, and he had to disarm one of the pupils who threatened him with a knife. But neither his intellectual dissatisfaction with Dartmouth (which could have been surmounted) nor his mother's difficulties (which could have been solved if he had gone home for a long weekend, thrashed the rude schoolboys and then returned to Hanover) explained why he left college. As Frost rather vaguely confessed: "I was glad to seize the excuse (to myself) that my mother needed me in her school, to take care of some big, brutal boys she could not manage. That wasn't the real reason. I had decided I was up to no good at Dartmouth, so I just went home to Methuen." The real reasons for his departure were less noble.

Frost could have stayed long enough to pass his first semester exams, so that he could later return to Dartmouth or transfer to another college. But he was longing for Elinor White, whom he loved and wanted to marry. She had gone to St. Lawrence University, a Universalist college which her father had attended, though he had not graduated. Located in Canton, New York, a town of three thousand people near the St. Lawrence River and the Canadian border, it had sixty male and thirty female students—so the girls were in great demand. Frost hoped to persuade Elinor to leave college, as he had done, and rejoin him in Massachusetts.

The cruel and constant bullying at Dartmouth was extremely discouraging. On the very first night he moved into his room Frost, who always had a night light, was suddenly shut up in terrifying blackness: "somebody opened my door and threw something in and upset my lantern; and then I was in the dark for a while. And then I heard strange noises: not hammering at all, but it turned out that somebody had driven screws into the door so you couldn't open it. And there I was. . . ." *The History of the Class of 1896* emphasized that the two newcomers, Frost and Shirley, were unremittingly victimized by the older students, who would smash into and destroy their rooms: "their sophomore neighbors did manifest considerable animosity. Night after night did Wentworth Hall resound with the tumult of the battles which they waged against the two lone freshmen, and the latter lived in a state of perpetual siege. Often their fortifications were broken through and their stronghold carried by assault and pillaged." No wonder that Frost, a nervous and delicate young man who was afraid of the dark and accustomed to spending the night in his mother's room, found it difficult to study and became depressed, dyspeptic and unable to sleep.

Frost said that he himself took an active part in one sadistic prank that had grave consequences. When students were bursting feather pillows on each other's heads, one of them said that Frost needed a haircut. He then told a boy preacher, known as "the minister": "I'll tell you what I'll do. If you let me cut your hair, I'll let you cut mine." Frost continued: "So Hazen and I cut his hair. We made a picture on the back of his head, so the skull showed through. Then . . . I did a dastardly thing; I said we'd have my hair cut another night—not that night. I refused to have mine cut. And do you know what happened to him? He left College." Frost concluded that "it was one of those things I ought to be ashamed of. . . . I ought to have been fired for doing that." In this version of the story Frost, who felt guilty about what he had done, made his classmate, rather than himself, the victim.

Frost gave several different accounts of this incident. In October 1915 he told the Dartmouth librarian that he had never done anything wrong. More than twenty years later, in June 1938, he told another friend that *Time* magazine (which had probed into his life and uncovered some damaging information) had just telephoned to ask why he had been expelled from Dartmouth. Frost denied the charge and told them he had not been expelled. He had been a good boy and earned high marks as long as his patience held out, but bored by the system of grading and by the quest for meaningless rewards, he had restlessly stolen away.

Despite Frost's denials (he loved to mislead biographers about his own life), the rumor that persisted until 1938 seems to be true. The students were clearly out of control, and the professors apparently used the head-shaving incident to punish them. William Jewell, the son of Frost's old friend and classmate Ernest Jewell, using the same word as Frost, told an interviewer that "the boys were both fired—and Robert Frost was one of them."[5] Frost and Hazen were expelled and they, rather than "the minister," had to leave in disgrace.

By leaving Dartmouth Frost threw away his chance for a good job and a professional career, and made it much more difficult to marry Elinor White. His abrupt departure led, in fact, to many years of poverty and to a series of domestic misfortunes. Since he had everything to lose and nothing to gain, he would not have left Dartmouth unless he was forced to do so, and his claim to have left voluntarily is unconvincing. But Frost's expulsion explains why he left so suddenly and secretly—without sufficient reason, without telling anyone but Shirley, without applying for permission to leave or for honorable dismissal. His expulsion also accounts for many other aspects of his character and later life: his insecurity, his need to retaliate by beating the rough boys in Methuen, his hostility to professors and higher education, his adversarial role in academia, his desire to have colleges bid against each other for his services, his delight in extracting maximum payment from all of them and his need to succeed at Dartmouth—which later awarded him *two* honorary degrees.

IV

The promising valedictorian, who seemed to have rejected his grandfather's generous offer of a college education, claimed that he had left Dartmouth of his own free will and returned to face the harsh disapproval of Lawrence: "A cloud of puzzlement hung over me as an obstinate, indecisive young fool." He seemed to have changed rather suddenly from the brightest boy in his class to the laziest lout in town. He had sold newspapers on the streets of San Francisco, and now took up the same sort of menial, short-lived jobs that had occupied him during his summers in primary school and high school, when he had tried to supplement his mother's meager income.

During 1886–88, while in high school, he had served as an apprentice in a shoe factory, hammering nails into soles and cutting out patterns in leather. After his freshman year in high school, in 1889, he cut hay for a farmer in Salem. The following summer he worked as a handyman and errand boy in a resort hotel on the coast of Maine. In 1891 he worked for a Scottish fruit grower, but lasted only three weeks because the farmer's teenaged son was cruel to Frost and woke him up in the morning by sluicing him with a pitcher of cold water. He then moved on to Braithwaite's woolen mill, where for six long days a week he collected empty thread bobbins. At Braithwaite's he once used a broom handle to shut the current off at a distant switch and then clumsily dropped it, cutting all the threads from the central spool, stopping production and infuriating the foreman. Like D. H. Lawrence, who used to hear the Nottinghamshire miners singing hymns in the cold dawn on the way to work and who praised their joyous spirit and fraternal bonds, Frost "used to think the mill people, scooting home in the dusk, were sad, till I worked in the mill and heard them singing and laughing and throwing bobbins up at me as I stood up on the ladder fixing the lights." After graduating from high school he was hired as gatekeeper at the Everett Mill, where the air was full of wool dust and a thousand yarns were pulled and twisted through the spools. Frost had to shut the entrance against the men who were late to work and lost a half-hour's pay. This experience inspired his most proletarian poem, "The Lone Striker" (1933), in which a tardy laborer, shut out of the mill, throws up his job and takes to the woods—a luxury few workers could enjoy.

Frost's jobs after leaving Dartmouth were even more unsatisfactory and ephemeral. He taught his mother's rough eighth-grade class in Methuen from January 1893 until the term mercifully ended in March. He spent that spring and summer on a farm in New Hampshire, doing chores for Elinor's mother and her two daughters: one a mentally unstable invalid, the other pregnant and estranged from her husband. In the fall he briefly tried to promote an elocutionist who read Shakespeare in public, but abandoned him after he roared his lines to an empty hall during an inept performance in Boston. Frost then returned to the Arlington woolen mill in Lawrence and had to climb up a ten-foot ladder to trim the carbon-pencil lamps that provided light. When not tending the lamps, he escaped to a kind of chicken coop on the roof of the building and read Shakespeare to himself. Though Frost was roughed up on the way home from work by the former pupils he had beaten with the rattan canes, he later felt quite nostalgic about the easy-going, paternal ways of his old boss on the lighting job.

In the spring of 1894 in Salem he instructed, for one term at $24 a month, a dozen children under the age of twelve in reading, writing, spelling, grammar, penmanship, arithmetic, geography and history. He did not work for the rest of that year. During the first two months of 1895, he followed his father's occupation and became a cub reporter for the Lawrence *Daily American* and weekly *Sentinel*. Newspaper work taught him to finish his writing instead of leaving it to complete later on. His main story described an eagle that flew into Lawrence, perched on a flagpole and was shot by a zealous hunter. All these low-paying and somewhat degrading factory, mill, farming, teaching and writing jobs exposed Frost to the rough realities of working life. They increased his knowledge of rural and urban New England and gave him the kind of practical experience that he finally valued much more than a college education. They also weaned him from his mother, deepened his sympathy with the people who had moved from the farms to the factories and provided material that he would use in "The Lone Striker."

In the fall of 1894, while Frost was vague and drifting but still keen to follow the career of a poet, his grandfather made him an offer. He would give Frost money for a year on the understanding that if he could not support himself by the end of that time, he would abandon poetry for a more secure profession. Frost realized that what appeared to be a generous offer would actually put an end to his poetic ambitions, for it would be impossible for a twenty-year-old to publish his work, establish a reputation and support himself within that time. Instead of expressing gratitude, Frost imitated the cry of an auctioneer and exclaimed before the startled old man: "I have one, who'll give me twenty; I have one, who'll give me twenty; one give me twenty-twenty-twenty-twenty. . . ." Shortly afterwards, he told Ernest Jewell that he would, if necessary, stick to his plan to become a poet for twenty years. In fact, he needed twenty years, and his first book of poems was not published until 1913. The auctioneering theme, which appealed to Frost's ironic sense of humor, reappeared in "The Self-Seeker." In that poem a young man, mutilated in a farm accident, is asked: "Have you agreed to any price?," bargains with an insurance agent and demands, "Five hundred. / Five hundred—five— five! One, two, three, four, five."[6]

Dartmouth provided a negative example of education that Frost reacted against in his own teaching, and led to a period of drifting into a series of dead-end jobs that marked him as a notable failure. But he did make three important literary discoveries while he was there: Palgrave's anthology of poetry, *The Golden Treasury,* Thomas Hardy's novels and the

New York newspaper the *Independent*—which was edited by a distinguished and quite unusual brother and sister, William Hayes Ward and Susan Hayes Ward. In March 1894, just after he completed the term at the Salem school, Frost sent them his first professional poem, "My Butterfly," which they published on November 8, 1894.

William, a Congregational minister and graduate of Amherst and Andover Theological Seminary, had been associated with the *Independent* since 1868. A leading authority on Assyrian and Babylonian seals, he had discovered the ancient city of Nippur in 1884. The old gentleman had once been a long-distance runner and still exercised by jogging around in his drawers. His younger sister, Susan, the literary editor of the newspaper, had studied china painting in Dresden in the 1870s and was an expert in needlework. An authority on hymns, she had also published several books on religion. The artistic, accomplished and well-bred New England spinster, six years older than Belle Frost, lived with her brother in Newark. The Wards, the first to discover the nascent poet, took a great interest in Frost's early career, published six more of his poems between 1896 and 1908, showed his work to established writers and became surrogate parents. They tried to give him good advice and were cross with him for having left Dartmouth. "They blamed me for that and reminded me of Milton, who was a very learned man," Frost remembered. In a review of September 28, 1899, Susan Ward linked Frost's first poem to his theory of poetry and wrote: "'My Butterfly' (November 8, 1894), which reads as if written with a practised pen, was, I believe, the first poem its author, Robert Lee Frost, ever offered for publication. He was hardly past boyhood at the time, and the poem was written, he says, when it first dawned upon him that poetry 'ought to sound well.'"[7]

Frost corresponded with Susan Ward for twenty years, sought her advice and visited her in December 1911. He later recalled that he had written "My Butterfly" by locking himself in the kitchen of his house in Lawrence. While he was composing the poem his sister, Jeanie, tried to batter down the door and break in. In January 1896, unsure of his talent and still trying to find his way, Frost wrote Susan Ward that he feared he was not a poet—or not a very comprehensible one. He later told another friend that in the pure, imagistic description of the second stanza ("The gray grass is scarce dappled with the snow") he had struck for the first time his characteristic note. He was sufficiently fond of this poem, inspired by Wordsworth's "To a Butterfly," to include it in his first book, *A Boy's Will*. Nevertheless, its archaic diction ("Snatched thee, o'ereager, with ungentle grasp") and sentimental thought (he finds its broken wing amidst the withered autumn leaves) made it distinctly inferior to the rest of the book. Frost's tremendous advance as a poet can immediately be seen by comparing it to "Blue-Butterfly Day" (1921), with its confident colloquialisms, striking imagery and frightening contrast in the razor-like last lines: "They lie closed over in the wind and cling / Where wheels have freshly sliced the April mire."

The publication of his first poem was a significant advance in Frost's career. But he still did not have a job or any clear plans for the future and could not live for long on the $15 fee. In the spring of 1893, while working for Elinor's mother on the farm in New Hampshire, he had paid such serious attention to Elinor's pregnant sister that Mrs. White had summoned Elinor back from college to reclaim him. In the fall of 1894, while still unemployed and after rejecting his grandfather's offer, he resumed (like his father) the ardent courtship of an older, reluctant woman. After Frost left Dartmouth, Mr. White had opposed the marriage. Elinor, quite reasonably, "said again and again I was willing to leave college and be married as soon as he was earning enough money to rent *one room* somewhere, but that I couldn't consent to be a burden to our parents." In order to persuade her to marry him at once, Frost made an extraordinary poetic gesture. He copied out "My Butterfly" and four other idyllic poems, had them printed on fine paper and bound in brown leather, with *Twilight* gold-stamped on the front cover, in an edition of only two copies. Like the secret exchange of wedding rings, one booklet would be for Elinor, one for himself.

Armed with these love tokens and encouraged by Mrs. White, Frost, who had heard that Elinor had acquired a handsome suitor, was determined to recapture her. He had left Dartmouth and now tried to persuade Elinor to leave St. Lawrence. But if his insistence on marriage without job or money was irrational, her behavior seemed incomprehensible, even cruel. He took the night train to Canton, went to Elinor's boarding house and knocked on her door. Surprised, shocked and clearly irritated by his arrival, Elinor, forbidden to admit him to the house, refused to meet him elsewhere and ordered him to take the next train home. She had rebelled against conventional behavior in high school, but behaved with extreme propriety in college. Hurt by this unexpected reception, he gave her the precious copy of *Twilight*. She took it casually, without understanding the significance of the gift, and closed the door in his face. As he walked out of town along the railroad tracks, enraged by her rejection, Frost destroyed his own copy. It now symbolized, like the Subverted Flower, the destruction of his hopes. He never published the other four poems, which were derivative and which he associated with this humiliating experience. Later on, he said that he had to cleanse himself of everything in *Twilight*.

Frost always maintained that Elinor had broken their engagement and almost immediately agreed to marry Lorenzo Dow Case, his rival at St. Lawrence. Her harsh rejection, her inability to understand his feelings, her disloyalty and betrayal, especially after they had slept together and pledged themselves to marriage, destroyed forever the essential foundation of his love. Though they would eventually marry, Frost became permanently convinced that Elinor did not love him as much as he loved her, and never recovered from this scarifying wound. In 1957 he recalled the effects of that traumatic visit: "I must have looked awful to Elinor. I looked worse than unpromising—everybody was broken up by the way I *looked*. I had no sense of being defiant—I just went this vague way. . . . I was persuaded at last that Elinor did not love me. . . . Since then I have never believed that life would turn out right. I still today feel I could lose everything and not be surprised."[8]

V

After returning to Lawrence Frost made the strange decision (never explained by himself or anyone else) to punish Elinor by disappearing into the Dismal Swamp. But if he wanted to kill himself, why did he not do so in Canton or Lawrence, where it would have the maximum impact? And if he wanted to end his life, why first travel nine hundred miles, from the Canadian border to the distant reaches of North Carolina? The reason, once again, was poetic. He was attracted to the Dismal Swamp, whose name suited his mood, because three important poets had described the place and drawn him to it.

Frost may not have read Harriet Beecher Stowe's *Dred: A Tale of the Great Dismal Swamp* (1856), in which a cruelly treated slave seeks refuge there. But he would have been familiar with the stirring Abolitionist work by Longfellow (one of his favorite poets), "The Slave in the Dismal Swamp" (1842), and could identify with the persecuted runaway— forced to hide out in that jungly landscape:

> In the dark fens of the Dismal Swamp
> The hunted Negro lay;

He saw the fire of the midnight camp
And heard at times a horse's tramp
    And a bloodhound's distant bay. . . .

Where hardly a human foot could pass,
    Or a human heart would dare,
On the quaking turf of the green morass
He crouched in the rank and tangled grass,
    Like a wild beast in his lair.

Frost's mother had read him the works of Poe—who had grown up in Richmond, not far from the Swamp—throughout his childhood. In the hypnotic "Dream-Land" (1844)—a land of death, of the unconscious and of nightmare—the narrator escapes from the agonies of the real world into a phantasmagoric landscape, where (like Frost) he confronts his own torments:

By the grey woods,—by the swamp
Where the toad and the newt encamp,—
By the dismal tarns and pools
            Where dwell the Ghouls,—
By each spot the most unholy—
In each nook most melancholy,—
There the traveller meets aghast
Sheeted Memories of the Past.

In November 1803 the Irish poet Thomas Moore, en route to a government job in Bermuda, visited Lake Drummond in the Dismal Swamp. Three years later, in "The Lake of the Dismal Swamp," Moore portrayed a grief-stricken lover who disappeared into that wilderness and was never seen again. Frost, rejected by Elinor, readily identified with the hero in the epigraph to the poem: "They tell of a young man, who lost his mind upon the death of the girl he loved, and who, suddenly disappearing from his friends, was never afterwards heard of." He had gone to the Dismal Swamp, "wandered into that dreary wilderness, and had died of hunger, or been lost in some of its dreadful morasses."

Away to the Dismal Swamp he speeds—
    His path was rugged and sore,
Through tangled juniper, beds of reeds,

Through many a fen, where the serpent feeds,
And never man trod before.

And, when on earth he sunk to sleep,
If slumber his eyelids knew,
He lay where the deadly vine doth weep
Its venomous tear and nightly steep
The flesh with blistering dew![9]

The heavily forested and almost impenetrable Dismal Swamp, which extends for twenty miles on the Virginia–North Carolina border, is, as the poets suggested, an extraordinarily menacing place. It was surveyed by George Washington in 1763, had a canal pushed through it in the 1790s, and during the Civil War became a base for Confederate guerrillas and a refuge for deserters from both sides. It has dangerous bogs and quicksands, fierce bears and bobcats, venomous rattlers and water moccasins. The coffee-colored, sandy-bottomed Lake Drummond, in the center of the Swamp, is surrounded by a dense undergrowth of briars, vines and mossy cypress trees. In the Dismal Swamp, as in Conrad's Heart of Darkness, "The great wall of vegetation, an exuberant and entangled mass of trunks, branches, leaves, boughs, festoons, motionless in the moonlight, was like a rioting invasion of soundless life, a rolling wave of plants, piled up, crested, ready to topple over the creek, to sweep every little man of us out of his existence. . . . It made you feel very small, very lost." The Swamp reflected Frost's despondent mood and was the perfect place to disappear—for a while—in order to frighten Elinor and make her understand the desperation of his love.

On November 6, 1894 the twenty-year-old Frost took a train to New York, boarded a steamer for Norfolk, Virginia, and, wearing ordinary clothes and carrying a small bag, walked about ten miles into the Swamp. Instead of finding death, he met a congenial group of drunken duck hunters. They invited him on board their boat, gave him a hearty meal, took him through the canal to Elizabeth City, North Carolina, and then across Albemarle Sound to Nags Head on the Outer Banks. After returning with them to Elizabeth City, he hopped a freight train north to Washington and Baltimore. Then, weary of his adventure, he wired his mother for money to buy a train ticket home.

More than sixty years later, after Frost had revisited Kitty Hawk (a few miles north of Nags Head), where in 1903 the Wright brothers took off in the first airplane, he celebrated his youthful journey. In "Kitty Hawk" he describes how the convivial duck hunters from Elizabeth City, loaded with guns and drink, included him in their revelry. But he stole off one night, where the Atlantic pounded the beaches, and met a solitary coastguardsman who told him how Aaron Burr's daughter, Theodosia, had been shipwrecked on that very shore. Frost, a son astray and at odds with men, identified with that drowned daughter.

Frost's half-hearted, not to say mythical, suicide attempt was no more serious than the young Evelyn Waugh's attempt to drown himself off the coast of North Wales, which was thwarted when he swam into a school of jellyfish. A month before his death, Frost told one of his biographers: "I suppose it was all nothing but my young way of having the blues." The main poetic legacy of the Dismal Swamp was not "Kitty Hawk" but "Into My Own," the first poem in his first book. After the narrator steals away into the vastness of dark trees, he wonders if those who love him will try to find him:

> I do not see why I should e'er turn back,
> Or those should not set forth upon my track
> To overtake me, who should miss me here
> And long to know if still I held them dear.
>
> They would not find me changed from him they knew—
> Only more sure of all I thought was true.[10]

As in Poe's "Dream-Land," the narrator of "Into My Own" finds himself (in the positive sense) by running away and becomes surer of what he felt was true—his love for Elinor.

During his first ten years in New England Frost felt angry about the degrading poverty of his family and about the humiliation his mother had suffered in her teaching jobs. He also brooded over and resented Elinor's rejection of his love, which would undermine the basis of their marriage. Emotional and insecure, he turned to poetry to direct his life and give it meaning; and poetry influenced and sometimes determined some of his most crucial decisions. He used Shelley's paean to free love to justify sleeping with Elinor, gave her the poems in *Twilight* to persuade her to marry him and was lured to the Dismal Swamp by its poetic associations. His expulsion from Dartmouth merely strengthened his ambitious commitment to a poetic career, which finally seemed possible after his first poem was published in the *Independent*.

3

Marriage

1895–1900

I

Frost's suicidal gesture made a powerful impression on Elinor. The dramatic adventure showed how much he loved her and led to the hoped-for reconciliation. She finally agreed to marry him. Having accelerated her education, she finished college in three years and graduated in June 1895. Belle Frost, after losing her job in Methuen, planned to start her own private school, with her daughter Jeanie and Elinor as teachers. She rented two offices in a commercial building in the center of Lawrence and converted them into classrooms. In the spring of 1895 Frost, in need of funds, briefly returned to his job in the Salem grade school where he had taught the previous year. When Belle's prospects improved, he became a teacher in his mother's modest academy.

Frost and Elinor, like his school-teacher parents, were married in the middle of the academic year, on December 19, 1895. He was twenty-one and she was twenty-three. Since neither of them was a believer, there was no church ceremony and a Swedenborgian minister officiated in the converted classrooms. They postponed their honeymoon until the summer and moved in with Belle and Jeanie. In the spring of 1896, when Elinor realized she was pregnant, Frost suffered severe—sympathetic or competitive—stomach pains. In the fall they finally moved into their own small flat, and their first blue-eyed, blond-haired child—whom they named Elliott, after Frost's ancestral town in Maine—was born nine months after the wedding, on September 25, 1896.

Elinor resembled D. H. Lawrence's first love, Jessie Chambers. She was a delicate, high-strung, introspective, dreamy, poetical young woman—"shy, questioning, a little resentful of strangers . . . a wild, quiveringly sensitive thing." Only five feet tall, she had a pale complexion, a low voice and a mild, inscrutable manner; an attractive, sweet, sad face with "blue eyes which looked straight at you, but without seeing you—even then her gaze seemed to be directed at some private inner world."

Frost's friends rarely mentioned Elinor—who seemed self-effacing and rather colorless—or, out of respect for him, merely offered a few mild platitudes about her. In letters to her family and friends she usually wrote about the weather, children and household affairs. She never considered more serious subjects and appeared to be a dull and utterly conventional woman, who liked to read Zane Grey and P. G. Wodehouse. The wives of English poets, who met her some years later and lived in close contact with her, were condescending. Catherine Abercrombie said Frost's "little wife Elinor was a charming little woman, quite an ordinary little woman, a rather shy person." And Helen Thomas "felt a sort of motherly compassion for her, for she seemed rather quiet and meek, and a little inadequate to cope with the wild ways of her husband" and growing family.[1]

In "Paul's Wife," a rather defensive poem, Frost dramatized his feelings about Elinor. People say Paul has married a wife who is not his equal and claim he is ashamed of her. Paul, extremely prickly and sensitive on this subject, keeps his wife hidden and his love secret, and will not be spoken to about his wife in any way the world knows how to speak. Frost was completely committed to Elinor, who shared his deepest thoughts and inspired his poetry, and felt her personal shortcomings were irrelevant. When a friend baldly told him that some people thought Elinor had no personality, he did not deny the description, but considered Elinor a part of himself and vehemently replied: "But she's *mine!*"

Though she made most of the children's clothes, Elinor, like Belle, was by all accounts an incompetent and chaotic housekeeper. Frost, following the custom of the time, rarely helped with the housework. He suffered strange pains when there was work to be done and used illness to excuse himself from domestic duties. At a time when there were few mechanical appliances, Elinor casually told a friend that the fewer dishes there were, the fewer one had to wash. In 1913 she also advised a younger woman, "you must learn the art of 'letting things go' just as I had to learn it long, long ago," and self-protectively asked: "How could I have ever lived through those years when the children were little tots if I had been at all fussy about my housework?" Like the "servant to servants," in Frost's poem, Elinor, overwhelmed and exhausted by work, might well say:

> It's rest I want—there, I have said it out—
> From cooking meals for hungry hired men
> And washing dishes after them—from doing
> Things over and over that just won't stay done.

Like the Swedenborgians, she was determined to concentrate on higher things.

Helen Thomas, who knew Elinor well and shared many household tasks with her, emphasized her physical weakness and impracticality: "Elinor . . . had a rather nebulous personality and had none of the physical strength or activity of her husband. House-keeping to her was a very haphazard affair and I remember that when dinner time approached in the middle of the day, she would take a bucket of potatoes into the field and sit on the grass to peel them—without water, to my astonishment—and that, as far as I could see, was often the only preparation for a meal." The Frost household had a chaotic routine, irregular mealtimes and casual diet. If Elinor made a special effort she would cook a huge roast beef, with only bread and tea, and would always leave the dirty dishes until the next morning. She tried to adjust to Frost's habit of staying up very late—so he could write when the children were asleep —and lying in bed till late the next day. In the mornings the children, who had to remain quiet and shift for themselves, often cut a chunk of cold meat from the leftover roast for their unconventional breakfast.

Eleanor Farjeon, a friend of Helen and Edward Thomas, saw the positive side of this regimen, which protected the exhausted Elinor and encouraged the children's spontaneity, independence and interest in the natural world: "Mealtimes (bedtimes too, I believe) were when you felt like them. Irregular hours for children meant an extension of experience for them; it was more important for a child to go for a walk in the dark than to have an unbroken night's rest. . . . When the children were hungry . . . they helped themselves to . . . bread, fruit, cold rice in a bowl. . . . Elinor Frost, fragile and weariable, was not the naturally joyful housewife that Helen was. . . . The centre of the Frosts was out-of-doors, and household standards mattered very little."[2] Elinor could rise to the occasion when she had to entertain distinguished guests. Later on, at a party for the poet Amy Lowell, she hired a caterer to serve good plain fare: chicken salad with rolls, cake and ice cream with coffee. One grateful guest at Amherst recalled a dinner of lamb chops, baked pota-toes, peas and carrots, with salted peanuts and apple pudding.

Elinor, who had been sick with fever for two years in high school, had a hard life. Her houses were quite primitive, she had a delicate constitu-tion, and frequently suffered from both physical and nervous illness. Frost, a complex and demanding husband, frustrated in his early career and often pressed for money, was sometimes difficult to live with. Soon after she married, doctors told Elinor that she had a heart condition which made it dangerous to have children. But she gave birth to her second child, Lesley, on April 28, 1899; to three more children (in less than three years) between 1902 and 1905, and to her sixth child in 1907. All these pregnancies wore her out and weakened her health.

When discussing the serious problems in marriage, Frost mentioned babies and the fear of babies, and (quoting Shakespeare) told Unter-meyer that the word "stork" was even more unpleasing to a married ear than cuckoo. His close friend Sidney Cox revealed that Frost emphasized the importance of improving the race and "doubted the beneficence of widespread [or even personal] birth control. . . . To have geniuses and powerful men, Robert said, a people must have many children." Thomp-son noted that Elinor had a difficult time in childbearing and "hated the indignity of having a doctor explore her before childbirth."[3] When Frost had established his reputation and began to give poetry readings throughout the country, Elinor, afraid he might be tempted by other women, became jealous. Frost, a handsome, strongly sexed man, did attract the ladies and "had many troublesome feelings" about them. But he was faithful to Elinor, who consented to have a large family and satisfied his sexual and emotional needs.

After his rejection at St. Lawrence, Frost may also have been jealous, despite the scrutiny of small-town eyes, when Elinor was left on her own. He expressed his fears about her infidelity in "The Middletown Murder" (1928). Elinor did not want him to publish this rough-hewn, serio-comic ballad, which he brought out in the *Saturday Review of Literature* but never included in his *Collected Poems*. In this poem a rural husband returns unexpectedly from a trip to the lumber camp to find his wife sleeping with his friend and bitterly exclaims: "The joke's on me for trusting a whore. / Wouldn't it make a rifle roar?" He gives the treacherous friend a chance to run, then shoots him through the heart and is arrested. The sheriff tells the woman, who will be responsible for the death of two men: "Let it be a lesson to you for life: / Next time you marry, be a wife."[4]

II

Frost's adult appearance, tastes, habits, character and beliefs had formed by the time of his marriage. He was about five feet, nine inches tall and had the penetrating, bright blue, deeply recessed—but color blind —eyes of his seafaring Scottish grandfather. He had a full, sensuous mouth, a square, blunt nose and moved his eyelids up and down very slowly. As he got older, his eyebrows shot out like an insect's antennae. His workman's arms were thick and hairy, his hands large and strong, his body broad-shouldered and athletic. When thinking, he often rubbed his nose with his right index finger. Fond of country speech and rustic expressions, he would say "f'rall," "presdint" and "doncha know." The poet John Gould Fletcher was later "struck by the Celtic dreaminess of his eyes, his quiet unworldliness, his serene detachment of manner." But Helen Thomas saw him as a more solid, earthy creature: "Robert was a thickset man. . . . His face was tanned and weatherbeaten and his features powerful. His eyes, shaded by bushy grey eyebrows, were blue and clear. It was a striking and pleasing face, rugged and lined. He was dressed in an open-necked shirt and loose earth-stained trousers held up by a wide belt. His arms and chest were bare and very brown. His hands were hard and gnarled. He spoke with a slight American accent."

Since Elinor had no interest in cooking, Frost's taste in food was, by necessity and choice, very simple. Food and drink, as well as furnishings, clothes and possessions, were not important to him. He would wake up late in the morning and have a simple breakfast: a raw egg in a glass of orange juice and a cup of milk with hot water. He would eat a hearty meal at noon and take a light supper. He claimed, in a book on masculine cuisine: "I cook nothing and have never cooked anything except potatoes outdoors in wood ashes. They can be cooked without burning." He then added that he was especially fond of this rustic recipe: "I like them with the skin burned black and hard as a shell."[5] He also loved sweets, ate candy by the box and cookies by the carton, and put plenty of sugar in his hot and cold drinks.

He was able, when necessary, to provide hearty American food for his friends. He served liver and bacon, sweet potatoes and canned cherries for Thompson, and a more elaborate meal for another guest: "There were two lamb chops on my plate and a mixture of rice and something else, a little chicken, I think. There was smoked cheese as a side dish. . . . Fruit, pickles, crackers, and candy were the other delicacies." Though "something else" and "I think" are slightly alarming, they seemed to have eaten the meal without serious incident. One of his relatives said his favorite dinner was pan-broiled steak, baked potatoes, corn muffins, lettuce leaves and ice cream. Like a good puritan, he scorned all culinary refinements, but would dine with gusto when taken to fine restaurants.

Frost did not smoke and, because of his father's notorious example, avoided liquor—though he always kept a congenial bottle of whiskey for visitors. He got drunk in 1894 to see if it would inspire his poetry but did not find it helpful. "I hated liquor," he told a biographer. "If I ever got drunk in my whole life it was to make somebody sorry for something he had done to me."

Always susceptible to bronchial illness, Frost kept his windows closed at night and liked a warm room with plenty of covers on his bed. He did a bit of fishing, but did not like hunting. Though athletic, like his father, and surrounded by country lakes and ponds, he almost never went swimming. He did not like to expose his bare body and may have feared the water after watching his father's dangerous swims in San Francisco Bay. He had played football in high school, but his two lifelong passions were tennis and baseball. He became actively interested in tennis, which he associated with good manners, as early as 1890 and took it up seriously when teaching at Plymouth in 1911. One observer reported that "he played badly, being slow in his reflexes and heavy of foot . . . [but] with quiet, stolid determination, remaining planted like a mountain and moving only when he had to go after a ball that was already over the net." At the Bread Loaf summer school in Vermont—with sleeves rolled up and suspenders hoisting his long trousers—he swung mightily in tennis and baseball. He played doubles with Kay Morrison, whose "life depended" on no errors or double faults. Later on, younger writers—including Untermeyer and Stanley Kunitz—were expected to defer to the vanity of the bard and gracefully accept defeat on the court.

Frost was also fiercely competitive about baseball, which he played with his children and pupils as well as with writers at Bread Loaf. He would round first base and slide into second, argue angrily with the umpire and, if his team was losing, claim the scorekeepers had somehow missed a couple of runs. In baseball as in tennis, Frost's side had to win or he would get into a dangerously grumpy mood. Late in life, he wrote a witty essay about baseball for *Sports Illustrated*.

When listing his likes, he alluded to his habitual late hours, a dramatic poem by Milton which he had memorized, taught and performed, his own poem "The Road Not Taken," his border collie and, rather surprisingly for a confirmed countryman, a big city. His dislikes included sloppy habits and his political *bêtes noires:* "*Things I like:* The time after midnight, 'Comus,' A path without road or stones, My dog, New York; *Things I dislike:* Incompleteness, Excuses for defects, Internationalism, War predictions, Nothing else as much as these."[6]

Many aspects of Frost's life and character were paradoxical: he was a New Englander, born in San Francisco; a Yankee named Robert Lee; a farmer who did not do much farming; an American poet, first recognized in England. He was ambitious but idle, famous yet insecure, sickly in youth but hearty in old age. He became a prolific author, but talked more than he wrote. He never seemed pressed for time, never looked at his watch or clock, and what seemed to be laziness was actually a period of mental reflection and sparkling conversation that was essential to his creative life.

He would slide down into his chair till his head rested on the back, and begin his genial and uninhibited, penetrating and revealing talk, which ranged from intimate gossip to philosophical speculations. Frost was an intriguing storyteller, with a great gift for dramatic narrative. He was also an attentive listener and questioned people closely on matters that interested him, but would talk until the early hours of the morning and "was a hard man to get away from when he was wound up." He loved the natural ebb and flow of his own rambling but fascinating discourse, which jumped from subject to subject but always circled back to the dominant idea. Most friends (especially as he got older) were content to listen rather than converse. Those who had the privilege of hearing his riveting talk considered him to be one of the greatest speakers of his time—comparable to Samuel Johnson and to Coleridge.

In one of his most charming poems, "A Time to Talk," Frost says that when he is working in the fields and a passing friend slows down his horse and calls to him from the road, he does not worry about all the work he has to do and always has time to exchange news and ideas:

> I thrust my hoe into the mellow ground,
> Blade-end up and five feet tall,
> And plod: I go up to the stone wall
> For a friendly visit.[7]

Conversation complemented physical labor, allowed him to break out of the solitude of farming and poetry, and stimulated him to formulate and refine his thoughts.

Frost often spoke about his attitude toward religion, and defined his lack of belief in his letters and talk more clearly than he did in his more cryptic and elusive poetry. He told Thompson that he respected his mother's spirituality and admired her devotion, but—like his father —had no religion himself. He also doubted if he had ever been religious and said he did not believe in the efficacy of prayer. Frost moved from a William Jamesian "Will to Believe" in his youth, through scepticism, to a final nihilism and even mockery of religion. He wrote Untermeyer that he would be "safely secular" until the very end, and told a scholar: "You know, there is nothing after this." He also mentioned his principal objections to Christian doctrine and declared that "reason sticks at two things and won't allow the mind to accept them: the first is that one man's sin would cause the downfall of all men. . . . The second is the idea of the immaculate conception." Frost, who had six children, could not bring himself to believe that "having children is sinful." Parodying a nursery rhyme, he even wrote a blasphemous quatrain about how Joseph was cuckolded: "Mary had a little lamb, / His name was Jesus Christ, / And God, not Joseph, was the ram; / But Joseph took it nice."[8]

Though Frost was usually genial and expansive, he was—even in his years of fame—cautious, defensive, touchy and extremely sensitive to slight. Always on his guard against everyone, he would bark at a well-wisher who inquired about his health: "Cut out the therapeutic!" Raymond Holden, a young poet who became a neighbor and intimate of Frost and his family, explained that the poet always concealed his deepest emotions: "One of the difficult things about Robert was that he never let me know what he was thinking or feeling. We would talk for hours about Poe, Shakespeare, George Meredith, Thoreau, nature or neighbors, but never about the things nearest us. My [first] wife had an affair with another man, and although Robert appraised it correctly before I did, he never let me know what he thought about it." In a letter to Harold Rugg, the librarian of Dartmouth, Frost (like the cunning drumlin woodchuck in his poem) was hyperbolically witty about the elaborate methods he used to defend himself against the demands of readers, critics, scholars and friends: "Lies, false promises, flattery, bribes, prayers, tears, tear gas, malingering, protective coloration, irony, hysterics, change of pace, tact." With keen self-insight he told his daughter how he protected himself against the possibility of rejection: "I was always too inclined to give up wanting anything that was denied me unjustly and take it out in a feeling of injured superiority." In a frank yet characteristically subtle letter to the poet Mark Van Doren, who had made a meager choice of Frost's poems for an anthology, Frost was at once confessional, imperious and engagingly minatory: "I'm too touchy —particularly with friends. Treat me well and you'll be expected to treat me better."[9]

Those who did not treat Frost well were subjected to his withering anger and risked the loss of his friendship. The independent-minded Frost, resenting any patronage, debts or obligations, repeatedly turned against those who had helped him in the early phases of his career: first, his grandfather, Carl Burell and Ernest Silver; then Pound, Amy Lowell and the editor William Braithwaite; and finally Raymond Holden, the author Stark Young and the college president Alexander Meiklejohn. Though Frost was ungrateful to some benefactors, he defused his anger by threatening to retaliate against his adversaries. But these threats were almost never translated into action. It's been a hard winter, he wrote Untermeyer, punning as usual to this friend, and when hard up he would harden his heart against almost everyone. He told another friend: "I won't be insulted without striking back." "Christ forgive me the sin of vengefulness," he exclaimed to his former student John Bartlett, "the worst you could reveal was my Indian vindictiveness." He also confessed to Thompson, with disarming candor, "I take a long time to wreak vengeance, when I've been wronged . . . but I never forget, and I never forgive a wrong." Frost liked to swagger a bit and appear as a tough hombre who could never be crossed. Thompson naively accepted and magnified this myth, and included a whole section on "Revenge" in his index. But with the single exception of Stark Young, Frost never actually tried to harm anyone. He confined his anger to caustic remarks and said: "I didn't mean any harm; I just meant a little harm."[10]

Frost's characteristic defensiveness, hypersensitivity and anger were all related to his insecurity. This began in childhood when Will's rage and cruelty made him doubt his father's love, and when Will's early death forced the family into an uprooted, humiliating and impoverished life, into a series of menial jobs (for both his mother and himself) and cramped tenement rooms in the slums of the town. This poverty continued, as his own family grew, in his years of struggle as a farmer and teacher in New Hampshire. During the first twenty years of his adult life the ambitious Frost, isolated in a rural region, tried to establish his reputation as poet, but was not able to publish his first book until he was nearly forty.

The poet John Holmes called Frost "an untamed, wary, stubborn, easily alarmed man." Theodore Morrison, a close friend, believed he was never "free from spells of acute self-doubt." Kay Morrison, who knew Frost better than anyone, confirmed that "he really needed to be told he was good. He was uncertain about himself until the last day of his life; he was uncertain of everything." Mark Van Doren, who respected Frost but kept his distance, perceived that his melodramatic threats were harmless and that his insecurity was not only personal but cosmic: "Frost should never have been allowed to say so many times in public . . . that he was a terrible man. . . . He enjoyed too much the telling of it. . . . In Frost, though, it was fear as well. Incredibly, he never seems to have known how good a poet he was, and so had to play games with fame. . . . He feared every living poet, and needed to fear none. It wasn't jealousy, it was terror."[11] Frost had a lifelong fear of the dark; he heard disturbing noises, knew insanity was rampant in his family and was afraid that he too would go mad.

III

In December 1896, three months after the birth of his son, Frost's rage exploded into a fistfight. To earn some extra money he had sublet rooms on the second floor of his rented house in Lawrence to a young man named Herbert Parker, who had worked with him in the Arlington mill. Parker had rebelled against his prominent family by marrying "a whore-house keeper's daughter" and had been unable to find a place to live. Frost objected to the visits of a woman who was known to be a prostitute, exchanged harsh words with Mrs. Parker and was called a coward for insulting her when her husband was absent. Frost later gave one of his biographers an exaggerated account of this incident and claimed that "the wife flared and attacked [him], and he was compelled in self-defense to hold her by the wrists until her rage subsided. . . . When he heard the husband come home, he went upstairs and thrashed him soundly."

In fact, according to a front-page story in the Lawrence *Daily American* of December 28, 1896, his conflict with Mrs. Parker was merely verbal. Stung by her charge of cowardice, he exclaimed:

> "Your husband don't dare call me that" and left the room.
> When Mr. Parker entered his kitchen Mr. Frost came in and asked him if he called him a coward.

"I do," he replied, "if you insult my wife in my absence."

"Do you want to fight?" . . .

"No, I don't."

Trouble seems to have followed and the black eye which Parker is wearing at present is said to have been given him by Frost.

Parker jumped up from his chair to defend himself and the two grappled with each other and in a second Parker was on a chair with Frost on top of him. Some scars on Parker's forehead and chest are said to have been received at this time.

Mrs. Frost, her daughter and her daughter-in-law then intervened and separated the combatants and both parties withdrew to their respective tenements.

Parker then went to the police station to swear out a warrant against Frost and told his story to the city marshal.

Frost pleaded guilty, was sentenced to a fine of ten dollars or thirty days and paid the fine.

The absurd, embarrassing and costly fight (ten dollars was more than a week's wages) made it clear to the young husband and father that teaching in his mother's school was leading nowhere. He had originally intended to follow his father to Harvard, and during his senior year in high school had gone to Cambridge to take the entrance exams. On that occasion he was shown around Harvard and found it extremely impressive: "Some boys from my high school asked me down. They were all three rich boys . . . one of them is [Fred] Robinson, who taught Chaucer at Harvard. . . . They were all very cultivated and all of cultured families, and they asked me down on account of something of mine they'd seen written [in the *Bulletin*]. And they entertained me for a day, and I went to their beautiful rooms and I saw walls of books and I thought to myself, isn't it lovely—college life with all books and things. I never saw such books again."[12] He must have longed for the gracious rooms and cultured life at Harvard when assaulted in his bare room by the drunken bullies of Dartmouth.

Frost had maintained his interest in the Classics and now decided that he wanted to teach Latin and Greek in high school. His grandfather, who may not have known about his expulsion from Dartmouth, once again agreed to pay the tuition. In September 1897 the twenty-three-old Frost (five years older than most of the freshmen) was admitted to Harvard as a special student. At first he lived alone in Cambridge, but missed his family and was lonely without them. Later in the term Elinor, with her mother and the baby, moved in with him.

Frost was required to take English composition and German as well as Latin and Greek. He mentioned his experience as a teacher, reporter and published poet and asked to be placed in the advanced composition class. The professor, in his most condescending Harvard manner, exclaimed: "Oh! So we're a *writer*, are we?" and rudely rejected his request. His instructor in English A was Alfred Sheffield. Only three years older than Frost and known as "the bearded lady," he was married to T. S. Eliot's sister Ada. He disliked Frost's work, sneered at important poems like "The Tuft of Flowers" and gave him a mere B– in the course. Frost thought his Latin teacher, Charles Parker, was both boring and pedantic. Though he never took a course from the English professor Barrett Wendell, he saw enough of him to despise his affectations. The only teacher he fondly recalled was Frank Cole Babbitt, who awarded him A's in Greek. Despite his bumpy ride in English, Frost won a Sewall Scholarship of $200 for excellent work during his first year.

In his sophomore year Frost continued with Latin and Greek and took two courses in philosophy. He had hoped to study with William James, who took medical leave that year, but used James' book *Psychology: The Briefer Course* (1892) in the class taught by the German Hugo Münsterberg. The History of Philosophy course was taught by Frost's most distinguished professor, the Spanish-born, Harvard-educated man of letters George Santayana. He had recently published *Sonnets and Other Verse* (1894) and *The Sense of Beauty* (1896), a major treatise on aesthetics. Still under the influence of his mother's piety, Frost was shocked by Santayana's sarcastic and even blasphemous attitude toward religion and preferred the more positive ideas expressed in William James' "The Will to Believe."

Frost remained at Harvard until March of his sophomore year, when he decamped in the middle of a term—as he had done at Dartmouth. He must have really "hated it" (as he told a friend) to risk provoking the wrath of his grandfather and scorn of his friends, and to sacrifice, for the second time and with a family to support, the teaching career that would have been open to him with a college degree. The main problem was that Frost felt intellectually and emotionally isolated at Harvard. Wallace Stevens and Witter Bynner, who later became his friends, were his contemporaries but—older, distant from most of the students and absorbed in his family—he never even heard of them till long afterwards. His lack of money and social polish, his rough clothes and blunt manners marked him as different from the privileged Harvard men. He did not live in the congenial Harvard houses or belong to any of the elite social clubs. He never wrote for the *Advocate* or the *Harvard Monthly,* never had time or money to go to the Boston Symphony or Museum of Fine Arts. When he became disillusioned with the academic work, there was nothing else to sustain him.

In the summer after his freshman year at Harvard Elinor became inconveniently pregnant with their second child and did not return to Cambridge with him. Though conscious of his own abilities, and keen to escape the limitations of his family and a shameful hand-to-mouth exist-ence, living alone in Cambridge was more than he could bear. Then his mother became seriously ill. He felt so lonely and out of place that his misery erupted in physical symptoms. As with Elinor's first pregnancy, he suffered severe pains in his chest and stomach. "I got very sick," he melodramatically told Elizabeth Sergeant, "terribly so, as if something were very wrong with heart or stomach. Trouble in the solar plexus. So I resigned from the sophomore class at the end of March [1899], to the Dean's regret. The doctor thought I would die. He sent me home to die." Instead of dying, Frost returned (as he had done after Dartmouth) to Lawrence and to an uncertain future. This time, however, he was able to secure a note of honorable dismissal from the dean. Frost now believed, more strongly than ever, that leaving college was more beneficial than staying there.

By the time he left Harvard, Frost had taken six years of Latin and five of Greek. Though he had abandoned the idea of becoming a Classics teacher, he had all the formal education that he needed. He would later teach Latin in high school, give a lecture on "The Discipline of the Classics and the Writing of English" at the January 1916 meeting of the Classical Association of New England and seriously consider offering a course in Latin at Harvard. Under the subtle but unmistakable influence of the Classics, Frost developed the most chaste and chiseled style in modern American poetry. A. E. Housman wrote of his own verse: "My classical training has been of some use to me in furnishing good models, and making me fastidious, and telling me what to leave out." In a similar way, Frost's long training in strict classical meter encouraged him to write in traditional forms and made him one of the ablest verse techni-cians of his time.

Ever since Pound's review of *North of Boston,* which he titled "Modern Georgics," Frost's pastoral poetry has been compared to Virgil's. Like Virgil, Frost used rural subjects and settings for social criticism and developed the ancient analogy between the farmer's craft and the poet's art. Because Frost was a real farmer, his daily life supplied him with the realistic details and human characters in his poems. In "Build Soil," his most conservative political poem, he adapted and parodied the two shepherds, Tityrus and Meliboeus, from Virgil's first *Eclogue*. As Theodore Ziolkowski writes: "precisely, as in the first *Eclogue*, we are dealing in Frost's 'political pastoral' with social turmoil, dispossessed shepherds, and political aspiration in a poetic dialogue that confronts the realistic fugitive Meliboeus with a somewhat complacent Tityrus, who defends the autonomy of the individual and, accordingly, of a *poésie pure*." The most specific allusion to Virgil, Ziolkowski observes, occurs in "the first line of 'The Mountain,' 'The mountain held the town as in a shadow,' [which] is not so much a translation as a paraphrase [or extension] of the two magical closing lines of the first *Eclogue*: 'And already smoke is rising from the housetops in the distance, / and longer shadows fall from the lofty mountains.' "

The most striking classical parallel is with the poems from the *Greek Anthology*, whose brevity, stylized diction, concise couplets, extreme concentration and striking immediacy Frost imitated in seven short poems from *A Witness Tree*. The famous Greek epitaph (for example): "At sixty I, Dionysios of Tarsos, lie here, / Never having married: and I wish my father had not,"[13] Frost deliberately echoes when he asks in "A Question": "If all the soul-and-body scars / Were not too much to pay for birth."

IV

While studying at Harvard in the spring of 1899 Frost had experienced mysterious chills, sharp chest pains, sweaty nightmares and physical exhaustion. These symptoms were probably psychosomatic (most of them disappeared when he left Harvard). But his doctor feared tuberculosis, which had killed his father, and recommended farming to get him outdoors and away from the strains of sedentary life. Frost knew Charlemagne Bricault, born in Canada in 1866 and trained as a veterinarian at Laval University, who owned a prosperous poultry farm in Methuen. Bricault advised him about how to raise Wyandotte hens and promised to help him market the fowl and eggs. In May 1899 Frost rented a place in Methuen.

Frost's second child, Lesley, was born in Lawrence in April 1899—the month after he left Harvard. Fourteen months later, the three-year-old Elliott became seriously ill with an intestinal infection. Elinor's mother and sister had become Christian Scientists and said that a doctor should not be called. Belle's physician examined him and left some pills, but the child got worse. After severe vomiting, diarrhea and loss of fluid, he went into a state of shock and collapsed. Frost then summoned his own doctor. Angry that he had not been consulted sooner, he called the case hopeless, blamed the stunned parents instead of the previous doctor and brutally told them: "This is *cholera infantum.* It's too late, now, for me to do anything. The child will be dead before morning." His prediction was accurate and Elliott died on the night of July 8, 1900. Belle, staying in their house and ravaged by cancer, made matters worse by declaring "it was God's punishment."

Even before their marriage, Elinor had been rather silent, sad and dour, and had always taken a dark view of life. She had held the sick child, willed him to live and begged God to save him. When he died, she was crushed and broken by the loss, rejected God and renounced any belief in a Supreme Being. Since a central tenet of the Universalist faith was a certainty of just retribution for all sins, she agreed with Belle that Elliott had been sacrificed by a malign Deity in order to punish her. As Frost wrote in *A Masque of Mercy:* "She's had some loss she can't accept from God." She withdrew into a desperate, fatalistic pessimism and combined the worst traits of Frost's parents: his mother's dreary incompetence, his father's bitter gloom. In an early poem, "My November Guest," Frost addressed Elinor as "My Sorrow" and identified her with the desolate winter landscape.

Frost's relations with Elinor deteriorated after Elliott's death. Embittered and withdrawn, she became increasingly critical of her husband, and seemed to turn against him as she had done when he visited her at St. Lawrence. Luxuriating in her grief, alternating between glowering silence and wounding accusations of selfishness and neglect, she opposed him with her stillness and her sharp retorts, and neither cared nor understood how he felt. Instead of consoling each other, the Frosts exacerbated each other's misery. The death of Frost's mother, at the age of fifty-six, occurred four months later, on November 2, 1900. He was close to his mother and his grief was deep, but he left no record of his response to her death.

Elliott was never mentioned again; no picture of him survives and we know almost nothing about the child's life. Four of his children predeceased Frost and another became insane, but he never—except in "Home Burial" (1914)—wrote directly about these personal tragedies in his poetry. Fearing excessive emotion or unseemly revelation, he said: "Something in me refuses to take the risk—angrily refuses to take the risk—of seeming to use grief for literary purposes." Though he gave perhaps a thousand readings of his poetry, he considered "Home Burial" too sad to read aloud.

"Home Burial" (whose title suggests both burial at home and the burial of home life) describes with startling honesty the effect of Elliott's death on Elinor and speaks of woe that is in marriage. The poem portrays two kinds of grief: the man hides his feelings and wants to resume life; the woman, overcome by her feelings, wants to mourn. He asks to be let into her grief; she shuts him out. Though the woman fails to understand the man, Frost sympathizes—as in "The Subverted Flower" —with her point of view, for the passion expressed in that poem had led to the death in this one. In this respect, his dramatic account of an agonizing situation resembles Hemingway's "Hills Like White Elephants" (1927). In that story, a young man, trying to convince his mistress to have an abortion, talks too much (as the woman remains rather silent) and alienates her affection. As Frost explained in his Notebook: "His wife listened to his ruthless talk and for a long time half-believed him. Reckless of losing her he still talked on." In Frost's poem, the man perceives: "My words are nearly always an offense."

As the man talks on, the woman becomes fearful, cowering and withdrawn. Their quarrel on the narrow staircase of their house concerns perception. She calls him a blind creature who cannot see; he claims to see what is bothering her. Her grief is focused on the family graveyard, visible from the house, where their recently dead first infant is buried. (The baby's mound of earth contrasts with the solid stones of the older dead.) When he dares to mention the fresh grave, she cries: "Don't, don't, don't, / don't," which echoes through the poem. It has the same effect as the "Never, never, never, never, never" in *King Lear* and the "please please please please please please please stop talking" in Hemingway's story. Frost told his friend Sidney Cox that "the four 'don'ts' were the supreme thing in it."[14]

The woman denies him the right to speak of her loss. Stifled by her existence, she threatens to leave as he pleads with her to stay. He claims her grief is excessive ("You overdo it a little"); she maintains that he has no feelings. She then condemns him for the way he—almost joyfully (for he was physically absorbed in the cathartic work)—dug the child's grave:

> Making the gravel leap and leap in air,
> Leap up, like that, like that, and land so lightly,

and for coming into the house "with the stains on your shoes / Of the fresh earth from your own baby's grave."[15] He replies that he is cursed, like Job, both by the death of his child and by his wife's imprecations. But she continues to condemn him by repeating his innocent but apparently callous words: "Three foggy mornings and one rainy day / Will rot the best birch fence a man can build." By saying this, he was thinking of fences—not their implications. But she connects the fence to the child in a horrible way, twists his words to mean that their baby was doomed to rot as surely and as quickly as the fence. Why make a fence, if it rots in only three days, he seems to be saying, and why make a baby, who now *rots* in the ground. She prefers to be alone with her grief ("I won't, I won't!" echoes her previous "don'ts"); he wants to make his "way back to life." When he utterly fails to persuade her by words, he threatens to follow her out of the house and force her back into life. Frost, however, could rarely force the strong-willed Elinor to do anything and was himself forced to live with the grief that had damaged their marriage forever.

4

A Hampshire Lad

1900–1906

I

After Elliott's death the Frosts felt the Methuen house was ruined for them by morbid associations. In any case, Frost was asked to move by the landlady, who could no longer tolerate hundreds of chickens running all over her property. In September 1900 Elinor's mother found an attractive farm—located in Derry, New Hampshire, just north of Salem—with thirty acres, a fairly new house and barn, an apple-tree orchard and a small brook. It had outdoor privies, and a horse and buggy to get into town. Despite his disappointment and anger about Frost's abortive education at Dartmouth and Harvard, Frost's grandfather now offered to buy the farm for him, though he intended to retain title to the $1,700 property. He also arranged for Frost's capable high school friend, Carl Burell, to live on the farm, do most of the work and instruct the novice, who had spent his entire life in cities and towns, and had worked mainly in schools and mills.

In October 1900 (between the deaths of Elliott and his mother) Frost became a farmer in a rural village when most farmers in the region were leaving the land for the city. The thin soil, short growing seasons and small yields, the rocky landscape, severe climate and long winters had forced the population of upper New England down to Boston. "Many farms, sometimes whole villages, had been abandoned during the past fifty years as the inhabitants emigrated to the west or to factory towns" in search of regular wages. Surveying the Northeast in 1904, Henry James painted a grim picture of "these scenes of old, hard New England effort, defeated by the soil and the climate and reclaimed by nature and time —the crumbled, lonely chimney-stack, the overgrown threshold, the dried-up well, the cart-track vague and lost." He could have been describing the characters in Frost's *North of Boston* when he observed that "a sordid ugliness and shabbiness hung, inveterately, about the wayside 'farms,' and all their appurtenances and incidents—above all, about their inmates." Despite its poverty and radical decline, Frost became deeply attached to this region and called New Hampshire "the state where my father was born and three-fourths of my children and practically all my poetry."[1]

In July 1901, nine months after Frost moved to Derry, his grandfather died and left an estate, including the farm, worth $17,000. His legacy to Frost was extremely generous. He gave him the free use and occupancy of the farm for ten years, after which time it would become his own property. He also canceled Frost's debts and left him a $500 annuity, which would increase to $800 after a decade. This money gave Frost a comfortable sum to live on and made him, compared to the marginal farmers in the region, relatively well off. It also aroused the envy of his neighbors. He recalled that when he first presented his trust fund check at the bank, the teller sarcastically asked: "How will you have your hard-earned money?" But Frost, poor at managing money and not allowed to draw funds in advance, was always short of cash before the annual payment. In May 1902 he borrowed at 15 percent interest the considerable sum of $675 from Ernest Jewell, his high school classmate, who had graduated from Harvard and returned to teach math in Lawrence. But he never repaid either the principal or interest. Twelve years later, writing to Jewell from England, he cavalierly dismissed the debt and tried to resurrect the ruined friendship. Frost regretted that Jewell was still angry. He insisted that his own feelings toward his old friend had not changed, and that his creditor must still be concerned about what became of him.

Agriculturally speaking, Frost was a loser. He would never have survived without his grandfather's annuity and Burell's help (which lasted until March 1902). "His awkwardness around livestock, his distaste for regular chores, his frail constitution, his fears of darkness, storms, and tramps, his difficulty in rising early in the morning, and his general inexperience with the basic elements of rustic husbandry all contributed to his unsuitability for farm life." Frost had no fixed time to feed the chickens, and gradually accustomed his cow to give milk at noon and midnight (instead of dawn and dusk) so he could continue to sleep late in the morning. He said "the cows got used to his hours more easily than his [ultra-conservative] neighbors."[2]

Frost's inexperience also made him prone to accidents and misfortunes. He nearly burned the house down when his huge bonfire, fanned by the wind, got out of control. In 1905 his frisky mare Eunice, rearing up on her hind legs when a steam train clanged into the station, turned over a sleigh with Lesley inside it. Two years later, during a "mad dog epidemic," his collie Schneider was bitten by a strange dog. Fearing rabies, Frost cut his head off, sent it to the university laboratory in Durham for examination and solemnly buried the trunk in back of the house. His Newfoundland dog Winnie later attacked a porcupine and got her mouth and muzzle full of quills. Frost had to give her chloroform in order to pull them out, but administered an overdose and accidentally killed her.

Frost had an easier time with the poultry and actually became quite fond of them. He had raised chicks as a boy in San Francisco. Later on, he brought chickens with him when he came to teach at the University of Michigan and always kept a farm in his backyard. "I had three hundred white Wyandottes," Frost said. "I knew something about the care of them, and I built a good henhouse for them. I learned to kill them for market, sticking them with a knife" and splattering himself with their blood. In "A Blue Ribbon at Amesbury," which celebrates the appearance of his prizewinner at a poultry show northeast of Lawrence, he describes his duties on the farm and dreams of breeding a new race with his superior bird. While Yeats idealized the wild swans at Coole, Frost made poetry out of the tame hens at Derry.

Frost supplemented his income between 1903 and 1905 by selling eleven stories, for ten dollars each, to two New England trade journals: the *Eastern Poultryman* and *Farm-Poultry*. These witty, ironic, disillusioned fables, written with the same laconic country talk he used in his poems and adopted in his own speech, were intended for practical-minded experts and gave an insider's view of the business. At the end of "Trap Nests"—in which a furious farmer fails to get his hens to lay—his wife, using a familiar proverb, tells him: "You can't get out of the hen business as easy as that. Your chickens will come home to roost." To which he replies: "'Will they? I'll stay here and see they don't.' And armed with a broomstick, he stayed."

The stories also allowed Frost to indulge his taste for amusing puns and broad American humor. In "The Original and Only" he tries out a pun on stayed-staid (as opposed to fancy) that he later used in "Take Something Like a Star." In the story the poultryman, who has bought an expensive hen, says: "She'd have been the making of us if we'd staid in the fancy, only she didn't let us stay." In the poem he writes: "We may take something like a star / To stay our minds on and be staid"—that is, be anchored and solemn. In "The Question of a Feather" (to pull or not to pull) a farmer asks a friend to advise him about the

> "feather on the leg of, I think, our best pullet."
> "Pull it?"
> "Yes, pullet."
> "Help you pull it, I mean."
> "Tell us whether it is right to pull it."

In "The Universal Chicken Feed" one farmer explains another's failure to get eggs by guessing "perhaps your hens weren't females."

The best story, "Old Welch Goes to the Show," was clearly influenced by one of Frost's favorite tales, Mark Twain's "The Celebrated Jumping Frog of Calaveras County" (1867). In both comic fables men meddle with the creature in order to change its natural appearance and habits. In Twain, the champion jumper is defeated when a stranger fills it with quail shot. In Frost, the hopeless cock is renovated and redesigned by his groomer, and put into a made-to-order corset to improve both his shape and his chance of winning a prize:

> "There's pretty nearly everything the matter with him. His comb
> don't fit, his eyes ain't mates. He's yellow, and his legs ain't. He's
> too highposted. He's whale backed and hollow chested."[3]

Frost's stories came to an end when he made a foolish blunder. Writing seriously about his older friend John Hall, who raised prize fowl and whose private life inspired Frost's poem "The Housekeeper," Frost boldly declared: "Mr. Hall's geese roost in the trees even in winter." The editor of the journal, who failed to catch the obvious error, asked Frost to respond to a farmer who wrote in and exclaimed: "I am 45 years old and have been among geese all my life time, and I can never remember seeing a goose in a tree. I thought if I could get a breed of that kind I could dispense with coops." Instead of admitting that he was wrong, the Harvard man decided to brazen it out with a hilarious, hair-splitting attempt to save face before the country yokels who knew much more about geese than he did: "Geese would sleep out, or float out, let us say, where hens would roost in the trees. To be sure. But what more natural, in speaking of geese in close connection with hens, than to speak of them as if they *were* hens? 'Roost in the trees,' has here simply suffered what the grammarians would call attraction from the subject with which it should be in agreement to the one uppermost in mind. That is all. But the idea will have to stand, viz., that Mr. Hall's geese winter out,—and that is the essential thing."[4] Only later did Frost confess to a friend that he should have let the geese alone.

II

His grandfather's annuity and the relatively light work on the farm allowed Frost sufficient leisure to read and to spend a good deal of time with his children. His friends confirmed that his extensive knowledge and wide-ranging conversation were based on a solid foundation of reading. Raymond Holden never actually saw Frost reading a book (he read mostly at night), but confirmed that he was very well informed about literature, religion, history, science and politics. Armour Craig, a younger colleague at Amherst, agreed that he had mastered the Classics and the major works in English: "He could quote Hamilton perhaps a little more readily than Jefferson, but he could set off Locke against Hobbes. He produced the spatial vision of Lucretius as easily as the elegances of Horace. He knew the wars of the Spartans as intimately as the battles of the 18th-century highland clans."

Frost often mentioned his most beloved books, though his choices varied at different times in his life. In 1911 he advised a student to buy Marcus Aurelius' Stoic *Meditations,* Wordsworth's *Complete Poems,* Emerson's *Representative Men* and especially Palgrave's *The Golden Treasury,* which had a profound influence on his own life and work. Responding to a questionnaire from the Massachusetts Library Association in 1936, Frost revealed both his taste and his cast of mind, and included many books whose independent spirit and adventurous content would also appeal to children:

> *The Odyssey*— "the first in time and rank of all romances. . . . I can permit myself but one translation out of ten books"
> *Robinson Crusoe*— "shows how the limited can make snug in the limitless"
> *Walden*— "Crusoe was cast away; Thoreau was cast away. Both found themselves sufficient"
> Poe's *Tales*— "every kind of entertainment the short story can

afford, the supernatural, the horrific, pseudo-scientific, inge-
nious and detective"

The Oxford Book of English Verse and

Untermeyer's *Modern American and British Poetry* [in which he was
generously represented] — "pretty well cover between them
the poetry of our race"

The Last of the Mohicans — "supplies us once for all with our way of
thinking of the American Indian"

[Anthony Hope's] *The Prisoner of Zenda* — "surely one of the very
best of our modern best-sellers"

The Jungle Book — "I shall read it again as often as I can find a new
child to listen to me"

Emerson's *Essays and Poems* — "the rapture of idealism."

Eighteen years later, in an essay on Thoreau's *Walden,* he included
two books from his previous list and wrote: "There we have a book that is
everything from a tale of adventure like *Robinson Crusoe* and *The Voyage of
the Beagle* (the three have a special shelf in my heart) to a declaration of
independence and a gospel of wisdom." In the *Chicago Sunday Tribune* of
November 1958, Frost again listed the *Odyssey,* mentioned an obscure
work that reflected his lifelong interest in archeology and "love of desolation": John Stephens' *Incidents of Travel in Yucatán* (1843), and added
three others: the Old Testament, Catullus' *Poems* and Gibbon's *The
Decline and Fall of the Roman Empire.*[5] Frost's various lists exclude all works
in foreign languages (except Greek and Latin) as well as the most
important novels and plays in English. They express his love of the Bible
and Classics, authors like Poe and Cooper who had been read to him as a
child, travel and adventure books that emphasize man's resourcefulness
and self-sufficiency, and the whole range of English poetry from medieval lyrics to the present.

Though Frost did not include many novels among his favorite books,
he did read them. He praised Turgenev's *Fathers and Sons,* said James'
short stories were "simply too good" and was familiar with contemporary
fiction by Zona Gale, Floyd Dell, Waldo Frank, his friend Dorothy
Canfield Fisher, Sherwood Anderson and Sinclair Lewis. He warmly
admired the stories and novels of Willa Cather and Ernest Hemingway.
Mainly, however, Frost read Horace and Virgil, Shakespeare and Milton,
the major English Romantic and Victorian poets: Wordsworth, Byron,
Shelley and Keats, Browning, Arnold and Francis Thompson as well as

Hardy and Kipling. The poet Wilbert Snow recorded Frost's views on the main American poets of the nineteenth century:

> Whitman lacked form. One poem of Whitman's, he acknowledged, moved him, the one entitled "To You." . . .
>
> Of all Emerson's poems the one he cherished most was "Uriel." "The greatest poem written in America," he asserted. . . .
>
> "You can damn all you want to," he told me, "Bryant, Lowell, Holmes and Whittier, but keep your hands off Longfellow. . . . Longfellow was the only poet that ever stopped a session of the United States Senate. It seems that the poet was once sitting in the Senate gallery when he was spied by a Senator who admired his work and called for a recess in order that they might all shake his hand."[6]

Frost also expressed his high opinion of "Uriel" in *A Masque of Reason,* and later received his own tribute from the United States Senate.

Though extremely well read, Frost had a very limited knowledge of music and art. He never listened to serious music, did not respond when a friend tried to arouse his interest by playing classical records, and declared that he liked band and glee club music best. He liked to visit the Metropolitan Museum in New York, but regretted that he had learned very little about art. His favorite painters were predictably American: Winslow Homer, Thomas Eakins and Andrew Wyeth. Apart from Gilbert Stuart, the poultry illustrator F. L. Sewall, and the popular sculptor John Rogers, there are no references to artists in Frost's poems.

III

The fear that life was precarious, which overwhelmed them after the death of the three-year-old Elliott, encouraged the Frosts, despite Elinor's weak heart, to have a number of children in close succession during the early years of their marriage. Their son Carol was born, three years after Lesley, in May 1902. He may have been named for Carl Burell, who had lived with the family and worked on the farm until just before Carol's birth. Irma followed a year later, in June 1903 and Marjorie, less than a year after that, in March 1905. All but one of Frost's children were born in the spring, between March and June, so his procreative season was the summer.

His sixth and last child, Elinor Bettina, was born on June 20, 1907, and lived for only two days. A high school friend gave a pathetic account of Elinor's "very unhappy state of mind. She had given birth to a baby that had lived only a short time, and she was miserable because they would not let her have the child in bed with her and cuddle it and love it for the short time it lived. She complained bitterly of her husband and said he was very heartless to her." Frost—recovering from a near-fatal bout of pneumonia—never wrote about this crushing blow, but he must have remembered Charles Lamb's sentimental yet moving "On an Infant Dying as Soon as Born" in his frequently read copy of *The Golden Treasury:*

> A flow'ret crushéd in the bud,
> A nameless piece of Babyhood
> Was in her cradle-coffin lying;
> Extinct, with scarce the sense of dying:
> So soon to exchange the imprisoning womb
> For darker closets of the tomb! . . .
> Riddle of destiny, who can show
> What thy short visit meant, or know
> What thy errand here below.

Frost was, according to the poet Donald Hall, "a devoted, assiduous, bossy, and affectionate father." After rejecting the conventional path through college to the middle class and getting nowhere in his career as a poet, he continued to work and write on the farm, and gave a great deal of attention to his son and three daughters. He drove them around the countryside with his horse and buggy, took them for walks and hikes up mountains, showed them where to find the rarest birds and flowers, explained the constellations, went berry-picking and swimming, played indoor games and baseball, let them share in the farm work and care for the animals, read them stories, encouraged their writing and taught them at home as he had been taught by his mother.

Frost wrote in "The Fear" that "Every child should have the memory / Of at least one long-after-bedtime walk." On clear nights he would sometimes let the children stay up late and take them out to see the midnight stars. He always went outside for a last look at the earth and sky before going to sleep. At a time when there were few toys for children, he carved little wooden animals for them. Always thinking of them and loving to tease, he played an elaborate joke on April Fool's Day in 1906. He cut flowers out of colored paper, put them in the snow around the house and woke the children with the news that the flowers had finally blossomed. He later told a friend that this charming deception had backfired. At first taken in, the children became furious when they realized he had tricked them into believing that spring had really come.[7]

Frost believed, before the stupefying incursion of television, that "the greatest dangers to the country" were the "three insipidities—radio, the comic strips, and the movies." He tried to protect his children from mindless entertainment and stimulate their cultural development by reading them amusing and instructive grown-up books. The Old Testament, the *Odyssey, Robinson Crusoe, Walden* and *The Voyage of the Beagle* were his own favorites. Shakespeare, Coleridge's "The Ancient Mariner," Longfellow's "My Lost Youth," Macaulay's *Lays of Ancient Rome* and Tennyson's *Idylls of the King* had been read to him in childhood. The children were encouraged to memorize these and other poems, and were rewarded for doing so. Marco Polo, Hakluyt's *Voyages* and Prescott's *Conquest of Mexico* were sources for his poetry. The *Aeneid*, Melville's *Typee* and *Omoo*, W. H. Hudson's *The Purple Land* and books on Stefansson and other Arctic explorers reflected his taste for heroism and adventure. *The Pilgrim's Progress*, Maeterlinck's *The Blue Bird* and Charles Gayley's *Classic Myths in English Literature* (1893) were popular with the children. He may also have read, because of its fortuitous subtitle, Horatio Alger's last book: *Out for Business, or, Robert Frost's Strange Career* (1900).[8]

The reading around the family hearth was complemented by instruction at home instead of formal schooling. Frost taught the children botany and astronomy; Elinor taught geography, reading, writing and spelling. In photographs taken during their early years, running toward the camera in front of the Derry farm or solemnly lining up in their best clothes, the children appear handsome, healthy and happy. Lesley was an athletic tomboy, Marjorie sickly but sweet; but Carol was sullen and Irma rather strange. Inspired by their father, all the children developed artistic gifts. Lesley, who kept an elaborate childhood journal, later published children's books and detective stories; Irma became a sculptor; Carol and Marjorie both wrote poetry, and Frost brought out a small volume of her work after her death.

Frost was a concerned and conscientious father, but confessed to Untermeyer (who would also have serious problems with his children) that there was no right way to raise a child. A reserved and undemonstrative New Englander, Frost did not show his affection by hugging and kissing his children and grandchildren. He and Elinor both had puritan reticence and Victorian inhibitions about sex, which (even within the family and on the farm) was never mentioned. Frost's daughters felt that their mother had never given them a clear explanation of sexual matters. When her sister-in-law had a child, the nineteen-year-old Marjorie asked her "how babies were conceived and about the length of pregnancy."

Frost maintained proper discipline in the household but, avoiding the brutal example of his father, never whipped the children. He once joked to a friend about the difficulty of controlling them, and maintained that recently he and Elinor had refused to rent a house when they discovered that it had no closets. They could not possibly bring up a family of unruly children if they had no closets in which to confine them. When punishments had to be administered, Lesley wrote as a child, "Papa generally pinches us where it hurts but mama where it doesn't." Frost expressed his practical yet tender attitude toward child-rearing in a letter to his editor, whose infants had whooping cough: "You must take good care of them, show them plenty of pictures, tell them plenty of stories and say 'Easy, easy' every time they get into a gale of coughing."[9]

The most traumatic incident of Lesley's childhood took place in the winter of 1905, when she was six years old. Her father suddenly woke her up in the middle of the night and led her barefoot through the cold, dark house to where a light was burning in the kitchen. Her mother, seated at the kitchen table, was holding her head and sobbing. Frost, pointing a pistol at himself and then at Elinor, screamed: "Take your choice. Before morning, one of us will be dead!" Terrified and clearly unable to choose, Lesley was embraced and led back to bed by her mother. Frost's wild gesture repeated his father's threat to shoot the San Francisco doctor who had come to deliver his son. The tension that erupted in this quarrel also resembled the agonizing domestic atmosphere, described in "Home Burial," after the death of Elliott. Frost meant to win the argument and punish Elinor by frightening Lesley, but his daughter held it against him for the rest of his life.

The death of two children and Frost's violent threat persuaded Elinor to adopt a protective attitude, and she bound the children to her in that close-knit and somewhat stifling household. Like Frost's mother, she first educated them at home and then allowed them to leave school whenever they wished. Frost's powerful personality dominated them all. The family led a compulsively isolated and emotionally turbulent life, which Lesley compared to the hermetic existence of the Brontës: "We lived in a similar isolation and world of our own, and a similar ferment. . . . We were all together all the time, indoors and out. We had no playmates among neighbor children. Our house was isolated. We were a little scared all the time."

Frost emphasized their solitude when he recalled: "We had lived in the farmhouse all those [ten] years, and only twice during all that time had we been away from home later than eight o'clock at night." But in March 1903 he did take Elinor, then pregnant with Irma, and the two older children for an unusual month-long visit to New York. Lesley, one of the two children who survived him, maintained an ambivalent but resentful attitude toward her father. She claimed, in a saccharine sentence, that "held by the hands of two loving parents, I was led into the realm of nature," and her Derry journal, *New Hampshire's Child*, confirms this idyllic view. But she also believed, till the very end of Frost's life, that he "had always ruled and dominated them with fear, fear, fear."[10] Lesley could never forget or forgive Frost's terrifying threat to kill himself or Elinor, and this incident later triggered her vitriolic condemnation of her father.

During his decade at Derry Frost used the farm and annuity to support him while he devoted the most precious part of his life to writing poetry. As he observed in "Build Soil": "The Muse takes care of you. You live by writing / Your poems on a farm and call that farming." But he told Untermeyer, who had set himself up as a gentleman farmer in upstate New York, that the farm did not earn him a living—and neither did poetry. He sold only five poems between 1894 and 1906, and earned only $200 from poetry during the first twenty years of his career. Part of the problem was caused by his physical and intellectual isolation, for in Derry artistic companions were as scarce as—hens' teeth. Folks in that rural region considered poetry an incomprehensible, feminine and even shameful occupation. As he wrote a fellow poet, quoting Luke 17:2: "I have lived for the most part in villages where it were better that a millstone were hanged about your neck than that you should own yourself a minor poet." "I was thirty years old" in 1904, he told another friend, "and as great a failure as anybody ever was at the turn of life." But he also said, alluding this time to Matthew 10:39, that "in order to accomplish anything he has repeatedly found that he had to be given up for lost by his family and his friends." Family responsibilities, subsistence farming and frustrating failure in his poetic vocation provoked mysterious periods of lassitude, frequent bronchial attacks and outbursts of violence that matched his father's rage.

Frost was fond of repeating that he combined farm work with poetry and that his three favorite kinds of labor were "mowing with a scythe, chopping with an ax, and writing with a pen."[11] He wrote "The Grindstone" about the scythe, "The Ax-Helve" about the ax, and in these poems (and many others) equated the perfection of agricultural labor with the creation of poetic art. In New Hampshire and later in Vermont, Frost always lived on small one- or two-man farms where the work —mowing fields, making hay, picking apples, tapping maples—was done by hand, without the assistance of electrical machinery. When machines appear—as in "The Self-Seeker" and "'Out, Out—'"—they mutilate and destroy men. A quaint photograph of Frost raking hay reveals that his labors were closer to the agricultural methods of the Middle Ages than to modern mechanized farming. It was precisely this kind of ruggedly independent life that inspired most of Frost's early poetry. Despite all the anxieties and frustrations of farming, he began writing during the long, solitary nights at Derry many of the poems that eventually filled his first three books. The years spent on that farm became retrospectively the most sacred in his entire life and prepared him for the astonishing poetic effusion that would take place in England in the years before the war.

5

Pinkerton and Plymouth

1906–1912

I

Farming provided leisure for poetry, but neither occupation earned much money. So at the age of thirty-two and with four children, Frost was driven, for the first time in his decade of married life, to seek regular salaried employment. "I always go to farming when I can," he later said, describing a recurrent pattern. "I always make a failure, and then I have to go to teaching. I'm a good teacher. But it doesn't allow me time to write." Frost was lively and talented in the classroom, but he associated teaching with his tedium and disillusionment at Dartmouth and Harvard, with the failure and humiliation of his mother's schools and with long hours of repetitive, low-level work. Bored with farming and pressed for money, he reluctantly decided (he told a friend) "to do what I hated to do—and what I didn't want to do, what I had never liked to do—go back to the drudgery of teaching."

Pinkerton Academy, in Derry village, was founded in 1815 by Scottish Congregationalists for the purpose of "promoting piety and virtue, and the education of youth in science, language and the liberal arts." Frost had lived within two miles of the school for more than five years but, leading a solitary existence, had never met anyone connected with it. In January 1906 he met William Wolcott, whom he had known as pastor of the First Congregational Church in Lawrence. Wolcott had friends at Pinkerton, urged him to apply for a vacancy there and wrote a letter of recommendation: "I know of my personal knowledge that [Frost] is a man of scholarly instincts and habits, and I have had testimony from former pupils that he was an efficient and inspiring teacher."

A trustee of the Academy, Charles Merriam, then suggested that Frost would get the job (despite his lack of a college degree) if he read one of his poems at the forthcoming banquet of the Men's League of the Congregational Church. Frost replied that he would never dare to read his work in public, but would give him a poem and sit next to him at the banquet while Merriam read it to the assembled guests. The poem Frost chose, "The Tuft of Flowers" (later published in *A Boy's Will*), was perfectly suited to the occasion. Composed of twenty couplets, it described —like "Mowing" and "An Exposed Nest"—the pastoral labor of cutting a field of grass and the careful preservation—as in "Rose Pogonias"—of a tuft of wildflowers. The narrator of the poem, who follows the absent mower and must turn the cut grass, finds himself alone: "'As all must be,' I said within my heart, / 'Whether they work together or apart.'" A butterfly then leads him to a tall tuft of flowers beside a brook: "A leaping tongue of bloom the scythe had spared / Beside a reedy brook the scythe had bared." The flowers, spared by the mower who rejoiced in their beauty, awaken his senses and enable him to "hear his long scythe whispering to the ground"—a fine line which Frost also used in "Mowing." The flowers also carry a "message," which contradicts his earlier assumption about the solitude of men and puts him in touch with the kindred spirit of his fellow toiler: "'Men work together,' I told him from the heart, / 'Whether they work together or apart.'"[1]

Frost's poignant poem symbolized his movement from solitude to society and made a favorable impression at the religious banquet. He was not exaggerating when he later told Untermeyer that he owed absolutely "everything I am" to poetry, which became the organizing principle in his life. On this strange and sweet occasion, he employed his poem in a particularly adroit way to alter the course of his life and secure a teaching position at Pinkerton Academy. His first use of poetry as an entrée to an academic job established the method he would later use to become poet-in-residence at many universities.

Frost began in March 1906 by teaching two sections of sophomore English. When negotiating the salary the principal said that Frost's work would amount to two-sevenths of a full-time job, which paid $1,000 or $1,100 a year. Insecure about his lack of a degree, Frost vaguely agreed. But he was annoyed with himself for accepting two-sevenths of the lower salary, $95 a term, when he could have earned $105.

In the fall of 1906 he began teaching full time. He taught all the English courses in the school, with occasional tuition in Latin, history and geometry—seven classes a day, thirty-five hours a week, with no rest periods. He also coached the debating team, advised the school newspaper and helped out with athletics. But he did have the opportunity to teach fairly small groups (the senior class had only thirteen girls and four boys) some of his best-loved books: the *Odyssey, The Pilgrim's Progress, Robinson Crusoe, Walden,* the poems in *The Golden Treasury* and others by Shakespeare, Wordsworth, Coleridge, Scott, Tennyson, Browning, Arnold and Kipling, as well as George Eliot's *Silas Marner.* Frost walked the four miles there and back, even in winter, and crossed West-Running Brook on the way.

The young and energetic Frost found unusual ways to stimulate his students. He used coins to arouse their interest in ancient history, and told them about the lives of the authors they were reading. He gave occasional exams to fulfill the school requirements, but rarely graded or returned them. Instead, he emphasized reciting poetry and memorizing lines. To encourage their active participation and bring literature to life he produced five plays a year, in versions he shortened and adapted for his classes. The students performed Marlowe's *Doctor Faustus,* the Renaissance tragedy of a mythic pact with the devil and thirst for infinite power; Milton's *Comus,* the Puritan pageant extolling chastity, and Sheridan's *The Rivals,* the witty eighteenth-century comedy of courtship and mistaken identity. Frost also included two contemporary verse dramas by Yeats. In *The Land of Heart's Desire* a fairy child lures a wife away from her husband; in *Cathleen ni Houlihan* the eponymous heroine (who symbolizes Ireland) lures the hero away from his prospective bride. Frost later recalled: "I went to the city and bought some masks—horrible masks, swine's heads and things like that—for the rout of *Comus,*" when the chaste Lady, captured by the evil Comus, is rescued by her brother. Frost's principal and quite revolutionary idea in education was that students should not be taught to absorb information from books and teachers, but must be encouraged to rely on their own personal experience, to think independently and to develop ideas of their own. "Don't write unless you have something to say," he would tell his students. "If you don't have it, go and get it."

His original approach inevitably aroused resentment among some of the faculty and students just as his poetry had provoked jealousy and suspicion among the farmers. One brash student enraged Frost by referring to his humble attempts to raise poultry and writing "hen-man" on the blackboard. Though unconventional in his teaching, Frost believed in traditional discipline. He recognized the student's handwriting and kicked him out of the class. Since there was no other class for the boy to join, the trustees expelled him from the school.

Frost's extraordinary ability was recognized and praised by Henry

Morrison, the State Superintendent of Public Instruction, who observed his "class of boys and girls of high school age listening open-mouthed to the teacher who was talking to them about an English classic . . . talking to them as he might talk to a group of friends around his own fireside. But he 'had them' as few other teachers ever 'get them.' . . . [I] saw, first, that he knew what he was talking about; and second, that he had some genuine love of his own apparently for the pieces of literature about which he was talking." Morrison invited Frost to speak on methods of teaching English at a New Hampshire teachers' convention. Though Frost was exceptionally nervous, with stomach pains and cold sweats, his provocative talk went over well. Reversing the traditional order, Frost argued that the teacher's responsibility was first to develop his own mind and "save his soul," second to teach the art of the author and third to help the student learn.

Frost made two new friends at Pinkerton. He established immediate rapport, partly because of their common interest in sports, with Ernest Silver. Two years younger than Frost, he had graduated from Dartmouth in 1899. He "was short, blond, pink-cheeked, with a great deal of tact, not quite so much principle" and became head of the school in 1909.[2] John Bartlett, Frost's prize pupil and lifelong friend, was the son of a small-town lawyer. Captain of the football team, editor of the school newspaper and president of the senior class, Bartlett fell in love with his future wife in Frost's classroom and, like his teacher, married his high school sweetheart. Frost took a sympathetic interest in Bartlett's love affair—as he would later do with younger friends like Joseph Warren Beach and Armour Craig—and was pleased when Bartlett dropped out of Middlebury College, as he had left Dartmouth and Harvard.

In the spring of 1909 Frost gave up farming, rented the upper floor of a house in Derry village and, for the first time, placed his three oldest children (ages six to ten) in school. The owner of the house, a young lawyer named Lester Russell, lived on the first floor and became Frost's good friend. Two years later, after Russell had gambled away a client's trust fund, he was arrested by the local sheriff. He went to get his coat, drank the arsenic he was using to spray the garden and died in agony the next morning.

Depressed by Russell's suicide, which he had difficulty explaining to his children, Frost also struggled with his own health problems. Beginning in 1906, he had to spend at least part of the summer in the mountains of New Hampshire or Vermont in order to escape severe attacks during the hay-fever season. The following year a bout of pneumonia forced him to miss the entire spring term. By 1911 he was so exhausted by the long hours of teaching at Pinkerton that he was "practically in a coma."

Frost was rescued that year when Ernest Silver became principal of the State Normal School, or teachers' college, at Plymouth in central New Hampshire, where Silver remained for the rest of his career. Though there were no jobs available in English, Silver invited Frost to accompany him. Frost took a part-time position at an annual salary of $1,000 (the same as for a full-time job at Pinkerton), and taught one course in the History of Education and another in Psychology to a hundred female students. He abandoned the standard textbook in education and used Plato's *Republic,* Rousseau's *Émile,* and *How Gertrude Teaches Her Children* (1801) by the Swiss educational reformer Johann Pestalozzi. In the second course he taught two books by William James: *Talks to Teachers on Psychology* and *Psychology: The Briefer Course*—the text in his philosophy class at Harvard. His less onerous duties at Plymouth allowed Frost to relax his dignity. One student recalled his characteristic arrival in class: "He would come hustling through the door, breathless and muttering embarrassed apologies. We were given to understand that the clock had either gone on strike, or his wife had failed to hand him his hat at the proper time. We always grinned knowingly at each other, knowing that the reason for his tardiness was a book and the old arm chair." The pupils felt that "he always seemed to be wandering around in a fog, mentally."

Frost, punning as he often did, said: "I am a great equalitarian: I try to spend most of my time with my equals." But it was difficult to find equals, or even people with common interests, among the farmers, faculty and students in rural New Hampshire. When the Frosts arrived, Ernest Silver shared his house on the Plymouth campus with them. But when he criticized Elinor's chaotic housekeeping, their friendship cooled. Opposed to traditional academic habits and trying to lead a life conducive to poetry, Frost appeared to most townsfolk as rough and eccentric. In 1911 a friend at Plymouth "first thought him uncouth. We were at a dance, and he wore an unpressed suit, and a gray soft-collared shirt; and he sat with crossed knees, and poked fun. After that . . . I still detected in his speech what seemed a lack of elegance, and in his attitude an absence of conformity. There was something earthy and imperfectly tamed about him." Frost's solitary life in the confines of his family, where he was the dominant figure, had made him egoistic and socially maladroit.

Frost later recalled that his lifelong friendship with the sympathetic

Sidney Cox, then teaching English in the local high school, got off to a rocky start: "It began one evening in 1911 when we met as strangers looking on at a school dance at Plymouth. . . . By saying something flippant about the theme papers he had to hurry away to correct I angered him to the point of his inquiring behind my back if it was because of alcohol I had got no further up in the world at my age."[3] Born in 1889 in Lewistown, Maine, the son of a Baptist minister, Cox had graduated from Bates College in that state and earned a master's degree at the University of Illinois. A gaunt, blunt, clerical man, with an odd, ascetic manner, Cox was (like Carl Burell and Preston Shirley) rather weird-looking. He had "a large and gangly body, oversized head, big ears, large pale blue eyes that seemed a bit runny . . . a most mobile mouth—a long pensive upper lip with a pendulous lower lip that was never at rest."

Cox said the domineering Frost was "always a tease, a fighter, a snapper of bonds he didn't forge." After their first contretemps Cox became, like John Bartlett, a loyal and devoted disciple. As his wife regretfully told Frost, who had overwhelmed Cox with the force of his personality and his poetry: "Sidney had substituted you for the God that his preacher forebears had worshipped, and the missionary spirit was rampant." Frost feared that his friend's "enthusiasm and exuberance, his near-idolatry, would make them both appear ridiculous." But Cox, after joining the Dartmouth English department, became his advocate and agent in Hanover. Comparing himself to the wise but garrulous old Greek statesman in Homer, Frost wrote that "Sidney and I were great friends and stayed so in spite of the bullying he often got from me in my letters. . . . Sometimes his evangelicality made me talk to him like a Nestor which is the way the thing usually winds up with me."[4] After long years of failure in college, in menial jobs, in farming and in poetry, Frost's recognition, success and friendships while teaching at Pinkerton and Plymouth did a great deal to strengthen his self-confidence.

II

Frost once contradicted Randall Jarrell, who thought poets were not helped enough, and insisted, from his own experience, that "poetry had always lived on a good deal of neglect." Though he published very little, he wrote most of his first book, more than half his second and quite a bit of his third during his decade in Derry and Plymouth. "I went to England with the material for several books," he told a friend in 1940. "In every book I ever published, there is material from that early period. If I ever publish another book, there will be pieces in it from those first efforts." Yet his poetry, in the philistine atmosphere of Derry, remained a secret activity. Lesley wrote that her father "never so much as hinted that he was frequently writing poems of his own, at the table in the kitchen of our farmhouse, long after we children had gone to bed."

Frost would sit up till the middle of the night in front of the open fire—alternately dozing and writing. At Harvard he had bought a Morris chair (with an adjustable back and loose cushions), and preferred to write there, on a shelf placed across its flat arms, rather than at a table or desk. He took the talismanic chair with him to England. When Frost could not take it with him during his travels around the country, Elinor would try to arrange for him to have a chair with high arms so that a board could comfortably lie across it. In 1926 he was pleased to "have at last developed a one-legged writing table," which rested on the arms of his Morris chair, "the materials of which can be found in almost any wood shed and assembled in a minute. . . . Strange chairs have no longer any terror for me."[5]

While teaching his classes and writing his first two books, Frost studied and memorized the poets who were most valuable to him, mastering their diction, their imagery and their formal techniques. "Poetry begins in reading of books," he declared, and the poet "writes out of the eddy in his mind of all the books he ever read. . . . The whole thing is performance and prowess and feats of association." The music of his verse, drifting through his head, set off associations of other poems he'd read and the rich bequest of his predecessors directly inspired his own poetry. To be fully understood, Frost's poems must be read not only in the context of his life, and in relation to other poems in the entire body of his work, but also in the tradition of English poetry, which he devoured during these solitary years in Derry. This devoted study was the most vital part of Frost's education.

Though their poetic content was quite different, Frost had a great deal in common with his contemporary T. S. Eliot. Just as Frost believed that "a poem is best read in the light of all the other poems ever written," so Eliot, in a characteristic passage of "Tradition and the Individual Talent," defined his own poetic method as well as the one Frost had adopted. It is extraordinary that while teaching in an obscure village, Frost discovered and practiced a method of composition that the high priest of modernism would also formulate in a more sophisticated way.

Both believed that the poet belonged to a historical tradition, which provided a storehouse of images and ideas that the modern writer could use and build on:

> We shall often find [Eliot wrote] that not only the best, but the most individual parts of his work may be those in which the dead poets, his ancestors, assert their immortality most vigorously. . . . The historical sense compels a man to write not merely with his own generation in his bones, but with a feeling that the whole of the literature of Europe from Homer and within it the whole of the literature of his own country has a simultaneous existence and composes a simultaneous order. This historical sense . . . is what makes a writer traditional. And it is at the same time what makes a writer most acutely conscious of his place in time, of his own contemporaneity.

Both Eliot and Frost drew extensively on other poets, ancient and modern. But while Eliot usually quoted directly, signaling his sources with quotation marks, foreign words and footnotes, Frost subtly disguised and transformed his allusions—in his letters as well as in his poems. He did not give the reader intellectual pleasure, through the shock of recognizing a familiar line in an unusual context, as Eliot did. But by subtly embedding quotations in his own text, he offered the reader the illusion that the whole new artifact, the poem by Frost, is familiar in a deeply satisfying way. "It's fun to quote something," he playfully said, "to make everybody wonder where you got that."[6] Frost and Eliot were actually doing the same thing: re-possessing the poetry of the past by bringing it to bear on the present moment. Eliot liked to startle by juxtaposing contemporary scenes and images with touchstones from the literary tradition, and Frost also used quotation for ironic contrast. But he more often transformed and renewed the source of his allusions. In the most sophisticated adaptations—like "After Apple-Picking"—he paid homage to the great poems he knew by heart, and let the mood of Keats' "Ode to a Nightingale" permeate and enhance his own very different work of art.

Helen Bacon observed that Frost's "direct allusions extend the sense and often give coherence and meaning to apparently incidental details, making the poem both more complex and more unified." The poetry that influenced and echoed through Frost's work was not, as with Eliot, from Dante, the Jacobean playwrights, the Metaphysicals and the French Symbolists, but from the Bible, the Latin poets, the ballads, Shakespeare, the English Romantics and the Victorians. Frost has been studied almost exclusively in the American grain and critics have overwhelmingly stressed his relation to Emerson, Thoreau, Dickinson and other writers of the New England Renaissance. In fact, Frost was more powerfully influenced by English verse, particularly the English pastoral tradition, than any other American poet of his time (see Appendix I).[7]

Frost's relation to the poetry of the past—and especially to the ballads, Wordsworth, Kipling, *The Golden Treasury* and to his kindred spirit Thomas Hardy—is worth emphasizing. Frost preferred popular to classical music and was very fond of ballads. He gave his guitar-playing friend and rival Carl Sandburg the tune and verses of "Whiskey Johnny" and "Blow the Man Down," which he had learned as a boy in San Francisco while "listening to sailors and dock-wallopers along the water front." Toward the end of the nineteenth century Hardy, Wilde, Housman, Kipling, Yeats and, later, Pound all wrote ballads, and Frost shared their interest in this form. The father of Stafford Dragon, the hired man on Frost's Vermont farm, was a well-known old ballad singer, whom Frost invited to sing and play at the Bread Loaf School. In his Introduction to a book on ballads, Frost connected them to spoken speech and compared them to the natural sound of birds: "Ballads lead their life in the mouths and ears of men by hear-say like lovebirds and flickers in the nest holes of hollow trees."[8] Frost quoted the ballad "Thomas Rymer" in *A Masque of Mercy* and used the ballad form in his own verse from "Love and a Question" through "Brown's Descent" to "The Bearer of Evil Tidings."

Frost adopted many of the principles expressed in Wordsworth's Preface to the *Lyrical Ballads* concerning the diction, people, places and social conditions appropriate to poetry. Like Wordsworth, he "chose incidents and situations from common life," described them in "language really used by men" and made these "incidents and situations interesting by tracing in them . . . the primary laws of our nature." He preferred people in "low and rustic life" because they "speak a plainer and more emphatic language," express elemental feelings and reveal "the essential passions of the heart." The "manners of rural life" are "more easily comprehended and are more durable . . . because in that condition the passions of men are incorporated with the beautiful and permanent forms of nature." In an early interview Frost traced the source of his fundamental theory back to Wordsworth: "As language only really exists in the mouths of men . . . Wordsworth was right in trying to reproduce in his poetry not only the words—and in their limited range, too, actually used in common speech—but their sound."

Richard Wilbur, Frost's friend and poetic disciple, recalled that Frost admired the tone of Wordsworth's most prosaic verse: "I remember Robert Frost, one time, talking about the dullness of Wordsworth. He used 'dullness' as a term of approval, speaking of Wordsworth's willingness to write prosaically so as to fulfill the structure of his longer poems and make bridges between his more intense passages." Frost clarified this idea in his extensive "Tribute to Wordsworth" when he praised the innocence and simplicity of "Michael," and defined the "essential Wordsworth" as "that lovely banality and the lovely penetration that goes with it. It goes right down into the soul of man, and always, always there'll be one line in it that's just as penetrating as anything anybody ever wrote. But always this insipid tone. Sweet, insipid tone. Now that's the Wordsworth I care for."[9]

Kipling was the most popular English poet in the 1890s, when Frost began to write and publish his own verse. He found in Kipling, as in Wordsworth, a poet who confirmed and strengthened his own artistic theories. As he told Susan Ward in 1894, Kipling says almost everything he says under the influence of sound. In the dramatic monologues in *North of Boston* Frost employed vernacular speech, as Kipling had done, to reveal the psychology of his characters. He adapted the title of Kipling's *Departmental Ditties* (1886) in his satiric poem "Departmental," compared Kipling's "Ballad of the King's Jest" (1890) to his own ballad "The Bearer of Evil Tidings," alluded to "Recessional" in *A Masque of Reason* and used Kipling's famous refrain from that poem—"Lest we forget—Lest we forget!"—in his early, uncollected poem "Warning." Frost said this poem was a "curiosity. It was accepted and in print about a month after the appearance of Kipling's of the same, or almost the same, refrain. My inference seems reasonably safe that it was written before I saw Kipling's. Yet I wouldn't believe it if it rested on my own unsupported story." In fact, "Recessional" was published on June 22, 1897, two and a half months before "Warning" appeared in the *Independent,* on September 9, 1897, and Frost probably lifted the refrain from Kipling.

The first book of poetry that Frost ever bought, while a student at Dartmouth in 1892, was Palgrave's immensely popular *The Golden Treasury* (1861). Frederick Turner Palgrave (1824–97) was an official in the Education department and Professor of Poetry at Oxford. He made his thematic selection, from the early Renaissance through the Romantics, of "the best original Lyrical pieces and Songs in our language, by writers not living,—and none beside the best," in consultation with his close friend, the Poet Laureate Alfred Tennyson. Frost loved the whole collection and read it "literally to rags and tatters." He memorized most of the poems in the anthology, and his children and Pinkerton students also had to memorize many poems from Palgrave. In his early poem "Waiting" he expressed the exaltation he felt from

> the worn book of old-golden song
> I brought not here to read, it seems, but hold
> And freshen in this air of withering sweetness.

He told an English friend that he went to England in 1912 partly because "he wanted his poetry to be printed first in the land which had produced the *Golden Treasury*."[10] Frost believed that anthologies were "the highest form of literary criticism." They not only reflected the poetic taste of the editor, but also allowed the reader to refine his own taste by choosing the best poems in the book.

Three of Frost's poetic touchstones, which he frequently quoted, appeared in Palgrave: Robert Herrick's "To Daffodils" (also included in the volume Frost's mother had reviewed), James Shirley's "The Glories of Our Blood and State" and William Collins' "How Sleep the Brave" (which had first awakened his interest in poetry). He used the last poem to teach Robert Lowell concision. These pure and perfect lyrics, composed with superb technical skill, all express the theme of mutability: the effect of time on man and nature. It is quite extraordinary that at least twenty-five of the poems—by Marlowe, Shakespeare, Herrick, Waller, Milton, Gray, Smart, Cowper, Burns, Wordsworth, Scott, Byron, Shelley and Keats—that Frost alludes to in his own work come from Palgrave. Moreover, of the fifteen poems that Frost included as examples in his "Tribute to Wordsworth" in 1950, eleven (including works by Shirley, Campbell, Southey, Wordsworth, Shelley and Byron) also came from *The Golden Treasury*. Palgrave's anthology not only motivated Frost to live in England, but also contained three more influential poems: Shelley's "Love's Philosophy" justified free love with Elinor, Burns' "Bonnie Lesley" provided the name of his first daughter, Lamb's "On an Infant Dying as Soon as Born" consoled him after the death of baby Elinor. *The Golden Treasury*, a lifelong source of inspiration for his prose, his poetry and his life, had a greater influence on Frost than any other book.

Frost discovered Hardy at the same time as Palgrave and read through his novels *A Pair of Blue Eyes* and *Two on a Tower* in the fall of 1892. Two years later he told Susan Ward that Hardy had taught him the good use of a few words and how to achieve a solemn simplicity. While in England he wrote Sidney Cox that "Hardy's my man." Alluding to Hardy's early career as a craftsman, he told John Bartlett that Hardy was almost never seen in public but was said to resemble a little old stonemason. Frost called Hardy an excellent poet and the greatest living novelist, and praised him as "one of the most earthly wise of our time."

At the turn of the century Hardy was, as Frost suggested, the most prominent and controversial poet in England. Hardy was a father-figure to the Georgians and war poets, Frost's allies when he lived in Gloucestershire. Ford Madox Ford maintained that he had founded the *English Review* in 1908 when no other journal would publish Hardy's "A Sunday Morning Tragedy." Frost's intimate friend Edward Thomas wrote an essay on Hardy in the January 1913 issue of *Poetry and Drama,* D. H. Lawrence composed his "Study of Thomas Hardy" the following year and Lascelles Abercrombie brought out his book on Hardy in 1919. Hardy's poetic reputation has continued to rise throughout the modern age. Pound included a tribute to Hardy in his anthology *From Confucius to Cummings* (1964) and ten years later Lowell called Hardy "by far the greatest poet of the century."

The poetic careers of Hardy and Frost—as well as their choice of subject, diction, characters, technique, mood and theme—were strikingly similar. Both had their early poems rejected and did not publish their first volume until relatively late in life (Hardy was fifty, Frost thirty-nine). Both brought out eight or nine volumes during a poetic career that lasted for seventy years and their last books appeared, near the time of their deaths, in their late eighties. Like Hardy, Frost established his methods and ideas in his early years and did not change them very much as he grew older. Both were regionalists, and Hardy's ambition, like Frost's, "was to have some poem or poems in a good anthology like the *Golden Treasury.*"[11] Frost, in fact, became the American Hardy, and eventually achieved the same kind of respect and influence as his predecessor.

Robert Langbaum's pioneering essay suggests the main points of comparison between Hardy and Frost. Both were influenced by Wordsworth and by the dramatic monologues of Robert Browning; remained hostile to modernist poetry; wrote about nature and pre-industrial values when most modernists concentrated on art, politics and urban life; portrayed nature as indifferent and even malevolent. "Hardy and Frost are important," Langbaum concludes, "because they show how to be modern without being modernist." David Perkins' discussion of Hardy's relationship to Wordsworth applies equally to the color-blind Frost: "he shares Wordsworth's primitivism to some degree; he finds in nature sources of beauty, resigned wisdom, and sympathy; but at the same time he rejects the Wordsworthian hopes and writes to expose them. The result is a natural world . . . composed of greys, bleakness, emptiness, chilling wind and rain, yellowing leaves, and mutely suffering creatures, with signs everywhere of dreariness, ominous threat, and blight." Perkins balances Hardy's characteristic somberness with the more positive qualities he also shared with Frost, and writes of his "compassion, reflectiveness, wistfulness, interest in character and story, elegiac and commemorative respect for human fates. Above all, there is the appeal of the firsthand, of experience and feeling that seem caught from life rather than literature." Like Hardy, Frost had memorized hundreds of lines of Browning and particularly admired "his power of catching tones of voice." He told Thompson that Browning had an even greater influence on him than Wordsworth.[12]

Both Hardy and Frost reproduce, as accurately and vividly as possible, the fluctuations in tone and mood of the natural but rather flat spoken word. As Hardy wrote of rural speech in *The Return of the Native:* "sounds intrinsically common become attractive in language, [just] as shapes intrinsically simple become interesting in writing." Both poets used ordinary, often monosyllabic, speech to achieve pathos, exaltation and tragedy. They were fond of metrical variety and complicated stanzas, and wrote with deceptive simplicity. They conveyed their ironical view of the world by dramatizing opposing feelings, ideas and values, by creating a dynamic tension of unresolved polarities. The wintry tones, self-centered bleakness, sense of foreboding, stoical unease and mournful serenity mark the characteristic mood and sensibility that Frost shares with Hardy. Their dominant seasons, as Samuel Hynes writes, "are autumn and winter—the gray, dead, twilight seasons . . . [with] falling leaves, bare trees, gray skies: 'It never looks like summer here,' as one poem puts it. . . . Wind, rain, fog, and snow—the weather of suffering—prevail." Both poets are consummate storytellers whose speakers reveal their emotions and dark truths by suppressing the violence and madness that swirl beneath the surface of their lives. As his best critic, Randall Jarrell, observed, Frost has "a final identifying knowledge of the deprived and dispossessed, the insulted and injured, that one matches in modern poetry only in Hardy."[13]

Frost used Hardy as a model for many poems that have the same imagery and themes. He also adopted several of Hardy's titles: "Bereft" and "The Wind and the Rain" (originally from Shakespeare). Hardy's "An Ancient to Ancients" influenced "A Servant to Servants"; and Frost, who liked to play on his own name, must have been delighted by Hardy's "A Light Snowfall After Frost." Images of a chalice or goblet, of swirling leaves and of flower stems appear in both poets. Drinking water from a symbolic glass unites the lovers in an almost mystical way in Hardy's "Under the Waterfall":

> By night, by day, when it shines or lours,
> There lies intact that chalice of ours,
> And its presence adds to the rhyme of love
> Persistently sung by the fall above,

just as it does in Frost's "Directive":

> (I stole the goblet from the children's playhouse.)
> Here are your waters and your watering place.
> Drink and be whole again beyond confusion. (*Poetry*, p. 379)

Dead leaves, swirling on the faded earth below the heavy sky, create the characteristically desolate mood in Hardy's "The Voice," in "A Night in November" and in the last stanza of his major poem "Neutral Tones":

> Since then, keen lessons that love deceives,
> And wrings with wrong, have shaped to me
> Your face, and the God-curst sun, and a tree,
>   And a pond edged with greyish leaves. (Hardy, 26)

Frost takes up this suggestive image and in "Bereft" makes it snakelike and menacing:

> Out in the porch's sagging floor
> Leaves got up in a coil and hissed,
> Blindly struck at my knee and missed. (Frost, 251)

In "The Darkling Thrush," in which "Frost was spectre-gray," Hardy makes a negative allusion to Apollo (the god of poetry) and establishes the mournful mood with a marvelous image as "The tangled bine-stems scored the sky / Like strings of broken lyres" (Hardy, 14). Frost employed the same image in two of his poems. In "The Death of the Hired Man" the woman tenderly "put out her hand / Among the harplike morning-glory strings" and again in "The Lone Striker" the mill spinner's "deft hand showed with finger rings / Among the harplike spread of strings."

In "Meeting and Passing" Frost portrays Hardy's theme, in "A Man Was Drawing Near to Me," of a mysterious epiphany between man and woman.[14] In "Near Lanivet, 1872," one of Hardy's many poems of tragic love, an anguished woman self-consciously assumes a martyred pose:

> Her white-clothed form at this dim-lit cease of day
> > Made her look as one crucified
> In my gaze at her from the midst of the dusty way,
> > And hurriedly 'Don't,' I cried. (Hardy, 41)

This poem inspired the pleading, dramatically forceful "Don't—don't go" in the husband's appeal to the self-tormented woman in "Home Burial." Like his novels, Hardy's verse contains dramatic scenes of hateful confrontation between husband and wife. In the penultimate stanza of "Neutral Tones," he compares the woman's expression to a bird of ill-omen:

> The smile on your mouth was the deadest thing
> Alive enough to have strength to die;
> And a grin of bitterness swept thereby
> > Like an ominous bird a-wing. (Hardy, 26)

In the intense, emotionally devastating but little-known "Beyond Words," which Frost said was about Elinor and did not publish until after her death, he compares his cold hatred to icicles in the first two lines and in the last two has the woman spit out "you" four times—just as she had cried "don't" four times in "Home Burial" (the spaced dots are in the poem): "That row of icicles along the gutter / Feels like my armory of hate; / And you, you . . . you, you utter. . . . / You wait!" (Frost, 393)

Hardy's belief, in "Hap" and "Nature's Questioning," that God is either hostile or at best indifferent to the fate of helpless men, finds expression in Frost's dark poems "The Night Light" and "Bereft." Hardy's use of distant stars to symbolize, in "Wanting Both," the littleness of man amidst the vast cosmos,

> A star looks down on me,
> And says: "Here I and you
> Stand, each in our degree:
> What do you mean to do?" (Hardy, 134)

precisely recurs in Frost's "Stars," where the goddess of wisdom is blind:

> And yet with neither love nor hate,
>   Those stars like some snow-white
> Minerva's snow-white marble eyes
>   Without the gift of sight. (Frost, *A Boy's Will*, 5)

The closest thematic parallels occur in three poems where Frost not only adopts Hardy's imagery and ideas, but also draws closer to his source by alluding to specific poems. Hardy's "The Darkling Thrush" made its mark on Frost's "Come In." In Hardy's ironic poem, published on the last day of the nineteenth century, a decrepit bird, who matches the landscape, sings without reason and offers illusory hope:

> At once a voice arose among
>   The bleak twigs overhead
> In a full-hearted evensong
>   Of joy illimited;
> An aged thrush, frail, gaunt, and small,
>   In blast-beruffled plume,
> Had chosen thus to fling his soul
>   Upon the growing gloom. (Hardy, 15)

In "Come In," which also alludes to the theme of death in Keats' "Ode to a Nightingale," the thrush's song at dusk beckons the man to enter the forbidding woods. Frost's speaker also rejects the thrush's song, which now stands for darkness and lamentation, and searches instead for the light of the stars. Hardy's apocalyptic war poem "In Time of 'The Breaking of Nations'" begins:

> Only a man harrowing clods
>   In a slow silent walk
> With an old horse that stumbles and nods
>   Half asleep as they stalk. (Hardy, 184)

In "The Strong Are Saying Nothing" Frost absorbs Hardy's harrowed field and stumbling horse, and moves from plowing, by way of the wind, to express scepticism about the afterlife:

> There is seldom more than a man to a harrowed piece.
> Men work alone, their lots plowed far apart,
> One stringing a chain of seed in an open crease,
> And another stumbling after a halting cart. (Frost, 299)

In "An August Midnight," Hardy assembles a cast of menacing entomological characters who smear the fresh ink on his manuscript and crash meaninglessly against his lamp, and who lead him to question the meaning of their existence—and his own:

> On this scene enter—winged, horned, and spined—
> A longlegs, a moth, and a dumbledore [bumblebee];
> While mid my page there idly stands
> A sleepy fly, that rubs its hands.
>
> Thus meet we five, in this still place
> At this point of time, at this point in space. . . .
> "God's humblest, they!" I muse. Yet why?
> They know Earth-secrets that know not I. (Hardy, 6)

In Frost's "Design" the predatory spider and victimized moth represent kindred spirits of death and blight and suggest the evil in God's design of the universe: "What but design of darkness to appall?— / If design govern in a thing so small?" Frost was saturated with Hardy, just as powerfully, though less obviously, as Hardy's self-proclaimed disciples: D. H. Lawrence, Robert Graves, W. H. Auden and Philip Larkin.

Frost felt the impact of younger contemporaries, as well as of older masters, and learned from his competitors even when he disapproved of their experimental techniques. When the title of a current novel caught his fancy, he made good use of it. He alluded to Hemingway's title for Martha Gellhorn's *A Stricken Field* (1940) in *A Masque of Mercy*, to Graham Greene's *The Ministry of Fear* (1943) in "Why Wait for Science," to John Kennedy's *Profiles in Courage* (1956) in "For John F. Kennedy" and to an ironic slogan from George Orwell's *Nineteen Eighty-Four* (1949), "Freedom Is Slavery," in "How Hard It Is to Keep from Being King." More surprisingly, he plays with Gertrude Stein's phrase "Rose is a rose is a rose

is a rose," from her poem "Sacred Emily" (1913), in "The Rose Family."
In *A Masque of Mercy* he sarcastically describes Joyce's technique in
Finnegans Wake (1939) as "combining / All language in a one-man tongue-
confusion," but varies the rhythm, repetition and alliteration of "snow
falling faintly through the universe and faintly falling," from the last
sentence of his story "The Dead" (1914), in the brilliant opening of
"Desert Places": "Snow falling and night falling fast, oh, fast." In *A Masque
of Reason* he alludes in one playful phrase— "the gold enameled nightingales / Are singing"—to both Yeats' "Sailing to Byzantium" and Eliot's
"Sweeney Among the Nightingales." More seriously, he rhymes "slices"
with "crisis" in "One Step Backward Taken" (1946), just as Eliot had
rhymed "ices" with "crisis" in "The Love Song of J. Alfred Prufrock"
(1915). He also alludes to another alliterative lyrical passage from Eliot's
poem,

> I have seen them riding seaward on the waves
> Combing the white hair of the waves blown back
> When the wind blows the water white and black,[15]

by transferring "riding seaward" into rode backward and adopting Eliot's
white and black waves in a rushing riverine passage in "West-Running
Brook":

> The black stream, catching on a sunken rock,
> Flung backward on itself in one white wave,
> And the white water rode the black forever. (Frost, 258)

III

The poet Anthony Hecht has observed that Frost opposed the prevailing
current of twentieth-century poetry: "He was an almost solitary defender
of formal poetic values during the modernist period when the formal
practices were being widely trashed." His unusual emphasis on meter
and rhyme made Frost scorn contemporaries who took pride in profess-
ing to know nothing about prosody. His great technical skill substanti-
ated his apparently egoistic but quite truthful claim in a letter to John
Bartlett of July 1913: "To be perfectly frank with you I am one of the
most notable craftsmen of my time." In one of his famous comparisons,

directed mainly against his popular rival Carl Sandburg, Frost refused to abandon the rules of poetry and said he would as soon write free verse as play tennis with the net down. When Sandburg took up the challenge and insisted that "you can play a better game with the net down," Frost triumphantly replied: "Sure you can play a better game with the net down—and without the racket and balls—but it ain't tennis."[16]

Frost made some terse but telling remarks, when writing to young poets, about rhyme and rhythm, and revealed the essence of his creative process. Rhymes, he believed, should be original, unforced and inevitable: "You know the weakness of verse: one line of it will be strong and good and the next will be almost anything for the sake of the rhyme. . . . We go on line by line in poetry, building up from the idea, trying to make a rhyming that will not seem the tiniest bit strained. . . . The most important thing about a poem . . . is how willfully, gracefully, naturally, entertainingly and beautifully its rhymes are taken."[17] Speaking, in a similar way, about rhythm, he maintained that his verse sprang from the strain or tension that evolves when a strong rhythmic pattern, based upon strict or loose iambic meter, is played against the irregular variations of common speech.

A brilliant teacher from his youth to old age, Frost had many valuable —and always pragmatic—ideas about the imaginative act, the rush of inspiration, the methods of revision and the pressures of publication. He was not a tormented, self-destructive poet—like Roethke, Berryman, Lowell and Plath—but one who loved the play of the imagination, took joy in his creation and believed that "poetry spoils you for anything else in life." Fond of social life and a great talker, he loved to draw large crowds and spent a great deal of time during his last fifty years lecturing around the country. But he also felt the need for solitude and reflection, and thought he should be walled in by himself most of the time. Reflecting on the apparent laziness of his early years, he declared that loafing was closely connected to being creative, and that for proper artistic growth there must be idleness, which had been the making of him. As confident of his creative powers as of his longevity, he told a friend: "The clearest hint I have of immortality is that I have time to burn. I've always known somehow that I've had time to burn." When a young poet and friend began a career in publishing, Frost—who almost always combined writing with farming, teaching or lecturing—approved of his decision and said: "Can't write poetry all the time, can ya?"[18]

Often asked about poetic inspiration—how a poem actually comes into being—Frost carefully formulated his ideas on this crucial subject.

He felt that transformations in his life — traveling around, changing jobs, moving houses, even a high fever — stimulated his writing. He emphasized the lively play of mind and play of words, and said: "You've got to snap the quip to make Pegasus prance." He wrote an essay in praise of extravagance and, like Thoreau, feared "only lest my expression may not be extravagant enough." The best way to get started, Frost told a correspondent, was with one original metaphor: "Write down your luckiest comparison simply and unaffectedly enough and you can hardly help having poetry. That's the whole game. . . . Make one good distinct figure of speech that's all your own and you are started on the road to poetry."[19]

Frost believed that a poem should be written in a single, free-flowing run. He compared composing verse to sliding down a hill on a sled and declared: "I never wrote anything without thinking: 'This is it!' " Like Plato's symbolic horses, whose creative energy had to be harnessed by a charioteer in order to be transformed into art, Frost wrote, in a punning passage, that the first rush of inspiration must be tempered by word play in order to avoid the twin dangers of cliché and aestheticism: "Emotional plunge comes first of course, but it simply must be harnessed to the wit mill to turn mots, phrases, stanzas and notions. Wit gives a poet something else to play with than the conventional old poetic resentments against machinery, money and the humdrum of instituted society. It protects the professor of beauty from becoming a kalomaniac [someone crazy about Beauty]. I may make too much of nimbleness. But even at my most serious give me nimbleness and 'spree.' "

Hemingway liked to stop writing when he knew what was coming next and could let his unconscious mind meditate on his art, but he also gave in to his overwhelming creative urge and once wrote three stories in one day. Frost also considered this problem and said that "he always tried to hold back after writing a poem before he started on a new one so that he didn't repeat himself, but this led to the problem of always being slightly rusty when he set out to write a new one." He also told an interviewer: "When I start a poem I can tell right away if I'm having my way. If I'm not having my way I quit."[20]

Quitting did not mean abandoning a poem entirely. Despite frequent assertions that he composed his verse in one inspired sitting, Frost's manuscripts reveal that he revised extensively and sometimes took a long time to complete his poems. He then kept them for further consideration and did not publish them for many years. When he rode in trains and lectured on the college circuit, he always carried his manuscripts with him and worked on "things of my own I haven't yet published or haven't yet put the last touch to." Early in his career, he was forced by frequent rejections to keep his work for a long time before publishing it. Even after he achieved recognition, he told the editor of *Poetry* magazine, he was still reluctant to hand over his poems: "I am so accustomed to having things around for years and years that I find them hard to part with under a year old," but "I couldn't keep [them] indefinitely and run the chance of spoiling [them] with too many last touches." Unlike Yeats, Frost did not continue to revise his poems after they had appeared in his books. Frost wrote about eight poems a year, averaged a book every seven years and produced about four hundred poems during the fifty years (1913–62) between his first and last volumes.

Frost formulated his principal theory of poetry, which he called "the sound of sense," before leaving for England. Victorian poets, especially Tennyson and Swinburne, had accepted Pater's belief that "All the arts may be supposed constantly to tend and aspire" to "perfect moments" of music, and had made music an essential element in their poetry. The Wards and other mentors urged him to study the musical notations of Sidney Lanier's work and make his poems "more poetic." But Frost made a radical break with this musical tradition, and based his innovative poetry on the tone of ordinary speech, the realism of the living voice, "the rise and fall, the stressed pauses and little hurries, of spoken language." He had heard mystical voices in childhood and used them in adult life to inspire his poetry. "You begin to hear little voices like hallucinations," he said, "many going on around you. You begin to phrase your feelings. . . . Words haunt you."[21]

Frost was drawn to lines of poetry in which one-syllable words convey the effect of common speech. He first heard this distinctive tone of voice, on the printed page, in Virgil's *Eclogues,* in Shakespeare's *Hamlet* and in Milton's *Comus.* He was especially fond of the subtle irony in Horatio's "So have I heard and do in part believe it" (*Hamlet,* 1.1.165), which he alluded to in "Never Again Would Birds' Song Be the Same" and quoted directly in "From Plane to Plane," and of the Lady's queries: "Shall I go on? / Or have I said enough?" (*Comus,* lines 779–80), which he also alluded to in "From Plane to Plane."

Frost believed that "tones, pauses and rushes and intensities of sound are more revealing than the definition value [that is, the specific meaning] of the words," and told John Bartlett: "I alone of English writers have consciously set myself to make music out of what I may call the sound of sense." But this theory, like his bountiful allusions, was firmly rooted (as his references to Shakespeare and Milton suggest) in the

English literary tradition. In "An Essay on Criticism" (1711), for example, Pope declares, "The sound must seem an echo to the sense" (2: 162) and in chapter nine of Carroll's *Alice's Adventures in Wonderland* (1865), the Duchess tells Alice: "Take care of the sense, and the sounds will take care of themselves." When advocating the primacy of sound over sense, Frost defined a sentence as "a sound in itself on which other sounds called words may be strung." Then, stretching his case to an unbelievable degree, he insisted that "the sentence sound often says *more* than the words. It may even as in irony convey a meaning opposite to the words. . . . I shall show the sentence sound saying all that the sentence conveys with little or no help from the meaning of the words."

Frost gave two examples to support his theory that the tone of voice conveys more than the precise meaning of the words. When walking in the English countryside with his poet friend Edward Thomas, Frost shouted something to a distant farmer, who could not hear his words, and the farmer shouted something back. Though it was impossible to distinguish what the farmer said, Frost maintained that "the cadence of the answer was as clear as that of the question" and, turning to Thomas, exclaimed: "That's what I mean." In the same way, Frost gave an American interviewer "the example of two people who are talking on the other side of a closed door, whose voices can be heard but whose words cannot be distinguished. Even though the words do not carry, the sound of them does, and the listener can catch the meaning of the conversation."[22] Anyone who tries these experiments can immediately see that Frost, passionately arguing against the prevailing trends in poetry, overstated his case. The *cadence* of the farmer's reply (whether hostile or sympathetic) was clear enough, but it was impossible (even with an inspired guess) to make out the actual *meaning* of his words. Nor is it possible to understand a conversation, however helpful the tone, with muffled voices through a closed door. But Frost's essential point, that the tone of voice is vital to the meaning of the words in his poetry, is valid.

Frost gave his best definition of poetry in his essay "The Figure a Poem Makes" (1939), which was used as the Introduction to various editions of his collected poems. He believed that poetry begins in the delight and ecstasy of creation, and ends in "a momentary stay against confusion"—a clarification of life as the poet makes artistic order out of chaotic experience. A poem is momentary when being composed, but once completed becomes permanent. He also said that poetry begins with suffering and a sense of wrong, with a homesickness or lovesickness and is "a way of taking life by the throat." Echoing Horace's *Ars Poetica*, "If you wish me to weep, you must first grieve yourself," Frost wrote. "No tears in the writer, no tears in the reader."[23]

IV

By 1912, when he was thirty-eight years old, Frost had lived in cities (San Francisco and Lawrence) for twenty-six years and on farms and in villages (Derry and Plymouth) for twelve. He had crossed the country three times by train and been as far north as the Canadian border and as far south as the Dismal Swamp. But he had never been outside America. He had studied for half a year at Dartmouth and for a year and a half at Harvard. He had worked in factories and mills, as a reporter and farmer, and had taught in every kind of public and private institution from grade school to teachers' college. He had always planned to sell the Derry farm as soon as it became his property and leave teaching for at least a year in order to write. As he explained in a Lawrencean passage: "My mind was made up. I would stop teaching. It was not for me. Why keep on working when you get nowhere for the effort? Why have only your labor for your pains? I said to my wife, 'It'll never do to go on like this. I'll just turn into a machine, and what will happen to my poetry? We must get away, somewhere, anywhere—only away.' I wanted to be as far away from the nosey relatives down Lawrence way as I could get, clear off. . . . They were good people who honestly were trying to save me from myself. I had no choice but to run away somewhere and hide."

He also wanted to leave because he hoped that new scenery and the stimulation of change would somehow offer him a better chance of publishing his work and revive his hopes for a poetic career. He lamented that "nobody ever sent me as good a letter of acceptance as some I got for rejections," that "I couldn't keep writing while rejection slips came in. Every one of these slips was hateful to me." The poet in him had nearly died and his confidence in his creative powers was not fully restored until he had lived for a year in England.

But there was still the problem of where to go. John Bartlett had married his high school girlfriend, moved to Vancouver on the west coast of Canada, and got a job as a reporter. Frost, tempted to join him there, told Thompson that they tossed a coin to decide between England and Vancouver, and that "the coin chose England."[24] It is extremely unlikely, however, that a coin decided this important matter. Vancouver was then a remote and raw frontier town. It had no literary life and was filled with the sort of philistine provincials Frost was trying to escape from in New Hampshire. Broken in health and with his career foundering, Bartlett had nothing to show for his years there and returned to America, defeated, in 1915.

But there were a great many reasons to go to England. It was cheaper to live there than in America or Canada, and Elinor had the romantic wish to live under a thatched roof. It had nourished the great tradition of English poetry that Frost so admired in *The Golden Treasury*, and London—filled with writers, editors and publishers—was the literary capital of the world. Unlike Pound, who went to England in 1908 to "learn from Yeats," or Eliot, who went to Oxford in 1914 to study philosophy, Frost did not go to England for a specific purpose or to meet a particular person. He had already developed his poetic theory and technique. He now needed leisure, stimulation and a more sympathetic response to his work.

In July 1911, ten years after his grandfather's death, Frost inherited the Derry farm and then sold it for $1,900. At the same time his annuity increased to $800. Third-class passage was only $50 for adults, and the children, keen for adventure, went free when accompanied by their parents. Frost eventually managed to accumulate $3,600 and the family of six lived on that sum for three years. They stored their furniture, and took only bedding, pictures, chair, rugs and books. They sailed from Boston to Glasgow on the *Parisian* on August 23, 1912. Despite some seasickness, they enjoyed the ocean voyage and saw the British fleet as they approached the coast of Scotland. After landing in early September, they traveled south from Glasgow by train, reached London that evening and took rooms at the Premier Hotel. In London Frost's literary career would be launched at last by a French widow and an American expatriate.

6

England and
Ezra Pound

1912–1914

I

In early September Frost looked for a modest house near London while
Elinor showed the children the sights of the city. In the evenings, leaving
the thirteen-year-old Lesley in charge of the younger ones, they went to
the theater. He also heard Shaw tease the suffragettes in a public speech
and acquired a library card at the British Museum. Alerted to the possi-
bilities of Beaconsfield, in Buckinghamshire, twenty miles north of London, he emerged from the suburban train station and was struck by the
sign of a real estate agent: A. C. Frost.

The town, from which Disraeli took his title, had impressive literary
associations. Edmund Waller, author of "Go, Lovely Rose," had lived
there and Edmund Burke was buried there. Milton had completed
Paradise Lost in Beaconsfield and Gray was buried a few miles south in
Stoke Poges. And that fierce, foaming Toby-jug, G. K. Chesterton, whose
essays in *Heretics* (1905) Frost had read in Plymouth, lived right in town.
For twenty dollars a month on a year's lease, Frost rented The Bungalow,
a five-room suburban villa on Reynolds Road, built a few years earlier, in
1909. Elinor, pleased with the place though it had no thatch, described
it as "a low cottage, built of stucco, with vines growing over it, and we
have plenty of land with it—a large grassy space in front, and a pretty
garden behind, with pear trees, strawberry beds and lots of flowers." By
Christmas, a newspaper headline proclaimed: "ENGLAND IN THE
GRIP OF FROST."

Frost visited the local school and was not impressed. The classes had
forty pupils each, the rooms were merely divided by a curtain and no one
had ever heard of the progressive ideas of Maria Montessori. Worst of all,
the children seemed malnourished and malformed—like the poorest

inhabitants of an American slum. No middle-class families enrolled their children in the free County Council schools, where they would pick up a cockney accent and an inferior education, and Frost could not afford to send his brood elsewhere. So Elinor prolonged their hermetic existence and taught them at home, and they had very little contact with English children. Nevertheless, they made an excellent impression on the English barrister and poet John Haines: "[Lesley] was very nearly grown up and well educated and very handsome. I fancy she read a great deal. The youngest girl (Marjorie) was very quiet and shy. Irma and Carol were most delightful children, very talkative and lively. Irma looked fragile but was lively enough and was the one who asked the most questions about everything. She was the most American of the four."

The English were also very fond of Frost. Catherine Abercrombie, the poet's wife, said that "you couldn't have had a nicer man, or more pleasant, gentle, humane man than Robert Frost." Eleanor Farjeon—author of children's books, friend of D. H. Lawrence and the poet Edward Thomas—found Frost frank, intelligent and deceptively "simple." She remembered "his figure as middle-sized and compact, his manner friendly and undemonstrative; he looked at you directly, his talk was shrewd and speculative, withholding nothing and derived from nobody but himself. His New England speech came readily and leisurely, and of all the writers of worth whom I had met he spoke with the least sophistication." When potatoes had to be dug up from the garden, Frost assumed his customary role of lord and master: "The only indolent member of the outfit was Robert, who, smoking blandly [a short-lived English habit], strolled up and down the patch, a self-appointed overseer of cheap labour."[1]

The family hiked all around the countryside. Though they were less than ten miles from Windsor Castle and only about twenty-five from Oxford, there is no mention of visits to these places. But in August 1913, at the invitation of Ernest and Mary Gardner, whom Frost met at a poetry reading and who also had young children, he rented a cottage near them in Kingsbarns, on the North Sea coast near St. Andrews. He had lost contact with his mother's family in Scotland, but was keen to see Edinburgh Castle and Arthur's Seat, which she had often told him about in childhood. The family took a boat up the east coast to Dundee and then a train to the village in Fifeshire.

Gardner, an eminent archeologist at the University of London and the British School in Athens, had discovered some nearby caves that contained an extraordinary treasure: the first, 10,000-year-old Paleolithic animal drawings in Britain. When Gardner proudly showed off his find, Frost contradicted the expert. He boldly declared that some of the figures were made by water on the soft sandstone and that none was older than five hundred years. (Excavations at these caves, completed in 1914, proved Frost much more accurate than Gardner. They "conclusively dated their earliest occupation to Roman times," placed the drawings at 800 A. D. and ruled out "any possibility of stone age habitation.") Frost's outspoken assertion inevitably caused strained feelings. By the end of August he wrote Bartlett that Mary Gardner, a would-be poet who liked to be flattered, had virtually forced him to go up to Scotland. He called the Gardners lion hunters who had picked him up as a bargain before he had made his reputation. Frost had better luck with a learned Scottish school inspector, J. C. Smith, who also edited Shakespeare for Oxford University Press. He wrote to Frost after his first book had appeared and in March 1914 organized a discussion of Frost's poetry at an Edinburgh literary society.

As soon as he had settled into Beaconsfield, Frost aranged the manuscripts of his early lyrical poems into the form of a book, which he planned to offer for publication. Bartlett had sent him copies of the London journal *T. P.'s Weekly* while he was still living in New Hampshire, and Frost claimed that he chose his publisher on the advice of a retired police constable who wrote a column for that paper. But there were better reasons to choose the now obscure but then prominent firm of David Nutt. According to Ezra Pound, it was "long known as a lover of good letters." In 1913 the firm had an extremely cosmopolitan list and published poetry books about "Greece, Africa, Ulster, Persia, Russia, Scotland and America." Above all, it was the discoverer and publisher of William Ernest Henley, who had died in 1903, and still had fifteen volumes of his work in print. Nutt also brought out the work of its literary adviser, John Drinkwater, the Georgian poet, playwright and actor, who recommended Frost's book for publication.

Alfred Nutt, who had succeeded his father, "was an accomplished and widely read man. . . . He was a publisher whose books reflected his scholarly tastes, and was something of an author as well. He was in the van of the Celtic revival; originator of the movement which led to the formation of the Irish Texts Society; founder of the English Goethe Society; and past-president of the Folk-lore Society, all the publications of which he issued through his own house. . . . In May 1910 Alfred Nutt was at Melun [southeast of Paris] with his invalid son, whose carriage somehow slipped into the river [Seine], and was swept away. His father sprang to the rescue, and was drowned. The son was saved."[2]

In October 1912 Frost entered the premises at 17 Grape Street, off New Oxford Street in Bloomsbury, and encountered a grasping French-woman who seemed to come right out of a novel by Balzac. Mme. M. L. Nutt had been Alfred's secretary, then his wife, and was now head of the business. In 1913 she would bring out under her firm's imprint her extremely bitter and idiosyncratic feminist novel, *A Woman of To-Day*. Though dressed in black, she never mentioned that her husband had been recently drowned and merely said that she would speak for him. Frost left the book with her and three days later, on October 26, she promptly accepted it.

Recently widowed, with an invalid son, and inexperienced in running the business, Mme. Nutt probably felt she had to be tough with the engaging but unknown American. She was a formidable adversary, as Stanley Unwin, an experienced publisher, discovered when he tried to buy her firm in 1914: "I received a letter from Mrs. Alfred Nutt—a French lady—suggesting that I should become her publishing manager. I don't think that I have ever encountered anyone so suspicious. The negotiations were interminable, but led nowhere. As soon as I looked like coming to terms with her solicitor she threw him overboard on the ground apparently that I was in some mysterious way in league with him. I would then start afresh, but as she could never finally make up her mind what she wanted, nothing ever came of the negotiations." Mme. Nutt, in fact, retained control of the business until it went into liquidation in 1921.

Poets usually paid for the publication of their first book; even Hous-man had to bring out *A Shropshire Lad* at his own expense in 1896. Since Mme. Nutt did not ask for money and even offered to pay royalties, she could dictate the terms of the contract. Frost consulted Thomas Mosher of Portland, Maine, the only publisher he knew, and then, with some misgivings about the terms, accepted her offer. The contract—dated December 16, 1912, signed by "David Nutt" and taxed with a sixpenny stamp—specified a large edition of 1,000 copies and a 12 percent royalty after the sale of the first 250. Frost gave her English-language rights throughout the world and (most unusually) the option on his next four books in verse or prose. He feared, he wrote Mosher before signing the document, that it might seem "traitorously un-American" if all his early work came out first in England. But he was pleased that she had such great faith in his potential value and wanted to acquire several of his books before they were even written.

A Boy's Will, published on about April 1, 1913, appeared in Nutt's Series of Modern Poets and cost one shilling and sixpence (7.5 modern pence). It was advertised in newspapers and sold directly by the publisher so that Mme. Nutt would not have to give a 40 percent discount to the bookstores. John Walsh, in his useful book on Frost's years in England, states that by the terms of the contract Frost would have handed over "to Mrs. Nutt the first twenty-four pounds of his book's earning, a sum equal to several months rent on the Bungalow." In fact, the total earnings on 250 copies came to £18.75, of which Frost's share (at 12 percent) was only £2.25 (or $11.25) — less than two-thirds of a month's rent. Despite the contract, Mme. Nutt never gave Frost either a royalty statement or a check for the two books she published. All he got from her were discouraging French shrugs, which he recognized from the French-Canadians in New Hampshire, and insulting remarks: "Oh poetry, you know, can't be expected to make money" and "Americans were all money chasers."[3] However, the whole question was academic since *A Boy's Will* probably did not sell more than 250 copies. She did owe him money for his second book, but shrugged off the obligation and never bothered to pay it.

Mme. Nutt was an irritating woman and gave Frost a good deal of unnecessary trouble, but on the whole he did rather well with her. She immediately recognized his talent and potential. In contrast to her dilatory tactics with Unwin, she took Drinkwater's sound advice, and accepted and published Frost's first two books at her own expense when very few editors in America would accept his poems. Partly through her extraordinary efforts (as well as his own), his two books were well and widely reviewed. She never paid royalties on his second volume, but he eventually broke his contract, forced her to surrender American rights, and did not give her his third and fourth books.

II

Frost arrived in England at exactly the right time to publish his poetry and the man, the moment and the milieu came together under optimum conditions. In October 1912, a month after he reached London, Harriet Monroe brought out the first issue of *Poetry* in Chicago and provided a valuable showcase for his future work. In December the first anthology of *Georgian Poetry* appeared. It was well received by the public and did a great deal to stimulate interest in contemporary verse. On January 8, 1913 Harold Monro, editor of *Poetry and Drama* and publisher of *Georgian Poetry,* officially opened the Poetry Bookshop. After browsing through the latest books, Frost heard the first public reading by the dashing and handsome Rupert Brooke, the Georgians' Philip Sidney.

Born in Brussels in 1879, the son of a Scottish engineer, Monro, a fervent Fabian Socialist, came down from Cambridge in 1901. He married in 1903, founded the Samurai Press three years later and lived for a time among the English expatriates in Florence. The Poetry Bookshop was located in an eighteenth-century house at 35 Devonshire Street, off Theobald's Road in Bloomsbury. It was in the slums of Holborn and across from a whorehouse, but only five minutes' walk from the British Museum. The Bookshop sold volumes of poetry, contained the offices of Monro's journal and small publishing house, had a large garret room for public poetry readings and several smaller furnished rooms that were rented to poets at modest cost.

Frost felt Monro was duplicitous and tactless. Despite pleas from his fellow poets, he and the editor, Edward Marsh, had excluded Frost from the anthologies of *Georgian Poetry.* Frost satirically described Monro as "horse-faced, wall-eyed, two-faced: arm around shoulder, then a nasty crack. . . . Remarked re an anthology, 'Only the best in this; you won't be in it.'" Though Frost also criticized the gloomy spirit and theological strain of Monro's *Poetry and Drama,* he sold six poems to this journal and in April 1914 accepted as partial payment a week for himself and his family in the rooms above the shop.

On the momentous opening night of the Bookshop the poet Frank Flint asked Frost if he were American. Frost said: "Yes. How'd you know?" Flint simply replied: "Shoes." He also told Frost that he ought to meet his fellow countryman Ezra Pound, and persuaded Pound to invite Frost round for a talk. Frost took almost three months to respond to Pound's offer. Flint, meanwhile, generously introduced Frost to many of the leading writers in the close-knit London literary world. Born (like Pound) in 1885, Flint was the son of a London traveling salesman. He left school at the age of thirteen, but taught himself a dozen languages, was knowledgeable about French Symbolist poetry and became a senior statistician in the Ministry of Labour. An ally of Pound in the Imagist Movement, he was rather harshly described by the American poet John

Gould Fletcher as "bespectacled, shy, apologetic . . . ashamed of his own Cockney antecedents . . . doomed perpetually to follow, and never to lead."

Speaking of the English writers he had met before the war, Frost once told a friend: "I knew a lot of them. I knew just about all of them." Frost knew the great modernists—Yeats, Ford and Pound—but felt more at ease with the traditional Georgian poets—W. H. Davies, Wilfrid Gibson, Lascelles Abercrombie and Edward Thomas—who were less self-consciously literary and more down-to-earth, closer to him in subject and technique, and far easier to compete with. Most of the writers Frost met had established their reputations well before he published his first book in 1913 and took little notice in their letters and memoirs of the shy American. But in his unobtrusive way, on frequent trips into London from suburban Beaconsfield, he did come to know Rupert Brooke, Jacob Epstein, T. E. Hulme, Laurence Binyon, Robert Bridges, Walter de la Mare and Robert Graves.[4] Though Yeats and Pound treated Frost with polite condescension, he received an extraordinarily warm reception from most other writers. He found the English charming and hoped to stay, if his money held out, for five years—or until he was deported. His love of England, he told John Haines, was his love of friends, who kept him up to date with the latest trends in poetry, painting and philosophy.

In London Frost made a great intellectual leap from his kind but limited friends, John Bartlett and Sidney Cox, to real poets like Ezra Pound and Edward Thomas. In contrast to the intense isolation of the Derry farm, where he had no friends, he was now constantly talking to writers who shared his tastes and interests. For the first time in his life, he met creative men with first-rate minds, who understood his ideas and appreciated his achievement. Though Frost's two and a half years in England did not influence the essential quality of his work, it strengthened his commitment to poetry. England freed him from poultry and pedagogy, gave him the necessary distance from his subject matter and provided tremendous stimulation.

Frost was taken up, praised and promoted by Pound, Ford and the Georgians in exactly the same way that Lawrence had been. A coal miner's son and, like Frost, an outsider, Lawrence had confidence in his ability and bitterly resented the patronizing attitude of the established—and sometimes less talented—middle-class writers: "In the early days they were always telling me I had got genius, as if to console me for not having their own incomparable advantages." Like Lawrence, Frost brought a lively new viewpoint into the rather stuffy atmosphere of the Georgians.

Though Frost and Lawrence never met, they knew each other's work. In June 1915 Frost, impressed by Lawrence's vivid technique, distinguished him from his contemporaries and wrote enthusiastically to Edward Garnett, a distinguished English critic and friend of Lawrence: "I'll tell you a poet with a method that is a method: D. H. Lawrence. I came across a poem of his in a new Imagiste Anthology just published here, and it was such a poem that I wanted to go right to the man that wrote it and say something." Two years later Lawrence, in an angry mood, indiscriminately lumped Frost with his inferiors, whom he accused of "puerile self-magnification": "I believe in America there is the courage of ultimate truth—which in Europe there *is not.*—But your Sandburgs and Untermeyers, even your Edgar Lee Masters or Robert Frosts—the vanity ticklers —no, they are not to be borne."

Frost and Lawrence also shared significant traits. Both were influenced by Hardy, responded intensely to nature and had an extraordinary ability to portray their regional landscapes. Echoing Lawrence's "Never trust the artist. Trust the tale," Frost once declared: "Don't trust me. Trust the poems."[5] Frost's "Me for the hills" in "New Hampshire" matches Lawrence's "When in doubt, *move,*" Frost's lovers in "Meeting and Passing" resemble those in Lawrence's *The Rainbow,* and in both "Home Burial" and *Women in Love* the man upsets the woman by coming in from the graveyard with fresh earth on his boots.

Frost's incisive and often satiric observations show that he kept close watch on his contemporaries. He said that Rupert Brooke affected a metaphysical sarcasm and tried to be a latter-day John Donne. Jacob Epstein, who had settled in London in 1905 and created shocking sensual figures, had rooms across the hall when Frost lived above the Poetry Bookshop. Frost amusingly described him as "the futurist sculptor, the New York Polish Jew, whose mind runs strangely on the subject of generation, whose work is such a stumbling block to the staid and Victorianly but who in spite of all is reckoned one of the greatest living geniuses." Frost attended the Tuesday "at homes" of Epstein's friend T. E. Hulme, in the house of his patron at 67 Frith Street in Soho, and discussed the French philosopher Henri Bergson, whom Frost had read in 1911 and Hulme had translated in 1913. Hulme's advocacy of the "hard dry image" influenced Imagism, and his own "Complete Poetical Works"—five poems—appeared in the *New Age* (to which Flint contributed) in 1912. Frost described the impressive Hulme as a hulking English squire, just back from Germany, who held forth on philosophy.

Another artistic venue—in addition to the Poetry Bookshop and the salon at Frith Street—was the Vienna Café, where Frost met the poet and art critic Laurence Binyon. On the second floor above the corner of New Oxford Street and Bloomsbury Street, furnished in the Danubian mode with red plush chairs and seats, it was a favorite rendezvous for European émigrés and for writers associated with the British Museum. In Canto 80 Pound noted that when the Austrian owner was forced to close the Vienna, after the war broke out and the waiters were interned, the Café was transformed into a bank. At the Vienna, Binyon introduced Frost to the seventy-year-old Robert Bridges, who had been a friend of Hopkins and was named Poet Laureate in 1913. Frost argued about metrics with the dogmatic Bridges, disagreed with his theories and called him, in a letter to Cox, "a fine old boy with the highest opinion—of his poetry you thought I was going to say—perhaps of his poetry, but much more particularly of his opinions." Frost intensely admired Walter de la Mare. He liked him personally and thought he was the "greatest of living poets." De la Mare visited Frost in Amherst in 1917; Bridges succeeded Frost at the University of Michigan in 1924.

Frost also met Robert Graves, then a young officer, at the Poetry Bookshop early in 1915. Graves became an admirer, disciple and lifelong friend. He saw Frost (who came up from Florida especially for the occasion) in New York in May 1959, when Graves received a gold medal from the Poetry Society of America, and wrote frequently and perceptively about him. In an early review of *New Hampshire,* Graves found "both passion and music in Frost, though the passion is under control and the music is an unusual idiom." In a moving tribute after Frost's death, Graves said he "was one of the very few poets alive whom I respected and loved."[6]

Though Frost met Yeats (through Pound) on only two occasions, in March and April of 1913, Yeats made a strong impression on him. He attended Yeats' "Monday nights" in his Bloomsbury flat in Woburn Walk and was surprised by the dark-curtained, candle-lit atmosphere of the rooms. Frost took the opportunity of discussing the plays by Yeats he had put on at Pinkerton. But most of their talk led to minor contretemps. Frost rashly claimed that he could tell from reading a poem whether it came easily or was difficult to write, and cited Yeats' "The Song of Wandering Aengus" as an example of the former. Yeats then contradicted him by declaring that it had been written in agony during a period of emotional turmoil.

Writing to Sidney Cox a few months after meeting Yeats, Frost declared that the Irish poet, like Bridges, was personally disappointing: "Yeats has undoubtedly been the man of the last twenty years in English poetry. I won't say that he is quite great judged either by the way he takes himself as an artist or by the work he has done. I am afraid he has come just short of being. . . . Let him be as affected as he pleases if he will only write well. But you can't be affected and write entirely well." His main criticism of both Yeats and Pound was that they were "always *faking*," in their lives as well as in their art. Frost gave as an example Yeats' story, which seemed to confirm his "wistful half belief" in fairies and revealed the ludicrous aspects of the Celtic Revival. Yeats claimed that he once saw a leprechaun who was kept in a cage and pined away in captivity. When his masters finally took pity and released him, he joined a companion who had hung about the house in mourning and the two "hurried off hand in hand down the glen." Frost remembered this story when he decided to drop his own fairy poem, "Spoils of the Dead," from his *Collected Poems*.

Pound introduced a note of realism, Frost recalled, by "taking the Irishman apart." He told Yeats: "'You're too full of adjectives and expletives. Let's wring you dry.' He then proceeded to take some of Yeats' poems and, as he put it, wring them dry." Yeats and Eliot meekly submitted to this well-intentioned maneuver, but Frost protested violently when Pound tried it out on him. He was delighted when Yeats told Pound that *A Boy's Will* (complete with the fairy poem) "was the best thing that had come out of America for some time"—though Yeats would not commit himself to this opinion in print.

Frost alluded to the famous opening line of Yeats' "The Lake Isle of Innisfree"—"I will arise and go"—in his early uncollected poem "Summering" and to the theory of masks, expressed by the heroine's "favorite poet," in *A Masque of Mercy*. Frost cchoed "Now shall I make my soul" from "The Tower" in "Triple Bronze," and may have been influenced by the cosmic rage expressed in "The Second Coming" in "Once by the Pacific." Frost's humorous one-page playlet, "The Cow's in the Corn" ("Go drive her into someone else's then!"), was his sole contribution to Celtic drama.[7]

III

Frost was on much more intimate terms with the Georgian poets. He was especially fond of W. H. Davies, three years older than himself, "a small narrow-headed blackhaired Monmouthshire man, with the childish slightly uncomfortable smile of Welsh people." Davies had little formal education, spent many years as a tramp and beggar in England and North America, and seemed like one of the eccentric characters Frost portrayed in *North of Boston.* When he tried to jump a train in Ontario in 1899, his right leg was severed at the ankle and then amputated at the knee. Davies walked like an old sea captain, with a wooden stump, sold shoelaces and penny rhyme-sheets in the streets, and consorted with prostitutes. He was befriended and helped by Edward Thomas at the beginning of his literary career and, Frost wrote, had the charming naiveté "of a lost child: he easily sees wonders." Poverty and physical pain had driven Davies to drink and he remained fond of the bottle after he became a famous poet. Frost captured his engaging speech and personality in an affectionate portrait: "Davies is lovely. . . . They gave him a pension to take him off the streets. Has done some good things in unconscious art. Said he to me, 'I remember you were there the other night. I spoke to you didn't I? But I was awful. After you went I went out of the restaurant a minute for one more drink and I never found my way back.'"[8]

Lascelles Abercrombie, "a small dark, shy man, with spectacles and straight, slightly greasy-looking hair," was born near Liverpool, the son of a stockbroker, in 1881. Educated at Malvern and Manchester University, he began as a literary journalist and published his first book of poetry in 1908. He worked as a munitions inspector during the war and then became a university professor. A partisan of Frost's work, he urged Edward Marsh to include Frost in *Georgian Poetry* and favorably compared him to Ford Madox Ford (then called Hueffer): "Frost, at his best, is far more genuinely and deeply original, much more beautiful and interesting, and however experimental, is firm, finely proportioned and intellectually constructed." Though Pound had been asked—and had refused —to contribute his "Ballad of the Goodly Fere" to the first volume of *Georgian Poetry,* Marsh excluded Frost because he was not British.

Wilfrid Gibson, four years younger than Frost, was born in Northumberland and graduated from Cambridge. He wrote on northern rural themes, published his first book in 1902, moved to London a decade later and served as a private in the war. Until he met Edward Thomas, Frost considered Gibson his "best friend" and contrasted his frankness to the literary fakery Frost so detested in Yeats and Pound: "He's just one of the plain folks with none of the marks of the literary poseur about him." D. H. Lawrence, who met Abercrombie and Gibson in Italy in 1913, liked them as much as Frost did and gave Edward Marsh a vivid account of their characters: "Abercrombie *is* sharp—he is much more *intellectual* than I had imagined. We both loved Mrs. Abercrombie. . . . She's most awfully jolly, and a fine true-metal sort that I love. . . . I loved Gibson still more than Abercrombie—perhaps because I know him better. But I think Gibson is one of the clearest and most lovable personalities that I know." Gibson himself described Frost's witty, wide-ranging and apparently endless conversation, which gripped the attention of his listeners. He also mentioned the almost professional "twinkle" in Frost's eyes that he summoned up at will to captivate his audience:

> In the lamplight
> We talked and laughed, but for the most part listened
> While Robert Frost kept on and on and on
> In his slow New England fashion for our delight,
> Holding us with shrewd turns and racy quips
> And the rare twinkle of his grave blue eyes. . . .
> Again Frost's rich and ripe philosophy
> That had the body and tang of good draught cider
> And poured as clear a stream.[9]

Frost aligned himself, professionally as well as personally, with the Georgian mode of poetry rather than with Pound's more experimental Imagists and Futurists. The Preface to the first of five volumes of *Georgian Poetry*, which ran from 1912 until 1922, alluded to the recent deaths of Meredith and Swinburne in 1909 and declared that "English poetry is now once again putting on new strength and beauty." The Georgians' rather sedate poetry portrayed "country cottages, old furniture, moss-covered barns, rose-scented lanes, apple and cherry orchards, village inns, and village cricket." Their lyrics, usually inspired by nature, tended to express a moral point.

In 1914 Lawrence, who contributed occasional poems to these volumes, cut to the heart of their weakness and frankly told Marsh that he was "*bitterly* disappointed" in "the red nose and the rough spun cloak of

Masefield and Wilfrid. . . . I hate and detest [Abercrombie's] ridiculous imitation yokels and all the silly hash of his bucolics." Four years later T. S. Eliot, justifying his own very different kind of verse and alluding to Keats' "Ode to a Nightingale," wittily attacked their bland insipidity: "What nearly all the writers have in common is the quality of pleasantness. There are two varieties of pleasantness: (1) The insidiously didactic, or Wordsworthian (a rainbow and a cuckoo's song); (2) the decorative, playful or solemn, minor Keatsian, too happy, happy brook, or lucent sirops. In either variety the Georgians caress everything they touch." Frost wrote of common folk in common speech and used pastoral themes in *A Boy's Will*. But the lovely English countryside did not inspire his poetry, and the Georgians' rustic sentimentality was very different from his tragic vision in *North of Boston*. The farther he got from New England, the more intensely he became attached to it. He proclaimed himself "a Yank from Yankville," and during his years in England got Yankier and Yankier.[10]

IV

A Boy's Will, published on about April 1, 1913, was dedicated, like all but one of his books brought out in her lifetime, to Elinor. It took its title from a favorite boyhood poem, "My Lost Youth," in which Longfellow wrote: "A boy's will is the wind's will, / And the thoughts of youth are long, long thoughts." In Frost, as in Longfellow, the boy tends to brood about the past and has emotions as variable as the wind. The original edition contained vague and not especially illuminating glosses on the poems, after the fashion of Yeats' *The Wind Among the Reeds* (1899). They suggest the considerable difference in age between the thirty-nine-year-old author and the youth in the book, and express the poet's gently ironic attitude toward his sentimental and self-pitying hero.

The thirty-two autobiographical poems (three were later dropped, along with all the glosses) reflect the annual cycle of the seasons and move from autumn to autumn, from "My November Guest" to "October." The first poem, "Into My Own," describes his flight from Dartmouth, Lawrence and Elinor into the Dismal Swamp. "The Tuft of Flowers," which got him the job at Pinkerton, appears toward the end and marks his return to society after five years of self-enforced solitude in

Derry. Frost described the book to the editor of the *Youth's Companion,* which had published three of the poems, as "a series of lyrics standing in some such loose relation to each other as a ring of children who have just stopped dancing and let go hands," and called it "The Record of a Phase of Post-adolescence."

A Boy's Will describes the natural elements that Frost would make his permanent poetic property: stars, clouds, leaves, flowers, brooks, birds. Nine of the poems had been published in minor American periodicals between 1906 and 1912; and he retained "My Butterfly" (from the *Independent* of 1894), which stuck out awkwardly amidst his more pol- ished work. Frost developed his ideas about the use of everyday language *after* he had written these poems, which are full of old-fashioned contrac- tions, inversions and lifeless archaic diction: "I wist . . . Thou didst . . . fain to list . . . full many a time . . . many and many a year . . . I knew not well myself . . . that frighted thee so oft." Frost's poetic progress from *A Boy's Will* to *North of Boston* becomes clear when one compares "Snatched thee, o'ereager, with ungentle grasp" (the worst line in the former) to the intensely colloquial "What help he is there's no depending on" in "The Death of the Hired Man."

"My Butterfly," "Into My Own," "The Tuft of Flowers" and the Hardy- esque "Stars," which carries the gloss "There is no oversight of human affairs," have already been discussed. "Ghost House" anticipates the abandoned farms in *North of Boston;* "My November Guest" expresses his sorrowful love for Elinor, in a grey Hardy-like landscape, as the lovers meet amidst "The desolate, deserted trees, / The faded earth, the heavy sky." In the ballad "Love and a Question," the bridegroom does not want to allow a woeful stranger into his house to spoil his love on his wedding night. In the powerful "Storm Fear"—thematically related to his later poems "The Fear" and "House Fear"—a blizzard, blowing high snow- drifts, blocks a small family into their house "Till even the comforting barn grows far away" and makes them doubt whether they have the strength to survive the storm. The supplicating "A Prayer in Spring" reflects the change of seasons and portrays a benign God (who becomes malevolent and menacing in greater poems like "Once by the Pacific"). It reveals Frost's intense response to the natural world and, when calling a white orchard "Like nothing else by day, like ghosts by night," contains the finest line in the book.

"The Trial by Existence," "Mowing" and "Reluctance" are the strong- est poems. Frost said that the theme, meter and imagery of Rossetti's

"The Blessed Damozel" (1846), which expresses the yearning of the loved one in heaven, inspired "The Trial by Existence." In Frost's poem, dead heroes awake in paradise (the fourth line echoes the Lord's Prayer), amid the fields of asphodel in Hades, where Odysseus found Achilles and Patroclus, to discover that they must continue the struggle they had made on earth. Heaven will also be a testing place of man's courage.

"Mowing" continues the pastoral theme which began with Marvell's "The Mower, Against Gardens" and continued with Wordsworth's "The Solitary Reaper," and which Frost himself took up in "The Exposed Nest" and "The Last Mowing":

> There was never a sound beside the wood but one,
> And that was my long scythe whispering to the ground.
> What was it it whispered? I knew not well myself;
> Perhaps it was something about the heat of the sun,
> Something, perhaps, about the lack of sound—
> And that was why it whispered and did not speak.
> It was no dream of the gift of idle hours,
> Or easy gold at the hand of fay or elf:
> Anything more than the truth would have seemed too weak
> To the earnest love that laid the swale in rows,
> Not without feeble-pointed spikes of flowers
> (Pale orchises), and scared a bright green snake.
> The fact is the sweetest dream that labor knows.
> My long scythe whispered and left the hay to make.

In this early poem, Frost said, he came so close to what he longed to achieve that he almost despaired of coming nearer. He was so fond of the second line that he used it again, a few pages later, in "The Tuft of Flowers." The sound of a blade cutting hay can actually sound like the whisper of a human voice, and during the consoling rhythm of repeated motion the mower hears the sound and tries to make out the unspoken sense of what it whispered. Echoing the song from *Cymbeline* ("Fear no more the heat of the sun"), Frost suggests that the truth lies in the physical conditions of summer toil, during which he cut the spiky orchis flowers and scared—but did not harm—the bright green snake. The mower-poet discerns from the whispering scythe, by the end of the morning and the end of the poem, that the thing he *makes*—the hay in the poem and the poem itself—"is the sweetest dream that labor knows."

In "Reluctance," the last poem in the book, Frost returns to the woods and season of the opening poem. After running away, he now comes home and expresses his individualistic credo by asking, in imaginative terms, three rhetorical questions:

> Ah, when to the heart of man
> Was it ever less than a treason
> To go with the drift of things,
> To yield with a grace to reason,
> And bow and accept the end
> Of a love or a season?

Reluctant to accept the norms of conventional behavior, he declares that he will go against the grain, follow his own intuition and resist what appeared to be the end of Elinor's love. The concluding stanza synthesizes the theme of mutability, which Frost admired in his favorite poems by Herrick, Shirley and Collins, and made the dominant theme in *A Boy's Will.*

Frost did not need other writers to stimulate his own poetry, but he did need them to review it. His English friends rallied round and gave his first two books an enthusiastic reception. *A Boy's Will* had brief paragraphs in the *Athenaeum* and *Times Literary Supplement,* a positive review in the *Academy* and favorable notices by Norman Douglas, Frank Flint and Ezra Pound. *North of Boston* was reviewed by Monro, Abercrombie, Gibson, Thomas and Pound as well as by Ford Madox Ford, Richard Aldington and Edward Garnett.

Since Frost had published very little poetry, most of it in obscure journals, his first book seemed especially original and surprising. The anonymous critic in the *Academy* exclaimed: "We have read every line with that amazement and delight which are too seldom evoked by books of modern verse. . . . It is undoubtedly the work of a true poet. . . . No one who really cares for poetry should miss this little book." The distinguished novelist Norman Douglas praised Frost's "image of things really heard and seen. There is a wild, racy flavour in his poems; they sound that *inevitable* response to nature which is the hallmark of true lyric feeling." Frank Flint, who had discussed Frost's verse with him, admired his characteristic qualities: "direct observation of the object and immediate correlation with the emotion—spontaneity, subtlety in the evocation of moods, humour, an ear for silence."[11]

V

The most important personal as well as critical response to Frost and his work came from Ezra Pound, with whom he had a brief, intense friendship. After Flint told Pound about Frost, Ezra invited him round to his flat at 10 Church Walk in Kensington, with a card that read: "At home, sometimes." Annoyed by the cheeky tone, Frost did not stop by until *A Boy's Will* was about to be published. In late March 1913 he made his way down the narrow path between church and graveyard, knocked on Pound's door and was told to wait inside while Ezra, drying his staircase of rufous hair, emerged from his bath. "Not improbable re Frost finding me in tub," he later said in imitation cockney, "but not hip, more likely byby's bawth."

Born like Frost in the American West but eleven years younger, the erudite and pedantic Pound had studied romance languages at Hamilton College and the University of Pennsylvania, and been dismissed, after a minor scandal, from Wabash College in Indiana. He had already brought out a formidable number of books and secured a beachhead in the London literary world. He had printed his own first book, *A Lume Spento* (With Tapers Quenched, 1908) in Venice; and after moving to London that year published with Elkin Matthews and Stephen Swift three more volumes of poetry—*Personae* (1909), *Exultations* (1909) and *Ripostes* (1912)—as well as a book on the French troubadours and three volumes of translations from Provençal and Italian. A fierce and contentious personality, he was deeply engaged in all the avant-garde movements: Imagism, Futurism, Vorticism.

D. H. Lawrence and Wyndham Lewis both met Pound, four years before Frost did, in 1909. Lawrence, who had recently moved to London to take up a teaching job, was impressed by Pound's generosity, bohemian digs, academic qualifications, eccentric poetry and swaggering cosmopolitanism: "He is a well-known American poet—a good one. He is 24, like me,—but his god is beauty, mine, life. He is jolly nice: took me to supper at Pagnani's, and afterwards we went down to his room in Kensington. He lives in an attic, like a traditional poet—but the attic is a comfortable well furnished one. He is an American Master of Arts and a professor of the Provençal group of languages. . . . He is rather remarkable—a good bit of a genius, and with not the least self-consciousness." The self-assured Lewis, more caustic and critical, described Pound as "an uncomfortably tensed, nervously straining, jerky, reddish-brown young

American,"[12] with polyglot propensities and encyclopedic pretensions. Pound aggressively asserted his superiority as poet and intellectual, and tried to be a portable substitute for the British Museum. He also affected the bombastic behavior and outrageous dress, with velvet coat and turquoise earring, of the *fin-de-siècle* Whistler.

Frost's encounter with the equally touchy Pound had the makings of high comedy. In London the respectable, rural paterfamilias, who believed in proper behavior and was concerned about what people thought of him, confronted the wild urban bohemian, who defied social convention and flouted public opinion. Frost had four children and cared deeply about them; Pound thought poets should not be burdened with them and did not bring up his own offspring. The personal clash between the conservative, traditional, reticent older American "farmer" and the anarchistic, experimental, brash younger continental bohemian reflected the diametrically opposed strains in contemporary American poetry.

After Pound had dried off and made himself presentable, he asked about Frost's book. Copies were supposed to be ready, but Frost had not dared to request one. He disliked personal confrontations with the unpleasant Mme. Nutt and, though eager to see the volume, was content to wait until she sent it to him. Not so Ezra. When he wanted something, he had to have it straightaway. Since they were both great walkers, they strolled several miles from Kensington through Hyde Park to Grape Street in Bloomsbury, where Pound grabbed and pocketed the only available copy of Frost's book.

Pound began to read it as soon as they got back to his flat. According to Frost, "He said, 'You don't mind our liking this,' in his British accent, slightly. And I said, 'Oh, go ahead and like it.' Pretty soon he laughed at something ["In Neglect"], and I said I knew where that was in the book, what Pound would laugh at. And then pretty soon he said, 'You better run along home, I'm going to review it.' And I never touched it. I went home without my book, and he kept it. I'd barely seen it in his hands."

During their long walk through London, delighted by Pound's company and carried away by the warmth of his response, Frost told Pound he had been disinherited by his grandfather. He also talked extensively about poetry and had some fun at the expense of an older American: "We talked of several poets in the limelight at the time, but mainly about E. A. Robinson. I remember what a good time we had with 'Miniver Cheevy,' and how we laughed over it—a laugh was something for

Ezra—especially how we laughed over the four 'thoughts' in the poem. The first three—*Miniver thought, and thought, and thought,* were all right. But when Robinson dragged in the fourth *And thought about it,* it was a sort of intolerable poetic touch."

Frost discovered, for all their differences, that he and Pound agreed about one fundamental principle, first stated in Wordsworth's Preface to the *Lyrical Ballads,* that the language of every good poem must "in no respect differ from that of good prose." Writing to Harriet Monroe in 1915, Pound insisted that "poetry must be *as well written as prose.*" This corresponded closely to Frost's belief that "a poem must at least be as good as the prose it might have been."[13] When Pound read the dramatic narratives in *North of Boston,* he told Frost that he was trying to write short stories and recommended Flaubert's *Trois Contes* (1877) as a model.

Dazzled and stimulated by Pound, Frost continued to see him at Yeats' "Monday nights" as well as on their own. "Don't forget our first moment together—Pound's and mine—was happy, even romantic," he told Elizabeth Sergeant. "Pound showed me London's Bohemia—he was boyish about it. He presented me with two little books of his verse, *Personae* and *Ripostes.* The last had recently appeared. I liked them and said so—then he backed off—'But it's all old stuff. I shall not go back to it.'" Pound took Frost to little Italian restaurants, like Pagnani's, where he could show off his knowledge of the language and order the dishes he had tasted in Venice. They recited their poems to each other at dinner and Pound spouted "The Goodly Fere" so loudly that a waiter hastened to place a screen around them. They talked about playing tennis but never got around to it. Pound demonstrated his athletic ability by showing Frost, between courses in the restaurant, how to practice jiu-jitsu. Frost recalled that Pound impatiently exclaimed: "'I'll show you. I'll show you. Stand up.' So I stood up, gave him my hand. He grabbed my wrist, tripped me over backwards and threw me over his head." The brawny Frost suddenly found himself on his back, looking up at the crowd of diners who had gathered round to see what had provoked the public disturbance. Ezra, meanwhile, was mighty pleased with himself.

Frost believed there were three types of poet in England: Grub Street hacks, gentleman poets with independent incomes and a few, like John Masefield, who had become popular. Pound, who stood between the first two categories, planned to remain an expatriate and wanted to write for the elite. Frost, who intended to return home when his money ran out, wanted to reach a wide audience in America. Frost admired the natural imagery in Pound's two-line, haiku-like "In a Station of the Metro," which would appear in *Lustra* in 1916: "His best passage was about the faces in the metro looking like wet petals along a bough. The nicety of the metaphor."[14] But he disliked Pound's urban subjects and experimental technique as well as the free-verse poets Pound promoted in his anti-Georgian anthology *Des Imagistes* (1914).

Pound—who would discover Hilda Doolittle, Eliot and Hemingway —wrote a proprietorial letter to a literary editor just after meeting Frost in March 1913: "Have just discovered another Amur'kn, VURRY Amur'kn, with, I think, the seeds of grace." His primary aims at that time were to promote Imagism, to attack American editors who had rejected his work and to help Frost. In his initial burst of enthusiasm, Pound "would have refashioned both the man and his verse had not Frost rebelled." In 1913 he tried to "improve" Frost poems for *Poetry* just as he had done, with their acquiescence, to Yeats' and Rabindranath Tagore's. Frost described how "Pound . . . took a poem of mine, and said: 'You've done it in fifty words. I've shortened it to forty-eight.' I answered: 'And spoiled my meter, my idiom, and idea.' " As Emerson said of Montaigne: "Cut these words and they would bleed; they are vascular and alive; they walk and run."[15]

As Frost saw more of Pound, he found him more and more irritating. He ran down American culture and praised freakish elements of the avant-garde, he was a "fake" (like Yeats) and a "self-boomer." He boasted about his classical learning, though Frost knew more Latin and Greek than Pound ever did, and embarrassed Frost by his intolerable kindness and "bullying generosity." In November 1913 Frost sent a satiric portrait of Pound to a colleague at Plymouth, who must have wondered at the strange company he was keeping:

> Ezra Pound, my fellow countryman, is one of the most describable of [the poets]. He is six inches taller for his hair and hides his lower jaw in a delicate gold filigree of almost masculine beard. His coat is of heavy black velvet. He lives in Grub Street, rich one day and poor the next. His friends are the duchesses. And he swears like a pirate and he writes what is known as vers libre and he translates from French, Provençal, Latin and Italian. He and I have tried to be friends because he was one of the first to review me well, but we don't hit it off very well together. I get on better with fellows like Gibson who are less concerned to dress the part of poet. Gibson is a much greater poet too.

Pound, the London representative of Harriet Monroe's *Poetry,* lost no time in publishing, in the May 1913 issue, the first American review of Frost's first book. He managed to pack a great deal into that short notice: quotations of several poems, a kick at American editors, a judicious appraisal of Frost's faults and strengths, a patronizing joke about his rustic subject matter, a condemnation of Frost's family for their harsh treatment of the budding poet and a concise judgment of his work:

> David Nutt publishes at his own expense *A Boy's Will,* by Robert Frost, the latter having been long scorned by the "great American editors." It is the old story.
>
> Mr. Frost's book is a little raw, and has in it a number of infelicities. . . . [But] this man has the good sense to speak naturally and to paint the thing, the thing as he sees it. . . .
>
> [Frost could say, like a man on a desolate bog:] "Faith, ye can sit on a midden and dream stars.". . .
>
> [The poems were] written when his grandfather and his uncle had disinherited him of a comfortable fortune and left him in poverty because he was a useless poet instead of a money-getter. . . .
>
> He is without sham and without affectation.

Having misled Pound about the way his grandfather had treated him, Frost became angry when Pound emphasized the family melodrama to enliven his review. Since he was living in England on his grandfather's annuity and on the money from the sale of his farm, Frost would seem to be guilty—if word of Pound's review ever reached Lawrence, Massachusetts—of both mendacity and ingratitude. Frost also disliked the way Pound had portrayed him as a literary refugee in London with a grievance against American editors. Though Frost had felt unappreciated in America, he feared Pound's review might count heavily against him when he returned to native grounds and sought his natural audience. Hilda Doolittle and John Gould Fletcher had both published their first work in England; and Pound's portrait of the neglected American genius, driven out of his own country to achieve recognition and fame in England, seemed much more like Pound than Frost. Yet, as John Cournos has pointed out, "everyone spoke with admiration of [Frost's] courage in coming to England with his family at this time to fight out a difficult destiny."

After scoring tactical points in his first review, Pound hastened to publish a second, little-known one in the feminist-Imagist *New Freewoman* of September 1, 1913. This notice concentrated on Frost's literary qualities: his language of actual speech, the reality of his experience as a farmer, his traditional yet impressively original verse: "Mr. Frost has sought the natural cadences of speech. Many of his opening lines are the lines of common conversation. His language is for the most part natural and simple. The wind working against him in the dark, the noise of his scythe in the grass are very real to him, and it is with little surprise that we learn that his knowledge is actual and not theoretic. He has written life as he has lived it. . . . What one gets from the book is not any pleasure in pyrotechnics but a conviction of poetic personality."[16]

Frost was both pleased and irritated by Pound's first review, which he saw in typescript. He was grateful for the qualified puff but fearful about the trouble it might cause: "Ezra Pound, the stormy petrel . . . has found me and sent a fierce article to Chicago denouncing a country that neglects fellows like me. I am afraid he over did it and it may be a mercy all round if it isn't printed." Frost wanted fame but felt that the review was a little too personal. He had taken a great deal of trouble over polishing his verse, disliked being called "raw" and thought it wiser to ignore—or at least not offend—the American editors. Frost also complained to Thomas Mosher that Pound had portrayed him as a simpleton and bullied him on the strength of his "stupidly wide of the mark" review in *Poetry*. Yet he had to acknowledge that Pound, for all his deliberate and unintentional offenses, meant to be generous and had been extremely effective in publicizing his book.

In letters to Frank Flint, who had introduced him to Pound, written several weeks after the first review appeared, Frost criticized Flint's abject deference to Pound. He bitterly resented Pound's phrase about Frost sitting on a "midden" or dunghill, was furious about Pound's condescending patronage and mentioned their quarrel about Pound's highhanded appropriation of his manuscript:

> You are in awe of that great intellect abloom in hair. You saw me first but you had to pass me over for him to discover. . . .
>
> Who will show me the correlation between anything I ever wrote and his quotation from the Irish, You may sit in a midden and dream stars. You may sit on a sofa and dream garters. . . .
>
> Pound can be cruel in the arbitrary attitudes he assumes toward one. It pleased him to treat me always as if I might be some kind of poet but was not quite presentable—at least in

London. Some of the things he said and others I imagined drove me half frantic. . . .

We will hate the arrivist in him and like what there is left to like. He wants to be good to us all. . . .

He likes [my poetry] because I have four children to feed and it flatters his vanity to be in a position to sell me to American editors.

Pound had compounded his crimes by sending "The Death of the Hired Man" to the *Smart Set* without consulting Frost (the title alone was enough to set Frost's teeth on edge). Then—mocking Frost for having a fit of nerves—he refused to withdraw it. Frost told Cox: "He *asked* for the poem he speaks of and then failed to sell it. It was even worse than that. I had demanded the poem back when I learned the name of the magazine he was offering it to but he went ahead in spite of me. And there began our quarrel."

In a letter to Flint of July 20, Frost enclosed an angry, amusing and revealing poem that parodied Pound's free-associating free verse. As his rage boiled over, he attacked Pound's condescension, signaled his change from gratitude to resentment, criticized Pound's megalomania, begged for recognition and confessed his fear of the younger poet. Pound had said that Frost could not read poetry, looked old and was slow-witted. He was willing to take these insults as long as he could hug the illusion that Pound liked his poetry for the right reasons. But Pound had arbitrarily praised Frost solely to exert his own power and took credit for showing that he could thrust his stuff upon the world. Frost clung to him, however, because he believed Pound thought he was a poet. "The truth is," Frost said, "I was afraid of you."[17]

In October 1913, the month after the appearance of Pound's second review, Frost told Mosher that he no longer saw Yeats and had fallen out with his "quasi-friend" Pound, an "incredible ass" who did more harm than good. In January 1915, still smarting from the well-intentioned but potentially damaging reviews of his first two books, Frost emphasized the crucial distinction between Pound's rejection of his country and his own commitment to America—which would have significant consequences during and after World War II:

I fear I am going to suffer a good deal at home by the support of Pound. This is a generous person who is doing his best to put me in the wrong light by his reviews of me: You will see the blow he dealt me in *Poetry* (Chicago) for December, and yet it is with such good intention I suppose I shall have to thank him for it. . . . The harm he does lies in this: he made up his mind in the short time I was friends with him (we quarreled in six weeks) to add me to his party of American literary refugees in London. Nothing could be more unfair, nothing better calculated to make me an exile for life.

In a 1949 interview, which showed that his grievance still rankled, Frost satirically summarized Pound's ludicrous appearance as well as his proprietorial attitude toward his "discovery": "He was a flashy dresser, but the Byron collars and Japanese dressing gowns didn't go with his shrill Idaho voice. He was full of generous enthusiasms, but possessive. . . . It was as though he were boasting to the world. . . . 'Look! I'm so powerful I can take even this New England yokel and make a celebrity out of him!' "

Pound took credit for puffing Frost and "hammering his stuff into *Poetry*." But he also maintained a rather disdainful attitude toward the man he considered a country yokel. He called the "dull and old-fashioned" Frost a "backwoods, even a barnyard poet."[18] In a letter to T. S. Eliot's brother, Pound took far too much credit, as Frost's reputation continued to rise, for *North of Boston,* which was virtually completed by the time Frost met Pound, and emphasized the superiority of his own verse: "Robert Frost has, let us admit, done a book of New England eclogues. (Incidentally, it was I who insisted or 'suggested' that he should do it. He brought me one or two poems that now appear in that book and spoke of more in the making. . . . I certainly had some part in getting him to do that series of 'eclogues.') Still, a set of provincial studies, local, a bit dull, is a very different thing from poetry which accepts the tone and difficulties of contemporary civilization."

Pound's rebarbative character, eccentric ideas, patronizing attitude and high-handed revisions, the polemics and distortions in his review of *A Boy's Will* and willful appropriation of Frost's poetry made the rupture —after a lively start—inevitable. Yet Frost, for all his anger, never forgot that Pound was "the most generous of mortals" and that "a lot of us owe him a lot for where we are."[19] Though Frost disliked Pound's vulgar self-promotion, Pound taught him the value of making the right contacts and generating publicity. If Frost wanted to earn a living from poetry, he had to sell himself to gain an audience and advance his career.

7

Gloucestershire and Edward Thomas

1914–1915

I

In April 1914 Frost's close friendship with the Georgian poets prompted his move from the suburbs to the country. Wilfrid Gibson and Lascelles Abercrombie were living in charming cottages in the depths of Gloucestershire, about a hundred miles northwest of London, and invited the Frosts to join them there for congenial conversation and the familiar pleasures of rural life. Frost borrowed money from Cox for the move, and they arrived at the house, Little Iddens, in Leddington near Dymock, at the start of the English spring.

Their sixteenth-century cottage, built in Shakespeare's time, still exists—bulging, collapsing, propped up by structural supports and decorated with "Danger: Keep Out" signs. Cross-timbered, with whitewashed brick, a shingle roof and leaded window panes, it was attractive but uncomfortable. The kitchen was tiny, the staircase narrow, the ceilings low, the stove old-fashioned, the water pump and lavatory outside the house. But it was down a quiet lane, surrounded by fruit orchards, and had a fine view to the south of May Hill. Two weeks after they moved in Elinor wrote her sister: "The cottage we are living in is very old—about 350 years old, and all the floors downstairs are brick tiled and the beams show above. We have five rooms and the rent is only $50 a year. Wilfrid Gibson and his wife live about a mile from us and Abercrombie with his wife and two children are three miles away. We see them all often." But, frail as always and used to a cloistered life, Elinor was completely exhausted by the housework and the frequent visitors: "I have been feeling quite worn out. The household and teaching and the excitement of meeting so many people constantly, have been almost too much for me. Three weeks ago I felt that I was on the edge of complete nervous prostration."

Frost's temper was also on edge. In July, after a heated argument with his landlord, he wrote to Flint, quoting *Hamlet:* "I almost ended my tenancy here this very morning by punching my own hand a number of times very close to my landlord's face to the accompaniment of words, words, words." Although Frost had paid a year's rent for the cottage, its primitive condition clearly made it uninhabitable in the winter. So he gladly accepted Abercrombie's generous offer to share his house, The Gallows (where a poacher had once been hanged), during the fall and winter months. The Frosts had lived, with varying degrees of success, with Herbert Parker and his wife in Lawrence, with Carl Burell and his grandfather on the Derry farm, with Lester Russell in Derry village and with Ernest Silver in Plymouth, and were used to sharing quarters with other people. They moved in September, and had a pleasant four months in The Gallows, where Elinor finally fulfilled her romantic ambition to live under thatch.

Despite the discomforts, Frost always remembered that spring and summer of 1914—when John Drinkwater, Rupert Brooke and Edward Thomas gathered in Gibson's house—as idyllic. "You wouldn't think all these great people could fit in this tiny place but we did," Frost later recalled, using a characteristically English word. "And, we had a cozy time there. Then the war spoiled it all."[1]

II

On May 15, 1914, David Nutt published—in a green buckram volume at three shillings and sixpence—Frost's second and finest book, *North of Boston*. He began writing this work in 1905 and completed "the bulk of it" in 1913. Assuming English readers would associate Boston with the town in Lincolnshire, Hulme wanted Frost to change the title to the Virgilian *Yankee Eclogues,* and Pound called his influential review "Modern Georgics." Other provisional titles were *New England Eclogues,* the more familiar *New England Hill Folk* and *Farm Servants, and Other People.* Its publication greatly enhanced Frost's status among the English poets.

This volume signaled Frost's change of emphasis from solitary to social beings. In his dedication to Elinor he called it "This Book of People," and in a note to the original edition said that "Mending Wall," which considers beliefs that separate men, takes up the theme where "The Tuft of Flowers" ("Men work together . . . / Whether they work together or apart") laid it down. Despite the social emphasis, most of the characters in *North of Boston* experience great loneliness.

The poems in *A Boy's Will* are short lyrics; those in *North of Boston* are ironic and often witty dramatic dialogues after the fashion of Browning and Kipling. In the second volume he moves from archaic diction to colloquial language and combines country lore with metaphysical conceits. As Lawrence Lipking observes: "Voices clash against each other. . . . A harder broken speech replaces the language of flowers. And through that act of reinterpretation"—of defining his new poetic identity— "Frost becomes Frost."

In *North of Boston* Frost staked out his poetic territory and began to set his regionalism against the cosmopolitanism of Pound, Eliot and Stevens. He had no interest in urban or industrial life and, unlike contemporaries from Yeats to Robert Lowell, rarely wrote poems on historical events, living or dead friends, painting and music. Though he lived for substantial periods in Michigan, Florida and Texas, and later traveled to France, Cuba, Brazil, Peru, Israel, Greece and Russia, Frost never wrote about these places. When he described exotic locales—Mexico, the Madeiras, the Vale of Cashmere—he used historical accounts by Prescott, Hakluyt and Marco Polo. Apart from a few poems about California and England, he was (wherever he lived) an exclusively New England poet.

Frost's New England "is really a nineteenth-century phenomenon . . . of subsistence farming." The desolation, decay and desperation; the exhaustion, estrangement and isolation; the violence, mutilation, terror, madness and death in *North of Boston* capture the last moments of a dying race. Amy Lowell, the grande dame of Boston, once told Frost that she had left her summer place in New Hampshire because she could not stand the people. When he asked her what was wrong with the people, she told him to read his own books and find out. Yet Frost's poetry, like Hardy's, is strengthened by his intense focus on and intimate knowledge of one region. He values country over city, worldly experience over school learning, personal independence over government interference. His magnificent description of the natural—but often threatening— world expresses his belief in self-reliance and rugged individualism. These qualities had largely vanished from the anonymous life of urban and industrial America, and lost city-dwellers still longed for them as part of their Puritan and frontier heritage.

Frost's poems set themes in ironic opposition and unite, as Jackson Bate wrote of Coleridge, "scope and depth, philosophical range and immediacy of detail, psychological insight and emotional suggestiveness." When Randall Jarrell asked Frost about the poems in *North of Boston*—"Home Burial," "A Servant to Servants," "The Housekeeper," "The Fear"—in which an emotionally oppressed woman finally reveals her deepest feelings, Frost said that "the woman loses," but "she loses in a strange way, she pulls the whole thing [down] with her. She has that satisfaction."[2] Frost understood the suffering and frustration of these hard-working yet impoverished women, who took grim pleasure in venting their anger and achieving revenge.

The sixteen subtle poems in *North of Boston* have great technical and thematic interest. "The Death of the Hired Man" includes three very different characters, one of them offstage, who are revealed entirely through dialogue. Silas, the hired man, has instinctively returned to his lair like a wounded animal. The farmer and his wife discuss how to deal with this unwelcome guest, for whom they feel partly responsible. The poem considers how much dignity is due to a useless and derelict old man. "A Hundred Collars" contrasts the countrified, expansive and witty bill-collector, Lafayette, with the urban, repressed and solemn teacher, Magoon. It is quite funny and contains two striking similes. The tight collars choke Lafe "like a nursery tree / When it outgrows the wire band of its name tag" and his spoiled horse Jemima turns in at every house along the road "As if she had some sort of curvature." "The Black Cottage" ends with the same visual power and dramatic intensity of Hemingway's early stories:

> He struck the clapboards,
> Fierce heads looked out; small bodies pivoted.
> We rose to go. Sunset blazed on the windows.

"A Servant to Servants" contains a hair-raising description of a crazy naked man, locked in a cage, who screams obscenities as the young bride and groom lie in the next room. "The Self-Seeker" is based on a mechanical accident that badly crushed Carl Burell's feet and crippled him. His casual negotiations with the company lawyer are interrupted by the charming intrusion of a little girl, who brings rare specimens of flowers he can no longer find himself and emphasizes the priceless value of what he has lost. The conclusion of "The Wood-Pile," with its faint echo of Gray's "Elegy" ("They kept the noise*less* tenor of their *way*"), contains the finest lines in the book:

> To warm the frozen swamp as best it could
> With the slow smoke*less* burning of de*cay*.

The best poems in *North of Boston* are "Home Burial," "Mending Wall" and his masterpiece, "After Apple-Picking." "Mending Wall" (like "The Road Not Taken," "Birches" and "Stopping by Woods on a Snowy Evening") has become overly familiar by endless reprintings in school anthologies. Like the frequently reproduced *Sunflowers* of Van Gogh, it has lost a good deal of its freshness and impact. Frost once saw the mindless statement "Good fences make good neighbors" (originally made by his Derry friend, the "old-stone savage" Napoleon Guay), used on an advertisement for a prefabricated picket fence.

Frost himself said the poem concerned "the impossibility of drawing sharp lines and making exact distinctions between good and bad or between almost any two abstractions." But he clearly stands with the narrator, who questions the very need to have a wall and repeats his belief: "Something there is that doesn't love a wall." That "something," a natural force which breaks down the wall and indicates the poet's point of view is—of course—frost. His allusion to Matthew 24:2 clarifies the theme by connecting the inevitable and proper destruction of the wall in the poem to Christ's fierce prophecy about the iniquitous Temple of Herod in Jerusalem: "There shall not be left here one stone upon another, that shall not be thrown down."

"After Apple-Picking" has often been compared to Keats' "Ode to Autumn," as if it were primarily a celebration of harvest. But its elevated diction (quite distinct from anything else in the book) as well as its images, mood and theme, all suggest a greater affinity with Keats' "Ode to a Nightingale." In that weary, drowsy poem the speaker longs to escape through art, symbolized by the nightingale, from the pain of the real world and melt into the welcome oblivion of death:

> My heart aches, and a drowsy numbness pains
>   My sense, as though of hemlock I had drunk,
> Or emptied some dull opiate to the drains
>   One minute past, and Lethe-wards had sunk.

Frost's narrator, standing on the earth but looking upward, is also suspended between the real and the dream world:

> My long two-pointed ladder's sticking through a tree
> Toward heaven still,
> And there's a barrel that I didn't fill.

The long and short lines, the irregular rhyme scheme, the recurrent participles (indicating work), the slow tempo and incantatory rhythm all suggest that repetitive labor has drained away his energy. The perfume of the apples—equated through "essence" with profound rest—has the narcotic, almost sensual effect of ether. Frost's speaker, like Keats', is suffused with drowsy numbness, yet enters the visionary state necessary to artistic creation:

> Essence of winter sleep is on the night,
> The scent of apples: I am drowsing off.
> I cannot rub the strangeness from my sight
> I got from looking through a pane of glass
> I skimmed this morning from the drinking trough.

The glassy piece of ice—which distorts, transforms and makes the familiar seem strange—is, like Keats' nightingale, a symbol of art. In his dream state (the word "sleep" occurs six times in the poem),

> Magnified apples appear and disappear,
> Stem end and blossom end,
> And every fleck of russet showing clear,

and he rhythmically sways on the ladder when the boughs bend with his weight. As the apples are gathered—and the poem written—he becomes both physically and mentally exhausted:

> For I have had too much
> Of apple-picking: I am overtired
> Of the great harvest I myself desired.

He needs to regenerate himself, like the hibernating woodchuck, by a long, death-like winter sleep, so he will be ready to re-enter the poet's dream world and achieve another spurt of creativity. In "After Apple-Picking" Frost achieves a perfect fusion of pastoral and poetic labor.

Frost was pleased to read the favorable reviews of his book—including those by Abercrombie and Gibson—while living near his friends in Gloucestershire. Ford Madox Ford mentioned his friendship with Frost, stated that he had transformed common speech into poetry and had made a significant contribution to American literature: "I have the privilege of knowing Mr. Frost quite well. . . . He seems to make people, or the narrator, talk with the abrupt sort of rhythms that do undoubtedly distinguish his compatriots north of Boston. . . . Mr. Frost's achievement is much finer, much more near the ground and much more national, in the true sense, than anything that Whitman gave to the world." The usually acerbic Richard Aldington, associated with Pound and the Imagists, enthusiastically recognized Frost's originality: "It would be very difficult to overpraise Mr. Frost's book. He is one of the extremely few American poets who have had sufficient individuality to be American. Mr. Frost is a better poet than Whittier. I hear it whispered that he is better than Whitman. . . . At any rate, he has put between his two green covers more of a certain kind of American life than any other American poet I have read."

Abercrombie, benefitting from extensive conversations about Frost's ideas and methods, praised his dramatic exploration of character: "Within their downright knowledge, their vivid observation, and (more important) their rich enjoyment of all kinds of practical life, within their careful rendering into metre of customary speech, the impulse is always psychological—to set up, in some significant attitude, a character or a conflict of characters." In *Poetry,* Pound, after unleashing his self-interested blast against American editors, adopted a patronizing manner, saw Frost as a modern Wordsworth and emphasized his truthfulness to actual experience: "The typical American editor of the last twenty years has resolutely shut his mind against serious American writing. . . . Mr. Frost is an honest writer, writing from himself, from his own knowledge and emotion. . . . Frost's people are distinctly real. Their speech is real; he has known them. I don't want much to meet them, but I know that they exist."[3]

The shrewd and industrious Mme. Nutt quickly took advantage of all the attention Frost's book had aroused. In August 1914 she issued a four-page publicity pamphlet quoting excerpts from anonymous reviews in the *Times* and *Pall Mall Gazette* as well as from those by Gibson in the *Bookman,* Ford in the *Outlook,* Abercrombie in the *Nation* and Edward Thomas in the *English Review* and the *New Weekly.* Having learned "self-booming" from Pound, Frost immediately sent a batch of them to Cox. He asked his friend to distribute the pamphlet in crucial places in order to arouse interest in his book both north and south of Boston.

III

In October 1913—between the publication of *A Boy's Will* and the move to Gloucestershire—the poet Ralph Hodgson introduced Frost, at a coffee shop in St. Martin's Lane, to the man who became the most intimate friend he ever had. Edward Thomas, of Welsh descent, was born in London in 1878, the eldest of six sons. His father was a clerk in the Board of Trade. Morbid and sensitive, Thomas attended St. Paul's School and had no contact with girls until he met his future wife, Helen Noble. She was two years older and sympathetic, and he wrote to her about his sexual problems, "his adolescent fight against erections, nocturnal emissions, and occasional masturbation." After an emotionally turbulent courtship, they became lovers.

At Lincoln College, Oxford, Thomas drank heavily, took laudanum and caught gonorrhea. But he somehow managed to graduate in 1900. Edward and Helen were forced to marry in June 1899, when she became pregnant, and their son Merfyn (a year younger than Lesley Frost) was born the following January. Bronwyn was born in 1902 (the same year as Carol) and Myfanwy (five years younger than Marjorie) in 1910. Unable to maintain the discipline of regular employment and with a growing family to support, Thomas became a tireless and ill-paid Grub Street hack. He wrote books on Richard Jefferies, Maurice Maeterlinck, Lafcadio Hearn, Swinburne, George Borrow, Pater, Marlborough and Keats. He published twelve books, just before he met Frost, between 1910 and 1912. By exhausting effort, for none of his books was commercially successful, he managed to earn about £400 a year. Frost described him as "a natural naturalist" in the tradition of Jefferies, Borrow and Gilbert White of Selborne. Dressed in country tweeds, even in London, Thomas was tall and slender, with a slight stoop. He had a handsome, hawklike face, piercing blue eyes, a sensitive mouth, fair hair worn slightly long and a ruddy complexion.

His melancholia was based partly on overwork, partly on marital unhappiness. Helen explained to a friend that "poverty, anxiety, physical weakness, disappointments and discouragement are making him bitter, hard, and impatient, quick to violent anger, and subject to long fits of depression." In 1911 he wrote alarmingly to her: "Tired is not what I am. I'm sick of the whole of life—of myself chiefly, of you and the children." He often left his family to wander about the countryside or work in solitude, but Helen knew he would remain sexually faithful and always care for her. She even encouraged his friendship with the vivacious and intelligent Eleanor Farjeon, who was in love with him. Helen thought the friendship would be good for Edward, and Eleanor soon became part of their family.

Frost and Thomas each had a troubled marriage, had threatened suicide, suffered long neglect of his work and toiled in uncongenial jobs as he slowly made himself into a poet. In October 1913, as Frost was just beginning to be known, Thomas was already established as a nature writer and literary critic. Though Thomas seemed cold and even arrogant, "Frost's personality drew Thomas toward him like a magnet" and they formed an instant rapport.[4]

They soon found they had similar ideas about poetry. Both were interested in the speech of rural folk—Thomas sang Frost ballads in Welsh—and believed that poetry should use common language and a natural voice. In his poem "The Mill-Water" Thomas adopted Frost's precise terms and wrote: "The sound comes surging in upon the sense." Thinking of Pound's intolerable domination, Frost recalled that he and Thomas met as perfect equals and encouraged each other's work. Thomas wrote four generous reviews of Frost's first two books. Frost, who cheered him up, strengthened his confidence and convinced Thomas that he was really a poet, later recalled their mutually nourishing companionship:

> I had written two and a half of my three books, he had written all but two or three of thirty. . . . The least rivalry of that kind would have taken something from our friendship. We were greater friends than almost any two ever were practising the same art. . . . He gave me standing as a poet—he more than anyone else, though of course I have to thank Abercrombie, Hueffer, Pound and some others for help too. I dragged him out from under the heap of his own work in prose he was buried alive under. . . . The decision he made in going into the army helped him make the other decision to be a poet.

Thomas agreed to spend a month with Frost in Gloucestershire in August 1914. His daughter Myfanwy remembered that on August 4, the day the Great War broke out, Helen, her two daughters, a Russian boy and a dog left Hampshire by train to meet Edward at Little Iddens. The sudden need to mobilize troops had thrown the system into disarray. Railway officials, infected with war anxiety, heard the Russian boy's odd accent and suspected they were spies. Helen was frantic with worry, and it took all day to get to Ledbury, where they had to hire a cab. At Little Iddens they found that Elinor Frost had not prepared a proper meal for them. Robert had attempted to provide for both families in the "siege situation" of war by laying in large supplies of shredded wheat, sweet biscuits and scented soap—all that could be obtained in the local shop.

The poets did their patriotic duty. Abercrombie failed the army physical exam; but Gibson, Monro, Ford and Graves served in the war. Brooke died of a fever on active service; Hulme and Thomas were killed in action. Frost idealized war—partly because he had never fought in one. He thought courage was the greatest virtue and wanted to test himself in combat. He talked to Graves about enlisting, going over to France and suffering with the others. But since he was forty and had four children, the closest he came to fighting was a run-in with his neighbors, who suspected his New Hampshire accent, decided he was a Hun and threw stones at his windows. He was also angry about the suspicious local constable, who took him for a German spy. Though Frost had no gun, he threatened to shoot the man if he came nosing round the house. He told Cox that he had two fervent, egoistic hopes about the future: "One is that the Germans may not sow the Western Ocean with mines before I cross with the family and the other is that I may find something to do to make up for lost money when I get across."[5] In a letter to Bartlett, nine months after hostilities began, he shrewdly predicted that even if Germany lost the war it would remain a formidable power and be strong enough to fight another round.

Though Frost worried about his loss of income, his uncertain future and his difficulty in returning home, he was insulated in that remote region from the direct impact of the war. August 1914 was probably the happiest month of his life. His daily conversations and intensely emotional friendship with Thomas took on great poignancy in the shadow of impending tragedy. Frost later said that Thomas, more "than anyone else, was accessory to what I had done and was doing. We were together to the exclusion of every other person and interest all through 1914 —1914 was our year. I never had, I never shall have another such year of friendship." After his return to America, he often longed for the sunny days when they had walked and talked on the footpaths and stiles of Leddington and Ryton. Elinor, who usually disliked visitors, felt the same way about Thomas and told her sister: "Rob and I think everything of him. He is quite the most admirable and lovable man we have ever known."

In "This England," a charming essay about his friendship with the unnamed Frost, Thomas gave an equally idyllic picture of the country-side and mentioned their topics of conversation: "Three meadows away lived a friend, and once or twice or three times a day I used to cross the meadows, the gate, and the two stiles . . . [to] the little house of whitened bricks and black timbers. . . . [It had] a vegetable garden in front with a weeping ash and a bay tree, a walnut in a yard of cobbles and grass behind, a yew on the roadside, an orchard on the other. . . . We talked—of flowers, childhood, Shakespeare, women, England, the war —or we looked at a far horizon, which some dip or gap occasionally disclosed." Thomas also recalled their precious, leisurely, comradely hours together, in which the silences were almost as meaningful as the discussions of poetry:

> The sun used to shine while we two walked
> Slowly together, paused and started
> Again, and sometimes mused, sometimes talked
> As either pleased, and cheerfully parted
> Each night.

On September 3, just after he left Little Iddens, Thomas told his poet friend Gordon Bottomley that he had quarreled with Gibson (whom he had supplanted as Frost's "best friend") but that his intimacy with Frost had deepened: "I saw too little of Abercrombie, too much of Gibson, and Frost daily—our families interwove all day long and we enjoyed many days but with all sorts of mixed feelings."[6] Thomas' ambivalence concerned his endless conflicts between married life and solitude, Helen Thomas and Eleanor Farjeon, salaried employment and hack writing, journalism and poetry, America and England, civilian life and military service, cowardice and courage. In their long conversations the two men explored Thomas' gnawing anxieties about his marriage, his career and his wish to be a poet. Thomas was also driven by the overwhelming feeling that he ought to enlist.

Thomas understood more clearly than anyone else what Frost was attempting to do in his poetry. His three reviews of *North of Boston,* which appeared just before and while he was with Frost at Little Iddens, rightly placed the emphasis on Frost's originality and technical skill. In the *Daily News and Leader* of July 22, 1914, he called Frost's work "one of the most revolutionary books of modern times" and then explained:

These poems are revolutionary because they lack the exaggeration of rhetoric, and even at first sight appear to lack the poetic
intensity of which rhetoric is an imitation. The language is free
from the poetical words and forms that are the chief material of
secondary poets. The metre avoids not only the old-fashioned
pomp and sweetness, but the later fashion also of discord and
fuss. . . . Yet almost all these poems are beautiful . . . often grand,
sometimes magical. Many, if not most, of the separate lines and
separate sentences are plain and, in themselves, nothing. But
they are bound together and made elements of beauty by a calm
eagerness of emotion.

In the *English Review* of August 1914, Thomas wrote that Frost had freed
himself from the personal lyrics and "poetic" diction of *A Boy's Will* and
achieved a unique type of homely, racy eclogue. The language ranges
from the colloquial to "brief moments of heightened and intense simplicity" and the poems are "masterpieces of deep and mysterious tender-
ness." In the *New Weekly* of August 8, he compared Frost (as Ford and
Aldington had done) to Whitman, the English touchstone for American
poetry, and, through his common language made truly poetic, to Wordsworth: "It is a beautiful achievement, and I think a unique one, as
perfectly Mr. Frost's own as his vocabulary, the ordinary English speech
of a man accustomed to poetry and philosophy, more colloquial and
idiomatic than the ordinary man dares to use in a letter . . . possessing a
kind of healthy natural delicacy like Wordsworth's."[7]

In the summer of 1914 Frost encouraged Thomas to write poetry. He
also convinced him that he *was* a poet by reading aloud Thomas' prose
work *In Pursuit of Spring* (1914), telling him it was poetry and insisting
that he had actually been writing poetry all his life. Frost's inspiring ideas
about poetry and his stimulating personal example released Thomas'
creative potential, and he published his first poem in December 1914.
His early work, which combined exact observation of the English countryside with a bleak but scrupulous clarity, clearly imitated Frost's. He
even proudly told Frost: "this one sounds like one of yours." W. H.
Davies, who was also on the scene that summer, "never forgave himself
for his unintentional blunder in telling Thomas, who showed him three
of his first poems without disclosing their authorship, that they certainly
were the work of Robert Frost." Davies crushingly confirmed Thomas'
"lack of faith in the individuality of his own work."

Thomas' doubts about his ability to fight in the war were also stirred up by a crucial incident that took place in late November 1914 during his last visit to Frost at The Gallows. As Thomas and Frost walked through the estate of Lord Beauchamp, who had rented the house to Abercrombie, they were threatened by the gamekeeper, armed with a shotgun, and exchanged sharp words. Thomas was obviously frightened. The ever-touchy Frost became furious when the gamekeeper, who called him "a damned cottager," challenged him for walking where the Abercrombies and Gibsons were allowed to go as "gentry." Frost had already quarreled violently with his landlord and threatened to shoot the village bobby, and was thoroughly disgusted with the English caste system.

In early December Abercrombie told a friend that "when the keeper takes to threatening Frost *in the road,* the affair is obviously intolerable and must be put a stop to." But he also had been placed in an awkward position by his egalitarian American guest and tended to blame Frost for causing trouble: "He is peculiarly sensitive to anything remotely resembling insult or deliberate annoyance to himself. This is not the first time he has been aggrieved.—As to the wood incident, he had, of course, no right there. I have permission, but that does not imply permission to my friend. . . . I believe the secret of the whole thing is that Frost does not know how to talk to such folk as keepers."

Thomas, like Abercrombie, thought Frost was hypersensitive and too fond of a fight. Frost, who valued courage above all other virtues and hated to seem unmanly, felt Thomas had not shown a fighting spirit and was critical of his humiliating response to the gamekeeper's threat. "I don't want you to die," he told Thomas, when discussing the war, but "I confess I wanted you to face the possibility of death." He always believed that Thomas had been propelled into the war by the fear of his own cowardice. Elinor, writing to Lesley in 1917, agreed that Thomas' "anxiety to try himself in danger had something to do with [his enlistment], after his encounter with the gamekeeper. Papa thinks his unhappiness at home, his irritability with Mrs. Thomas and Merfyn, had a good deal to do with it."[8]

IV

Frost had published his two volumes just in time. During the war the market for poetry suddenly dried up, along with his money, and after two and a half years in England he was forced to return to uncertain prospects in America. The Frosts sailed on the *St. Paul* from Liverpool to New York on February 13, 1915. They did not leave until dark, proceeded slowly from port and were escorted down the coast of Ireland by two British battleships. They crossed in a convoy with the *Lusitania,* which was sunk by a German submarine three months later, with twelve hundred casualties.

Thomas wanted to get the fifteen-year-old Merfyn out of England during the war and Frost took him along as a hostage to draw Thomas after him to America. Since Frost had no house or job, Thomas arranged for the boy to stay in New Hampshire with a schoolmaster friend, who had eloped with his wife's half-sister and left England. Frost warned Thomas, just before leaving, that no alien under the age of sixteen could enter the United States without at least one parent and that Merfyn should appear on the ship's manifest as sixteen years old. The immigration officials somehow discovered that Merfyn was ten months under age, and he was imprisoned for a day on Ellis Island until Frost sorted out the trouble and got him into the country. According to his sister Myfanwy, no harm was done. Merfyn was fascinated by the experience and even learned how to do card tricks during his day in jail.

When Frost returned to America he repaid Thomas' generosity by placing his work with his own publisher. Frost shared Thomas' divided sense of what his friend should do with his life. Though he had wanted Thomas to test his courage in war, he also kept up the campaign to bring him across the ocean so he could continue to write poetry and prosper in America as Frost had done in England. In early March 1915, just after Frost reached home, Thomas told Bottomley: "I now gather that Frost's idea is that helping him on the farm will set me up and set me free from English journalism; and that I might find a market out there for what I really want to do. . . . If I have to lecture or help Frost at a school in America I shall be so much the better trained." With typical ambivalence and indecision, Thomas also wrote: "I am beginning to think of [America] as the only possibility . . . though really not thinking of it as quite possible either."[9] If Thomas had listened to Frost and come to America, he would have lived to write more poetry.

Though Thomas kept thinking about going to America, he felt compelled to join the army. He was thirty-seven, with three children, and had no obligation to enlist. But he told Frost that only poor health and his mother's fears still kept him out of the army. "Frankly, I do not want to go," he wrote in June, "but hardly a day passes without my thinking I should." Influenced by the chauvinistic atmosphere of the day, he believed that England "was not mine unless I were willing and prepared to die." As he said in "An Old Song," "I've thrown away a chance to fight a gamekeeper," and was now "rather impatient to go out and be shot at." By July 1915 his desire to escape from journalism and from marital discord (he and Helen had been throwing dishes at one another) as well as the call to patriotic duty and the need to test his personal courage prompted him to enlist as a private in the Artists' Rifles. He knew Frost would intuitively understand his decision and wrote: "If there is anything to forgive you would forgive me, I believe. But I don't feel inclined yet for explaining myself, though if you were here I should."[10] Thomas became an artillery officer in July 1916. He took Frost's third book, *Mountain Interval,* with him to France in January 1917, and dedicated his *Poems,* published posthumously that year, to his best friend.

Even on the Western Front, Thomas continued to be haunted by his cowardly confrontation with the gamekeeper. In his last letter to Frost, on April 2, 1917, he confessed that he had to force himself to climb a chimney, which was used as an observation post, and had come under enemy fire:

> The unendurable thing was having to climb up the inside of a chimney that was being shelled. I gave up. It was impossible and I knew it. Yet I went up to the beastly place and had 4 shells burst very close. I decided that I would go back. As a matter of fact I had no light and no information about the method of getting up so that all the screwing up I had given myself would in any case have been futile. It was just another experience [like the gamekeeper] but it was far less on my mind, because the practical result of my failure was nil.

In April the British General Allenby launched the battle of Arras in northern France. He attacked the German lines and "the ill-omened Vimy Ridge, which had so long proved an impregnable barrier to the Allied forces." But his "gamble failed — the preparations were too hasty, the resources inadequate, and the front too narrow." During this battle on Easter Monday, April 9, Thomas directed artillery from the Beaurains observation post as the waves of British troops left the trenches, crossed into no man's land and charged toward the enemy trenches. At 7:30 that morning he was blown to pieces by a direct hit from a German shell.

In a premonitory letter to Helen Thomas of March 8, Frost, alluding to St. Matthew, feared the worst yet hoped for the best: "I can't help wishing he could have saved his life without so wholly losing it and come back from France not too much hurt to enjoy our pride in him. I want to see him to tell him something. I want to tell him, what I think he liked to hear from me, that he was a poet."[11] On April 27, after hearing the news of his friend's death, Frost told Helen that Edward was the bravest, best and dearest man he had ever known, and called him the only brother he ever had. He dedicated his *Selected Poems* (1923) "To Helen Thomas, In Memory of Edward Thomas" and for the rest of his life idealized their friendship.

Frost wrote four poems about Thomas. In the film *Voices and Visions* he mentioned that "The Road Not Taken" was in part a gentle satire on Thomas' inability to resolve his eternal conflicts: "No matter which way he went he was always sorry he didn't go the other way. And he could go on like that until eternity." "A Soldier" compares the body of the dead warrior to a fallen lance that strikes the ground but shoots the spirit up toward God. In "Iris by Night," which alludes to the goddess of the rainbow, Frost complements Thomas' "The Sun Used to Shine" by describing an extraordinary natural phenomenon he and his friend had witnessed in August 1914. As they were walking near the Malvern Hills they saw a "miracle" that Frost, like the Ancient Mariner, "alone of us have lived to tell." Instead of receding as they approached it, the rainbow lifted off the ground and gathered its many-colored ends into a ring that seemed to symbolize the eternal friendship of the two "elected" (or divinely chosen) friends. Thomas also gave an account of this experience in a letter to Eleanor Farjeon: "I like your rainbow, but mine that I saw with Frost seems like the first that ever was except that I knew it was a rainbow. I can't imagine a painter interfering with either. Mine was too much of a pure rainbow, a new toy discovered by Apollo, for anyone to paint. It was more for a mythologist clad in skins."

Frost's "To E.T." (1920) is the only elegy he ever wrote. The poem opens as Frost sleeps with the half-read poems, which Thomas dedicated to him, open on his chest like dove's wings on a tomb. Repeating the idea he had expressed in the letter to Helen Thomas, he hopes that he will be able to tell Thomas in his dream, as he never could do in real life, that he was indeed a true soldier and poet. Frost calls him "brother," as he did in his letter (Gibson was merely a friend), and claims that Thomas' death, as he met the shell's embrace of fire on Vimy Ridge, was a victory over fear. For all his depth of feeling, Frost was not very good at expressing conventional sentiments and the elegy seems rather forced and stilted ("The foe thrust back unsafe beyond the Rhine"). Though Frost was fond of Helen, he was then very puritanical about personal, especially sexual, revelations. He became bitterly angry when, in *As It Was* (1926) and again in *World Without End* (1931), Helen described, with shocking and quite intimate Lawrencean detail, their youthful love affair and marital problems. Frost thought she had insulted Edward's manhood by disclosing his lack of experience with women and broke off relations with her.[12]

Frost kept in touch with his other English friends. He entertained several of them in America, and looked them up when he returned to England in 1928 and 1957. Though he lost contact with Pound, he remained grateful for his help, and that irascible poet came back into Frost's life, in an unexpected way, in 1958. Frost's years in England were a major turning point in his life. He was encouraged by some of the most important writers of his time, published his first two books, attracted wide recognition, established his reputation and returned with new confidence to America.

8

The Return of
the Native

1915–1916

I

Frost's personal and poetical reception in America was strikingly similar
to his enthusiastic welcome in England. He immediately charmed all the
writers and critics he met in New York and Boston, and soon found many
new friends who were keen to help him establish a reputation in his own
country. Just as his fortunate arrival in London in 1912 had coincided
with a resurgence of interest in verse, so his return in 1915, before
America entered the war, caught the wave of a new popular eagerness
about poetry. "Suddenly," wrote the Irish author Padraic Colum, "there
were poetry-societies and poetry-magazines and interesting poets. Into
an atmosphere of expectancy he came with an audience ready and even
prepared for him." In 1915, as in 1912, every aspect of his life seemed to
fall luckily into place.

While Frost was still in England Mrs. Henry Holt, the wife of the
publisher and a keen reader of verse, had seen Pound's lively review of *A
Boy's Will* in the May 1913 issue of *Poetry*. She ordered a copy of *North of
Boston* from David Nutt and in August 1914, while on holiday in Stowe,
Vermont, wrote to Frost in praise of it. She also recommended it to
Alfred Harcourt, the head of Holt's trade department. He liked it and so
did his leading Vermont author, Dorothy Canfield Fisher, who urged
Harcourt to publish it. When he sailed from England Frost knew that
Holt (who also published William James) had accepted his first two
books, but did not know when they would appear.

On February 22, as he walked from the New York docks to the center
of town, Frost stopped to look at the current issue of the *New Republic*. He
was astonished to find a favorable review of *North of Boston* (which had

been published that day) by the influential poet Amy Lowell. He proceeded to Holt's office and met Alfred Harcourt, who presented him with a $40 check for "The Death of the Hired Man," which had appeared in the *New Republic* on February 6. At Harcourt's suggestion, Frost remained in New York to lunch with the editors of the *New Republic* and attend a meeting of the Poetry Society of America. His family went up to the White Mountains of New Hampshire, as they had often done during the hay-fever season, to stay as paying guests with the Irish farmer John Lynch. While Robert pursued his literary interests, Elinor looked around for a farm that would suit the family and recapture their idyllic days in Derry.

After traveling north to Lawrence, Frost had a cold meeting with Ernest Jewell, to whom he still owed a considerable debt, and a warm reunion with the Bartletts, who had returned from Vancouver. In Boston he met two important editors: William Braithwaite of the *Boston Evening Transcript,* who wrote several articles about him, and Ellery Sedgwick of the *Atlantic Monthly,* who accepted "An Encounter," "Birches" and "The Road Not Taken." While Frost was living in England, before the success of *North of Boston,* Sedgwick had rejected his work and curtly written: "We are sorry that we have no place in the *Atlantic Monthly* for your vigorous verse." Now he was full of false bonhomie and genuine condescension. Though Frost had just returned from the English literary scene, Sedgwick saw him as a latter-day Robert Burns and told Edward Garnett: "I found him quite delightful—as unspoiled as when he left his Vermont plough." Still smarting from the rejections, which Sedgwick naturally tried to ignore, Frost adopted a role he had previously tried out with his grandfather. Taking the poems out of his pocket and holding them high, as if he were an auctioneer, he teased Sedgwick by asking: "Are you sure—that you want to buy—these poems?" Then, after soliciting a bid, he graciously concluded: "They—are—yours."[1]

In 1915 Frost had an anomalous position in American poetry. He was about ten years older than the modern poets who began to publish at the time of World War I—Williams, Pound, Jeffers, Moore, Ransom and Eliot—and by age belonged to the earlier, and at that time dominant generation of Masters, Robinson, Amy Lowell, Sandburg and Vachel Lindsay. But Frost soon surpassed his major rivals. Lowell died in 1925, Lindsay committed suicide in 1931, and the work of Masters and Robinson declined sharply in the latter part of their careers. Sandburg, four years younger than Frost, also lived until his late eighties. During his lifetime he equaled Frost's popularity among readers and on the lecture circuit. But Sandburg's reputation has now disappeared while Frost stands with Pound, Eliot and Stevens as one of the major American poets of the twentieth century.

Though he had joked about "Miniver Cheevy" with Pound, Frost respected Edwin Arlington Robinson. William Braithwaite introduced him to Robinson and they drank bitters together in a Boston bar. Robinson had also dropped out of Harvard; and his poems about stinginess, lechery, alcoholism and suicide in Gardiner, Maine, had a good deal in common with *North of Boston*. Both New England poets used the words and rhythm of ordinary speech, portrayed the characteristic mood of late autumn, emphasized individualism and self-reliance, and adopted a Hardyesque view of human suffering and defeat. Frost particularly liked Robinson's "A thousand golden sheaves were lying there, / Shining and still, but not for long to stay" in "The Sheaves" and alluded to these lines when he wrote, in "Nothing Gold Can Stay": "Nature's first green is gold, / Her hardest hue to hold. . . . So dawn goes down to day. / Nothing gold can stay." In 1915 Frost told Robinson that he had taken real satisfaction in every one of his poems. Two years later, after reading *Mountain Interval,* Robinson returned the compliment and said: "you seem undoubtedly to have added something permanent to the world."

In later years Frost's admiration was tempered by reservations about Robinson's regression into the "Arthur twaddle" that had been popularized in the Victorian age by Tennyson. During a dinner in the early 1930s, when Frost chided him for wasting time on the Arthurian legends, Robinson politely changed the subject by mentioning Frost's best poems. Despite Robinson's weaknesses, Frost admired him more than any of his contemporaries and declared that "Robinson was the only man from whom I took advice in poetry matters." In one of his rare introductions, to the posthumously published *King Jasper,* Frost praised Robinson's work and paid him a subtle personal compliment by observing that "he knew how to forbid encroachment" on his personal life.[2]

Frost's relations with Amy Lowell—the literary field marshal of Boston, struggling with Pound for control of the Imagists (or Amygists) —contained, as with Pound, an element of comedy. She had written an important review of *North of Boston,* but had ignored Frost's humor and fondness for his country characters. Instead, she portrayed him as a disillusioned rustic who described an arid, dying culture: "It is certainly the most American volume of poetry which has appeared for some time. . . . [a] work of a color so local as to be almost photographic. . . .

Mr. Frost's book reveals a disease which is eating into the vitals of our New England life, at least in its rural communities. . . . [He] has reproduced both people and scenery with a vividness which is extraordinary. . . . Frost's is not the kindly New England of Whittier, nor the humorous and sensible one of [James Russell] Lowell; it is a latter-day New England where a civilization is decaying. . . . His people are left-overs of the old stock, morbid, pursued by phantoms, slowly sinking to insanity. . . . The result is a book of unusual power and sincerity. . . . If the book is not great poetry, it is nevertheless a remarkable achievement."

Frost thought it prudent, while in Boston, to call on Miss Lowell and thank her in person for her favorable notice. The rich, well-connected, cigar-smoking versifier—who worked through the night and slept by day with sixteen pillows—was the sister of the president of Harvard and belonged to the same poetic dynasty as James Russell Lowell. As he entered the lavish library of her Brookline mansion, Frost found the Gertrude Stein of Imagism: obese, ambitious, domineering, egoistical, eccentric and emotionally deprived. Though good-natured, she combined execrable poetry with a patronizing manner and demanded constant flattery. Frost expressed his gratitude and was suitably charming and deferential. He made a favorable impression and left on good terms.

Two years later Amy expanded her review into a chapter on Frost (the first essay about him to appear in a book) in *Tendencies in Modern American Poetry,* which also included sections on Robinson, Masters, Sandburg and two Imagists: Hilda Doolittle and John Gould Fletcher. After a long biographical introduction, based on material supplied by Frost, she described him as an intuitive writer, a true bucolic and a poetic realist who based his "very sad book" on actual experience and portrayed a decaying New England. She discussed the major poems in *North of Boston* and came to some negative conclusions: "The Death of the Hired Man" is "very simple and slight," "he feels the people, but has no ear for their peculiar tongue," "his canvas is exceedingly small, and . . . he cannot attain to the position held by men [and presumably by Amy herself] with a wider range of vision." By rescuing Frost from England and by reclaiming him for New England, categorizing him as a regional poet and looking down from Boston at the rude mechanicals of the countryside, Amy—like Ezra—came up with a generous and well-intentioned, but condescending, misguided and potentially harmful interpretation of his work.

In "A Critical Fable," based on James Russell Lowell's "A Fable for

Critics" (1849) and published anonymously in 1922, Amy supplied some doggerel lines on Frost. She described his characters as crazy and himself as the perfect cliché of a dreamy poet:

> There's Frost with his blueberry pastures and hills
> All peopled by folk who have so many ills
> 'Tis a business to count 'em, their subtle insanities.
> One half are sheer mad, and the others inanities.
> He'll paint you a phobia quick as a wink
> Stuffed into a hay-mow or tied to a sink.
> And then he'll deny, with a certain rich rapture,
> The very perversion he's set out to capture. . . .
> He's a foggy benignity wandering in space
> With a stray wisp of moonlight just touching his face,
> Descending to earth when a certain condition
> Reminds him that even a poet needs nutrition.[3]

Her ruse was discovered in January 1924 when she listed the poem among her works in *Who's Who*.

Frost had lost patience with Amy by 1920, when he threatened, in a letter to Untermeyer, to attack and expose her: "I don't believe she is anything but a fake, and I refuse any longer to let her wealth, social position, and the influence she has been able to purchase and cozen, keep me from honestly bawling her out. . . . I shouldn't wonder if I tried my hand at exposing her for a fool as well as fraud." Like most of Frost's threats, this one was never carried out. He held his fire and tried to remain on decent terms with her, and she continued to provide a rich fund of anecdotes. He later told Thompson that on his first visit Amy Lowell had a great number of dogs that caused bedlam. When Frost came back later they were gone and he asked where they were. Amy said that they interfered with her work and she had to kill them. "Why didn't you give them away?" he asked. "I couldn't do that because I loved them too much. Now I have a little yellow cat which I love dearly, but I'm afraid I shall have to kill her, too." To which Frost responded: "I'm glad you don't love me."

Two other major reviews of *North of Boston* appeared after Amy Lowell's, in the summer and fall of 1915, and immediately made Frost's name in America. Alerted by Edward Thomas, who had given him Frost's book, Edward Garnett sent an essay to the *Atlantic* that arrived just before Sedgwick accepted Frost's poems. In a letter of April 1915 Garnett compared Frost to Whitman, as Ford and Aldington had done (apart from Poe, Whitman seems to have been the only American poet the English had ever heard of), and told Sedgwick that "since Whitman's death, no American poet has appeared, of so *unique a quality,* as Mr. Frost." In his long essay, which appeared in the August issue of the *Atlantic* along with Frost's three poems, Garnett shrewdly prophesied that Frost was "destined to take a permanent place in American literature."

The following month the eminent novelist and editor of *Harper's* magazine, William Dean Howells (whom Frost's mother had known, before her marriage, in Ohio), also paid him a handsome tribute. In his "Editor's Easy Chair" column of September, Howells wrote that Frost's poems "merit the favor they have won" on both sides of the Atlantic: "They are very genuinely and unaffectedly expressive of rustic New England," his "fine intelligence tingles with a sense of life" and his poems have a "very distinctive power."[4] Howells followed up the review with an invitation to visit him in New York. When Frost appeared, Howells presented him with a volume of his own, similarly realistic poems, *The Mother and the Father* (1909). After Howells' death in 1921 Frost remembered that precious gift and told a mutual friend (exaggerating Howells' influence and accommodating the older writer to his own poetic theory) that he had learned from Howells to use the voices of people. No writer, he said, ever had a more attentive and imaginative ear for tones of voice.

II

Holt began very cautiously by importing from England only 150 unbound copies of *North of Boston.* But when the reviews by Lowell, Garnett, Howells and many others created an unexpected demand, they printed 1,300 of their own copies in March. The book then went through four more printings, reached the best-seller list and sold a phenomenal 20,000 copies. The *Nation* called *North of Boston* one of the four best books of poetry in 1914, and the English author Viola Meynell used "The Pasture" as an epigraph for her latest novel, *Columbine* (1915).

Amidst all this excitement—and the comparatively quiet publication of 750 copies of *A Boy's Will* in April 1915—there was more trouble with the hard-headed Mme. Nutt, who still controlled world rights to Frost's current and future books. In September 1914, while Frost was in England, Alfred Harcourt had been blind to Frost's commercial value and had absolutely no idea of his impending success. He told Mme. Nutt that though Holt liked *North of Boston*, "we cannot see a paying market here for this particular volume" and asked to buy rights to Frost's *next* book. She responded with justifiable pride in her own perspicuity, took credit for all she had done for Frost and shot back a rocket that was right on target: "We think that if you recognize the value of Mr. Frost's work you will also see that his books will make their way steadily. We could not offer you rights of his new book if you do not push the present volume to some extent. . . . We consider that under the present political circumstances [the war] American publishers ought to show some willingness to help English publishers who have had sufficient daring and intelligence to recognize the talent of one of their countrymen." Stung by her note, Harcourt immediately backed down and imported the first copies in sheets.

Meanwhile, that formidable lady firmly—but quite unreasonably—rejected Frost's request to publish his new poems in Harold Monro's chapbook and refused to send him an account of the modest sales in Britain. In the summer of 1915, when American sales became brisk, Frost desperately asked Harcourt if he could somehow get out of her clutches: "I am anxious to hear of any hope of being wrested from Mrs. Nutt. It seems to me that if I am to remain that lady's for life there will be no more poetry. What would be the use of writing just to be cheated out of royalties by her?" In a witty letter of October 1915 to Harold Monro, with whom he was now on cordial terms, Frost expressed his fervent wish that at least one of the German bombs now raining down on London would land on her office safe and blow his contract to bits. He hastened to add that as a good Christian he wished her no personal harm.

In his memoir, Harcourt assumed a superior attitude and condemned Mme. Nutt for not playing cricket: "The British edition of *North of Boston* was published by a rather obscure house, David Nutt, whose widow was running the business. Mrs. Nutt was uncommunicative, obviously not interested in anything but making the largest profit possible. When we saw the book might have a considerable sale, we tried to get permission from her to set it in this country and pay her a royalty on American sales, but we met with a flat refusal. We must buy her sheets, and at a high price. . . . She had never taken any steps to copyright his poetry in America, or even to bring it to the attention of American publishers. She had never given him reports of sales or sent him any royalty."[5] Though Mme. Nutt certainly had her shortcomings, there was nothing wrong with trying to make "the largest profit possible" and selling her now valuable sheets "at a high price." That was merely good business. But if (as Harcourt claimed) she *had* wanted to make the greatest profit, she would have made Frost publish the books at his own expense and printed far fewer than a thousand copies of his first work. In fact, it was Mme. Nutt (not Harcourt) who not only recognized Frost's talent, but also forced Harcourt to publish *North of Boston* when he did not want it. She made him realize that Frost's books would have a considerable sale and "make their way steadily" in America.

To protect Frost's interests, and his own, Harcourt put his lawyers to work. Since Frost had received neither accounting nor royalties, they considered his contract void. Following their instructions and repeating their words, Frost wrote to her in April 1916: "You are hereby notified that all my obligations under my contract with you dated December 16, 1912, and also all your rights thereunder are at an end." She threatened to sue, and the matter dragged on until her firm went bankrupt in 1921—hastened, no doubt, by Holt's grabbing her most profitable literary property. Even bankruptcy did not conclude this unpleasant though ultimately satisfactory affair. In July 1921 Frost told Raymond Holden, who had bought his farm but had not taken legal possession, that Mme. Nutt's receivers were claiming all the royalties Holt had paid him since 1915. Though he felt their claim was merely a joke or a formality, Frost thought it better to transfer the title of the farm to Holden's name. It is sad to think that the shrewd and infuriating Mme. Nutt lost Frost, and perhaps went into bankruptcy, only because she stubbornly refused to render accounts and pay a tiny £2.25 royalty on the first 250 copies of *A Boy's Will*.

Speaking of his numerous editors at Holt, Frost told Robert Francis that "they had fought among themselves—palace revolutions—blood flowing under the doors—but to him they had been only tenderly solicitous." The first crisis occurred in 1919 when Harcourt left Holt to start his own firm and tried to persuade Frost to come with him. Frost originally agreed to leave but, when he discovered that Harcourt could be as duplicitous as Mme. Nutt, decided to stay. According to Holt's historian: "It was his fixed wish to have all his books with one publisher, and Harcourt had assured him he would arrange the transfer. When Frost visited Harcourt in the fall, he asked him if Holt had released his books and was told that the arrangement had been made. Frost asked to see the letter of transfer. Harcourt pretended to look for it, but failed to produce it. Frost then suspected that Harcourt was not being frank with him and decided to remain with Holt."

Harcourt was replaced by Lincoln MacVeagh. Born in Rhode Island in 1890, he had studied philosophy and modern languages at Groton and Harvard, and served in World War I. To compensate for Holt's earlier refusal to release Frost's books, MacVeagh arranged a stipend of $100 a month, paid his permission fees in full (instead of dividing them equally) and arranged for the English publication of his work. Heinemann brought out his *Selected Poems* in 1923, Grant Richards did *New Hampshire* in 1924, Longmans Green published his *Collected Poems* in 1930 and beginning with his *Selected Poems* in 1936 Jonathan Cape took over as his English publisher. In 1924 MacVeagh left to found the Dial Press. A friend of President Roosevelt, during World War II he became ambassador to Yugoslavia and to Greece, and ended his distinguished diplomatic career as ambassador to Portugal and to Spain.

Frost single-handedly made Holt's name as a publisher of poetry and attracted a great many authors to the firm. Two profitable writers, Carl Sandburg and Louis Untermeyer, joined Holt in 1916 but moved with Harcourt three years later; Stephen Vincent Benét and A. E. Housman became Holt authors in the early 1920s. Frost also performed a valuable service by reading and recommending manuscripts by a number of distinguished poets who were eventually published by Holt: Walter de la Mare in 1916, Edward Thomas in 1917, John Crowe Ransom in 1919, John Drinkwater in 1931, Mark Van Doren and John Holmes in 1937 and John Ciardi in 1940. After his reading at the New School in the 1930s, Frost asked Van Doren: "Why don't we see more of each other?" Van Doren replied: "I don't know, Robert. Maybe it's better as it is." The gentle Van Doren was intimidated by Frost, but he was always immensely grateful to Frost for recommending him to Holt when he had been dropped by his own publisher and when his fortunes were low.[6]

III

Eager to capitalize on the success of *North of Boston,* in November 1916 Holt brought out his next book, *Mountain Interval,* in an edition of 4,000 copies. Always rather reluctant to part with his poems, Frost felt he had been pressed into publishing his third book. He thought it lacked formal unity and "was just a bunch of poems slapped together, not judged and weighed like the previous volumes." He had written part of the book before he went to England and several of the poems—"Birches," "Putting in the Seed," "The Hill Wife" and "The Sound of Trees"—while living near Abercrombie and Gibson in Gloucestershire. Firmly rooted in the English pastoral tradition, the book includes both rhymed lyrics and dramatic narratives in blank verse, along with a ballad and three poems for children. Frost's characteristic themes of isolation, loneliness and fear are expressed in "An Old Man's Winter Night," "The Hill Wife" and "Snow," of sudden violence and death in "The Vanishing Red" and "'Out, Out—'."

In "Christmas Trees," a holiday poem, a city slicker tries unsuccessfully to swindle a country man. In "The Exposed Nest," partly inspired by Burns' "To a Mouse" and Clare's "Mouse's Nest," the narrator saves vulnerable young birds whose nest has been exposed by mowing. "The Telephone" describes a fanciful talk, through the medium of flowers, between the speaker and his wife. "Meeting and Passing," like Hardy's "A Man Was Drawing Near Me," recounts a brief but telling moment of recognition.

"The Cow in Apple Time," a charming and witty poem with tragic implications, imitates the dramatic repetitions of John Clare's great poem "Badger." Clare describes the savage and pitiful pursuit of a badger in an urgent series of pronouns and active verbs—"He tries . . . He turns . . . He drives . . . He falls"—and concludes with sudden horror. Frost's poem describes a cow, crazily drunk on fallen apples and "having tasted fruit" (or evil):

> She scorns a pasture withering to the root.
> She runs from tree to tree where lie and sweeten
> The windfalls spiked with stubble and worm-eaten.
> She leaves them bitten when she has to fly.
> She bellows on a knoll against the sky.
> Her udder shrivels and the milk goes dry.

"Hyla Brook," where late the tree frogs sang, opens suddenly with "By June our brook's run out of song and speed." The water has gone underground and the frogs' shouts through the mist now seem "Like ghost of sleigh bells in a ghost of snow" (which echoes Frost's earlier line: "Like nothing else by day, like ghosts by night"). Though the brook is now nothing more than a precious memory, the speaker asserts his

unqualified love for the change of seasons in his native region, whatever
its defects:

> A brook to none but who remember long.
> This as it will be seen is other far
> Than with brooks taken otherwhere in song.
> We love the things we love for what they are.

"The Oven Bird"—about an American warbler with an oven-shaped
nest—follows and complements "Hyla Brook." The poem opens with
"There is a singer everyone [around here] has heard" and then describes
the harsh, midsummer song that reverberates through the wood, when
other birds have already stopped singing, and announces the coming of
autumn. Echoing Keats' "Ode to a Nightingale," and linking the oven
bird's song to the similarly diminished Hyla Brook, Frost emphasizes the
need to persist, as powers weaken, in singing—or loving or writing:

> The bird would cease and be as other birds
> But that he knows in singing not to sing.
> The question that he frames in all but words
> Is what to make of a diminished thing.

Though *North of Boston* is Frost's greatest book, each subsequent
volume contains a few masterpieces. The outstanding poems in *Mountain Interval* are the justly famous "Birches" and "The Road Not Taken" as
well as "Putting in the Seed" and "'Out, Out—'." "Birches" connects
poetic aspiration and physical love. It begins with a fanciful image ("I like
to think") of a boy swinging on and bending birches. It then shifts to a
brilliant description of ice-laden branches blown by the wind that "cracks
and crazes [suggesting cracked glazes] their enamel." Inspired by medieval cosmology and by a famous passage from Shelley's "Adonais" (an
elegy for Keats, about poetic power cut off in mid-career by death), Frost
writes of all the broken ice-glass: "You'd think the inner dome of heaven
had fallen." He then returns to the swinger-of-birches theme as the boy,
like the future poet, launches out at the proper time, keeps his poise and
climbs carefully. Swinging himself on the branches "*Toward* heaven,"
he'd

> like to get away from earth awhile
> And then come back to it and begin over. . . .

> Earth's the right place for love:
> I don't know where it's likely to go better.

Opposing the Platonic view of idealized love, Frost believes Earth, not Heaven, is the right place because love should be physical and tested against the realities of life.

"Putting in the Seed," one of Frost's most sensual poems, is also a celebration of physical love. The man puts the seed in the woman as well as in the ground and, as metaphor merges with reality, the procreative poem works perfectly on both levels. The speaker invites the responsive woman to "become like me, / Slave to a springtime passion for the earth." He capitalizes the life-giving moment, inspired by both passion and love, and the birth of the child follows naturally from the arched bodies in the sexual act. The infant shoulders its way out of the womb and into the world just as a new seed comes alive by pushing through the earth:

> How Love burns through the Putting in the Seed
> On through the watching for that early birth
> When, just as the soil tarnishes with weed,
> The sturdy seedling with arched body comes
> Shouldering its way and shedding the earth crumbs.

Though "'Out, Out—'" is one of his greatest poems, Frost always felt that (like "Home Burial") it was too cruel to read in public. The poem was based on an actual incident that took place in Bethlehem, New Hampshire, in March 1901. Raymond Fitzgerald, the son of Frost's friend, was cutting wood with a sawing machine when he accidentally hit the loose pulley, and badly cut and lacerated his hand. Raymond was taken into the house and a doctor was called, but he died of shock.

The title refers to the blood gushing out of the mutilated body as well as to Macbeth's speech on the death of his queen. Shakespeare's tragic hero emphasizes the brevity and meaninglessness of human existence:

> Out, out, brief candle!
> Life's but a walking shadow, a poor player
> That struts and frets his hour upon the stage
> And then is heard no more. It is a tale
> Told by an idiot, full of sound and fury,
> Signifying nothing. (5.5.23)

Frost's poem opens suddenly with the dangerous, menacing machine producing sweet-scented sawdust in a tranquil mountain setting. The first line is repeated more emphatically in the seventh as the setting sun that marks the end of the day's work foreshadows the extinction of the brief candle of life. Just at that moment the saw seems to take on a life of its own by leaping "out at the boy's hand" and causing a pathetic wound:

> The boy's first outcry was a rueful laugh,
> As he swung toward them holding up the hand,
> Half in appeal, but half as if to keep
> The life from spilling.

The boy begs them not to cut his hand off, but the hand is already gone. The ending, as life leaks out in a series of short phrases, is truly terrifying —and seems to recall the death of Elliott Frost:

> The doctor put him in the dark of ether.
> He lay and puffed his lips out with his breath.
> And then—the watcher at his pulse took fright.
> No one believed. They listened at his heart.
> Little—less—nothing!—and that ended it.
> No more to build on there. And they, since they
> Were not the one dead, turned to their affairs.

The conclusion of this poem—which echoes the magnificent last line of "The Fear": "It touched, it struck, it clattered and went out"—is a bitter comment on the callous indifference to human suffering. It inspired (along with Brueghel's painting *The Fall of Icarus*) the ending of Auden's "Musée des Beaux Arts" (1940):

> and the expensive delicate ship that must have seen
> Something amazing, a boy falling out of the sky
> Had somewhere to get to and sailed calmly on.

"The Road Not Taken" is a mildly satiric comment on Edward Thomas' self-tormenting ambivalence. But it has deeper roots in an uncanny experience that Frost described in a letter to Susan Ward on February 10, 1912, six months before leaving for England. While walking on "two lonely cross-roads," neither "much travelled," after a winter storm, Frost met a silent, approaching, Poe-like figure who seemed to be his spectral double—"like myself . . . my own image . . . this other self":

> Judge then how surprised I was the other evening as I came down one to see a man, who to my own unfamiliar eyes and in the dusk looked for all the world like myself, coming down the other, his approach to the point where our paths must intersect being so timed that unless one of us pulled up we must inevitably collide. I felt as if I was going to meet my own image in a slanting mirror. Or may I say I felt as we slowly converged on the same point with the same noiseless yet laborious strides as if we were two images about to float together with the uncrossing of someone's eyes. I verily expected to take up or absorb this other self and feel the stronger by the addition for the three-mile journey home. But I didn't go forward to the touch. I stood in wonderment and let him pass by. . . .

The words "lonely cross-roads," "converged" and neither "much travelled" in the letter become "Two roads diverged" and "less traveled by" at the beginning and end of the poem, and the inevitability of "converged" turns into the perplexity of "diverged." The two figures in the letter (Frost and his *Doppelgänger*) merge with Frost and his "brother" Thomas (since Frost was deeply involved in all of Thomas' conflicts) to produce in the poem the impossible desire to "travel both [roads] / And be one traveler." Though the poet takes the other road because it wanted wear and has the better claim, he also realizes that both roads are really about the same. The most important thing, therefore, is not the road itself, but the *decision* about which road to take:

> I shall be telling this with a sigh
> Somewhere ages and ages hence:
> Two roads diverged in a wood, and I—
> I took the one less traveled by,
> And that has made all the difference.

The first two lines in this final stanza are weak—the "sigh" is unequal to the emotion expressed, the near-cliché "ages and ages" is surrounded by two vague adverbs. The statement that one road is "less traveled by" contradicts "just as fair," "about the same" and "both . . . equally lay." Yet

Frost manages to convey the feeling of a momentous and life-changing resolution by repeating the opening line ("Two roads diverged in a yellow wood") and by the clinching word *difference*. He also draws on the associative power of the last lines of Wordsworth's great lyric "She Dwelt Among the Untrodden Ways" to emphasize, in a single word, the crucial opposition to all the sameness in the poem:

> She lived unknown, and few could know
> When Lucy ceased to be;
> But she is in her grave, and, oh,
> The difference to me!

The concluding sentence of William James' "The Will to Believe" (a quotation from Virginia Woolf's uncle Fitzjames Stephen), which Frost had read at Harvard and taught at Plymouth, suggests the philosophic difficulty of such momentous decisions and the positive, stoical attitude one has to adopt in order to survive: "If we take the wrong road we shall be dashed to pieces. We do not certainly know whether there is any right one. What must we do? . . . Act for the best, hope for the best, and take what comes." In May 1915, three months before the poem appeared in the *Atlantic Monthly,* Frost revealed in a letter that its ambivalence was his own as well as Edward Thomas' and asserted that he had always been right to choose the less practical and more poetical way. Like Thomas, Frost had to deal with the momentous question of what to do with his precious talent: "I have been pulled two ways and torn in two all my life. But by the Lord Harry every time I have taken the way it almost seemed as if I ought not to take, I have been justified somehow by the result. It scares me to say it. . . . I don't say I have done well for my family—I have done badly, but I've always made some little gain for them when I took a [chance]."[7]

IV

Mountain Interval received favorable reviews from Cox, Braithwaite, Untermeyer and Padraic Colum. It strengthened Frost's reputation and stimulated his competitive spirit. As early as 1894 the young Frost had spoken of the "astonishing magnitude" of his ambition. Twenty-one years later, after his return from England, he told Bartlett how he

intended, after his long wait for recognition, to win this poetic contest—even if the victory was posthumous: "I am but a timid calculating
soul always intent on the main chance. I always mean to win. All that
distinguishes me from the others that mean to win . . . is my patience. I
am perfectly willing to wait fifty, seventy-five or a thousand years as the
fates may decree."

Unwilling to leave the final decision to fate, Frost felt he had to take
active steps to advance his career. Befriending various writers, critics,
editors and publishers who might help him was perfectly natural. Getting friends to publicize and write about his work was also quite acceptable. But Frost provoked considerable criticism in poetic circles by his
hostility to those he liked to call his "enemies"—though they were
unaware of being cast in this role and rarely did anything, apart from
publishing their own work, to harm him. Frost felt that every living poet
was his potential or actual rival and made nasty cracks whenever a
"contemptuary" poet was mentioned. Apart from these malicious comments, he rarely did actual harm to his presumed opponents.

"Before I had published a book," Frost told Louis Mertins, with considerable exaggeration, "I was never conscious of the existence of any
contemporary poet. But as soon as my first book came out I became
jealous of all of them—all but Robinson. Somehow I never felt jealous of
him at any time." Frost must have been thinking only of American poets,
for after he broke into the big leagues with his first two books, he did
not seem to envy Abercrombie, Gibson and Thomas, who were actively
engaged in furthering his reputation. Frost, who eventually outlived
them all, liked to tell friends that "he wished some of his rivals were
dead." His sense of rivalry extended from poets of the past, who had
inspired his own work, to members of the same family. During World
War II, he felt overshadowed by his greatest predecessor and hoped that
the Germans "could, with one shell, blow Shakespeare out of the English
language. The past overawes us too much in art."[8] When William Jay
Smith told him that he had married a fellow poet, Frost replied: "That's
not a good thing. There will be too much competition"—and he proved
to be right.

Frost, who liked war because it tested man's courage, introduced the
dangerous concept of competition into modern American poetry. He
damaged his own character and reputation by equating poetry with war
and words with weapons: "I've always thought of poetry as something to
win or lose—a kind of prowess in the world of letters played with the
most subtle and lethal of weapons." On television, when discussing world

peace, he fiercely declared that "we were sent here to destroy each other in honest competition." Though Frost recklessly exaggerated these half-serious concepts, he did believe "there's room for only one person at a time . . . at the top of the steeple . . . [and] I always meant that person to be me." Like Hemingway and Norman Mailer, he liked to think of himself as the heavyweight champion of literature, who had won the crown by knocking out his adversaries. At a literary conference he declared: "I wish we had something like the prize ring where we could fight to a finish, where work went down on the mat or had its arm lifted by the judges at the end."[9]

Frost's combative attitude hurt himself as well as other poets. He told Untermeyer that he had suffered nervous collapse from the "strain of conscious competition." In one of the films about him, Frost freely acknowledged his self-destructive jealousy of all poets, and then engagingly added that he *genuinely disliked* some of them. After winning his fourth Pulitzer Prize, in 1943, he assumed an unusually benign attitude and disingenuously told a friend: "Prizes are a strange thing for me to have come by, who have hated competition and never wanted to be anybody's rival." As the poet John Ciardi shrewdly observed, Frost's great achievement *had* placed him on top of the steeple, and though his competitive attitude did more harm than good, he still felt the need to secure his position by engaging in petty plots: "Frost had a talent for living in a reef of tangled . . . people around him. I never understood his talent for creating intricacy. At least up to c. age 80 when he seemed to mellow considerably and to mend emotional fences around him, or not so much to mend, as to tear them down. Why should a man of such talent, and of such seeming self-control, involve himself in such bitter and petty political intrigue?"

Frost felt most at ease when he was in control: in his family, among friends, when teaching, on the lecture circuit, at conferences, prize-givings and celebrations. He therefore formed friendships with Bartlett and Cox, preferred the Georgians to Yeats and Pound, dominated a circle of would-be biographers and aspiring poets, and after the death of Edward Thomas never had a close friend who was his personal or poetic equal. When he achieved fame and honors he enjoyed his power to dominate people. He told Untermeyer that he so hated to be crossed that he had come to believe that not being crossed was the thing that mattered most in life. His biographer Robert Newdick was completely absorbed in Frost's life and chose to dance attendance whenever the Master honored the household with a visit. His wife, Marie, resentfully

—and somewhat unfairly, since Newdick eagerly courted the poet—called Frost "a despot." During domestic crises, Frost would sometimes react against his willfulness, castigate himself and mislead friends by exaggerating his own faults. In a guilt-ridden letter to the young poet Charles Foster, Frost called himself "a God-damned son-of-a-bitch, a selfish person who had dragged people roughshod over life. . . . He was always a person who had his way."[10]

To compensate for and disguise this harsh side of his character, and to counter the hostility aroused by his competitive, power-hungry streak, Frost began to create—as soon as he returned from England—a likable and engaging public image. Born and raised in towns until he was an adult, he deliberately transformed himself into a distinctive rural Yankee. This earthy, hayseed-sage persona was cultivated, by the poet who had twice dropped out of college, in direct opposition to the sophisticated but sterile academic circles in which he cautiously began to move. George Whicher, who became a close friend, reported that at a faculty reception after his first reading at Amherst College, in 1916, "Frost was dead set not to appear either academic or literary. He was all farmer. When it came my turn to speak to him, we spent an animated ten minutes describing the healthful properties of horse-manure."

In 1919 H. L. Mencken called Frost "Whittier without the whiskers." By the time he won his first Pulitzer Prize, in 1924, his public image was fully established. During scores of interviews, Frost's piercing blue eyes seemed to "twinkle" whenever the occasion demanded. One dazzled interviewer exclaimed: "he even *looks* like a symbol." The poet Stanley Kunitz ironically commented that Frost's "most successful work of the imagination was the legend he created about himself."[11]

V

In June 1915, four months after returning to America, Frost bought for $1,000 from his grandfather's annuity a farm in Franconia (about forty miles north of Plymouth) in the White Mountains of New Hampshire. Though the house was very small and lacked both bathroom and furnace, Frost wrote an enthusiastic description to Frank Flint: "Our forty-five acres of land runs up to the mountain behind the house about half a mile. In front of us the ground falls away two or three hundred feet to the very flat flood plain of the . . . river. Beyond that, right over against us not three miles away, are Lafayette and the Franconia Range of Mountains rising to five thousand feet. Not Switzerland, but rugged enough." The fourteen-year-old Carol did most of the work around the farm, and the place was wild enough to have six of their neighbor's sheep devoured by bears. But Frost remained restless as ever, continued his childhood pattern of frequent moves and lived in about forty different houses during the seventy years between his marriage and his death. The one constant factor in his houses, unchanged by fame and comparative wealth from the beginning to the end of his life, was their extreme simplicity. The cabin in Vermont and the bungalow in Florida that he occupied during his last twenty-five years were just as spartan as the rented apartments and hotel rooms of his early years in San Francisco.

While living in Franconia in 1915 Frost met the young poet Raymond Holden. He came from an old New York family that had made a fortune in tin, coal and railroads. After withdrawing from Princeton in 1915, he fought under Pershing when Pancho Villa invaded Texas. He married in 1918, had two children and worked for Macmillan publishers in New York. Holden had been spending his summer holidays in New Hampshire since boyhood, and in 1919 began to live year round in Franconia. Frost befriended him, encouraged his writing and recommended his work to the poetry editor of the *New Republic*. But Holden's wife, Grace, disliked living in that remote region. The marriage became troubled and they were divorced in 1923. Frost disapproved when Holden began to court his beautiful daughter Lesley.

Frost's dealings with Holden reveal his willingness to extract money from a rich disciple, in return for friendship and advice, when he needed cash to buy a farm. In 1919 Frost sold Holden, who had a substantial inheritance, the upper half of the Franconia farm (for which he had paid $1,000 only a few years before) for $2,500. In their contract Holden also agreed to buy the remaining half, if and when Frost wanted to sell it, for an additional $2,500. Holden had bought the farm and built a house there to be near Frost. But in 1920 Frost sold Holden the rest of the farm, moved to Vermont and realized a considerable profit. In 1921 he borrowed the lower house from Holden during the hay-fever season. These transactions made Holden feel wounded and exploited, and he later wrote: "Robert had come to think of me as a member of a class—a class of disturbers—and he didn't want to be disturbed. . . . I reluctantly felt that he had used me as a convenience. I even, for a time, believed that his friendship for me was insincere and motivated by what he thought he could get out of me."

Before their friendship cooled, Holden had some precious moments with Frost. He later described the experience that inspired Frost's "Evening in a Sugar Orchard," which was written in March 1930 after they had stayed up all night in the sugar house and tended the fire to keep the maple sugar flowing: "The firelight flickering through the stove doors on his face as he sat crouched, fingering a piece of wood, the smell of the thickening sap and its wavering stream, have never left me." Frost's face "showed the happiness coming from the kind of work which [unlike poetry] blended effort and will without too much pressure upon either and which resulted in the making of something, the importance of which did not have to be considered."[12]

Frost lived on poetry by a combination of frugality, shrewdness and enterprise. He said that he never earned more than $25 a week until he was forty, and survived on his grandfather's annuities, which eventually came to a total of $13,000, until the final payment in 1923. After he returned from England, where he had exhausted his savings, Frost supported himself and his increasingly extended family by college teaching, public readings and lectures, book royalties, magazine and reprint fees and, later on, by fine press limited editions and by selling his manuscripts to collectors. At first, he earned $50 to $100 for each reading, $15 to $30 each for poems in magazines and (after *North of Boston*) only a few hundred dollars a year from books. In August 1916 he told Helen Thomas that in the year and a half since leaving England he had earned a thousand dollars from poetry and another thousand from lecturing. Though he could not live only on royalties from poetry, there were limits to what he would do to make money. He did not apply for foundation grants, and in May 1916 told Amy Lowell that he had refused an offer to read his poetry at a silent movie theater. His poems were meant to give people time to get into their seats before the main part of the show began.

Frost had great expenses for his family and for his unprofitable series of farms. As his children married and had children of their own, one left a widow, others got divorced, became physically or mentally ill and were unable to support themselves. Frost generously paid their bills and gave them money. When he traveled on the lecture circuit, he handed extravagant tips to porters, waiters and cab drivers. He often asked friends: "Have you given him enough?" and his travel expenses seemed so high that they were actually questioned by the Internal Revenue Service. Though his family always resented him tipping any more than was absolutely necessary, he gave more than ever—sometimes as much as 50 percent of the bill. Thompson said that during their trip to Ireland, "Frost threw money around on tips, *scandalously*." John Ciardi confirmed that when he went down to Florida to interview Frost, "He absolutely insisted on paying the dinner check, and when I went to pay the motel check, he paid it. I pointed out that Good Heavens, I was on the *Saturday Review* expense account; there was no need for it. He said, 'You came down to see me, and you are my guest. That's the way I was brought up.' "[13]

VI

In the spring of 1915, while trying to establish himself in America, Frost met the man who became, after the death of Edward Thomas, his closest friend. The restless and sparkling, generous and warm-hearted Louis Untermeyer had a high forehead, thick glasses, a beaked nose, thin lips and a witty tongue, and was especially fond of bow ties and outrageous puns. He was born in New York in 1885, dropped out of high school and for nearly twenty years commuted from Manhattan to Newark to run the family jewelry business. After 1923 he devoted himself entirely to the business of poetry. He was a talented pianist, a prolific, successful and influential anthologist and editor, a popular teacher and lecturer, an energetic translator and mediocre poet. In later years, he worked for Decca Records and appeared on the panel of the popular television program "What's My Line?" The German-Jewish Untermeyer honestly described himself as "flippant, and unfaithful . . . too facile, too prolific."

Untermeyer's messy personal life was a constant source of amusement and concern to the respectably monogamous Frost, who was embarrassed by his friend's domestic quarrels when he stayed with him in New York. Untermeyer was married to the poet Jean Starr from 1907 to 1926, to the poet Virginia Moore from 1926 to 1927, to Jean Starr (for the second time) from 1927 to 1933, to the lawyer Esther Antin from 1933 to 1948, and to the editor of *Seventeen*, Bryna Ivens, from 1948 until his death in 1977. In 1926, Frost reported, Untermeyer's school anthology, *This Singing World*, included two poems by his last wife and two by his next. He usually put in Jean's poems when he was married to her and took them out when they were divorced. When her ex-husband dropped her poems from his anthologies, Jean complained to Frost, who kindly replied: "I shall have something to say to him if he could find it in his heart to hurt you with a last blow like this."

Untermeyer had a son, Richard, with Jean, a son, John, with Virginia, and adopted two sons, Laurence and Joseph, during his second marriage to Jean. In later years, he had a farm in the Adirondacks, near Elizabethtown, New York, and lived as a country gentleman in Newton, Connecticut. Untermeyer and Frost were also drawn together by similar tragedies. Richard Untermeyer hanged himself in his dorm room at Yale in January 1927; Carol Frost shot himself in Vermont in October 1940.

Frost lived in rural New England and kept his distance from other writers, but he loved to hear Untermeyer's lively accounts of the latest literary gossip from New York. Frost was a Vermont conservative, Untermeyer a New York socialist; and though they constantly argued about politics, it never interfered with their friendship. They shared a passion for sports and were tennis partners at the Bread Loaf Conference. Frost's daughter-in-law remembered that they always talked about "writing and writers, or baseball teams. Elinor liked Louis very much, as did all the children . . . [who] had fun when he was around."

Frost and Untermeyer also punned as wildly in their letters and conversations as Swift and Sheridan had done in the eighteenth century. Untermeyer punned so excessively that one of his wives tried to stop him by threatening to cut his necktie in half—and even that did not work. She cut it off, he went on punning. On one memorable occasion—alluding to William Douglas' poem "Annie Laurie" (which begins "Maxwelton's braes are bonnie")—Untermeyer actually brought two donkeys (named Max and Welton) to Bread Loaf so that the assembled poets could hear their bonnie brays. Frost referred to Untermeyer as Yahweh (the Hebrew word for God) and both he and Untermeyer would joke about his Jewish background. Four years before Israel became independent, Frost wrote in an epistolary poem that he sympathized with the Jews: "Give them back I say / All Palestine. . . . I have no pull with Arabs. / I am no Lawrence of Arabia."[14]

Frost genuinely liked Untermeyer, a lively and amusing companion, who brought out the playful side of his character. Louis was also a sympathetic and encouraging listener, and in a letter of July 1921 Frost apologized for his unpardonable self-absorption during his friend's recent visit: "The rest of me is swallowed up in thoughts of myself. All the time you were here I read and read to you from my own works. . . . But there's this redeeming consideration. It did occur to me of my own motion though not until too late that you also may have had works to read from and were only diffidently waiting to be asked like the decent person you are. I'll be damned. It shows how far we can get along in our egotism without noticing it."

But Frost also courted and flattered him, made good use of him and privately criticized his foolish vanity. Stroking the fur in 1916, he told Untermeyer that he feared he might "lose" him because he had not sufficiently praised him. Puffing up his feeble reputation when introducing him to Abercrombie in 1923, Frost absurdly called him one of our best poets and our best critic. Yet Frost told Thompson that since the time of his first anthology in 1919 Untermeyer "has been selling out to one thing after another." In about 1919 he wrote to Lesley about the gross disparity between Louis and Jean Untermeyer's talents and overweening ambitions, but warned that he had to maintain his useful friendship: "They are busy every minute they are awake talking of fame. They don't think of it any more than they talk of it because they talk of it all the time. The absurdity of it never strikes them. . . . [But] we must have no trouble or break with them. . . . Louis means to be a good backer."

Untermeyer adored Frost and did everything in his power to help his career. Beginning with his favorable review of *North of Boston* in April 1915, he dedicated many poems and books to Frost, included countless reprints of Frost's work in his anthologies, wrote eight reviews and articles about Frost, two reviews of books about him and two introductions to editions of Frost poems. He also edited an important volume of their correspondence and gave a memorial lecture on Frost at the Library of Congress. Untermeyer served on the Pulitzer Prize jury for nearly twenty-five years, was instrumental in awarding Frost four of these prizes and was extremely proud of what he had done for his friend. Frost turned to his ebullient companion in times of crisis, appreciated his help, confided in him and wrote Untermeyer his most revealing letters. After five marriages, Untermeyer remained an unregenerate ladies' man. On his eighty-fifth birthday he told Arthur Miller: "I'm still chasing them. The only difference is that now I can't remember why."[15]

9

Teaching at
Amherst

1917–1920

I

In October 1914, after the war had broken out and he was still living in Gloucestershire, Frost wrote Sidney Cox about his return to America and his plans for a career. Despite his critical success in England, he knew he would not be able to support himself entirely on poetry and would have to rely on teaching for most of his income: "I should awfully like a quiet job in a small college where I should be allowed to teach something a little new on the technique of writing and where I should also have some honor for what I suppose myself to have done in poetry."

In April 1916 Frost began to realize this goal, and resume what would become his lifelong occupation, when he accepted an invitation from the writer Stark Young to read poems from his first three books at Amherst, a small men's college in central Massachusetts. Frost made a favorable impression and was offered his first academic job as Professor of English. He began in January 1917 at an annual salary of $2,000, taught two courses of his own choice each term (instead of the regulation three) and was allowed to miss classes when invited to read at other colleges.

Though Frost needed an academic position, he actually disliked the idea of teaching and doubted whether it was possible to teach writing. But he thought he could serve as a personal and poetic example to aspiring writers. He considered himself an *agent provocateur* in the universities, and mocked college education while living as a teacher and accepting many honorary degrees. Generalizing from his own unhappy experience at Dartmouth and Harvard, Frost believed that the cloistered college life cut young men off from actual experience. "Anybody with an active mind lives on tentatives rather than on tenets," he said. "It's a sad life when it gets too bookish and too shut in from life."

He also thought that formal education created barriers to learning, simplified complex issues and encouraged intellectual passivity. "College seems artificial," he told an Amherst colleague, "in its way of subdividing wisdom and absurd too but at least it never hurt anyone who took it obediently." He felt obliged to warn Bartlett by asking: "Aren't you afraid of sending your boys to college? Aren't you fearful of what it might do to them?" Frost justified his ambiguous position by declaring (with a certain irony, since he believed that his students were profiting from *his* tuition): "Every day I feel bound to save my consistency by advising my pupils to leave school. Then, if they insist on coming to school it is not my fault: I can teach with a clear conscience."[1]

Frost's hostility to college education was closely related to the way his poetry was treated by pedantic academic critics, who lacked insight into a poet's imagination. He claimed to have "suffered terribly from doctors' theses. No one wants to read them, and you have to pay to get them published." He also thought that reading analyses of his own poems could make him self-conscious and even inhibit his creative impulse. When the poet William Meredith sent his Princeton senior thesis on Frost's poetry, Frost tactfully wrote in the margin: "My gratitude to the author for taking all these pains over work of mine yet not insisting on my evaluation of his results. . . . No man is supposed to look at himself in the glass except to shave."

Frost felt that "a poem had to be handled as delicately as one handled a butterfly, for fear of rubbing off some of the dust or sheen." Though convinced that heavy-handed critics could not do justice to his work (which had also been misunderstood by Ezra Pound and Amy Lowell), he wittily declared: "I'm entitled to every meaning to be found in my poem!"[2] Like Edmund Wilson, who was also ambivalent toward universities and opposed academic critics, Frost wanted serious attention but not dull pedantry. Frost was more closely associated with universities than Pound, Eliot and Stevens, and was annoyed when their erudite and puzzling poems received much more academic recognition than his cunning and complex work.

Frost's hostility extended to treacherous literary journalists like Burton Rascoe. In the *New York Tribune* of January 14, 1923, Rascoe published what Frost considered to be their private conversation and also garbled Frost's criticism of the obscurity in Joyce and Eliot, who had published major works in 1922. After stating that Frost was "earnest, earthy, humorous, without put-on, very real, likable, genuine. I admire him very much as a person," Rascoe flatly dismissed his poetry: "I regret that I find almost nothing to interest me in his poems. They are deft, they are competent, they are of the soil; but they are not distinctive." Frost vented his spleen in two letters to Untermeyer and included (as he had done with the satiric poem posted to Flint about Pound) a letter addressed—but not sent—to "You little Rascol." Frost told the sympathetic Untermeyer that "my grounds for wanting to let him have both fists in succession in the middle of the face are chiefly that he stated me so much worse than I know how to state myself."

Determined to oppose the traditional academic ideas and methods at Amherst—as well as, later on, at Michigan, Harvard and Dartmouth—Frost became an iconoclastic, innovative reformer in education. He disliked all rules—including compulsory morning chapel, course requirements, textbooks, reading lists, assigned topics, formal lectures, organized classes, note-taking, papers, examinations and grades—and was determined to give his students something entirely different and more exciting. Rejecting lectures that offered dull facts and stale ideas to passive students, Frost emphasized spontaneity and playfulness. He never planned his classes (or his remarks on poems when giving readings) and never spoke from a prepared text. Commenting on Harry Levin's notoriously difficult Shakespeare course at Harvard, Frost noted: "I'd never take Shakespeare that way. Shakespeare has been a playground for me. I would revel in it." Imitating his mother's lax discipline—a strong contrast to his strictness at Pinkerton and Plymouth—Frost sometimes skipped classes, ignored the students who had no interest in the subject and concentrated on those who did. One Amherst student, disturbed by the chaotic class, recalled that Frost "required virtually no papers. He hardly gave any tests or exams. His class was the most loosely run and undisciplined of any of the classes I attended in college. I used to talk to him about that, because the boys in the back row would actually be playing cards together while he was holding forth."[3] Though there was an element of self-indulgence in Frost's method, most students found him a stimulating teacher.

Frost thought that correcting and grading student papers—a tedious but essential part of a teacher's job—was a complete waste of time and did all he could to avoid them. Quoting *As You Like It,* he told the Columbia poet-professor Mark Van Doren: "Most teaching is mere correcting mistakes just as most loving is mere folly." Since pupils could not be *taught* to avoid grammatical mistakes, which did not in any case make much difference, it seemed beneath his dignity to deal with them: "Nothing is so deadening as to have to correct those tiny minor errors. It does no good anyway, for they will make the same errors four years from now." He boasted that he had "never touched a paper with a red pencil" and told his students: "I'm not here to worry your writing into shape for you. Look to it yourself."[4]

Frost wanted his students to ponder and revise their papers (as he did with his poems) and not hand them in until they had produced their very best work. To encourage careful and serious rather than hasty and slapdash college essays, he demanded audacity, sincerity and tenacity. He told his Amherst boys to write only when they had something to say: "This is a class in seeing how long I can keep from reading what you write. Keep things till you have an accumulation and make a choice. . . . The first thing you show me this year is what you're going to get your mark on, so gird yourself and take your time. . . . I'm no perfunctory reader of perfunctory writing."

Frost took final grades no more seriously than papers and exams, and tried to judge students on their originality, taste and judgment. On one final exam he simply told them: "Do something appropriate to this course that you think would please me." Some filled their bluebooks with elaborate answers, others came to his office and told him how much they had enjoyed the course. "One boy, who merely signed his name to the blue book and went home, got the only A." On another occasion he gave the highest mark to a student who had memorized and copied out a poem by Thomas Hardy. Since Frost felt grades were arbitrary and meaningless, he was generally lenient: "he was fair to average, never gave a failure mark, rarely reproved or exhorted—save by silence or evasion—the reprobate or the inattentive."[5] As Frost gradually drifted out of the classroom and assumed more honorific positions, his pupils had as little assigned work as their teacher.

II

In contrast to his orthodox colleagues, Frost had taught every age level from kindergarten to graduate school and had offered a wide range of subjects from Latin and English to mathematics, history, philosophy and psychology. Drawing on his broad experience, he emphasized free-flowing conversation, which contained elements of "performance" and surprise, made students active rather than passive participants and placed primary responsibility on the pupil rather than on the teacher. His principal aim was to provoke independent thought, to get "young people to the point, somewhere before college ends, of valuing themselves on an occasional generalization they make of their own." Frost inspired his students by his provocative insights—both in and out of class. When a young Amherst man asked: "Do they say that?," Frost responded: "No, *I* say it but *they* would say it too if I pointed it out to them." "The best way to teach students to do original work," he told a New England scholar, "is for the teacher to do original work himself, and in real scholarship as in art, he who lives most to himself lives most for other people, his disciples included."[6]

In his first courses at Amherst—Pre-Shakespearean Drama and the Appreciation and Writing of Poetry—Frost proposed "a lot of reading just off the main line of English Literature" as well as a new way to approach the subject. He used J. M. Manly's *Specimens of the Pre-Shakespearean Drama* (1897), which included early plays by Lyly, Greene, Peele and Kyd. As at Pinkerton, the students gave public performances of his own abridgments and got to know Frost more informally during rehearsals. He also advanced, through his ideas and his own work, the cause of American literature, which had barely been taught or studied in colleges or universities. At Frost's suggestion, a course in this subject was added to the Amherst curriculum in the fall of 1917. In the early 1920s, he also taught an unusual course on moral "judgments in history, religion and the arts. A study by the case method [as in law school], of how such judgments are arrived at and evaluated." Frost revealed his spontaneous, intuitive approach, his emphasis on the creation and effects of poetry in his course description at the New School for Social Research in New York:

> The method of this course, as appropriate to an inquiry into pure poetry, will be one of soundings for meanings, rather than one of general analysis. Some attention will be given to . . . sense and music in poetry, to the truth of metaphor; to the capacity of poetry to transcend all boundaries. Because the truth about poetry is infinitely subtle, all formal requirements of the lecturer's procedure are excluded. The program of each session will remain tentative to the last moment, in order that the lecturer, after experiencing the needs of his audience, may have free choice among the means for satisfying such needs.[7]

Frost was also far ahead of his time in believing that extracurricular activities, especially sports, were an important part of education. He had compared boxing and poetry as competitive endeavors and declared that athletics "are nearer the arts than scholarship ever thought of being." Writing in 1921 to Untermeyer, who also took a keen interest in baseball, Frost said that John McGraw, the famous manager of the New York Giants, had just recruited to his pitching staff an Amherst graduate who had taken Frost's course in writing. Pleased by his pupil's success, Frost claimed it was he and no one else who had taught the young man "style and control."

Frost took a personal interest in many of his students and encouraged them to stop by his house—a "perpetual at-home charity clinic" for young poets—to talk until the middle of the night. He said that Reuben Brower was the best student he ever had at Amherst, and Brower justified the compliment by becoming a professor at Harvard and writing one of the best books about his old teacher. True to his iconoclastic principles, Frost told Gardner Jackson that he was wasting his time at Amherst and ought to follow Frost's example by leaving college and bumming around for a couple of years. He encouraged and helped the Amherst student-poet Merrill Root in a different way by warning him about the influence of Frost's poetry and urging him to find his own voice.

Frost reserved the most extraordinary treatment for another promising poet, James Hayford. At Frost's prompting, Hayford wrote, he was awarded the first and only Amherst special student fellowship, with the following conditions: "Receive $1,000 (perhaps like $10,000 now); Stay away from graduate schools, art colonies, big cities, and Europe; Produce a book of poems in 20 years; Be terrifyingly on my own. . . . Frost wanted the Fellowship to spare its holder the necessity, at least for a while, of taking more degrees; to prevent his getting mixed up with literary cliques; and to save him from winding up as a professor, a critic, or an expatriate—in short, to save him for American poetry." Frost's plan to protect Hayford from malign influences was effective and he became, according to the poet X. J. Kennedy, a first-rate New England writer.[8]

Frost had three close friends and allies on the Amherst faculty. When his family first arrived in their battered old car, complete with chickens in coops, his hospitable next-door neighbors, Otto and Ethel Manthey-Zorn, lent them blankets and Otto slept under his overcoat that night. Born in Wisconsin in 1879, Manthey-Zorn earned his B.A. at Western Reserve and his Ph.D. at Leipzig. He joined the Amherst faculty in 1906, became Professor of German in 1918 and published *Germany in*

Travail, about the postwar scene, in 1922. Later on, he wrote a book on Nietzsche, and translated Kant into English and Frost's "The Death of the Hired Man" and "West-Running Brook" into German. Manthey-Zorn, who became Frost's close confidant at Amherst and a frequent correspondent after he left, admired Frost's "rebel side, his personal gifts, element of surprise, electrification of others, his genius."

George Whicher, a member of the English department, shared Frost's interest in Latin poetry, translated *The Goliard Poets* (1948) and wrote a life of Emily Dickinson. Whicher seemed to Wade Van Dore "a rather mild sort of person—neutral in color and in his convictions," but he could arouse Frost's anger when he opposed him in academic controversy. In a letter to Untermeyer of 1924, Frost called Whicher "the petty sort of half-friend. I've found him out in several deceits and concealments I don't admire." Generally speaking, however, their relations were cordial, and Whicher wrote three admiring biographical and critical essays on Frost. Another younger English department friend, George Roy Elliott, was born in Canada and had taught at Bowdoin before coming to Amherst. Though Frost disliked his fanatical religious views and heavy drinking, he respected his scholarly books on Shakespeare and modern poetry, and was grateful for Elliott's two appreciative essays on his work.

Frost's English friend Walter de la Mare visited him in January 1917, just after he arrived in Amherst. The poet stayed with Frost and when he took him to the train station the next morning, during a heavy rainstorm, their trolley car knocked over a wandering cow and broke her leg. The violent incident reminded Frost of the war in Flanders.[9]

Frost's pioneering ideas and provocative techniques of teaching, his privileged position and assault on conventional academic methods and values aroused considerable hostility. He fanned the flames by freely expressing his "violent prejudices and hatreds," not only about the literary scene in general but also about specific dead-wood colleagues at Amherst. One student recalled that Frost's "denunciation of the life of the Bohemian intellectuals in New York would have delighted the ears of any fundamentalist preacher in that wicked town. . . . He descended to gossip with a genuine relish and abused even teachers close to him on campus."

Frost himself acknowledged the reasons for his colleagues' disapproval: "Always I was under the suspicion of the old-timers that I was dodging work. I was. I responded [only] if something interested me." His fellow teachers wondered whether he was doing anything significant

—or even anything at all. One faculty member sneered at him with: "You teach courses in genius, I hear." Another angry professor, who collected Wordsworth, made a gratuitous comparison between Frost and his illustrious predecessor. "The only thing Wordsworthian he could conceive me capable of," Frost told Felix Frankfurter, referring to Wordsworth's youthful indiscretion, "would be having had an illegitimate child in France in the French Revolution."[10]

Despite occasional jibes from old-guard faculty members, Frost's controversial views were tolerated, even encouraged, by the liberal president, Alexander Meiklejohn, who had hired him on Stark Young's recommendation. Meiklejohn was born in Rochdale, England, in 1872 and came to America in 1880. He graduated from Brown, where he was a philosophy professor and dean, and became president of Amherst in 1912. A stimulating teacher, he would provoke class discussion with questions like: "Is Hardy's best novel better or worse than Meredith's?" "On the [lecture] platform he had personal charm, pungent wit, dazzling dialectical skill, and the eloquence of a convinced crusader." He inspired students, hired new teachers, revised the curriculum—which he felt should have a clear design—and brought the college "wide and favorable recognition."

In 1918 Frost, who seemed to have a good deal in common with Meiklejohn, mentioned that he "has been faultless in the honor he has done poetry in the person of me." But by 1919 Frost had become increasingly intolerant of Meiklejohn's radical, socialistic, even communistic views, which opposed his own belief in individualism and self-reliance, and said he was quite out of sympathy with the many changes the president was making in the college. In November 1919 Elinor wrote Lesley that he was thinking of leaving Amherst: "The atmosphere here is rather unpleasant. Papa has nothing to do with Mr. Meiklejohn, and I think the end will probably be that Mr. Meiklejohn will make things so disagreeable in return that papa will want to leave. That might not be such a great misfortune, for I feel that he is wasting his life here. The boys are after him nearly every evening, and he is tired all the time."

Their ideological disagreement reached a crisis that fall when Frost launched an attack on his former admirer Stark Young—a follower of Meiklejohn and frequent subject of Frost's gossip and abuse. A Mississippian, seven years younger than Frost, who had taught at Texas before coming to Amherst, Young published poems, plays, fiction, essays and translations, and later became drama critic of the *New Republic*. Frost knew Young was homosexual, and heard from students that he invited young men to his dimly lit, incense-filled apartment, read them homo-sexual literature and tried to attract them to abnormal behavior. He had advised Holt to reject Young's poems. Believing him to be a bad moral influence, he also went to Meiklejohn and demanded that Young be fired. Meiklejohn explained that in college, as in the real world, men would always be subject to temptation and had to learn to establish their own defenses against immorality. He thought Frost could counteract Young's influence. Frost replied that he did not come to Amherst to "counteract" anything. Dissatisfied with Amherst, Meiklejohn and Young, Frost submitted his resignation.

Young survived the attempted purge, but was bitter about Frost's ingratitude and betrayal. He later gave a jaundiced account of how Frost had wormed his way into Amherst and tried to expose the flaws in Frost's character: "I was the one that started Frost off at University classes. I persuaded Mr. Meiklejohn to that for *six months*. Frost worked the tuber-cular pallor, mussed hair, sensitive feelings to get it all extended—against, I think, Mr. Meiklejohn's better judgment. I know very well Frost's poses, his grudging and jealous (and piously admitted) nervous-ness about other living poets." Frost, as Elinor suggested, left the college in June 1920 with no regrets and told Bartlett: "I served my time at Amherst (four years), the same as at Pinkerton . . . to show that as the father of a family I could do what I had to do and then turned to something I liked better."[11]

III

Frost found the mountain farm in Franconia, New Hampshire, too cold, even in summer, to grow fruit and vegetables. In the summer of 1920, after resigning from Amherst to devote himself to poetry and apple farming, he began to look for a more temperate location, about a hundred miles south, near Bennington, Vermont. He was helped in his search by the novelist Dorothy Canfield Fisher, who had advised Holt to publish his poems and whom he had first met in Boston in 1915. Fisher, "square-jawed, graying, and with deep-set blue eyes, was [forty-one] and of Vermont pioneer stock; she had studied at the Sorbonne and at Columbia and had spent much time abroad. Now she lived a quiet domestic life on a farm near Arlington, Vermont."

Invoking his extortionate agreement with Raymond Holden, Frost

sold him the lower half of the Franconia farm and in November 1920
moved to the new farm at South Shaftsbury, near Arlington, in the
southwestern corner of the state. The half-stone, half-wood house, built
in 1779, had fine views of the mountains to the east and west. It had a
leaky roof and no running water, bathroom or furnace, but the Frosts
liked to live in a rough and rugged way. On November 10 Fisher wrote
Alfred Harcourt: "The Frosts are on their own farm now and the Lord
only knows whether they will make a go of it. [We] are ready to do
anything we can, from cookstoves to plumbing. If they only keep well."

In August 1922, after repairing and renovating the house, Frost and
three of his children explored the countryside by hiking and camping
out along the 261-mile "Long Trail," which ran the length of Vermont
from Massachusetts to Canada. As in Gloucestershire when the war
broke out, he bought some weird provisions along the way: steaks and a
two-pound box of chocolates; and one night had to break into an empty
mountain cabin to find a place to sleep. The vigorous children all
completed 225 miles; the forty-eight-year-old Frost did 125 miles before
he dropped out, slept alone on the ground and spent the next day
soaking his feet in a running brook.

Elinor, always something of an invalid, never took part in such energetic activities. She looked after Frost's business matters, but was as
disorganized about arranging readings as she was in the kitchen. She
wanted his poetry, which bound them together, to remain private and
strictly for themselves, and felt that his increasing success merely de-
based his work. After he became famous, she resented the many outsid-
ers who sought him out and came between them. Forced into the
background, she complained: "It is rare when anyone pays much attention to a poet's wife," but when the talk "turned to poetry she entered
into the conversation and spoke with authority."[12]

The poet John Holmes, like most of Frost's friends, found the reclu-
sive Elinor—the guardian of family privacy—rather difficult to understand: "She was inscrutable in many ways, shy and untamed, and fiercely
watchful. She never went to his readings more than once or twice, but
suffered at home"—probably because she disliked his public persona,
his mesmerizing performances and his personal revelations. She also
censured and restrained his unseemly vanity and malicious comments
about other writers. After his first success in 1915, Elinor kept up a
barrage of criticism and "began to point out all his little shortcomings."
She complained about her frequent pregnancies but was stoical about
her illness: "She used to talk about the sufferings of women in child-

birth. . . . [But later on,] when she was going through all her cancer troubles, she never complained of her sufferings."

To one faculty wife, who did not know them well and could not perceive the tensions swirling beneath the surface of their marriage, the Frosts (who kept up appearances) seemed to be a perfectly harmonious couple: "She gave the impression of being content to be her poet-husband's helpmate, supportive of his wants, protective of his health, and happy to be in the background on social occasions. Robert, in turn, seemed to us completely dependent upon her advice and judgment not only on domestic matters but on literary problems as well." The truth, as Frost bitterly confided to Untermeyer, was quite different. Elinor preferred the obscurity of Derry to the years of fame. He therefore resented Amy Lowell's unpardonable attempt to portray his wife as "the conventional helpmeet of genius." He exclaimed that the ethereal Elinor, wary of worldly honors that detracted from their "poetic life," never did anything at all to help his education, career, finances, well-being or public esteem: "Elinor has never been of any earthly use to me. She hasn't cared whether I went to school or worked or earned anything. She resisted every inch of the way my efforts to get money. She is not too sure that she cares about my reputation. She wouldn't lift a hand or have me lift a hand to increase my reputation or even save it. And this isn't all from devotion to my art at its highest. She seems to have the same weakness I have for a life that goes rather poetically; only I should say she is worse than I." As Frost's poetic conscience, Elinor felt his work had to be idealistic and pure, and that performance degraded its inner truth.

Yet Frost also told Newdick, in a significant phrase, "how much of my thinking was wound around Elinor's silences"—or her silent disapproval.[13] Most of the love lyrics in *A Boy's Will*, especially the conciliatory overtures after their quarrels—"My November Guest" and "A Dream Pang"—were addressed to Elinor. "A Servant to Servants" and "Paul's Wife" seemed to reflect on her character; "The Subverted Flower" and "Putting in the Seed" obliquely described their passionate sex life; "Home Burial" openly portrayed her response to Elliott's death; "Beyond Words" was as bitter and fierce as "The Pasture" (his prelude to *North of Boston*) was tender and gentle. There is no doubt that from their first meeting in high school until her death in 1938 Elinor, Frost's first reader and principal adviser, both inspired and nurtured his poetic flame.

Elinor's delicate, sometimes dangerous state of health remained a persistent worry. In the fall of 1915, eight years after the death of her last baby, she became pregnant for the seventh time. She got seriously ill and the doctor issued grave warnings about her heart. After Untermeyer put her in touch with a doctor in New York, she had an abortion. In December—when he took over her duties as family nurse, cook and chambermaid—Frost said he had no time for poetry and felt they were lucky to be alive. Ten years later, at the age of fifty-two, Elinor's miscarriage during her eighth pregnancy led to her complete nervous collapse.

Frost also had family troubles, in the years just after the war, with his daughter Lesley and his sister, Jeanie. According to Lesley's daughter, Frost was an overprotective, Victorian paterfamilias, who meddled in his children's personal affairs, tried to supervise Lesley's love life and disapproved not only of her friendship with Raymond Holden but also of her early romance in New York. Peter Davison, who knew both father and daughter, said the strikingly blond and blue-eyed Lesley wondered whether her boyfriends—who would stay in the house to talk to Frost instead of going out with Lesley—came to see her or the famous poet. Holden, whose intentions were honorable, thought Frost was unduly suspicious: "Robert expected trouble and trouble troubled him. He had an idea that as an unhappy man [in marriage] I would be sure to turn to his daughter Lesley, with whom I had a very pleasant but completely innocent relationship."

Frost had very little money during the war. Elinor tried to make Lesley's clothes, but had no sense of style, and Lesley went to college with only one dress. During her freshman year at Wellesley College, her English teacher was the same dull and pedantic Alfred Sheffield who had disliked "The Tuft of Flowers" and had been unpleasant to Frost at Harvard in the late 1890s. Worse still was her Latin teacher, Miss Waite, who emphasized the fine points of grammar and had neither love of the language nor a sense of literary values. The absolute antithesis of Frost, she criticized Lesley's background in Latin (which Frost had taught her), did everything possible to make the subject painful and stifled Lesley's enthusiasm by giving low marks for trivial mistakes. In a furious letter to Lesley of November 13, 1917, Frost supported his daughter, defended his own emphasis on giving the spirit a chance and cursed "the Latin-bitch": "I was sick all night last night with anger and so was mamma. You ought to have heard what mamma called them all every time she woke up. It's not so much anything as it is our own stupidity in letting such people get one on us. Damn their loathsomeness."[14]

Lesley felt like a prisoner at Wellesley and pleased her father by transferring to Barnard College. But she was also unhappy in New York and withdrew from Barnard after her sophomore year. Frost took some responsibility for this and told Harriet Monroe: "My line of talk isn't calculated to make her like any institution. You know how I'm always at it against colleges, in a vain attempt to reconcile myself with them." Later on, when she could not get the kind of job she wanted, Lesley accused Frost of discouraging her and ruining her chances of a decent career. "I needed my degree," she exclaimed; "why didn't they *make* me see it?"

Four years after she dropped out of college, Frost thought Lesley had turned out quite well and told a friend: "She is 23, inured to all sorts of college society and at once bookish and a girl of action." Hart Crane, who encountered Lesley in May 1919, during her year at Barnard, was tremendously impressed: "I met Robert Frost's daughter at a theatre party the other evening, and had the pleasure of taking the very interesting and handsome young lady back to her Columbia dormitory. I am hoping to see more of her at a near date, as she is worth looking at." Fortunately for Lesley, the homosexual, suicidal Crane was not really interested in women.[15]

Frost had never been on good terms with his younger sister, Jeanie, who had had a traumatic childhood and a troubled adult life. He told Thompson that she "had once been toyed with by an older boy when she was about three years old." Later on she suffered long periods of weeping and hysteria. In high school (which she never finished), Frost once had to slap her to make her stop crying and she had called him a coward for hitting her. During childhood she also had typhoid fever, was operated on for curvature of the spine and was thought to be epileptic. After her mother's death in 1900 her eccentric behavior seemed to increase, and she always frightened Frost's children with her wild talk. In her twenties Jeanie, an attractive young woman, adopted what was then considered a dubious profession and became an artist's model. She slept with a friend of Frost's named Mills, who sexually traumatized her, abandoned her and "broke her life."

In 1914 Jeanie wrote two lucid letters to Wilbur Rowell, who administered her grandfather's estate, asking him to send money to Frost in England. In 1918, when she was forty-two, she managed—with help and money from Frost—to graduate from the University of Michigan. But she also suffered from nervous instability, moods of depression and fits of raving. She became a teacher but, like her mother, was frightened by her rough male pupils and unable to keep her job. In 1917 she espoused unpopular communist and pacifist views, opposed American entry in the war and took part in protest marches. But she also sympathized with Kaiser Wilhelm and the German enemy. She went to a Red Cross meeting where ladies were knitting clothing for the soldiers overseas and provoked them by remarking: "Send the boys home, and their mothers will knit for them." On Armistice Day in 1918 she refused to salute the American flag, was mobbed by both her students and fellow teachers, and driven out of town.

Jeanie had for many years been obsessed with the idea that she would be captured by criminals and forced into prostitution. In Portland, Maine, in March 1920, she became hysterical about the war and fought the police when they were called to a drugstore to subdue her. She was locked in a cell, diagnosed as demented and destined for an insane asylum. Summoned by the police, Frost went up to Portland and found that Jeanie had been rescued by a lady friend and been placed in the care of a doctor. But Frost agreed with the medical authorities and felt she ought to be committed to the state hospital in Augusta. He secured the necessary legal documents and brought the police to Jeanie's home. While her friend scratched Frost's face until it bled, the police pushed Jeanie into a taxi and drove her to the asylum. Frost visited her there several times a year.

In April, between her confinement and his first visit, Frost told Untermeyer that Jeanie had a nervous sensibility and a horror of the physical, and had been destroyed before the war by a coarse and brutal world. He also revealed the reason for their estrangement: "She has had very little use for me. I am coarse for having had children and coarse for having wanted to succeed a little. She made a birth in the family the occasion for writing us once of the indelicacy of having children."

In 1914 Frost had written in "A Servant to Servants":

> They kept him
> Locked up for years back there at the old farm.
> I've been away once—yes, I've been away.
> The State Asylum. I was prejudiced;
> I wouldn't have sent anyone of mine there;
> You know the old idea—the only asylum
> Was the poorhouse, and those who could afford,
> Rather than send their folks to such a place,
> Kept them at home; and it does seem more human.

But he could not possibly keep Jeanie at home, and wrote Lesley: "We will do all we can for her short of darkening our lives with what we are not to blame for." In 1922 he told Wilbur Rowell that though Jeanie had long lucid intervals during which she spoke and wrote normally, she was never in control of herself. Whenever she seemed to be recovering, she cracked up again. Suffering from both depression and delirium, Jeanie was confined to the violent ward. In September 1925 she wrote a heart-wrenching letter to Frost, which described her childhood fears, traced the origins of her disease to the turn of the century and provided terrifying insight about her madness:

> I am very peculiar and did not start right. If I ever was well and natural it was before I can remember. I hate to have anyone understand how I feel in a way. To the mind of anyone who could understand the condition of my mind, there could not be any worse horror. . . .
>
> When I have been sick here as I have been twice, delirious, so that I couldn't recognize anyone, I imagine myself forever unable to move and without any feeling or interest, or else I pace back and forth feeling forever glum, caring for nothing. . . . Few people realize how entirely this depression cuts me off from things so that only for occasional moments I might as well be stone deaf and blind. . . .
>
> When there's a party now sometimes there's nothing to do for the very insane ones can't play cards. . . . At times I feel almost sure I am incurable—at others afraid. . . . When I get these excited spells I feel quite a little better, my nose bleeds slightly. When I put my handkerchief in just once there's blood on it and my hands won't stop bleeding.[16]

After nine years of mental deterioration, Jeanie died in the asylum in September 1929.

Despite his spectacular return to America, the postwar years were difficult for Frost. His extraordinary teaching at Amherst provoked the wrath of his conservative colleagues and after a dispute with Young and Meiklejohn he resigned from the college—without prospects of other employment. He had to sell the Franconia farm. The success of his poetry caused his estrangement from Elinor, who became seriously ill in 1915. Lesley dropped out of college—and then blamed her father for her decision. He went through the agonizing experience of seeing

Jeanie go mad and committing her to a bleak state institution. These failures and tragedies made him feel guilty and afraid that he might also become insane. They had a disastrous effect on his work and during 1917–19 he published only four poems. Now and in the years to come he would have to draw on his great resiliency and courage in order to maintain his equilibrium and keep on writing.

10

Michigan and
the Lecture Circuit
1921–1926

I

Frost adopted as his motto a line from his current poem "New Hampshire": "Me for the hills where I don't have to choose." He had established his itinerant pattern early in life and continued to move around restlessly, frequently changing academic positions and constantly setting off for another speaking engagement. He was always on the lookout for a new farm if it had an old house and a good view, and could be bought for a modest price. As he wrote in "A Hundred Collars":

> What I like best's the lay of different farms,
> Coming out on them from a stretch of woods,
> Or over a hill or round a sudden corner.

Though always on the move, he had a powerful sense of place and instinct for building his nest, and wanted his wife and family around him. He acquired a second farm in 1929, but continued to search for his ideal spot.

"I no sooner get settled in South Shaftsbury," he told Bartlett in June 1922, "than I am at it again for some reason, looking for another likely farm that could be bought right. I believe I'll end by buying a number of five hundred dollar farms in all sorts of places . . . for a change of residence when I get restless." He realized that his frequent moves stimulated his thought and helped define his sense of identity, and added: "I can't get over the strangeness of having been in so many places and yet remained one person."

Speaking of colleges, Frost playfully told Cox: "I ran away twice and I walked away a good many times," and explained to Bartlett that "my early detaching of myself twice over from colleges when young leaves me with a certain detachment in viewing their troubles now I am old."[1] Though he now wanted patronage and security, he also believed that poetry needed hardship in order to flourish. He taught, from the postwar years until the end of his life, at Amherst, Michigan, Harvard and Dartmouth. Though always regarded as a treasure and treated as a privileged figure, he loved to be courted and have colleges compete for him, and left Amherst three times and Michigan twice.

Though he preferred New England to the Midwest, he did not much care where he taught and was not particularly concerned with the difference in prestige, atmosphere, colleagues and students at his various colleges and universities. He was mainly interested in good pay, light duties and freedom to write. Like many academic stars, he kept changing colleges when offered a higher salary with fewer responsibilities. Since Frost always dealt on the highest level with the president (rather than with the dean or chairman), and was dependent on his generosity, good will and personal friendship, a change of president often signaled a change for Frost. His "permanent" and "lifetime" appointments were rarely permanent or for life.

In the early and mid-1920s Frost shifted back and forth—while playing one against the other—between Michigan (1921–23), Amherst (1923–25), Michigan (1925–26) and Amherst (1926–38). He had resigned from Amherst in 1920 after quarreling about Stark Young with Meiklejohn, whose liberal policies he detested. In 1923, after Meiklejohn was forced to resign, Frost left his two one-year appointments at Michigan and returned to Amherst. He left Amherst for Michigan in 1925 when he was offered more money and was not required to teach regular classes. He finally left Michigan for Amherst in 1926, after the death of his friend President Marion Burton, because he preferred a men's college, missed New England and was too far away from his family and farm (see Appendix II).

After resigning from Amherst in 1920, Frost spent a year without an academic salary and soon felt the pinch. He realized he had to find ways to earn more money and was especially responsive to Michigan's offer. At this moment the role of creative writer in the university was being created and defined. For the first time in American higher education, Miami University in Ohio had recently appointed a poet-in-residence, Percy MacKaye, who helped Frost secure a similar position at Michigan, for one year at $5,000. The contrast to Amherst was striking. Michigan is a large, coeducational, Midwestern state university on a sprawling campus in Ann Arbor, an attractive college town along the Huron River, about twenty-five miles west of Detroit. It had 10,000 students and many graduate schools.

Frost had no assigned work and was supposed to concentrate on his writing. But as the local lion he was frequently invited to dine out, had to give many informal speeches (in which he expressed his ideas about poetry and education), and was not able to write very much. He took an active part in the student literary society, and arranged readings by the leading American poets: Amy Lowell, Carl Sandburg, Vachel Lindsay, Louis Untermeyer and Witter Bynner as well as the British writers Padraic Colum and J. C. Squire.

Amy drew a crowd of 2,500 people, who were more interested in her bizarre appearance and eccentric behavior than in her mediocre verse. Frost could not help trying—in a farcical way—to sabotage and steal her show. He first pulled the wire of the special reading lamp she always carried with her, which blew a fuse and plunged the vast audience into darkness. While the janitor made the necessary repairs, he and Amy amused the invisible spectators with their jokes. After the lights went on, Frost tripped over the cord of the restored lamp and upset her pitcher of ice water.

In April 1925 Amy tried to bully Frost and Untermeyer into attending a party in her honor. She even invited Frost to her mansion so he could rehearse, under her direction, what she thought he should say. Annoyed by her imperious manner and by the satirical passage in her *Critical Fable,* they decided not to attend. When she suddenly died the following month, Frost made amends by writing an obituary tribute for the *Christian Science Monitor* in Boston and praising her in the vaguest possible way: "She helped make it stirring times for a decade to those immediately concerned with art. . . . Her poetry was forever a clear resonant calling off of things seen."

Though Frost had taught girls at Pinkerton and Plymouth, he found, after a couple of years at Michigan, that he disliked teaching female students. He told Lesley that they knew he was married, but made seductive advances and became hostile when he rejected them. They also unexpectedly challenged his authority by advocating feminist ideas made popular during the war: "I'm not fond of teaching girls in their new state of mind. They started out escorting me home from night classes and proposing canoe rides and when I blocked that turned on me in some sort of sex resentment and gave me one of the worst classes of wrangle and flat contradictions I ever had. . . . I had the most scratching, screeching row of females all over me in my class last night that ever befell me in pedagogy. The little she devils lit into me . . . for nothing but to assert their equality."

The first year at Michigan ended acrimoniously when Frost got into an absurd dispute with his formidable landlady, Mrs. D'Ooge, about a chamberpot. The university had found him a large and imposing house on Washtenaw Avenue, which required a servant (though they decided to do without one), and wanted him to live, Frost said, in a style worthy of his exalted position. When describing the quarrel in a hilarious letter to Untermeyer, Frost mocked her name by connecting it to a line ("Get along little dogie") in a cowboy song, revealed his taste for classical archeology and indulged in a scatological pun: "the distinguished Greek and Latin Professor's Widow (pronounced Dogie as in the Chisholm Trail) accused me out of a clear sky of having stolen or otherwise nefariously made away with one of the five iron pisspots she would swear she had distributed to the five bedrooms of the house she rented to us in Ann Arbor. She wouldn't claim it was an Etruscan vase. Neither was it Mycenaean or Knossian ware. Nevertheless it represented a loss of fifty cents and she proposed to make a stink about it if not in it. I haven't admitted that I could have stolen a thing I no longer have any use for since I stopped drinking."[2]

In the spring of 1923, when Frost was completing his second year at Michigan, the controversy surrounding President Meiklejohn reached a crisis at Amherst. He had alienated the conservative elements of the fifty-member faculty by his high-handed manner and pursuit of reform. He forced inert professors to resign, shifted the emphasis from a classical to a contemporary course of study and changed the teaching methods from formal lectures to class discussion. The faculty split into hostile camps, and his enemies, claiming he had failed to support religion on campus, called for his resignation.

Meiklejohn survived the initial attacks, but was finally brought down by excessive personal debts. He enjoyed the comforts of life and had an extravagant wife. For years he had overdrawn his annual salary and then "accepted private contributions from trustees to cover the excess." When the trustees (who included Vice-President Calvin Coolidge, an Amherst graduate) called for his resignation, he declared that they—rather than he—ought to leave. But the pressure continued to mount, his personal integrity was damaged and after eleven years as president he was forced to resign. Though asked to remain as Professor of Logic and Metaphysics, he chose to leave the college and took nine other professors with him. Felix Frankfurter supported Meiklejohn in the *New Republic,* and in the *New York World* Walter Lippmann wrote: "He could inspire but could not manage. He did magnificently with students and failed lamentably with grown-ups, yet he made Amherst one of the most distinguished small colleges in America."

Meiklejohn's departure paved the way for Frost's return. George Olds, a professor of mathematics who succeeded Meiklejohn, actively recruited Frost in an attempt to restore the depleted faculty. He also offered him the position of poet-in-residence, with only two courses a year and no other duties. In his literature course, loosely defined as "The Writing of Rebels," Frost taught Cellini's *Autobiography* (written in the sixteenth century but not published until 1728); Gibbon's *Memoirs,* 1796 (in which he submissively wrote, after giving up his fiancée: "I sighed as a lover, I obeyed as a son"); George Borrow's *Lavengro* (1851), on his wanderings with the Gypsies; Melville's *Typee* (1846), on his adventures among the cannibals of the Marquesas Islands; Emerson's *Representative Men* (1850), on Plato, Swedenborg, Montaigne, Shakespeare, Napoleon and Goethe; Thoreau's *Walden* (1854), an old favorite; and, rather incongruously, the conventional poems of Christina Rossetti.

Frost's regular courses left him less time to write at Amherst than at Michigan. In March 1924, toward the end of his first year, he longed for another long trip to Europe and regretfully told Untermeyer: "Amherst goes sadly, I'm afraid I have to admit. I'd like to look at it receding from the deck of an outward bound ship." By November the *Boston Evening Transcript* announced that Frost had accepted a better offer, with no teaching, and was returning to Ann Arbor: "His fellowship at the University of Michigan has been created especially for him, and will exist for life. The fellowship entails no obligations of teaching and it provides for all living expenses. He will have entire freedom to work and write."[3] But in pursuing the Holy Grail of a regular salary with no duties, Frost soon realized that if he did not teach regular classes, he would be called upon by faculty and students and used to generate publicity for the institution.

During his second stay at Michigan Frost lived in a double-columned Greek Revival house on Pontiac Road. Remembering his former occupation, he wittily described it as "poultry architecture": two legs in front and two wings on the side. He also published three poems in Henry Ford's *Dearborn Independent,* which had once been virulently anti-Semitic but now adopted a more temperate approach. (Ford later bought the house Frost had lived in and moved it to Dearborn Village.) But he was plagued by the same problems in 1926 as in 1922, when a local newspaper reported: "The social whirl has kept up for him ever since he arrived in Ann Arbor and we surmise that he has had but little time to devote to his own work." Frost told the reporter: "When I sit down to write I must see before me a few days of undisturbed concentration"—and never seemed to find those days. In January 1926 Frost told Bartlett that he was being drawn back to his region, and his children, who were now in their twenties and had begun to lead their own lives:

> I am not sure of hanging on long at Ann Arbor though the position is supposed to be for life. It's too far from the children for the stretch of our heart strings. Carol probably won't be budged. And here are Lesley and Marjorie in the book business in Pittsfield. We've just come on to be with Marj for an operation for appendicitis. She's been having bronchial pneumonia. We don't like to be scattered all over the map as long as we don't have to be. Elinor stands being separated from the children worse than I do. What I want is a farm in New England once more.

In 1926 Amherst topped Michigan's offer by paying him $5,000 for a ten-week, part-time position. Frost, finally weary of the constant moves, remained on their faculty for the next twelve years. In September 1932 he bought a big Victorian house at 15 Sunset Avenue in Amherst. He was succeeded as Michigan poet-in-residence by the eighty-two-year-old English Poet Laureate, Robert Bridges, whom he had met in London. Unfamiliar with transatlantic flora, he told Frost: "You have no trees in America." Then, mentioning his professional credentials, he asked: "Are the boys rough there? . . . I was a child specialist when I was a doctor."[4]

II

Frost's personal contact with the poets he invited to read at Amherst and Michigan enabled him to cast a cold eye on his competitors. In 1924 his list of the best living American poets included the older traditional writers: Lindsay (whose "General William Booth Enters into Heaven" Frost parodied in his own "John L. Sullivan Enters Heaven"), Robinson, Sandburg, Lowell and Conrad Aiken. About ten years later he told Newdick that "Robinson [was] the best of the moderns. Then Lindsay.

Isabelle Moodie Frost, 1876: an auburn-haired, high-colored woman, who spoke with a strong Scotch burr.

William Prescott Frost, Jr., 1872: a dark and brooding man, like Heathcliff in his sullen silences.

Robert and Jeanie Frost,
c. 1879: "Bob is as beautiful
as a little bear."

Jeanie Frost, c. 1900: "I am
very peculiar and did not
start right. If I ever was well
and natural it was before I
can remember."

Elinor White at the time of her marriage, December 1895: "shy, questioning, a little resentful of strangers . . . a wild, quiveringly sensitive thing."

Robert Frost at the time of his marriage, December 1895: One was "struck by the Celtic dreaminess of his eyes, his quiet unworldliness, his serene detachment of manner."

Lesley, Carol, Marjorie and Irma Frost, Plymouth, New Hampshire, 1911: Lesley was an athletic tomboy, Marjorie sickly but sweet; but Carol was sullen and Irma rather strange.

John Bartlett, 1910: Frost said: "You were the best pupil I ever had."

Sidney Cox in army uniform, c. 1917: a gaunt, blunt, clerical man, with an odd, ascetic manner.

Louis Untermeyer, c. 1950: A generous
and warm-hearted man with a high forehead, thick glasses, a beaked nose, thin
lips and a witty tongue.

Frost in England, 1913: "His face was tanned and weatherbeaten
and his features powerful. His eyes, shaded by bushy grey eyebrows,
were blue and clear."

Ezra Pound, London, c. 1910: "He is six inches taller for his hair and hides his lower jaw in a delicate gold filigree of almost masculine beard."

Edward Thomas in dejection, 1907. Frost said: "We were greater friends than almost any two ever were practicing the same art."

The Frost family, New Hampshire, 1915. Elinor, Robert, Lesley, Irma, Marjorie and Carol: "Lesley was grown up and very handsome. Marjorie was very quiet and shy. Irma and Carol were most delightful children, very talkative and lively."

Frost, 1920s: "His figure was middle-sized and compact, his manner friendly and undemonstrative; he looked at you directly, his talk was shrewd and speculative."

Frost and Elinor, summer 1928: "She was inscrutable in many ways, shy and untamed, and fiercely watchful."

Lesley, Carl Sandburg, Frost and Elinor, Rockford College, Illinois, 1934: Frost said that Sandburg "would deliberately rumple his white hair and strum his 'geetar' while talking sentimental, infantile politics."

Bernard DeVoto, 1934: The short, porcine DeVoto had thick glasses, thick lips and a broad flat Babe Ruth nose with tunnel-like nostrils.

T. S. Eliot at Faber & Faber, 1920s: A tall, sibylline figure "with features of clerical cut," he had a prim demeanor and fastidious manner of speech.

Frost and Wallace Stevens, Key West, 1940: "The trouble with you, Wallace, is that you write about *bric-à-brac*."

Bread Loaf Writers' Conference. Top row, third from left: DeVoto; middle row: Untermeyer, Frost and Ted Morrison; bottom row, second from left: Kay Morrison, summer 1939. Kay Morrison, Frost's "devoted, astringent, and affectionate amanuensis," had a slight build and bright auburn hair. The handsome, tweedy, pipe-smoking Ted Morrison was a Roman stoic and stiff-upper-lip New Englander.

Frost on his Vermont farm, 1954: "Time had whitened the poet's hair and marked deep grooves in his face. But he had a kind, lively, and even mischievous expression."

Frost in the Library of Congress, 1958: "The old man sat still, talking and talking, a mischievous grin playing over his strangely wrinkled face."

John F. Kennedy, with Senator Leverett Saltonstall and Secretary of the Interior Stewart Udall, presenting Frost with the Congressional Medal on his eighty-eighth birthday, March 26, 1962. Frost said of Kennedy: "You can't imagine how gifted the lad is."

Frost and Nikita Khrushchev, Gagra, Russia, September 1962: Frost said: "He is very good-natured, hearty, jolly, rough in a way. Probably a good deal deeper than I fathomed."

Next Sandburg—not much or often. Finally, Millay, in early things."

Advising George Roy Elliott about which writers might be willing to read at Amherst, Frost expressed rare admiration of the fiction of Willa Cather. He also made some amusing comments about the notorious sexual life and highly charged verse of Edna Millay, who had written "My candle burns at both ends; / It will not last the night":

> Robinson won't speak for love or money. He stays off the plat-form on principle. I doubt if you could get [Eugene] O'Neill. He makes too much out of his plays for lecture fees to tempt him. . . . Willa Cather is A No. 1. You *must* have her, and you may tell her I said so. Besides being a real figure in letters, she's both thinker and speaker. Miss Millay is a great audience-killer. . . . She loses nothing of course by her reputation for dainty promis-cuity. . . . She is already a love-myth. I don't have to tell you how much I admire her less flippant verse.

Millay's beauty and charm, passionate love affairs and dangerous aura clearly fascinated the puritanical Frost. Keenly aware of how personal appearances influenced a poet's reputation, he felt obliged to express his disapproval. As his former student Merrill Root told the poet Rolfe Humphries: "He doesn't like Millay's work much, says too many of her poems are propaganda for sleeping with a different man each night. Says he wouldn't care if she did, but he wishes she wouldn't insist on telling us about it. Sex poems he doesn't like."[5]

In 1928, when considering the younger poets, Frost predicted that Jeffers, MacLeish, Raymond Holden, Stephen Vincent Benét and Joseph March would achieve prominence. Emphasizing the need for courage in poetry as well as in war, he said the crucial question was: "Did they have the guts to go on?" Jeffers became a good and MacLeish a successful second-rank poet; the other three are now forgotten. It is worth noting that several years after the publication of three important modernist works—"Hugh Selwyn Mauberley" (1920), *The Waste Land* (1922) and *Harmonium* (1923)—Frost did not think Pound, Eliot and Stevens were serious rivals.

Frost also made typically caustic remarks about both his older and younger contemporaries. He particularly disliked Edgar Lee Masters, the prolific Chicago lawyer, who had gone rapidly downhill after the initial success of the *Spoon River Anthology* (1915). Frost told Untermeyer that Masters was too romantic and "false-realistic" for his taste, and scorned "the stagnant stuff he spigots out by the gallon." Elinor Wylie, another glamorous, scandalous and popular poet of the 1920s, had the same defect as Masters. Her appointed task "was to make a false heart ring false. . . . The falser she was the truer she rang."[6] Frost had qualified praise for Marianne Moore (she had published her first book in 1921 and was editor of the *Dial* in the mid-1920s), who was cultured and intelligent, and seemed to channel her sexual energy into poetry. "She gives nothing for the ear," he told Robert Francis. "But she's an intense Bryn Mawr old maid, and that's something." When a Texas professor compared E. E. Cummings to Keats, Frost got angry and told Bartlett: "Keats is hard, clear; cummings is weak, sentimental, nothing else!"

All Frost's judgments, however subjective, were characteristically shrewd, playful and witty. He found it great fun, especially with the worshipful Untermeyer, to demolish the opposition. His malicious observations were bruited about and gave him (as Ciardi noted) a reputation for ferocity. But when the kindly William Carlos Williams finally met Frost in 1939, he emphasized in a letter to his publisher the difference between what he had heard about Frost's notorious malice and provincial persona, and his impressive character and intellect: "He's all right, improved with age in spite of what has been said of him. I hope to see him again soon, a more cosmopolitan person than I had been led to believe. He's a good talker, witty, loaded with information and well able to take care of himself anywhere, anytime—unless I'm greatly mistaken."[7]

Frost's guarded respect for, even fear of, Carl Sandburg—his most formidable competitor in popular anthologies and on the lecture circuit —inspired a stream of corrosive comments. But the good-natured Sandburg, like Robinson, refused to quarrel. Though Frost made fun of Sandburg, as he did of Untermeyer, he was also quite fond of him. He often invited Sandburg to speak and they had, for nearly fifty years, many friendly if contentious meetings. The monkey-faced Sandburg, son of a Swedish immigrant railway worker, was born in Galesburg, Illinois, in 1878. He left school at thirteen, tried many proletarian jobs and was a soldier in Puerto Rico during the Spanish-American War. He eventually worked his way through Lombard College, in his hometown, and became a socialist, journalist, poet and biographer of Lincoln. (Frost would have agreed with Edmund Wilson, who said that Sandburg's *Life* was "the cruellest thing that has happened to Lincoln since he was shot by Booth.") Sandburg capped his career in 1960 by earning $125,000 for working on a Hollywood film, *The Greatest Story Ever Told,* about the life of Christ.

At their first meeting, in 1917, Sandburg "liked him immediately." Noting Frost's solitude, he called him "the strongest, loneliest, friendliest personality among the poets today." Though Frost was drawn to Sandburg, he found his public persona irritating—partly because it resembled his own. He mocked Sandburg as "the hayseed" and condemned his folksy props and naive brand of socialism: "In his stage appearances he wore a blue working man's shirt, and he would deliberately rumple his white hair and strum his 'geetar' while talking sentimental, infantile politics." When confused with Sandburg—as he often was, since they were linked in the public mind—the unmusical Frost would irritably exclaim: "Look! I don't have a 'geetar.' "[8]

Frost, whose own hair was perennially rumpled, disliked Sandburg's hair even more than Pound's, and was always annoyed, even infuriated, by his habit of combing his long silky hair *into* his eyes. Putting the knife in Sandburg, he attacked his personal and poetical defects, and told John Ciardi: "You know the way he dresses, that hair of his and those [string] ties. Everything about him is studied—except his poetry." Referring to Sandburg's first book, *In Reckless Ecstasy* (1904), Frost wisecracked: "Carl's got no brains. That's why he can be ecstatic." In May 1922 Sandburg's successful performance at Michigan provoked a stylish and funny letter from Frost, who was both mesmerized and outraged by his absurd mannerisms:

> We've been having a dose of Carl Sandburg. He's another person I find hard to do justice to. He was possibly hours in town and he spent one of those washing his white hair and toughening his expression for public performance. His mandolin pleased some people, his poetry a very few and his infantile talk none. His affectations have almost buried him out of sight. He is probably the most artificial and studied ruffian the world has had. . . . I heard someone [i.e., Frost] say he was the kind of writer who had everything to gain and nothing to lose by being translated into another language.

Their later meetings always brought out Frost's competitive spirit and tendency to be childish when challenged or thwarted. In 1949, when Frost appeared at Wofford College in South Carolina, Sandburg, living close by, attended the reading. Informed that Sandburg was present, Frost, who always had to be the center of attention, got alarmed and declared: "Carl is here? I'm not going in. . . . Carl is just here to steal the limelight." After the reading, Frost took his usual jab at Sandburg's free verse. Sandburg said: "I came down a mountain forty miles to see you," to which Frost aggressively replied: "Do you live on a high mountain? Higher than mine?" Ignoring Frost's sparring, Sandburg presented him with an inscribed copy of one of his Lincoln volumes. Frost left it on a ledge in the reception room. Sandburg retrieved it and presented it once again. Frost slyly managed to lose it a second time.

In 1960, when Sandburg (who liked Frost and often sought him out) unexpectedly turned up at the Library of Congress, Frost greeted him belligerently and reverted to his old obsession: "Don't you know enough to take your hat off when you come in the house? . . . Don't you ever comb your hair?," to which Sandburg replied: "You could use a comb yourself." When the host asked for speeches after the formal dinner, Frost declared: "Let Carl pay a tribute to me. He oughta praise me, my poetry." A bit later, he wondered if even he had gone too far and, not the least bit contrite, asked his host: "Was I really bad?"[9] Frost's egoism was so transparent that it had a certain charm.

III

On November 15, 1923, Frost re-entered the poetical arena against Sandburg and his other antagonists with his fourth book, *New Hampshire,* which followed the first volume of his *Selected Poems* (March 1923). *New Hampshire* was published in a trade edition of 5,350 copies and, for the first time, in a signed limited edition of an additional 350. Playfully subtitled *A Poem with Notes and Grace Notes,* it is divided into three sections. The first contains the title poem. The second, or "Notes" section, is an ironic jab at Eliot's pedantic footnotes to *The Waste Land,* published the previous year. It contains the longer, blank verse narrative poems from "A Star in a Stoneboat" to "I Will Sing You One-O." The section of "Grace Notes" (not essential to musical harmony but added as an embellishment) contains thirty shorter, rhymed, lyrical poems. Frost's autumnal and wintry poems (which match the season in which they first appeared) are grounded in an expert knowledge of geology and archeology, of botany, ornithology and astronomy. "Frost never wears his learning on his sleeve," Joseph Brodsky observed, "mainly because it is in his bloodstream."

The title poem was partly inspired by an invitation from the *Nation* in the spring of 1922 to write an essay on New Hampshire or Vermont in its current series of critical articles on "These United States" (Edmund Wilson published a piece on New Jersey on June 14). Instead of the essay Frost, most unusually, wrote the first draft of the long title poem—extolling the quiet virtues of the state—straight through a summer's night. When he looked up from his writing board, he was surprised to see the first rays of sunlight and the front lawn coming out of the darkness.[10] The rambling, sententious and irritating "New Hampshire" was Frost's first major failure. Like Hemingway in *Death in the Afternoon* (1932) and *Green Hills of Africa* (1935), he adopted an affected public persona, and moved from the subtle self-questioning of his earlier poems to dogmatic self-assertion. "New Hampshire" anticipated the self-conscious mannerisms of "Build Soil" and his two masques, and damaged his reputation.

Despite the shaky, off-putting start, the book includes no less than ten major poems. In "A Star in a Stoneboat," a fallen meteorite, pulled in a horse-drawn sledge and used as building stone, leads Frost to speculate about man's relation to the celestial universe. "The Grindstone" and "The Ax-Helve," which feature Frost's French-Canadian neighbor Napoleon Guay, subtly connect (like "After Apple-Picking") farm work to the craft of poetry. "The Grindstone" repeatedly contrasts the themes of stasis and motion. The scythe that is being sharpened holds the wheel back as it madly spins around. In this discord between power and intellect, frenzy and reason, the grindstone seems to take on a life of its own and produces tears, hate, bitter thoughts, fears, danger and threats of disaster. All these qualities are somehow needed to make the keen edge of the tool and the near-perfect poem.

In "The Ax-Helve" his neighbor Baptiste expertly catches the speaker's ax while he is chopping wood and insists on substituting a hand-made hickory handle for his machine-made one. As he shapes the helve, Baptiste talks about "knowledge" and defends his decision to keep his children out of school so they can learn from experience rather than from books. After Baptiste has finished his work and stands the axhead upright, Frost (in a startling simile) compares it to when the snake "stood up for" evil in the Garden of Eden. By doing so, he merges the colloquial meaning of "defended" evil with the vivid image of the devilish snake rising from its coil to tempt Eve with fruit from the Tree of Knowledge. In an interview of 1917, the year the poem was first published, Frost suggested the theme: "The Canadian woodchoppers whittle their axe-handles, following the curve of the grain, and they're strong and beautiful. Art should follow lines in nature, like the grain of an axe-handle."

"The Witch of Coös" (named for a county in northern New Hampshire) is a ghost—or skeleton—story inspired by the heroines in the tales of Edgar Poe who burst the confines of their coffins. The down-to-earth narrator confirms the reality of the supernatural events, which were told to him by the witch and her son (two "old-believers," or old-fashioned mediums) when their desire to confess overcame the need to keep their long-held secret. Forty years ago, they told him, a skeleton locked in the cellar carried itself "like a pile of dishes" up two flights of stairs and into the attic. The bones belonged to the woman's lover, whom her late French-Canadian husband, Toffile Lajway (Théophile LaJoie), had killed and buried under the house. Punning and quoting Chaucer's "Prioress' Tale," Frost said the theme of the poem was "murder will out—he's murder trying to get out."[11]

The concise, laconic, perfect and perfectly savage "Fire and Ice," the antithesis of the long-winded "New Hampshire," belongs with the apocalyptic "Once by the Pacific." The alternatives in the title represent passion and hatred, two ways of destroying the world. The poem was inspired by a passage in Canto 32 of Dante's *Inferno,* in which the betrayers of their own kind are plunged, while in a fiery hell, up to their necks in ice: "a lake so bound with ice, / It did not look like water, but like a glass . . . right clear / I saw, where sinners are preserved in ice." The last, understated word in Frost's poem, "suffice," clinches the meaning (like "difference" in "The Road Not Taken") by rhyming with the two lines that end in "ice" and enclosing that thematic word within itself.

Another brilliant, complex and resonant short poem, "Nothing Gold Can Stay," reconsiders (like several lyrics in *A Boy's Will*) the perennial theme of mutability. The opening line—"Nature's first green is gold" —is extremely ambiguous. It could mean either that nature's first green in the springtime has now turned to autumnal gold or that nature's first growth is golden, or precious, because it lasts such a short time, cannot hold its color and fades as soon as the leaves fall in autumn. The fall of the leaves is connected to the Fall of Man, when "Eden sank to grief." Just as the dawn inevitably "goes down" (like the leaves) to day, so the negative thought in the title—which suggests the transience of all things —is inevitably and tragically repeated in the last line of the poem.

"For Once, Then, Something," written in eleven-syllable lines that Frost adopted from Catullus, is about the difficult search for Truth—in life and in art. The speaker seeks Truth by looking into the deep water of a well, which merely gives him back his own reflection. On one notable occasion he does manage to see beyond and through the solipsistic image to something more meaningful in the depths. But he loses it when a drop falls to "rebuke" the clear water and a ripple blurs and blots out the elusive abstract truth he thinks he sees. The title, once again, is repeated in the last line as the speaker reaffirms that he has seen *something*, even if it is only a vague glimpse of what he truly seeks.

"The Need of Being Versed in Country Things" has six quatrains, rhyming in the second and fourth lines of each. The first quatrains describe a burnt, forsaken house, with only its chimney left standing, like a pistil after the petals go. Halfway through the elegiac poem the birds fly through the broken windows of the barn, recalling the sad memories associated with the abandoned farm. The fifth quatrain brings a sudden change of mood as the lilac renews its leaf and the sunlit elm seems touched with a fire that recalls the "glow" and "flame" of its earlier destruction. For the birds who rejoice in the nest they kept, there is really nothing sad about the forsaken house: "One had to be versed in country things / Not to believe the phoebes wept." The speaker would like to believe the phoebes—small American flycatchers whose cry resembles a human lament—"were sorrowful when the master's house burned, but he assures us they were not." The birds sing and nature renews itself, unconcerned with the disasters of men.

"To Earthward"—like "The Subverted Flower," "Putting in the Seed" and "The Silken Tent"—is a poem about physical passion. Frost signaled its personal significance by telling a close friend that one of the great personal changes he had experienced was recorded in "To Earthward." The first four quatrains describe the almost intolerable bliss of his youthful sexual ecstasy: "Love at the lips was touch / As sweet as I could bear; / And once that seemed too much; / I lived on air"—and on a woman's sweet breath. After the sudden change to the present in the fifth stanza, love turns bitter and painful. But "The hurt is not enough: / I long for weight and strength / To feel the earth as rough / To all my length." These lines obliquely suggest the weight of a woman's body as they make love on the rough earth (which clarifies the title) and even a longing for death (as in "Stopping by Woods") with the rough earth above, rather than below, the length of his body. This Hardyesque poem, about the bliss and anguish of love, records (as his letter suggests) a disastrous change in Frost's relations with Elinor.

The masterpiece in *New Hampshire* is the justly famous "Stopping by

Woods on a Snowy Evening." Like "The Road Not Taken," it suggests vast thematic implications through a lucid narrative. And like its predecessor, it has the same technical perfection as the poems by Frost's greatly admired touchstones: Herrick, Shirley and Collins. Frost said that he wrote this poem, "my best bid for remembrance," right off at dawn, after completing "New Hampshire"—though he later revised the second stanza. The most amazing thing about this work is that three of the fifteen lines (the last line repeats the previous one) are transformations from other poems. "He gives his harness bells a shake" comes from Scott's "The Rover" (in Palgrave): "He gave the bridle-reins a shake." "The woods are lovely, dark and deep" comes from Thomas Lovell Beddoes' "The Phantom Wooer": "Our bed is lovely, dark, and sweet." The concluding "And miles to go before I sleep" comes from Keats' "Keen Fitful Gusts": "And I have many miles on foot to fare." Though these three lines are variations from other poets, Frost, writing in the tradition of English verse, makes them original and new, and integrates them perfectly into his own poem.

The theme of "Stopping by Woods"—despite Frost's disclaimer—is the temptation of death, even suicide, symbolized by the woods that are filling up with snow on the darkest evening of the year. The speaker is powerfully drawn to these woods and—like Hans Castorp in the "Snow" chapter of Mann's *The Magic Mountain*—wants to lie down and let the snow cover and bury him. The third quatrain, with its drowsy, dream-like line: "Of easy wind and downy flake," opposes the horse's instinctive urge for home with the man's subconscious desire for death in the dark, snowy woods. The speaker says, "The woods are lovely, dark and deep," but he resists their morbid attraction.

Two years later Hemingway wrote of resisting a morbid impulse in "Big Two-Hearted River" (1925): "In the swamp the banks were bare, the big cedars came together overhead, the sun did not come through. . . . In the half light, the fishing would be tragic. . . . Nick did not want it. He did not want to go down the stream any further today." Frost's character, like Hemingway's, is only *half* in love with easeful death: the other half wants to move on and fulfill the promise of life and the promise of poetry. Vladimir Nabokov, an impressive poet as well as novelist, paid Frost a perceptive tribute in *Pale Fire* (1962) by praising his masterful repetition and closure, showing how the last two lines move from the realistic to the philosophical realm: "Frost is the author of one of the greatest short poems in the English language, a poem that every American boy knows by heart, about the wintry woods, and the dreary dusk, and the little horsebells of gentle remonstration in the dull darkening air, and that prodigious and poignant end—two closing lines identical in every syllable, but one personal and physical, the other metaphysical and universal."[12]

New Hampshire, Frost's most underrated book, revealed his supremacy in shorter poems. It received superficial but favorable reviews from Padraic Colum, Mark Van Doren, Mark De Wolfe Howe and the faithful Louis Untermeyer, and won his first Pulitzer Prize, in 1924.

IV

Frost's teaching jobs at Amherst and Michigan were originally intended to free him from the need to earn money by reading and lecturing around the country. But after he began teaching, and especially after he was released from regular class hours, Frost supplemented his income by "barding around" almost continuously for nearly fifty years—from 1915 until just before his death in 1963. In his round of public readings Frost joined the nineteenth-century tradition that ran from Dickens and Trollope to Oscar Wilde, and from Poe, through Emerson and Twain, to his bombastic but popular contemporary Vachel Lindsay. "Among American writers," John Kemp observes, "perhaps only Mark Twain was a more effective performer."

Like the ancient bards and troubadours, Frost performed his poetry and brought it directly to his audience. He learned to avoid his father's mistakes as a public speaker and soon developed an extremely effective platform manner. His growing fame was based on his persona as well as on his poetry. In contrast to Pound and Eliot, who lived and wrote as expatriates, Frost stayed in close touch with all of America and his verse, spoken in person, seeped into the national consciousness. He also remained in the public eye, whenever he arrived in town, through many newspaper (and, later, television) interviews, and through poems that were constantly reprinted in anthologies and widely used as school texts.

As soon as he returned from England in 1915 Frost began his career as a forty-year-old smiling public man. He started reading at Boston colleges—Tufts, Wellesley and Harvard—and then roamed as far west as Chicago. He eventually abandoned lecture bureaus and began to manage his own affairs, charging $50 at first, reaching $200 to $300 in 1950 and finally getting as much as $1,000 for each appearance. Equating academics with merchants, Frost told Bartlett in 1920: "It is a miserable business being a poet among professors and business men. The only way to make them respect you is to make them pay."

Frost's readings meant physical discomfort, long journeys and psychological strain. A typically grueling three-day schedule in 1916, during which he gave only two talks, involved two sleepless nights on a train. It began when he left his farm at 1 P.M., caught a southbound train from Franconia at 2, arrived in Boston at 9, took a midnight train for New York, got in at 7 A.M. the next morning, left for Philadelphia an hour later, arrived at 10, gave his reading that evening, departed for New York at midnight and caught the northbound 7 A.M. train for his next appearance in Providence. In contrast to his habitual lateness at Pinkerton Academy, Frost was—despite formidable hurdles—always prompt. Though travel meant getting up very early to catch the trains, he told Untermeyer that he had never missed a lecture or been even a minute late to one. The more readings Frost gave, the more he earned, and as his expenses mounted he drove himself mercilessly. He gave forty readings in 1922; fourteen talks, traveling two thousand miles in fifteen days, in 1939; and was still barding around in his eighty-ninth year.

The demands on Frost, once he arrived for his readings, were also emotionally and physically exhausting. Though he told his hosts that he hated to have tiring dinners before his talk, they were often scheduled as part of his performance. A typical day would normally include a boring lunch with university officials, with whom he had little in common, an informal class with untalented students in creative writing, dinner with university professors who pumped him with questions, an evening lecture before 2,000 people and a reception afterwards with local dignitaries, who considered his conversation the main amusement of the evening. Everywhere he went, a shower of meaningless and tedious compliments were heaped upon him. No wonder he told Lesley: "I feel on draught from dawn to dark."[13]

He loved to lecture around the country, but feared the new and strange, which compounded the terror of speaking with the risk of rejection and failure. Reading, to Frost, was the physical representation of the emotional and intellectual risk of writing a poem. It put him in the front line, in the flesh before his audience, and required, he soon learned, a good deal of personal courage.

Frost never conquered his fear of performing. During his first readings his voice trembled and his words came awkwardly. An early listener at Wellesley noted that he had to overcome an acute self-consciousness and nerve-wracking anxiety: "the reading was evidently so difficult for him that I wondered how he would be able to keep up for a continuous hour. . . . I see that he talks more easily than he reads. I only wonder that so sensitive a poet can bring himself to face an audience at all." His friend Richard Wilbur recalled that even when Frost was a famous and celebrated poet, with a warm and receptive audience, he suffered from acid stomach and last-minute panic. Just before Wilbur introduced him at Wesleyan, Frost threatened: "I may not go on!"

When Frost drew a large audience, he worried about whether the hall was big enough to accommodate everyone; when neglected, he became nervous about whether he would receive any more invitations or draw any audience at all. When the lecture room was far too small in Iowa City, Frost, like an old trouper, angrily berated his host: "What the hell do you think I am, a rural schoolteacher that nobody wants to hear? Last week I talked to two thousand in Philadelphia, and they turned five hundred away!" Robert Lowell "heard him say mockingly that hell was a half-filled auditorium." In a poignant letter to Kay Morrison, written in the late 1930s (after the critical failure of *A Further Range,* 1936), Frost expressed his hypersensitivity to anything less than complete triumph: "You'd think I wouldn't have to brag to you about all the success I have in my lectures, but I have to a little to get over the humiliation I have had lately in your eyes and my own from the difficulty of getting me engagements. So many things seem to fall through. I feel like an unwanted child."[14]

Even when the invitations came, the house was full and the audience responsive, Frost still faced the dangers of failure and humiliation. He could not always be at his best, and in July 1921, after six years on the circuit, he was still finding his way. He told Raymond Holden that he felt indifferent about his readings, had not given a good public talk all year and had just failed in New York; he had either to buck up and improve his style or quit the platform and return to his desk. In June 1937 his commencement address at Oberlin College was described as "one of those rambling talks, interesting to hear, with very little relation to the occasion." Reginald Cook, who taught at Middlebury College and recorded many of Frost's talks, noted that "his devices—repetition, alliteration, word play, suspended phrases, verbal indecisiveness, digressive spin-offs, spontaneous asides, and audience interrogation—were those of practiced platform speakers." But he also admitted that the printed transcripts of Frost's discursive ramblings seemed rather banal. Anyone who has attended Frost's performances, or seen him charm his listeners on film, would agree that "invariably the lectures *sound* better than they read. The voice on the sound track, with its pauses, hesitancies, repetitions and stresses, enlivens the talk and evokes a remarkable presence."

Even when his reading went well (as it usually did) Frost often had to deal with unexpected intrusions, with hostile, fatuous or irritating questions, and with boorish behavior. At Allegheny College in March 1924, a bat flew into the lecture hall. As the ladies shrieked and covered their heads with their coats, Frost armed himself with a broom and took some violent swings at the creature. Finally, by climbing into the balcony, he managed to push the bat out through an open window. Frost usually deflected dull or aggressive queries after his talk by saying: "There are some questions I won't answer because I can't and some because I don't want to and some because I'm scared to." When asked, for example, about the quality of education at the Bread Loaf School, he testily replied: "It insults me. I won't answer that."

Richard Wilbur reported that "a woman once said to Robert Frost, who had never actually seen any of her work, 'Should I go on with my poetry?' He said, 'Try and stop and *see* what happens' "—a wise answer to a foolish question. He not only wondered if she had an irresistible urge to write, but also urged her to reflect more deeply on this matter—as she had clearly failed to do before asking him the question. The poet W. D. Snodgrass revealed that provocative inquiries could lead to the kind of startling revelations that the audience hoped to hear at his readings. At Wayne State University some of Snodgrass'

> students must have got hold of Frost before his appearance and asked him about their teacher's idea that "Stopping by Woods" had something to do with suicide. During his reading, he talked about how scandalous it was that certain academics would say such things about him and his work. . . . The next day he appeared in Ann Arbor and read the poem again. Friends who were present told me that after reading it, he looked up startled and said, "Well, now, that does have a good deal of the ultimate about it, doesn't it?" Is it possible that he really had forgotten? He wrote about suicide so obviously elsewhere.[15]

A notorious incident occurred at Connecticut College in 1937 when the president, Katherine Blunt, who had no interest in poetry and ruled like a despot, officiated at Frost's reading. As he proceeded in his characteristically spontaneous, intuitive, associative manner, Miss Blunt suddenly interrupted him and exclaimed: "Mr. Frost, you are not doing what *I* want you to do. I brought you here to explain poetry to my girls. You're just talking at random. Now please talk to us about poetry." Frost continued in his usual oblique fashion, throwing ironic shafts at his blunt adversary, who waited impatiently for ten more minutes and again interjected: "Tell my girls about poetry. Tell them about rime and meter, and explain to them how you write your own poetry." The impasse was finally broken when Frost asked the audience, appalled by the president's behavior, what poems they would like him to read.

Why did Frost, especially when he no longer needed the money, continue to read under such harrowing conditions until two months before his death? He gave readings primarily because fame had come to him so late. He had waited twenty years for recognition and could not get enough of it. He was certainly a first-rate actor, liked performing and was excited by appearing on stage. His ego craved the adulation and sense of power that went with his theatrical performance. His kind of affair, he told Bartlett, was the "one-man show" where he was the star attraction. He disliked the formality of hand-shaking receptions, he informed a friend, and preferred to talk to those who sat at his feet when the lecture was over.

Alluding to the last lines of Keats' "Ode on a Grecian Urn" and emphasizing his ability to produce the right effect when reading his verse, Frost told a young poet: "My whole anxiety is for myself as a performer. Am I any good? That's what I'd like to know and all I need to know." Declining invitations for twenty-five years to read at Williams College, Frost maintained that he had no friends there. But when William Jay Smith was poet-in-residence, he accepted an offer to speak. Frost had a great turn-out, the largest ever at Williams, and Smith assured him that he had attracted more people than Mrs. Roosevelt (whom Frost strongly disliked). Smith was then running for the legislature in nearby Vermont. Pleased with his reception, Frost told the audience to vote for Smith (who was elected) because he was a fine poet.

Despite his doubts, Frost *was* a good performer. In addition to his control of tone, sense of timing and dramatic power, he also had good humor and an instinctive feeling for what would appeal to a particular audience. Speaking to a sophisticated, bohemian group in about 1960, he artfully played on the current use of the word "swinger." He would read "One could do worse than be a swing—er," then pause to stare at the audience and heighten their attention, and conclude "of birches" to roars of laughter and applause. His warmth and affection seemed to flow from his person into his poetry. Though he still kept something back from the public by refusing to read a few private and painful poems, he was willing to come downstage to chat informally or philosophize. He was always eager to hold forth, at length and in public, on any subject that might come up.

Pound and the other avant-garde artists had driven away the audience that had been so keen for poetry at the beginning of the war. Frost, who continued the tradition of Romantic nature poetry that Eliot scorned and rejected, drew people back to the poems. He seemed, as Leslie Fiedler observes, "a reproach to those others who made [readers] feel inferior with their allusions to Provençal and Chinese poetry, their subverted syntax and fractured logic, their unreasonable war against the iambic, their preference for strange, Mediterranean lands and big cities."[16] Frost's health and sanity also seemed a salutary contrast to the alcoholism and madness of the manic poets—Lowell, Berryman, Roethke, Jarrell, Schwartz and Sexton—who began to dominate the poetry scene after World War II. Frost's riveting performances interested and won over not only the general audience of students and readers, but also the more specialized professors, who began to recognize, interpret and publicize his poems in both popular magazines and learned journals. By pretending that it was neither difficult nor complex, Frost made tens of thousands of people interested in serious poetry. His pioneering efforts also persuaded his vast audience to be receptive to the verse of his successors, and enabled many less talented poets of the next generation to enjoy comfortable berths by teaching creative writing at colleges throughout the country.

Yet Frost paid a high price for these achievements. The long, tiring train rides, the poor meals at peculiar hours, the restless nights in one-night cheap hotels, the effort of making polite conversation with fawning people he did not know or care about, the fear and tension before and after his performance, the constant strain of being lionized and flattered, undermined his health and weakened his creative powers. In "On the Circuit," Auden was offhand and witty about his catholic audience and his enslavement to a bewildering reading schedule:

> I bring my gospel of the Muse
> To fundamentalists, to nuns,
> To Gentiles and to Jews,
>
> And daily, seven days a week,
> Before a local sense has jelled,

> From talking-site to talking-site
> Am jet-or-prop-propelled.

Robert Lowell, writing to Elizabeth Bishop, was more grimly realistic about the devastating effects of the lecture circuit: "One half of hell was the specter of 'forever meeting a new English faculty, coed, all older than one is, cup of coffee in paper cup, in the other hand a cookie and cigarette, and always standing, and signing copies of one's least-liked book.' The other half was 'the pre-reading cocktail party meant to last half an hour and lasting two, so that you can hardly walk or see.' "

Frost never got used to these lucrative ordeals, always had a terrific let-down after coming home and felt so nervously exhausted that he could not get any work done for several weeks. Putting Frost to bed after a long trip, Elinor expressed her dislike of his degrading public performances—a constant source of marital conflict—and told Lesley: "Your father *must* give this up. His health is failing. His life is being ruined. His poetry is suffering. It *can't* go on." Frost was forced to agree, when discussing his grand tours with a collector, that he needed tranquillity and solitude in order to do his work. Alluding to Christ's forty days in the wilderness, he said: "There has been too much public Me in it. It's the hardest thing to bring myself back to an interest in my own affairs. . . . I should have got off the train somewhere coming east and taken a month and ten days in some likely desert all by myself for a rest from smiling at my fellow man."[17]

V

Frost's annual visits to many colleges—often to pick up an honorary degree—enabled him to become involved in the personal affairs of a wide range of friends. His arrival was always a major event and his hosts took great pains to please him. Though the adults enjoyed his visits, the children often resented all the attention he received. In Amherst Armour Craig's little boy asked, with considerable irritation: "Is *he* coming again?" Dining with Bernard DeVoto in Cambridge in 1938, Frost mentioned that he might begin to write prose ten years from now. He was delighted when DeVoto's eight-year-old son exclaimed: "You'll be dead in ten years."

He had a more amiable time with the four children of Gordon

Chalmers, who became president of Kenyon College in Ohio. Chalmers told his children that Frost was waiting to see them in the study and both sides were slightly embarrassed by the formality of the occasion. Frost broke the ice by lining them up in front of him and saying: "This is the buckeye state. You go out and find me some buckeyes." When the children, excited by the hunt, brought back the horse chestnuts, Frost taught them how to string and play games with them.

On another occasion Chalmers drove Frost into Cincinnati to give a talk. Habitually late and now in a great rush, he dropped Frost off, explained the situation to the campus police and parked illegally. To protect Chalmers from being ticketed by someone else, the policeman wrote a bogus citation and put it on the windshield. Returning with Frost after the talk, Chalmers, to tease him, boldly tore it up. Frost was horrified that such a respectable citizen would break the law. A few years later, when Ann Chalmers was at Radcliffe, she and her mother visited Frost's house in Cambridge. During the conversation Mrs. Chalmers (herself a poet) mentioned Milton, Frost recited "Lycidas," one of his favorite poems, and Ann, who also knew the poem by heart, spoke the lines with him. As they finished, Frost looked at her with "delighted ferocity" and said: "Take that for your star."

A bizarre event occurred during his otherwise routine visit to the University of Minnesota in 1916. In a letter to Lesley, which may also have been a warning to his daughter, the lascivious old puritan exaggerated the amusing incident: "I personally conducted the elopement of Joseph Warren Beach that awful sinner with an assistant of his in the graduate school. I never saw craziness as near the surface as it is in Beach. He's a darn fool but he makes me laugh when I'm near him—laugh and cut up. It was cruel of me to marry him off, but I had to do it. I was cutting up. It was like some Shakespearean confusion."[18]

The comedy of errors began the previous summer when Beach, a thirty-five-year-old widower and English professor, visited Frost in Franconia and boasted about his sexual exploits. Frost was as intrigued by Beach's affairs as he had been by Edna Millay's. The following year in Minneapolis, Beach told Frost he was sleeping with his beautiful graduate student, Dagmar Doneghy, who (according to Richard Wilbur) was the daughter of his department chairman. The affair was further complicated by Dagmar's romantic interest in a local circus owner. Realizing that Beach loved Dagmar and was in a dangerous situation, Frost urged him to marry her immediately and offered to be best man. In one of Frost's milder versions of the story, they cruised around the campus in

Beach's car until they found Dagmar walking home and drove her into the country. Beach asked Frost to remain in the car and took her for a dalliance in the woods. They returned after a while to announce their engagement, secured a license, got married that very day and were treated by Frost to a champagne dinner. The marriage was a happy one and lasted until Beach's death in 1957. Using poetic freedom, Frost later told many friends that Beach had kidnapped Dagmar and that, after their passionate time in the woods, he had forced them to get married. When Frost heard that his ribald account of their courtship was hurting Beach's career, he wrote a formal retraction and apology. Beach was duly promoted, but their friendship ended.

11

Acquainted
with the Night

1927–1934

I

Frost's time in England had been cut short by the war and he soon had the urge to go back to Europe. Three years after returning to America, he had talked of taking a whole year abroad, perhaps in Madrid, to write poems and learn Spanish. In the late 1920s the desire to travel resurfaced. His daughter Marjorie had been ill, and he thought a trip abroad would improve her health and enable her to learn French. Dorothy Canfield Fisher arranged for her to live with a family in Sèvres, outside Paris. Taking advantage of his loose ties with Amherst to be poet-out-of-residence, Frost sailed with Elinor and Marjorie on the *Montnairn,* on August 4, 1928, from Quebec to LeHavre.

The strong dollar and the postwar desire to escape Prohibition and enjoy personal freedom had drawn thousands of Americans, including Hemingway and Fitzgerald, to Paris. But the atmosphere repelled Frost. He had studied Greek, Latin and German, but was embarrassed by his ignorance of French. He hated to be a tourist, distrusted the cunning and extortionate natives, and was disappointed by the sin and greed in the City of Light. Instead of broadening his horizons, his time in France made him feel homesick and strengthened his attachment to America. Two weeks after he arrived he told Lesley that traveling and sightseeing were a complete waste of time and money:

> We had a lot of opera both at the Opera and the Opera Comique. . . . We like French bread. The wine doesn't mean much to us. . . .
>
> You know how acute our homesickness always is. . . . Our realest anguish ensues from our being caught on what looks like

touring. . . . What the Hell am I so far out of my bailiwick for
anyway. . . .

The detestable thing is the greedy leer and wink everybody
has for us and our money. . . . What we are most aware of is not
the beauty of Paris, but the deceitful hate all around us.

The trip improved in September when Frost and Elinor, leaving
Marjorie in Sèvres, crossed the Channel. England seemed happier than
before the war and was not "whining and sullen" like France. His old
friends had helped him establish an international reputation. He could
now greet them as an equal rather than a novice, and was even in a
position to bestow a few favors of his own. Frost left only a skeletal
account of this journey. He planned but never took a motor trip with
J. C. Squire to his ancestral home in Devon. But he visited Gloucestershire, where the owners of The Gallows—at war with their neighbors
and ashamed of the run-down condition of the property—refused to let
him visit the old place. He saw Helen Thomas and expressed disapproval
of her all-too-frank memoir of Edward. He entertained John Gould
Fletcher at the Imperial Hotel in Russell Square and spent two nights at
the poet John Freeman's house. Prosperous, amiable and dull, Freeman,
the head of an insurance firm, had become as prominent in business as
in poetry. In Berkshire Frost visited Walter de la Mare, recuperating
from a near-fatal operation, whom he called "one of the best of the best."
Reviewing the *Collected Poems* later on, de la Mare expressed his own
admiration by calling Frost "the most original and vivid painter of common life that America has ever produced."

Frost had a warm reunion with Gibson, whose poetic reputation had
declined and who seemed to exist on his share of the income from
Rupert Brooke's estate. Friendly and sweet as ever, he forgave Frost for
quarreling with him about Edward Thomas and addressed a poem to his
old companion. In Leeds Frost saw Abercrombie, who was teaching at
the university, had several more children and was ill with diabetes. Frost
disliked the "stilted vernacular" of his recent play, which had been
condemned as immoral. John Cournos had a sick wife and Frost gave
him $50 for her hospital bill. Declining an invitation to dine with Edith
Sitwell, he paid a formal call in Oxford on the eighty-four-year-old
Bridges, who was working on his long poem "The Testament of Beauty."
Frost dined at the Garrick Restaurant with his early supporter Frank
Flint, who then introduced him to Edward Garnett. Though Garnett was
a friend of Edward Thomas and had praised Frost in the *Atlantic,* their

meeting was unaccountably touchy. Only the childishly egotistical Davies, who had married a young, wild and part-Gypsy wife, "was the same old Davies." Frost told a friend: "The minute Elinor and I got there he rose and presented us with an autographed poem as a 'souvenir of our visit.' He hasn't aged a hair. Still harping on why he isn't read in America. Wants to come over lecturing." Though Frost felt that Monro had resented him and treated him shabbily, he thought the highlight of the trip was a nostalgic reading at Monro's Poetry Bookshop, which had moved to Great Russell Street.

Things were a bit livelier during Frost's first visit to Dublin. Leaving Elinor to rest in London, he spent five pleasant days with Padraic Colum and with George William Russell ("A. E."), who talked for days and nights on end, and later dedicated the limited edition of *Enchantment and Other Poems* to Frost. Colum and Russell (both friends of Joyce) took him to a dinner party where Yeats was the guest of honor. Though Frost heard that he had become even more pompous after being nominated to the Irish Senate in 1922, Yeats was in fine form and recognized Frost in both senses of the word. But Frost got on with him no better in Dublin than when Pound had introduced them in 1913. Frost later told a poet-friend: "During the meal Yeats spoke up and said, 'You know I was the first poet in modern times to put that colloquial everyday speech of yours into poetry. I did it in my poetic play *The Land of Heart's Desire.*' Frost, who felt he had a monopoly on plain talking verse, said nothing."[1] Travel in Europe did not improve Marjorie's health nor Frost's temper. They sailed back on the *Olympic* on November 15, 1928 and suffered another bout of seasickness on the way home.

II

Four days later, while Frost was still at sea, Holt published his fifth volume, *West-Running Brook,* in an edition of 9,400 copies. Highly valued by the firm and now a more skillful negotiator, Frost got much better terms for this book: a 15 percent royalty on the first 5,000 copies, rising to 20 percent thereafter, a limited as well as a trade edition, a $2,000 advance and a monthly payment of $250 (up from $100) for the next five years.

In her review of this volume in the *Bookman,* the poet Babette Deutsch noted that it "contains several pieces that are unworthy of inclusion." Though it includes some minor poems and shows a slight decline from *New Hampshire*, *West-Running Brook* (one third as long as its predecessor) has two interesting poems: "The Egg and the Machine" (added in 1930) and "The Bear," and four major works: "Spring Pools," "Once by the Pacific," "Acquainted with the Night" and the title poem. (We have already discussed, from this volume, "The Lovely Shall Be Choosers," a tribute to his mother; "A Peck of Gold," about his childhood in San Francisco; and the Hardyesque "Bereft.")

"The Egg and the Machine," a witty Lawrencean diatribe that equates the mechanical with evil, expresses hatred of machines that invade and despoil natural life. Thinking of various ways to wreck the oncoming train, the speaker finds and arms himself with a buried turtle's egg. He then threatens: "The next machine that has the power to pass / Will get this plasm in its goggle glass." He realizes, however, that though he must make a symbolic protest against the engine, he will kill the life in the egg by shattering it against the headlight of the train.

"The Bear"—continuing the dominant theme of *contraries* in this book—contrasts the natural freedom of the bear with the caged intellect of man. The first twelve lines vividly portray the amiable bear gorging on chokecherries and rambling across the countryside. The rest of the poem describes a man either pacing a confined cell between his telescope and microscope or sitting on his "fundamental butt" (a Frostian pun on fundament-buttocks) between two metaphysical extremes: "And back and forth he sways from cheek to cheek, / At one extreme agreeing with one Greek."[2] Frost offered a rare explication of his poem in an unpublished letter to Morris Tilley, an English department colleague at the University of Michigan: "I wrote a poem about bears caged and uncaged. I made man out like a bear in a cage. When he walks back and forth from the telescope end to the microscope end of his confinement he is a scientist. When he sits back and sways his head from side to side between metaphysical extremes he is a philosopher. So now you know."

"Spring Pools," like many of Frost's finest poems, was inspired and enhanced by a Romantic lyric. Shelley's "To Jane: The Recollection" provided the original inspiration:

> We paused beside the pools that lie
> Under the forest bough,—
> Each seemed as 'twere a little sky
> Gulfed in a world below. . . .

In which the lovely forests grew,
As in the upper air,
More perfect both in shape and hue
Than any spreading there.

In Frost's poignant poem the spring pools that perfectly reflect the sky through the leafless forests will soon be dried up and darkened by the roots and leaves of the summer woods (rather than by the traditionally destructive winter season). The beautifully reversed adjectives and nouns in the flower-filled and water-soaked "flowery waters" and "watery flowers," which reminded Reuben Brower of Monet's paintings of water lilies, derive from the "watery bier" and "watery floor" in Milton's "Lycidas." The snows that melted only yesterday—from Villon's famous lament, "where are the snows of yesteryear?"—were the original source of the spring pools that have now been extinguished by the natural seasonal process of creation and destruction. Ford Madox Ford's praise of Hemingway's style applies equally to the perfection achieved in Frost's "Spring Pools": "[His] words strike you, each one, as if they were pebbles fetched fresh from a brook. They live and shine, each in its place. So one of the pages has the effect of a brook-bottom into which you look down through the flowing water. The words form a tessellation, each in order beside the other."

"Once by the Pacific" and "Acquainted with the Night" belong with a group of dark poems in the section subtitled *"Fiat Nox"* (Let there be night), an ironic allusion to *Fiat Lux* (Let there be light), the divine command in Genesis 1:3, when God "created the heaven and the earth." The destructive shattered water in the opening lines of the sonnet "Once by the Pacific" alludes to Shakespeare's Sonnet 64: "When I have seen the hungry ocean gain / Advantage on the kingdom of the shore." The last line not only negates the Biblical injunction but also echoes Othello's, "Put out the light, and then put out the light," just before he strangles Desdemona. As in Frost's "The Flood," "Sand Dunes" and "One Step Backward Taken," nature is hostile, menacing and dangerous. The ocean smashes against and threatens to destroy the edge and perhaps the whole of the continent. Like the slouching beast in Yeats' "The Second Coming," the night of dark intent refers (Frost said) to past wars and all the wars that would still have to come. The vague menace of "doing something," "you could not tell" and "someone had better be prepared" adds to the palpable yet indefinable threat.

In "Acquainted with the Night," written in *terza rima,* the noun expresses a powerful sense of urban anxiety, isolation, terror and meta-physical despair. As in "Good Hours," the concluding poem of *North of Boston,* the solitary and perhaps insomniac speaker in this poem walks out of the sleeping city, through the rain and into the blackness of night. The watchman evades him, unwilling to explain the pervasive sadness. He hears an "interrupted cry," which seems like a wail of desperation that he cannot answer and that intensifies his loneliness. The high clock tower, which proclaims the time was neither wrong nor right, echoes Hamlet's lament: "The time is out of joint; O curséd spite / That I was ever born to set it right!" (1.5.190). Whereas Hamlet accepts the fatal challenge to try to set a rotten world right, Frost, repeating the title and the first line in the ironic understatement of the last, portrays the troubled acceptance of his Kafkaesque fate.

The West-Running Brook, which flows west rather than east into the Atlantic, seems contrary to nature yet is perfectly natural. John Kemp explains that "Since New England's Appalachian ridges run north-south, brooks and streams in the back-country are as likely to flow west as east. In fact, the three regions north of Boston that Frost knew best are on the west side of the mountain systems and hence drained by rivers and streams flowing westerly. All the brooks near the Frost farm in Derry, for instance (including Hyla Brook, as well as the original West-Running Brook), drain west from Warner Hill into the Merrimac."[3]

This love poem takes the form of a philosophical dialogue between a newly married couple. The wife is idealistic, the husband grimly realistic (as in "The Death of the Hired Man") when interpreting what the brook means and how it reflects their marriage. The woman believes that they can "go by contraries" (and be in love despite their differences) in the same way the brook does. The man, more fully acquainted with this watery phenomenon, takes a darker view. He sees the brook—a univer-sal cataract of death that spends to nothingness—as a dangerous threat to their love, even to their very existence. But he also tries to reconcile their contrary viewpoints by connecting the brook to the source of life. He alludes to Heraclitus' belief that all things are in a state of flux, to Lucretius' theory of the stream of atoms and to Henri Bergson's idea in *Creative Evolution* that the human *élan vital* resists and dominates the forces of dissolution as the spirit fights against death.

"West-Running Brook" is thematically related to the four-line love poem "Devotion," in which the heart is compared to the shore of the ocean. By holding the curve of one position during an endless repetition of breaking waves, the ocean and the shore subtly symbolize the movement and climax of the sexual act. But love (as Frost revealed in "To Earthward") soon fades and becomes bitter. "The Thatch" (in the "*Fiat Nox*" section) concludes the series of intensely personal poems on the decline of love. It portrays the grim antagonism between a married couple who are intent on giving and taking pain, and reveals the bitterness in his marriage to Elinor. The husband leaves the house in anger and will not return until the wife turns out the light and goes to bed. She will not do this until he comes back into the house for a reconciliation before they sleep. The husband, grief-stricken during their unyielding battle of wills, vents his anger by forcing the summer birds (who symbolize his family) out of their nest in the thatch of his house and driving them into the darkness. The psychological force of the poem comes from the speaker's recognition that he has achieved pleasure and eased his pain by behaving cruelly to an innocent victim—as Frost had once done to Lesley when he quarreled with Elinor. Frost dramatizes his own grief, but also acknowledges that he has made others suffer: "Well, we should see which one would win, / We should see which one would be first to yield."

Frost's first volume of *Collected Poems,* which included his first five books, was published two years after *West-Running Brook,* in the fall of 1930. It received extremely favorable reviews and beat Hart Crane's *The Bridge* to win Frost's second Pulitzer Prize. James Southall Wilson, a distinguished professor at the University of Virginia, declared: "no richer volume of poetry has been produced in America since Poe's volume of 1845." Granville Hicks, a Communist critic writing in the *New Republic,* praised the consistently high level of his work: "*Collected Poems* shows and shows clearly that Frost has written as fine poetry as any living American and that the proportion of first-rate poetry to the whole is greater than in the work of any other contemporary." In England Geoffrey Grigson, known for his fierce criticism as well as for his responsiveness to pastoral poetry, agreed that "it is the most important poet's collection which has appeared for several years. It is rare to find three hundred and fifty pages of verse so consistently good from cover to cover."[4]

In the late 1920s Frost also began to publish his work in signed limited editions and privately printed pamphlets. As he told the master-printer Joseph Blumenthal in February 1930, "my sympathies have long been enlisted on the side of small presses and hand setting." Blumenthal —who was born in 1897, graduated from Cornell and was a naval aviator in World War I—began printing Frost's Christmas booklets at the Spiral

Press in 1929. His editions ranged from 275 copies in the beginning to 16,555 in 1962.

At first Frost was willing to sign anything but a check, but soon wearied of writing his name on slight poems and ephemeral works. As early as September 1930 he told Blumenthal: "I'll never write autographs again for a dollar and a half apiece. It is too ignominious, degrading and debilitating."[5] But his price went up and he kept on signing until the end of his life. When in a generous mood, he would write entire poems in his friends' books. One librarian claimed to specialize in the rare volumes that were *not* inscribed by Frost.

III

Frost was strongly opposed (as we have seen from his interview with Burton "Rascol") to obscurity in modern literature. He claimed that Joyce wrote *Ulysses* as a joke and mocked his wrong-headed "cloacality," but actually bought a copy of *Finnegans Wake* in 1939. "Looking it over," he told a friend, "he decided he was 'out' five dollars. He did not understand it. In fact, the only thing he did understand was a quotation he had previously learned and given to audiences as an example of obscurity." Though he joked about the "one-man tongue-confusion" in that opaque novel, he kept an eye on the competition and made good use in "Desert Places" of the elegiac conclusion of "The Dead."

Frost was eager to meet Joyce's friend and fellow modernist T. S. Eliot, his American rival, when he journeyed to England in 1928. Eliot, a close friend of Pound, was born in St. Louis in 1888 and educated at Harvard, Marburg and Oxford. A tall, sibylline figure with "features of clerical cut," he had a prim demeanor and fastidious manner of speech. Unhappily married to an attractive but mentally unstable Englishwoman, he had worked as a schoolmaster and bank clerk at Lloyd's in London before becoming the magisterial editor of the *Criterion* and prosperous publisher at Faber & Faber.

Frost was introduced to Eliot by Harold Monro, who had promised a stag dinner in return for Frost's reading at the Poetry Bookshop. Frost disliked the way Eliot affected an English accent and assumed the snobbery of his adopted country. With both poets on guard, the entire evening was rather strained. Frost confessed to Elizabeth Sergeant that he began the dinner with a bit of antipathy, "a touch of the old jealousy and suspicion that Tom Eliot had replaced me in the not too good graces of Ezra Pound," from whom he had long been estranged. On another occasion he asked Eliot if he thought Pound was crazy. "'Well,' Eliot hesitated, coming finally to the point, 'well, you know how it is.' "[6] Eliot's characteristically vague and cautious response suggested that since Frost knew Pound and his craziness, there was no need to seek confirmation from a friend. Frost wanted to break the ice and have some frank talk, but Eliot rejected his attempt at intimacy.

Their second meeting took place at the St. Botolph Club in Boston on November 15, 1932, when the forty-four-year-old Eliot was in America to give the Charles Eliot Norton lectures at Harvard. Frost did not much care for the way the Harvard poets obsequiously fawned on the younger poet. Eliot provoked his anger by dogmatically declaring that, apart from one sixteenth-century poem by William Dunbar, no good poetry had ever been written in Scotland. After Eliot had brusquely dismissed Robert Burns, Frost, feeling his ancestral honor was at stake, ironically asked whether he would admit that Burns was a good songwriter. In an intolerably patronizing manner, Eliot conceded: "One might grant that modest claim."

Frost had a chance to retaliate when a guest asked Eliot to read his poem "The Hippopotamus," and Eliot graciously agreed if Frost would read one of his own. Frost said he would do even better and offered to *write* a poem while Eliot was reading his. He then borrowed a pencil, fussed about with the place cards, faked an inspired moment and produced "A Record Stride" (between the Atlantic and the Pacific oceans), which he had composed a few months earlier. Frost felt impelled to lark around when Eliot was taking himself so seriously. "Wearing his pretentiousness haughtily to the end," Frost told Newdick, "Eliot was baited all evening but didn't seem to become aware of the fact." Eliot had just left his wife after a long struggle to sustain the marriage and was in a miserable state of mind. A few months later, in Baltimore, Scott Fitzgerald found him, despite all the public acclaim he was receiving, "very broken and sad and shrunk inside."

Six weeks later Frost wrote a friend that he had been in rotten health ever since his dinner with Eliot and was suffering from "modernism in the throat." He also told Thompson that Eliot (like Yeats and Pound) was a fake. Quoting Eliot's second wife, Valerie (or perhaps attributing his own opinions to her), Frost said his character and work had been fatally weakened by a restless expatriate life: "[He] thought there was an unpleasant falseness about him as a man, thought he was a sad one, that he Frost had once been told by the woman who took Eliot under her wing and bedclothes, 'The trouble with T.S. is that he has lost you and hasn't found us.' "[7]

Though they both believed that a poet should work within the literary tradition of the past, Frost's and Eliot's poetic themes and techniques were antithetical. Eliot, who disliked Kipling's "excessive lucidity," believed that "poets in our civilization, as it exists at present, must be *difficult* . . . more comprehensive, more allusive, more indirect, in order to force, to dislocate if necessary, language into [their] meaning." Since Frost's poetry did not seem to be difficult in the same way as Eliot's (though it was much more complex than Eliot assumed), he tended to dismiss it. In 1920 Eliot had rejected most American poets and told his mother: "I have never taken much interest in Frost's poetry, although I know he is much better than most others." Writing in the *Dial* two years later (and six years before he first met Frost), Eliot condescendingly dismissed his work as boring: "Mr. Frost seems the nearest equivalent to an English poet, specializing in New England torpor; his verse, it is regretfully said, is uninteresting, and what is uninteresting is unreadable, and what is unreadable is not read. There, that is done."[8]

Frost was stung by Eliot's criticism, irritated by his affected manner and antagonistic to his mode of poetry. He lashed out at Eliot (as he had done with Pound, Lowell and Sandburg) with a number of witty remarks. He conceded that "Eliot was unquestionably the best of the whole group of obscure poets," but felt that his obscurity masked an inability to express human emotions. He believed that "the need of being versed in country things was far greater, and often harder to achieve, than the need of being versed in pseudo-intellectual myths and symbols."

Though Eliot's fondness for literary allusions was rather similar to his own, Frost claimed Eliot was derivative and phony. Eliot's fakery, Frost told audiences on the lecture circuit, consisted of making "an Anthology of the Best Lines in Poetry," running the lines loosely together into a sort of narrative and copyrighting the result. Writing to Lesley in 1934, after their second meeting, Frost—proud of his solid knowledge of the Classics—condemned Eliot's pretentious scholarship and gloomy prognostications, and questioned his reputation for profundity: "From Pound down to Eliot they have striven for distinction by a show of learning, Pound in the old French, Eliot in forty languages. They quote and you try to see if you can place the quotation. Pound really has great though inaccurate learning. Eliot has even greater [pretensions]. . . . Eliot has written in the throes of getting religion and forswearing a world gone bad with war. That seems deep. But I don't know." Referring to the mystifying oriental words at the end of *The Waste Land*, Frost quipped that Eliot was "used to a lot of people who talk Sanskrit." He called Eliot's *The Cocktail Party*, a successful religious play of 1950, "Cocktailian Episcopalia."[9]

Writing about baseball for *Sports Illustrated* in 1956, Frost (playing to a low-brow audience) mentioned a collector friend and then punned in an amusing way about egghead poets and academic critics: "I have with me as consultant the well-known symbolist, Howard Schmitt of Buffalo, to mind my baseball slang and interpret the incidentals. . . . He didn't mean to represent himself as a symbolist in the high-brow sense of the word . . . ; he was a common ordinary cymbalist in a local band somewhere." In a letter to Manthey-Zorn (as well as in "The Lesson for Today") Frost strongly objected to Eliot's despairing depiction of the world and took a more positive view of human experience: "Some fellow has written about the world as Waste Lands. Nothing has been laid waste that was not always waste. Nothing has gone loose that was ever really firm. Some of the stars are comparatively fixed and so's friendship."

Despite the extreme contrasts in their personalities and poetry, Frost borrowed rhymes and lines from "Prufrock" in "One Step Backward Taken" and "West-Running Brook," and alluded to "Sweeney Among the Nightingales" in *A Masque of Reason*. In "The Generations of Men" (1914) Frost referred to the still-novel cinema and said: "It's as you throw a picture on a screen"; in "Prufrock" (1915) Eliot used a similar image and wrote: "as if a magic lantern threw the nerves in patterns on a screen." Both men published poems called "New Hampshire" (in 1923 and 1934), though Frost's work was satiric and Eliot's described his childhood memories in that state. In his poem Frost confessed that he has been "the author / Of several books against the world in general." In the same way, Eliot rather disingenuously said of *The Waste Land:* "To me it was only the relief of a personal and wholly insignificant grouse against life; it is just a piece of rhythmical grumbling."[10] Critics like Randall Jarrell revealed the dark side of Frost and explained that his dominant themes, like Eliot's, are alienation, loneliness and metaphysical desolation. But Frost's poetic characters have an inner strength—completely missing in neurotic aesthetes like Eliot's Prufrock—which allows them, even as they suffer, to take a more affirmative stand against the prevailing darkness.

IV

In May 1926, before Frost's troubles with his children intensified his tragic sense of life, he courted disaster by boasting to George Roy Elliott that his real success lay in being "so uncursed" in his family. Eight years later he asked Bartlett if he were a mild domestic tyrant, and then naively and mistakenly answered his own question by reassuring himself that he "had never had any trouble with any of them." Though John Haines had found the Frost children charming in England, Untermeyer—who met them after they returned to America and knew them well—called the spoiled and socially maladjusted teenagers "the most obnoxious and unattractive children he had ever met." When the grown-up children began to have their own grave problems, Frost's family and friends sought explanations for their misfortunes. He told Newdick that since Elinor had always done everything for the children, they were relatively helpless on their own. But even after the children grew up and got married, they lacked self-reliance and remained heavily dependent on their parents. Sergeant (who knew the family) observed that the Frosts were either followed by their children or dragged after them by magnetic attraction. During emergencies, and there were many, Frost was always on hand to provide moral, practical and financial support.

Frost's granddaughter believed that Elinor had sacrificed her own ambitions to devote herself to the family and wrapped herself up in the lives of her children. Elinor thought they would all become successful and was sadly disappointed when they failed to meet her expectations. Frost's son-in-law Willard Fraser blamed the young Frosts' later troubles on their lack of contact with normal children and on the unhealthy, self-enclosed world of their youth. Frost tended to blame himself and felt his family had paid dearly for his extraordinary success: "His career had been hard on his children. . . . There had been jealousy involved, unexpressed jealousy. . . . [They] had been pushed too much in the background."[11]

In the late 1920s and early 1930s Frost—like the biblical Job or a Greek tragic hero—suffered a series of family tragedies that lasted until there was no one left to devastate. In 1928 Lesley married Dwight Francis, a rich, divorced playboy. She had daughters in 1929 and 1931; but Francis was unfaithful and had a nervous breakdown, and the marriage was in ruins before the second child was born. In 1931, taking a realistic view and trying to reduce Lesley's unhappiness, Frost urged her

to cut her losses and dissolve the marriage: "Your question to decide is
whether Dwight's not being right in the mind and his having wronged
you come to the same thing for practical purposes. . . . The conclusion
you reached was whether he was psychopathic or merely spoiled and
misbehaved, you couldn't imagine him becoming possible to live
with. . . . Only if you can contemplate a life of self-sacrificing and child-
sacrificing tragedy could you begin over with him. Some people can't
resist tragedy." After her divorce the following year, Frost helped support
Lesley and her two young children.

In May 1932, when Lesley had published a pseudonymous detective
story, Frost told Untermeyer that he could understand her reckless
plunge into self-expression after all the "inhibiting" she had from him.
The following year Lesley, who did not have a college degree, was
teaching English at Rockford College in Illinois, where Gordon Chalmers was president. When Chalmers urged her to finish her degree, Lesley
became furious. Using her privileged position as Frost's daughter, she
boasted in a letter to her parents about how she had intimidated her
father's friend: "I am sitting pretty—but whether that is temporary, and
Gordon only bides his time for revenge, is a matter of speculation. . . .
[Mrs. Chalmers told a friend] that Gordon would *never* mention degrees
to me again—that he had had a headache for four days in consequence
of my explosion."

Frost criticized Lesley for lacking common sense, gadding around and
courting celebrities. But when she took her young daughters to Mexico,
he felt he had to forgive her adventurousness since she had so much life
and energy (if not direction). In 1945 Lesley—who by then had labored
in an aircraft factory, owned a bookstore, run a shop on a round-the-
world cruise, taught school, worked for a publisher, lectured on her
father's poetry and done many other jobs—was in charge of the American library in Madrid. Three years later, after two more of his children
had died and one become insane, Frost recalled her childhood. He
praised the strong and adaptable Lesley as the sole survivor among his
children, and again expressed guilt about what his success had cost his
family: "You typed at the age of twelve some of my earliest manuscript
going into a book and you have campaigned for it ever since in bookstores and editorial offices and from the platform. You came along at just
the right age to get some satisfaction out of my strange career. Not
everybody in the family had the same luck. I can be very very sad for the
little good Carol and Irma got out of being my children. . . . You are left

to cheer me with your pleasure in what I do and your participation in it."[12]

Though Frost did not mention Marjorie, his youngest and favorite child, her protracted illnesses caused greater pain and suffering than anything else in his entire life. In the fall of 1925, while Frost was still teaching at Michigan, the always delicate Marjorie had an operation for appendicitis, suffered from heart disease and (like Jeanie, Elinor and Irma) had a nervous breakdown. She entered Johns Hopkins Hospital in Baltimore three times and was in bed for several months. Marjorie recovered from this ordeal, and in 1928 began her nurse's training at Hopkins, where only two years before she had been an invalid.

But the rigors of the course undermined her health. By the fall of 1930 both Marjorie and her childhood friend Lillian LaBatt—who had married her brother Carol in 1923—had contracted tuberculosis. Carol had left the South Shaftsbury farm in Vermont (which Frost had given him as a wedding present) and taken Lillian to recuperate in the milder climate of Monrovia, California, just north of Los Angeles. Marjorie became a patient in the sanatorium in Boulder, Colorado (5,000 feet above sea level), where John Bartlett had moved and become a writer for trade journals. Frost and Elinor, having moved back to Amherst, traveled across the country to see their children in Colorado and California, and paid their expensive hospital bills.

Frost irrationally blamed himself for these calamities and in a letter to Untermeyer expressed a nostalgic longing for his years of obscurity and poverty in Derry: "All this sickness and scatteration of the family is our fault and not our misfortune or I wouldn't admit it. It's a result and a judgement on us. We ought to have gone back farming years ago or we ought to have stayed farming when we knew we were well off." By 1931 all his children were causing intense anxiety. Marjorie and Lillian were gravely ill and Lesley's marriage had broken up. Irma, who had married John Cone in 1926 and had a son the following year, had run away from her husband's wheat farm in Kansas and also asked for a divorce. They were reconciled and had another son in 1940, but finally got divorced, after her mental collapse, in 1947.

After a long illness, Lillian eventually recovered her health, and is still alive. While Marjorie was recuperating in the sanatorium, she met Willard Fraser, an archeology student at the University of Colorado. They married in his hometown, Billings, Montana, in June 1933. The following March she had a baby girl and, through the carelessness of her doctor, became infected with puerperal fever. She was delirious for four weeks and hovered at the verge of death. On April 26, after Frost had heard of a new serum used to combat the disease, Marjorie was flown to the Mayo Clinic in Minnesota, where few things begin and many things end. At the Mayo she had a fever of 110°, the highest ever recorded at the clinic, and developed an infected blood clot in "veins leading from the left leg." On April 29 the terrified Frost wrote George Whicher: "I must not say it but I fear Marjorie loses ground. . . . Her delirium seems more unbroken. The precious human serum so rare and bestowed on us by special favor has failed." Marjorie died, at the age of twenty-nine, on May 2, 1934. Two weeks later, remembering the death of Edward Thomas, Frost told Untermeyer:

> The blow has fallen. The noblest of us all is dead and has taken our hearts out of the world with her. It was a terrible seven weeks' fight—too indelibly terrible on the imagination. No death in war could more than match it for suffering and heroic endurance. . . . It was in a hospital she was caught to die after more than a hundred serum injections and blood transfusions. We were torn afresh every day between the temptation to let her go untortured or cruelly trying to save her.[13]

Marjorie's death was particularly heartbreaking. Always a sickly child, she had a talent for poetry and was Frost's darling. She had made a brave recovery from her nervous breakdown and tuberculosis, and had started a new life by enrolling in nursing school. She had fallen in love with a man Frost admired, been happily married for less than a year and had a healthy baby. With everything to live for, she had struggled to survive in two different hospitals, held on for seven weeks as her parents watched anxiously at her bedside—then died. Frost's hopes for Marjorie had led only to agonizing disappointment and despair.

Elinor took Marjorie's death harder than Frost did and suffered even more than when Elliott died in 1900. She expressed her stoical anguish and overwhelming grief in letters to her close friend Edith Fobes, who lent the Frosts her New Hampshire cottage during the hay-fever season: "With Robert I have to keep cheerful, because I mustn't drag him down, but sometimes it seems to me that I *cannot* go on any longer. . . . The pathos of it was too terrible. I long to die myself and be relieved of the pain that I feel for her sake. Poor precious darling, to have to leave everything in such a cruel and unnecessary way. I cannot bear it."

Unlike many poets, Frost never wrote a poem about the death of his child. But in "Maple" (1921), which mentions Marjorie by name, he had anticipated her death in an uncanny way. In this poem a girl is called Maple by her mother, who dies after giving birth to her, and tries to understand why she was given that unusual name. Her father explains that "Your mother named you. You and she just saw / Each other in passing in the room upstairs, / One coming this way into life, and one / Going the other out of life."

Frost, who said he could stand sorrow better than evil, sought wisdom and consolation—as he had so often done—in poetry. He often quoted Matthew Arnold, identified with him and wrote that "the old school-teacher . . . not a teacher, maybe—but a school man, [was] a good deal like me that way, I suppose. I feel a certain affinity with him. His sad old face always haunts me." As Marjorie was hovering near death, Frost told Untermeyer that his favorite poem, long before he realized what it was going to mean to him, was Arnold's "Cadmus and Harmonia." In this section of "Empedocles on Etna" (1852), Arnold relates the story, from Book IV of Ovid's *Metamorphoses,* of the man who gave his wife a necklace, as a wedding present, which led to many misfortunes:

> They had stay'd long enough to see,
> In Thebes, the billow of calamity
> Over their own dear children roll'd,
> Curse upon curse, pang upon pang,
> For years, they sitting helpless in their home.[14]

12

Poets and
Biographers

1934–1938

I

Frost had often suffered from pulmonary illness during the harsh northern winters and in Michigan one year had been repeatedly confined to bed after five attacks of influenza. Both he and Elinor had agonized over Marjorie's long illness and in November 1934, six months after their daughter's death, Elinor had a heart attack. The doctor advised them to spend the severest months in a warm climate. From 1934 to 1938 —trying out various places—they spent the cold season first in Key West and then in Miami, San Antonio, Texas, and Gainesville, Florida. Frost invited his children for Christmas reunions in the South, and felt he got more heat in the Florida winter than he had all summer in Vermont.

Key West, the southernmost town in America, is the last in a string of small subtropical islands that stretches southwest from the tip of the Florida peninsula and divides the Gulf of Mexico from the Atlantic Ocean. The maritime atmosphere of the seedy, unpretentious town of clapboard houses and open balconies was a mixture of Nantucket and New Orleans. It was then an exotic, almost foreign locale. Spanish was spoken everywhere, though the rollers of big cigars had moved to Tampa and the Cuban tourists had stopped coming during the Depression. Far from urban distractions, the island had two tennis courts (which Frost used), exotic cockfights, thriving whorehouses and several fine saloons. Hemingway had moved to Key West in 1928 and built a grand house on Whitehead Street three years later. Though Frost admired Hemingway's fiction and knew he was in town, he did not get to know him.

Writing from Key West, Frost told Joseph Blumenthal: "I expected to find it a busted cigar town. It turns out to be a busted land boom

town—all cut up into speculators' lots, with hardly a house on them."
In 1934, during the Depression, most of the inhabitants were on relief
and the town was bankrupt. The federal government had declared a
"civil emergency" and local authority had been transferred to the Federal Emergency Relief Administration. Elinor, who equated President
Roosevelt's New Deal with Soviet Communism, angrily told Sidney Cox
that "Key West has been taken over by the United States government,
and is ruled by a dictator. It is an experiment in state socialism." Frost
liked Gainesville much better, mainly because it was "uncontaminated"
by winter visitors.

In Florida Frost met a popular novelist and a prominent poet. The
tall, blond, florid Hervey Allen, fifteen years younger than Frost, was
born in Pittsburgh, attended the U.S. Naval Academy and limped badly
after being wounded while fighting in France during World War I. He
had written *Israfel* (1926), a popular life of Edgar Poe, and *Anthony
Adverse* (1933), a picaresque romance of the Napoleonic era that sold
half a million copies. Hervey Allen (like his friend Amy Lowell) was a
grandee who lived in luxury. "Once on the train," Frost told a friend, "he
had demanded a pillow; when he was refused, he telephoned ahead for
one. Two officials boarded the train later with a pillow for him. Hervey
was like that, always kicking up a rumpus." Impressed by Allen's imperious manner, Frost called him a great friend and said he was almost as
devoted as Untermeyer. In 1940 Allen found a suitable plot of land near
his estate in Coconut Grove, south of Miami, which Frost bought for his
permanent winter home.

Allen's son Richard remembered being bounced on Frost's knee, in
the back seat of their big blue Buick, as the old poet sang interminable
verses of "The Erie Canal." Frost was unusually tolerant of boys with
matches when Richard nearly burned down his house; and later used his
influence to prevent his expulsion from Exeter for flooding his room.[1]

Wallace Stevens, five years younger than Frost, had been his contemporary at Harvard. Trained as a lawyer, he became an insurance execu-
tive in Hartford and often vacationed in Key West. Frost disapprovingly
said that Stevens, who once had a drunken fistfight with Hemingway, was
frequently under the influence of alcohol. His first book of poems,
Harmonium (1923), was the absolute antithesis of Frost's earthy lyrics
and grim pastorals. In one of their sharp exchanges, Stevens said:

> The trouble with you is that you are too academic.
> The trouble with you [Frost said] is that you are too executive. . . .

> The trouble with you, Frost, is that you write about *things*.
> The trouble with you, Wallace, is that you write about *bric-à-brac*.

They maintained a guarded friendship, however, and Stevens good-naturedly sent his next book with the inscription: "Some more *bric-à-brac*."

In Key West in 1940, Stevens' adolescent daughter, Holly, complained that she was being treated like a small child. Frost tried to "lighten the situation" by taking her to a cocktail party without telling her parents and succeeded "in pulling one off on old Wally." When Frost visited Hartford, Stevens' eccentric wife, Elsie, insulted their rather touchy guest. Upset by her behavior, Stevens lamely explained: "You know, she insults everybody." Randall Jarrell's second wife, Mary (who knew both poets and was influenced by Thompson's consistently negative portrayal), exaggerated Frost's jealousy and misjudged both his poetry and his philosophical cast of mind: "There was a deep, smoldering, incurable resentment that Frost had about Stevens. It was partly the result of Frost's acute sensitivity at being a nonintellectual poet, somebody for *Saturday Evening Post* readers [though Frost never published in that magazine] or *Atlantic Monthly* readers, and Stevens being such an intellectual. Frost always divided the world into intellectuals and himself." Frost described their friendship more accurately when he assured Stevens: "Take it from me, there was no conflict at all, but the prettiest kind of stand-off."[2]

II

Frost also formed significant friendships with John Crowe Ransom and with Stevens' Harvard contemporary Witter Bynner. The mild and gentlemanly Ransom was born in Tennessee in 1888, studied at Oxford as a Rhodes Scholar and taught for twenty-five years at Vanderbilt. As leader of the conservative Southern Agrarians, editor of their journal, the *Fugitive*, and New Critic par excellence, he included Allen Tate, Randall Jarrell and Robert Lowell among his devoted disciples. In 1918, when the war had dampened the public's enthusiasm for poetry, Frost had "discovered" Ransom and persuaded Holt to bring out his first book, *Poems About God* (1919).

They did not actually meet until 1935, when Ransom invited Frost to lecture at Vanderbilt. At the formal party after Frost's reading, they had an exhilarating conversation that lasted until three o'clock in the morning. After Ransom had driven him back to the hotel they continued their riveting talk, still dressed in tuxedos, until dawn. Ransom then rushed home to change his clothes and complained to his wife: "I must go to class, but Robert Frost can sleep." Ransom's biographer concludes that Frost was "a poet whose achievement he considered of lasting importance and a man whose companionship he cherished beyond almost all others."

Though Eliot scorned Frost, and Tate said: "Mr. Frost is . . . an end, not a beginning," he was consistently praised by Ransom and his follower Cleanth Brooks, both of whom had enormous influence in academic circles. In a perceptive review in the *Fugitive* of June 1925, Ransom emphasized Frost's use of irony, his romantic strain and his philosophical content: "Mr. Frost's poetry is anything but pretentious, it is trim and easy and sometimes apparently trifling, yet it contains plenty of irony. . . . It is immensely metaphysical. . . . Always the natural processes are personalized, and art consoles us with its implication of far-flung analogies between our order and the natural order. Mr. Frost is more than ordinarily delicate in making this implication. . . . Like all inveterate poets, he commits this irony in a context sprinkled with sly romanticisms." Surveying poetry in English during the first half of the twentieth century in the *Kenyon Review* of January 1951, Ransom again expressed his admiration by ranking Frost—with Hardy, Yeats, Robinson and Eliot —as one of "the five major poets of our period."[3]

In 1937, after Gordon Chalmers had become president of Kenyon College, he invited Frost (then at Amherst) to join the faculty and become founding editor of the *Kenyon Review*. Frost declined and recommended Ransom, who got the job. Ransom's appointment, however, did not at first work out as well as Frost had hoped. Writing from Kenyon in April 1941, fulminating against Ransom's parochialism and the dominance of the New Criticism in American universities, Frost told Kay Morrison: "I have been brought out to see if anything I can say will save the college from his priggishness, his narrowness, his schoolmarmishness and his proselytizations. All he wants is disciples and all he talks about is Tate, Penn Warren, [Donald] Davidson and [George] O'Donnell." Frost was in a much more magnanimous mood when he returned to Kenyon in 1956 and told a student audience: "You have right here on this campus the greatest living American poet."[4]

Witter Bynner, seven years younger than Frost, was an extremely wealthy poet and benefactor who had traveled and collected extensively in China. Bald and bespectacled, with a minor talent and a waspish tongue, he was once considered an important writer and is now mainly remembered as a friend of D. H. Lawrence. In *The Plumed Serpent* (1926), Lawrence portrayed him as Owen Rhys and satirized his vacuity: "[He was] so empty, and waiting for circumstance to fill him up. Swept with an American despair of having lived in vain, or of not having *really* lived." After Frost had read Lawrence's Mexican poems in that novel he told Bynner: "the very first poem ["La Noche Triste"] I ever wrote myself was about how the children of Quetzal and Huitzil once gave Cortés One Very Bad Night."

Both Frost and Bynner were prickly and got on each other's nerves. After he had been invited to read at Michigan, Bynner coupled Frost with his old rival and remarked that his face was "a little too nervous and a little too satisfied. . . . Frost has a smuggish conceit, not unlike Sandburg's."[5] Frost, extremely punctilious about time, told Bynner that he had never been late for an appointment. When Bynner invited him to read in Santa Fe in the fall of 1935 and was supposed to introduce him, Bynner arrived ten minutes late and Frost had begun to read without him.

Bynner's homosexuality was another sensitive point. Frost, who had an old-fashioned puritan morality and sense of decorum in art, had disliked Stark Young's seductive relations with Amherst students and was disgusted by the poems of George Sylvester Viereck. "This thing of sodomy and perversion in poetry," he told Mertins, "doesn't strike me right. It is all an unnecessary cess pool." Speaking of Bynner's sex life in Santa Fe, he told Thompson, with Rabelaisian exaggeration: "Down there he had a boy who was finally so worn in the bung by this great hulk of a man that the boy needed an operation to straighten him out." But homosexuality did not prevent Frost's friendships with the poets W. H. Auden, Robert Francis and William Meredith. When asked if he ever discussed this subject with Frost, who sometimes stayed in his house, Meredith replied: "My goodness, no!"[6]

Frost's attitude toward homosexuality led to an extraordinary quarrel with Bynner during his visit to Santa Fe. The ostensible subject of dispute was *A Book of Leaves* (1935) by Horatio Colony, a prosperous textile manufacturer in Keene, New Hampshire. Colony's uninhibited titles, not calculated to appeal to Frost, included "Lust of the Sun," "Satyr Lullaby," "Sensuous Night," "Spring Longing," "Birth and Desire" and "Cravings." "Bacchic Revel in Rome" depicted

The heads of girls thrown back in dance divine,
The breasts of them in undue prominence,
The blood in them warm with a decadence,
The eyes of them full of the old delusion
Of gods and beasts and sexes in confusion.

Most of Frost's friends, fearful of provoking his wrath, carefully avoided personal confrontations, especially about "sexes in confusion." But Bynner was more bold. After Bynner had praised Colony's poems, Frost condemned their transparently Whitmanesque glorification of homosexuality, and ironically declared that Bynner was too young and innocent to understand their sexual implications. The exasperated Bynner ended the argument by grabbing a handy mug of beer and pouring it on Frost's head. Instead of exploding in anger at this outrage, Frost took it good-naturedly. He assumed the libation had been offered in a spirit of fun, and merely said: "You must be drunk." Bynner was certain he had mortally offended Frost and feared reprisals. But in March 1939 Frost, mentioning that he had not been properly anointed, genially wrote: "I hope you keep up in Santa Fe the high spirits of the days when you poured beer (mind you, not wine or oil) on my head for not agreeing with you that in Horatio Colony you had made your second greatest discovery in poetry. Long may you flourish the beer mug."

Many years later, when Frost had achieved great eminence and Bynner's reputation had declined, he saw Frost in the dining room of the Hanover Inn in New Hampshire. Still contrite, he approached Frost's table and said: "'Robert, do you remember me? I apologize for pouring that beer on you.' Frost looked at him in silence for a brief moment, as if, Bynner felt, taking his measure, and then recited two of Bynner's poems. A great compliment had been paid."[7]

III

Just as the Jazz Age, Prohibition, speakeasies and expatriate life in Europe during the 1920s made no impression on Frost's rural life, academic work and pastoral poetry, and might never have existed as far as he was concerned, so in the 1930s he tended to ignore not only the wars in Europe and Asia but also the unemployment, dust-bowl farms, bankruptcies, bread lines and suicides that came with the Depression. When most American artists and intellectuals were on the Left, he was adamantly opposed to the prevailing ideas about Communism, the proletariat, industrial conflicts and social welfare.

His father had been actively engaged in Democratic politics in San Francisco. During his boyhood Frost had been exposed to radical works like Edward Bellamy's *Looking Backward* (1888), which described a utopian, communistic Boston in the year 2000, and Henry George's *Progress and Poverty* (1879), which attacked private ownership of land and advocated a Single Tax. He thought that Grover Cleveland, Theodore Roosevelt and Woodrow Wilson were great men and had voted for Democratic candidates for president until the 1920s. But, writing to George Roy Elliott just after the war, he criticized Wilson's naively idealistic belief that "nothing permanent is ever achieved by force" and declared, with characteristic understatement, that both men and countries had to know how to defend themselves: "Of course nothing permanent is ever achieved by anything, though I sometimes half feel as if the end of Carthage was pretty permanently achieved by the Romans."

In his famous two-line poem "Precaution," published in *A Further Range* (1936), Frost maintained that he had never dared to be radical when young for fear of becoming conservative when old. But as a young man he had been radical enough to have premarital sex, raise a family without a regular job or salary, live a bohemian life, advocate progressive education and vote for Democratic candidates. And he certainly became conservative by the time he reached fifty. Though Frost had lived on his grandfather's annuity for twenty-three years, there was a certain consistency in his thought. He had praised Robinson Crusoe and Henry Thoreau for their self-sufficiency. He had urged a friend to be individualistic and "go it alone. You are stronger that way." His personal quarrel with President Alexander Meiklejohn, in which he opposed socialism with self-reliance, clearly anticipated his dislike of President Franklin Roosevelt. Far from courting popularity, Frost deliberately opposed the prevailing tide in his frequent criticism of the New Deal.

John Bartlett's daughter said that Frost did not share her father's conservative Republican views. But in 1927, after one of the most notorious trials of the decade, Frost had defended what all liberals considered to be the unjust execution of the Italian Anarchists Sacco and Vanzetti. Arguing illogically and speciously that they deserved to be killed for merely planning a crime, even if they did not actually commit one, he told Mertins: "I have no sympathy with them. They may not have been guilty of the specific crime [murder] with which they were charged; but it was just as well. They intended to commit some similar crime, carrying firearms to do it." By the time Roosevelt began to implement the New Deal in the 1930s, Frost had become a rock-ribbed Vermont Republican, strongly opposed to a minimum wage, labor union legislation, Social Security and medical insurance. Acutely summarizing Frost's political beliefs, Theodore Ziolkowski wrote: "In the atmosphere of the early 1930s, he worried more about a move toward socialism that would disenfranchise private property owners and he feared a movement away from republican democracy toward a totalitarianistic welfare state. The position that Frost developed constituted a kind of Emersonian self-reliance and classical laissez-faire conservatism that was specifically opposed to collective action."

Frost said he wanted not a New Deal, but a New Deck, and referred to the Popular Front, a coalition of Left-wing parties opposed to Fascism, as the "Popular Behind." He believed that Socialism, which took money from those who worked and gave it to idlers, was theft. He mocked welfare planners who felt social problems could be cured by legislation, and thought that in a homogenized society the cream would never rise to the top. A Social Darwinist who believed the strongest should prevail in the struggle for existence, he argued that man's first duty was to protect himself: "I discovered from Bellamy that socialism is everybody looking after Number Two. My criticism was the same then as now; just as conservative. It's harder to look after Number Two than Number One, for how do you know what Number Two wants?"[8]

Instead of restraining Frost's extreme tendencies, as she did with other aspects of his life, Elinor actually encouraged his conservative beliefs. Van Wyck Brooks recorded that Elinor hated Roosevelt for stealing their hard-earned money and handing it out to the unemployed workers of the cities. Newdick stated that the usually mild and unassertive Elinor was rabid on the subject of the New Deal and "hated FDR. A passion with her. She said she would kill him, if she had the strength." Brooks also believed that after Elinor's death Frost continued to attack Roosevelt "by way of making amends to his wife."

Frost expressed his beliefs in interviews as well as in poetry. On February 26, 1936 the *Baltimore Sun* reported: "Robert Frost has descended from the poetical Parnassus to the political arena. . . . He asserted he was anti-Roosevelt. He declared he once had held high hopes for Henry Wallace [Roosevelt's Secretary of Agriculture] but had lost them. He bitterly condemned an alleged administration policy regarding farmers as possessors of what he called sub-marginal minds, and with something of a flourish he produced a new poem, 'To a Thinker.' The verse, he indicated, was written about the President." Frost not only attacked Roosevelt in "To a Thinker" (in *A Further Range*), cruelly referring to his paralyzed walk as "rocking, or weaving," but also condemned "beneficent beasts of prey" in "A Roadside Stand" (also in *A Further Range*), "collectivistic regimenting love" in "A Considerable Speck" (1939) and "a holy impulse towards redistribution" in *A Masque of Mercy*. But in May 1943—when he won another Pulitzer Prize, for *A Witness Tree*, a year before Roosevelt's fourth presidential campaign—Frost wittily wrote that "Getting [the Prize] for the fourth time rather stops me from saying anything against a fourth term as president."[9]

Elinor's negative influence reveals that Frost's political ideas were more personal than ideological. He had known real poverty from the time of his father's death in 1885 until he began to teach at Pinkerton in 1906. He helped support his four children throughout their adult lives and came to believe that he had harmed them by undermining their independence. In October 1930 he frankly told a younger poet that he was a selfish artist and would not give a cent to see the world made better. He wanted the world to stay the way it was, like all conservatives, so he could continue to write poetry about it.

IV

Frost's political views influenced the negative reception of his sixth book, *A Further Range*, published on May 29, 1936. The title referred not only to the Green Mountains of Vermont beyond the White Mountains of New Hampshire, and past them to the Rockies and the Himalayas, but also to a new range of didactic poems with political themes. As reluctant as ever to bring out his later books, in 1936 Frost told George Whicher that since publication of *West-Running Brook* in 1928, "my seven [i.e., eight] years of writing are up and I must once again face print. Lucky I got the publisher to accept the seven-year formula early. I should go crazy or barren or something if I had them at me all the time." Though *A Further Range* had a greater number of mediocre poems than any previous book, it exhibited formidable technical skill and contained a dazzling range of genres: dramatic monologue, lyric, comedy, satire, ballad, epithalamium, epigram, recipe, animal fable, historical narrative and "political pastoral." It also had at least seven first-rate poems.[10]

"Two Tramps in Mudtime" opens in early spring when (as in "The Ax-Helve") the speaker is interrupted while chopping wood. Two intimidating tramps want to "take"—not do—the job for pay. Frost then shifts away from the main subject, as he often does, to a brilliant description of the treacherous New England spring, which suddenly changes from May to March. He returns, three stanzas later, to describe the intense pleasure he takes in physical labor and to consider the demands of the tramps. They are professional lumberjacks, who have left the forest and chosen *not* to work, and therefore have no pressing claim on his charity. The argument finally comes down to the speaker's love of work against their need of work for gain. He concedes that they have the better right, but the "But" that begins the final stanza suggests that his point of view will prevail. Using a daring Metaphysical conceit (like Donne's "twin compasses" in "A Valediction: Forbidding Mourning"), he says his aim in life is to write poetry *and* chop wood, just as his two eyes focus into single sight. Though it would be socially beneficial to give employment to the tramps, Frost believes—since the physical pleasure of chopping wood while observing the hesitant coming of spring is absolutely essential to the creation of his poetry—that his personal needs are paramount. The speaker looks after Number One rather than Number Two. As he told Untermeyer, he was brought up to think of self-preservation as a virtue, not an instinct. Just as "The Lone Striker" disappoints Left-wing expectations by advocating an individual's flight from industrial disputes rather than workers' solidarity and communal effort, so "Two Tramps in Mudtime" resists the liberal impulse and sends the tramps back into the mud instead of responding to their urgent but unspoken demand for money. As the speaker cunningly says when describing the spring, the lurking *frost* will show its crystal teeth.

"Provide, Provide," composed in seven savage triplets, was inspired, Frost said, by "a strike at Harvard College of the women who washed the steps, the front: scrubwomen." In the poem the withered hag washing the steps had once been a beautiful Hollywood film star. But she failed to take care of herself and provide for the future, and has now fallen on hard times. Some people, like professors, rely on knowledge for security; others, like their wives, on their fidelity. In order to avoid degrading poverty in old age, Frost argues, it would be better to buy the friendship of those who could take care of you rather than have no friends and no care at all. The forceful injunction of the last two words, "Provide, provide!," were usually followed during his public readings by Frost's statement: "Or somebody else'll provide for you! . . . And how'll you like that?" In this satire on the sentimental humanitarianism of the New Deal, which tries and fails to provide for all, Frost urges his readers to avoid the two alternatives offered at the end of the poem—hardship or boughten friendship—by providing for themselves.

Frost called "A Drumlin Woodchuck" a "smug poem" about "making his own freedom and security." A drumlin is a smoothly rounded hill; a woodchuck, or groundhog, hibernates for half the year and (in this witty poem) hides for the rest of the time. The frightened, defensive yet resourceful and cunning creature—who has been so instinctively thorough about his crevice and burrow—is very like the animal narrator in Kafka's "The Burrow," who begins: "I have completed the construction of my burrow and it seems to be successful. All that can be seen from the outside is a big hole; that, however, really leads nowhere; if you take a few steps you strike against natural firm rock." Frost's poem, like Kafka's story, describes how a writer must protect himself by hiding from people who make unwelcome demands and interfere with his work.

Another animal fable, "Departmental" (whose title comes from Kipling's *Departmental Ditties,* 1886), is a witty, cunningly rhymed satire on the mindless and boring bureaucracy of academic departments. Frost told Andrei Sergeev that formic, the acidic language of the ants, was in fact "the language of critics."[11] In "Departmental," the ants, like the professors, all have their narrow specialties and do not even stop their hurried tread when they come across one of their dead. Instead, they summon a solemn mortician whose official duty it is to drag away the obstructive corpse. Frost also satirizes, as in the conclusion of "'Out Out—'," the general indifference to the death of a friend or colleague: no one wastes time staring at the body, which is not their affair.

"Neither Out Far Nor In Deep" has been read by sophisticated critics like Lionel Trilling as "the response of mankind to the empty immensity of the universe." In fact, as its negative title and hopeless quest for truth suggest, it considers the same question as in "The Star-Splitter": "We've looked and looked, but after all where are we?" The poem is closely related to "Departmental" and mocks Frost's imperceptive critics, who turn their backs on the reality of the land and look pointlessly at the sea all day. They cannot either look out far to see the whole design of his work, nor in deep to scrutinize the exact details. Frost concludes by ironically alluding to Christ's words to his disciples at Gethsemane: "tarry ye here, and watch with me" (Matthew 26:38). The manifest limitations of his dull-witted critics, he says, never prevented them from searching for meanings in his verse, and their stupidity was never a bar to any watch they keep. This poem could be called, like the actual confection of ice cream encased in chocolate, "Frost-Bite."

"Desert Places" develops the themes in "Acquainted with the Night": loneliness, fear and despair. The fine opening line, which balances snow falling fast with night falling fast, equates the deathly aspect of the snow that covers the ground with the night that covers the sky. The fifth line, which describes the fallen snow that smothers the animals in their lairs: "The woods around us have it—it is theirs," follows the rhythm and structure of the first line of Matthew Arnold's sonnet "Shakespeare": "Others abide our question. Thou art free." The nothingness of the "benighted snow"—an apparent (black-white) contradiction, but actually an exact description of snow at night—and the vast immensities between the empty stars do not frighten the speaker nearly as much as the desolate, desert places within himself.

"Design," a perfectly executed sonnet, is Frost's greatest poem. The title refers to the idea, as William James writes in *Pragmatism* (1907), that "God's existence has from time immemorial been held to be proved by certain natural facts. . . . Such mutual fitting of things diverse in origin argued design, it was held; and the designer was always treated as a man-loving deity." The idea of a benign deity is mentioned, for example, in Matthew 10:29, which teaches that God oversees every aspect of the world, even unto the fate of the most common bird: "Are not two sparrows sold for a farthing? and one of them shall not fall on the ground without your Father" knowing it. The idea of a perfectly created world also appears in Genesis 1:31, where "God saw everything that he had made, and, behold, it was very good." In "The Tyger" (1794) Blake admired the power of a God who could create, in his divine order, the most fierce and gentle hearts, and rhetorically asked: "Did he smile his work to see? / Did he who made the Lamb make thee?"

To poets, the spider could represent different purposes in God's design. Whitman's "A Noiseless Patient Spider" is benign; but the Black Widow in Robert Lowell's "Mr. Edwards and the Spider" is a symbol of the damned soul. Frost, like Hardy in "An August Midnight," uses the spider to emphasize the evil aspect of God's design and offers, as Randall Jarrell notes, an "Argument from Design with a vengeance. . . . If a diabolical machine, then a diabolical mechanic . . . in this little Albino catastrophe."[12]

In "Design" the normally black spider and blue heal-all (the ironic name of the medicinal flower) are both wickedly white—a play on Elinor's maiden name. The spider, fattened by a previous victim, holds a dead white moth like a rigid piece of satin cloth (or a rigid waxy corpse) in a coffin. These three characters of death and blight, like the elements of a witches' broth, are ready to begin the morning right—or evil rite. Frost asks what evil force made the blue flower white and what malign power brought the spider into deadly conjunction with the moth. His dark answer suggests that this awful albino death-scene refutes Genesis, St. Matthew and the comforting belief recounted by Blake and William James: "What but design of darkness to appall?— / If design govern in a thing so small." In the horrible but inevitable logic of "Design" Frost replaces God's design with the artist's.

V

In 1936, for the first time since the publication of *North of Boston,* a number of high-powered and highly regarded critics reviewed Frost's work. This time, however, irritated by the weaker political verse, they ignored the great poems in *A Further Range.* They accused Frost of being completely out of touch with the spirit of the time and claimed that his poems, which had once balanced polarities in a delicate way, had moved toward assertiveness and dogmatic opinions, that his rugged individualism had hardened into reactionary ideas. "Build Soil" combines Frost's worst faults. It is tedious, long-winded, prosaic and dull, and wavers between what James Dickey called "elephantine levity and cracker-barrel philosophizing." As Granville Hicks wrote, Frost had become "Self-satisfied and yet at times regretful, / Profoundly smug but growing rather fretful." When Frost wanted to collect his "short pieces and poems about his political ideas and thoughts on man in the modern world," his publisher wisely dissuaded him.[13] Frost reacted defensively, claiming that he had antagonized the critics by not writing for the little magazines and by not "playing ball" with radical journals like the *Dial* and the *Little Review.* He claimed that Malcolm Cowley, the literary editor of the Left-wing *New Republic,* disliked him because he did not "hammer away" at their cause.

The poet Horace Gregory thought Frost was already *vieux jeu* and called him "the last survivor of the 'Georgian movement.'" Malcolm Cowley—repeating Hicks' criticism, that Frost was hopelessly old-fashioned and "cannot give us the sense of belonging in the industrial, scientific, Freudian world in which we find ourselves"—declared that

Frost was a reactionary, "opposed to innovations in art, ethics, science, industry or politics." Morton Zabel, a Unversity of Chicago professor writing in the *Southern Review,* said Frost had failed to develop from his earlier books, that "a certain vanity has bred stiffness in his sympathies and vision," that "uncritical indulgence has allowed pieces of dull writing and petulant wisdom to enter this volume."[14]

Other eminent critics were even harsher. Dudley Fitts, a distinguished translator of the Classics, noted "an obvious didacticism, a ponderous kind of playfulness" and "a sterility," and concluded (despite "Design" and the other fine poems) that "the diction is faded, the expression imprecise, and the tone extraordinarily tired and uneasy." Richard Blackmur (whom Frost referred to as Blackamur), an influential New Critic at Princeton, condemned Frost's "poetic failures" and said: "The good lines emphasize the bad, the careless, and the irrelevant, and make them intolerable." Newton Arvin, a Left-wing critic who taught at Smith, was the most severe of all. In the *Partisan Review* he lashed out at Frost's "profitless" philosophy, "fruitless and rather complacent skepticism," "dryness, emptiness, caprice, and even banality," lack of feeling and intellect and (fatal omission) "complete silence on the savageries of Fascism in Italy and Germany."[15]

In the 1930s the mixture of Left-wing ideology, resentment and envy of Frost, and legitimate criticism of the banality and smugness of the political poems devastated his book in the critical journals. Rolfe Humphries, a minor poet and classicist writing in the Communist *New Masses,* mocked the title of the book and called his review "A Further Shrinking." Condemning Frost's irritating didacticism and lack of originality, he blindly dismissed the poems as "defective in tone, color, and atmosphere . . . fuddled, garrulous, deaf, and ordinary." Humphries' letter to Frost's pupil and disciple Merrill Root, who had favorably reviewed the book in the obscure *Christian Century,* reveals that there was a great deal of personal jealousy and animosity behind all these reviews. In July 1942 Humphries (relying on gossip, for he did not know Frost well) asked: "Why is he so frightened, so mean, so envious, so jealous? He must know how false is much of the adulation that wreathes him round, yet he plays up to it." False or not, it *was* adulation and Frost (like most people) loved it.

In December 1936, Frost responded to Humphries' charge that he was a "counter-revolutionary" by punning and calling him, during a lecture at the New School for Social Research in New York, "a bargain-counter revolutionary." After his talk, a volatile bearded man stopped

Frost, said he was a friend of Humphries and threatened him. Frost remembered the threat, soon after he returned to Amherst, when he received a suspicious-looking package with no return address that seemed to contain a cigar box. Fearing that it was a bomb, he took it into the backyard, threw it against a tree—and scattered the cigars all over the yard.

Accustomed to praise for the last twenty years and knowing full well what he had achieved in *A Further Range,* Frost was hurt and disheartened by the onslaught of criticism. His pain was not mollified by favorable but relatively feeble hosannahs from John Holmes, his former Holt editor Herschel Brickell, his Texas friend Leonidas Payne, the serviceable Newdick, the prolific sonneteer Merrill Moore and the faithful Untermeyer. Frost's reputation still remained strong in England, however, where the Irish poet James Stephens, who had met him in Dublin in 1928, gratifyingly declared in the *Sunday Times* that "Mr. Frost now occupies in his own land the position which Mr. Yeats now occupies in ours. . . . More than any other American poet he is securely in the tradition of English verse."[16]

By 1936 Richard Thornton had succeeded Herschel Brickell (who had followed Lincoln MacVeagh) as Frost's editor at Holt. Born in Virginia in 1888, Thornton was educated at Lynchburg College and did graduate work at Columbia and Chicago before becoming an instructor in English at the University of North Carolina. He had served in the Navy in World War I, and commuted from suburban Scarsdale while working for Holt. Just as Mme. Nutt had capitalized on the good reviews of *North of Boston* by bringing out a publicity pamphlet in 1914, so Thornton attempted to bolster Frost's reputation by publishing and editing in 1937, twenty-four years after *A Boy's Will,* a book-length anthology of praise. *Recognition of Robert Frost* contained more than fifty essays, including important early reviews, verse tributes by his English friends, memoirs by Sidney Cox, Dorothy Canfield Fisher, George Whicher and Padraic Colum, homage from French and German critics, and appreciative essays by Untermeyer, George Roy Elliott and Mark Van Doren. The book concluded with disappointingly bland prefaces to the English edition of his *Selected Poems* by three important British poets: Edwin Muir, C. Day Lewis and W. H. Auden. It received positive notices from Theodore Morrison, Bernard DeVoto and several other critics, who did not think the tribute to Frost was premature or inappropriate.

Despite the negative reviews, Frost's "barding around" the country paid off and his sales went up as his quality seemed to go down. The limited edition had 800 copies; the trade edition had a first printing of 4,000 and a second of 6,000; and the Book-of-the-Month Club (with the faithful Dorothy Canfield Fisher on the selection committee) took an astonishing 59,000 copies, which earned $10,000. In 1937, the year the book of tributes appeared, Frost triumphed over the politically biased criticisms and won his third Pulitzer Prize, for *A Further Range*.

In 1939 Frost published his most important statement about poetry, the brief but metaphorically dense essay "The Figure a Poem Makes," as an Introduction to his *Collected Poems* and used it in all later editions of this work. Emphasizing *sound* as the gold in the ore of poetry, he says that he tries to make all his poems sound very different from one another. When defining true poetry, he advocates wildness, an unforeseen but predestined outcome, a series of revelations, the free play of wit, and the elements of freshness and surprise. Some of Frost's most famous and now proverbial phrases appear in this essay. Echoing Horace's *utile dulci*, he insists that a poem begins in delight and ends in wisdom; that its artistic order represents a momentary stay against confusion in the world; that the poet must experience tragic tears in order to move the reader to tears; and that the poem must ride on its own melting like a chunk of ice on a hot stove.

VI

By the 1920s Frost was sufficiently famous to attract a number of would-be and mostly ill-fated biographers. Since the distortions in the early reviews and essays by Pound and Amy Lowell, he had been extremely sensitive about interpretations of his life and work. This biographical activity both pleased and upset him, and intensified his ambivalent attitude toward his critics. Obsessed by his own life, which he frequently discussed in late-night conversations, he wanted to be perpetuated and wanted the world to know about him, but he did not want to reveal his private affairs or be "told" about himself. In one of his famous and most cryptic statements, he insisted in *A Masque of Mercy:* "But I want you to understand me wrong." He probably meant that he wanted his meaning to be understood on his own terms and in exactly the way he wished to be taken, revealing what he wanted to make public and hiding the more intimate aspects of his life.

The first candidate was Wilfred Davison, the dean of the Bread Loaf

School, who planned the book in 1926 and died, without doing much work on it, three years later. He was succeeded by the promising young English poet Edward Davison (no relation to Wilfred), who had been introduced to Frost by J. C. Squire. But he made the fatal mistake of criticizing Untermeyer in his first draft. To compensate for Davison's disappointment after he was urged to abandon the project, Frost invited him to lecture at Amherst, successfully recommended him for a Guggenheim Fellowship to England and helped get him a job as director of the Rocky Mountain Writers' Conference in Colorado. Frost was fond of Davison, often appeared at the Conference and remained on cordial terms with both him and his son, the poet Peter Davison. The first short but competent book on Frost, *Robert Frost: A Study in Sensibility and Good Sense* (1927), was finally published by Gorham Munson in George Doran's series of Murray Hill Biographies. About half of the book, based on information from John Bartlett and Sidney Cox, was biographical; the rest dealt with Frost's literary techniques.

In 1935 the dogged Robert Newdick, a Professor of English at Ohio State University, entered Frost's life. Newdick, whom his editor calls "a most obedient and adoring servant," was an enthusiast who sought Frost out and impressed him with his fanatical commitment, scholarly research and serious articles about his work in academic journals. In the mid-1930s he did a great deal of basic research into Frost's family background and early life, and transcribed many of his long conversations with Frost. But when Newdick found some early poems in the files of the *Independent,* which had been sold to the Huntington Library in California, Frost was alarmed. He did not want his current reputation to be harmed by the publication of his juvenile efforts, and flatly denied that he had written them. Frost told him: "The article in *American Literature* [May 1935] frightened me with the closeness which it follows on my trail. I shall have to walk in water for a mile to see if I can't throw you off." When Newdick showed him an article on "Robert Frost and the Classics" before publishing it in the *Classical Journal,* Frost responded with some annoyance. "'Tis ever thus with the biographer," Frost told him; "he will be making the most of everything. You are going to have me a classical scholar." Though he was proud of his knowledge of classical languages, and the high grades he had received in Greek at Harvard, he felt Newdick exaggerated his expertise.

Wanting to be left to "self-forgetfulness," Frost felt he had to take forceful measures to throw academic pathfinders off the trail. He told their mutual friend John Holmes that Newdick was all right and that he liked him most of the time, but asked Holmes' help in abating his excessive zeal. Holmes dutifully told Newdick to stop grilling Frost and warned him about Elinor, who had a strong desire for privacy and had cautioned Frost not to tell Newdick "everything": "If I were you I wouldn't follow him with many questions about his past in your search for records during the next few weeks. Both he and Mrs. Frost have a way of backing away from the responsibility of digging up material from the past." Frost also warned Newdick that he was not always a reliable source about his own life. Alluding to "The truest poetry is the most feigning" in *As You Like It,* he told his pursuer: "I was a very hard person to make out. . . . I might easily be most deceiving when most bent on telling the truth."[17] Canny yet indiscreet, sometimes manipulative and domineering, Frost enjoyed the attentions of his biographers but was also irritated by their revelations.

As early as November 1937 Frost feared the industrious but well-intentioned Newdick might inhibit his creative powers. He said he had carefully saved many experiences to use in his work and did not want anyone else to write about them. The people most interested in his poetry, Frost felt, could actually choke it off. He warned Newdick that "he had spent his life heaping up piles of building material—friends, experiences, memories—and leaving them behind him unused to be used sometime when, as and how he wished. He said that this material he feels is his, possibly for poems, and that once shaped by another hand isn't quite his any more." Newdick finally showed some awareness of Frost's uneasiness by recording a number of delicate (though not scandalous) matters that could not be mentioned in his future biography: "Extreme sensitiveness to criticism. . . . Remembers old wrongs. . . . No ear for music. . . . Intolerant of new currents, trends, movements, experiments in poetry, e.g., Eliot, MacLeish. . . . Negligent of correspondence. . . . Unusual closeness of union with his wife. . . . Children disappointing."

Newdick died unexpectedly during an operation for appendicitis in July 1939, raving about Frost, according to Mrs. Newdick, in his final delirium. For the moment Frost seemed free from the obsessive prying of his biographers. He discouraged the California collector and bibliographer Louis Mertins, whose "degree of devotion surpassed that of Newdick," and said he did not want Mertins to come east and "start nosing about in the years that are over. . . . I went through all this with Newdick." The scholar's basic research was "nosing about" to the poet. With grisly humor Frost ascribed Newdick's death to biography: "I suppose it killed him. . . . I told him I wouldn't stand for it, and he'd have to stop it. It broke his heart and he died."[18]

Sidney Cox, who had helped Munson, brought out his own forty-page booklet, *Robert Frost: Original "Ordinary Man,"* in 1929. He had his career to make at Dartmouth, and also wanted to expand his memoir and enter the biographical sweepstakes. But Frost, like his cunning and elusive drumlin woodchuck, was all for secrecy and guile. He sent Cox a series of monitory letters, urging him not to disillusion Frost's admirers by revealing the factual basis of his "sources and processes." He had told both Bynner and Untermeyer that his letters would be spoiled if they became collectors' items or biographical trophies, and frankly informed Cox that he had to protect himself against intrusions: "I have written to keep the over curious out of the secret places of my mind both in my verse and in my letters to such as you. . . . My objection to your larger book about me was that it came thrusting in where I did not want you." Like the bear in his poem, he was (he said) "such a free wild animal that being defined is as hateful to me as being trapped and caged." But the main reason for his woodchuck wariness, he told Alice Cox in 1956, four years after Sidney's death, was that personal revelations and critical analyses threatened his creative process: "I have never been able to go deeply into anything, review or article, that concerned my life or work for fear it would overwhelm me with self-consciousness."[19] Despite all these reservations, Frost's friendship with and gratitude to Cox prevailed, and in 1957 he agreed to the posthumous publication of Cox's *A Swinger of Birches: A Portrait of Robert Frost.* Taking advantage of his uncanny ability to outlive those who tried to write the story of his life, he added a sly preface that described his first meeting with Cox.

Margaret Bartlett, one of Frost's favorite pupils at Pinkerton, did not fare as well as Cox. The apparently generous dedication of Frost's last book, *In the Clearing* (1962), read: "Letters in prose to Louis Untermeyer, Sidney Cox, and John Bartlett for them to dispose of as they please." Since Bartlett had died in 1947 and Cox five years later, they were not in a position to dispose of anything. Soon after John's death, however, Margaret asked if she could publish an edition of Frost's letters to her husband in their biographical context. Using a familiar argument, Frost begged her to spare him that ordeal in his lifetime. He said that several biographies were being written or threatened, and that they were even worse than photographs and portraits for intensifying his self-consciousness and blocking his imagination. Two years later, Margaret poignantly renewed her plea by telling Frost that she was dying of cancer but still had time to edit the letters. Though her fortitude in the face of approaching death made it difficult to refuse her request, he stood firm. *Robert Frost and John Bartlett: The Record of a Friendship* was eventually published by her daughter, Margaret Bartlett Anderson, after Frost's death, in 1963.

VII

Frost needed an official biographer, not only to control access to his life and discourage other researchers, but also to ensure his place in literary history. After Newdick's death the biographical baton was passed to Lawrance Thompson, who was then curator of rare books at the Princeton University library and editor of its *Library Chronicle*. Before entering this high-mortality race, he modestly told Frost that Bernard DeVoto, Mark Van Doren or Louis Untermeyer should write his life. But Frost thought Thompson would be more dedicated and pliable, and suggested that he write it.

Thompson—a handsome, charming, industrious and apparently devoted man—was born in New Hampshire in 1906, graduated from Wesleyan and got his doctorate at Columbia. He helped organize a Frost exhibition at Wesleyan in 1936, published a book on Longfellow in 1938 and would bring out *Fire and Ice*, a study of Frost's poetry, in 1942. Apart from his service as a commander in the Navy in World War II, Thompson devoted most of his professional career to writing about Frost. Being the poet's biographer completely changed Thompson's life and absorbed him into Frost's. The biography gave Thompson status, grants, prestige and reflected glory. Recommended by Frost, he won a Guggenheim Fellowship in 1946 for this purpose and, after moving up the academic ladder, became a professor of English at Princeton in 1951. He was also offered a job at Harvard, but Princeton was eager to keep him and gave him more free time to work on the book.

Thompson's biography, begun in 1939, was an immense labor. It could not be published before Frost's death and consumed nearly thirty-five years of Thompson's life. He began research on it at the age of thirty-three, when Frost was sixty-five. Since Frost's father had died at thirty-four and his mother at fifty-six, it was reasonable to suppose he might also die within the next five or ten years. Instead, Frost lived for another twenty-five years, postponing indefinitely the long-awaited publication of the book. Thompson became seriously ill with a brain tumor while writing the second volume and, like several of his predecessors, died before he could complete the biography. The third volume was eventually put together by his student R. H. Winnick.

Thompson was well aware of Newdick's uneasy relations with Frost and should have been warned by his example. Though Frost was willing to talk expansively about his life, exaggerating the truth whenever he felt so inclined, he did not feel responsible for getting all the facts right and thought Thompson should find them on his own. He liked to talk, but disliked being interrogated, and misled Thompson as he had Newdick. Thompson did not have access to the material Newdick had gathered, which was finally published in 1976 as *Newdick's Season of Frost*.

Thompson was a critic as well as a biographer, and Frost resented critical interpretations of his poetry. When *A Masque of Reason* appeared in 1945, Thompson irritated Frost by distorting his religious views, by criticizing his character and by writing, in an unenthusiastic review, that "Frost's familiar cunning and slyness flash constantly through varied twists of words and phrases." Later on, Frost felt obliged to warn Thompson not only of the danger of seeing symbols where none exist, but also of the critic's presumption that he can surpass the poet by telling him what he is really up to. In the educational film they made together, *Princeton '55: The Enjoyment of Poetry*, Frost gets rather testy as Thompson labors through a dull explication of "The Witch of Coös." As Thompson hesitates and repeatedly asks Frost if his interpretation is on the right track, Frost tears his argument to shreds and insists that the meaning of his poem is perfectly clear. Just as a comedian expects his audience to get the point of his joke, Frost maintains, so a poet intends his readers to understand the meaning of his poem.

Thompson's extensive correspondence with Frost (now at Dartmouth) reveals that their relations were often—as in the film—strained and awkward. Thompson never managed to get on easy terms with his subject. Alternately fawning, sycophantic and irritable, he worried about becoming inappropriately familiar but constantly overstepped the mark. His unremitting research frequently annoyed Frost, who vented his anger on Thompson and subjected him to his demanding authority. A much more considerable figure than Newdick, Thompson wanted for professional reasons to spend as much time as possible with Frost, but deeply resented his role as factotum. Watching Frost at close quarters, and sometimes acting as his servant, Thompson had endless opportunities to observe his personal faults. As Archibald MacLeish perceived:

"Thompson saw too much of him—learned to dislike him very heart-ily!"[20]

Thompson himself believed that his relations with Frost began to deteriorate as early as 1946, when he returned from the war, spent the first of nine summers near Frost's cabin at Ripton, Vermont, and frequently saw the negative side of his character. Thompson confessed that it was "easy enough to get mad at the old bastard." Noticing Thompson's irascibility, Frost asked him: "Wasn't it possible that [he] had been working so hard and so long on Frost that [he] was actually sick of the whole thing?" Thompson's pathological hatred extended from Frost to his whole family. In a particularly splenetic outburst, he called Frost and Elinor "good examples of psychotics" and said "Lesley is [also] insane, though still at large." Thompson's Introduction to his edition of Frost's *Selected Letters* (1964) clearly expressed his attitude toward Frost. "His private correspondence," Thompson wrote, "reveals periods of gloom, jealousies, obsessive resentments, sulking displays of temper, nervous rages, and vindictive retaliations"—all of which now seems to describe Thompson rather than Frost.

No wonder, then, that Frost regretted naming Thompson his biographer and was fearful of the result. Stanley Burnshaw, his last editor at Holt, remembered when Frost insisted:

> "I'm counting on you to protect me from Larry.". . .
> "But he's your official biographer! *You* picked him."
> "I'm *counting* on you," he repeated gravely. "You will be here. I won't."
> "If you need protection, simply undo what you did."
> "Too late now."
> "*Anyone* has the right to retract for a valid reason."
> "I gave him my word."

But Burnshaw never convincingly explained why he, Frost's editor, and Holt, Frost's publisher, brought out a violently hostile biography of their most prominent author or why Burnshaw later wrote a whole book attacking the biography that he himself had edited.

While Thompson was toiling away in the third decade of his labors, Frost—to cover his bets when relations with Thompson deteriorated —encouraged Elizabeth Sergeant, who had published a good essay on him in the *New Republic* of 1925, to bring out her own book in 1960. Thompson, livid but impotent, exclaimed: "I'll never forgive that bitch, no matter how long I live."[21] Nor did he ever forgive Frost. Though he constantly sniped at Sergeant's inaccuracy in his lengthy footnotes, he used a good deal of her solid and serviceable biography.

When Thompson's biography eventually came out, most readers accepted his apparently authoritative view, but friends and scholars who knew Frost's life were shocked by the rabid bias. Reginald Cook declared that Thompson exaggerated "Frost's fierce professional jealousy, unforgiving vindictiveness, ruthless cunning, intense illiberalism, and sly playing of the career-advancing game." William Pritchard's Introduction to his 1984 study of Frost documented Thompson's manifest resentment and heavy-handed bias, and criticized him for portraying Frost as "a species of monster in human form."

Leon Edel, the eminent biographer of Henry James, cited Thompson's book as a notorious example of a negative "transference" between author and subject. "By the time Frost died," Edel observed, "Thompson was ready to arraign his subject as arrogant, jealous, resentful, sulky, vindictive and addicted to tempers and rages. Readers of Thompson's biography, which was never fully completed, remember that what emerged was a merciless portrayal of Frost's egotism and its devastating effect on those close to him." Robert Lowell, a friend and admirer of Frost, condemned Thompson's biography as "a work mediocre, poisonous, tone deaf, unable to animate a single character."[22]

During his quarter-century with Frost, Thompson gathered documents, letters and manuscripts, interviewed family and friends, and made notes on Frost's conversations. He spent many summers in Vermont, took care of Frost in Florida and traveled with him on trips abroad. He witnessed and recorded Frost's chaotic reaction to Elinor's death and, at the same time as Frost, became involved with Kay Morrison. Thompson's emotional entanglements with his subject made them both frustrated and angry. But except for the war years, he became Frost's persistent shadow, performing essential services and never leaving the scent of his trail.[23]

13

Death and Chaos

1938

I

Elinor, an invalid in high school, had a long history of chronic heart disease, complicated by the physical strain of eight pregnancies, an abortion, a miscarriage and a nervous breakdown in 1925. She had a severe heart attack in October 1934. Three years later, when she was operated on for a malignant growth and had her right breast removed, she was in mortal danger from both heart disease and cancer. This put a great strain on their marriage. While she was recuperating in October 1937 Frost, writing to Untermeyer, emphasized two crucial aspects of her life: she had inspired many of his poems and had experienced a great deal of suffering.

The Frosts spent the winter of 1937 with Lesley and her daughters in two apartments in Gainesville, Florida. Lesley thought her family should take the upper apartment so that her mother would not have to strain her heart on the stairs, but Elinor decided that she and Robert had to live above Lesley so that he would not be disturbed by the children's noise. On March 18, 1938 she had a severe heart attack. She became temporarily unconscious and the doctor warned that she would probably die. During the next two days, while Frost waited in the hallway outside her room, Elinor had seven more heart attacks and hovered on the verge of death.

According to Thompson, Frost waited for Elinor to call him into the room so he could say goodbye to her. In this scenario, he resembles the hero of Kafka's Existential parable "Before the Law" who, filled with guilt and dread, waits passively outside the door until the end of his life and is never admitted. But Elinor was clearly too weak, confused and exhausted during her intermittent consciousness to realize Frost was waiting and summon him for a deathbed discussion. She died on March 20, at the age of sixty-six, without speaking to him.

If Frost wanted some kind of final forgiveness from her, some reassurance that his art had justified her sacrifice, he should have gone in. Knowing her bitter resentment and fearing she would punish him by not granting the longed-for absolution, he could not bring himself to enter her sickroom. He thought it was better *not* to know her final feelings, and to place the responsibility on Elinor for refusing to call him in and make her final peace. A year after her death, Frost revealed his fear of a final confrontation and told Lesley: "I wish I hadn't this woeful suspicion that toward the end she came to resent some thing in the life I had given her."[1] Elinor had refused to see him in 1894 when he had gone up to St. Lawrence University to persuade her to marry him, and had often reproached him with her agonizing silence. To Frost, her silent rejection at the end of her life seemed to match her traumatic rejection during their courtship.

After Frost collapsed and took to his bed, Lesley arranged the cremation in Jacksonville. Following her parents' instructions, she put a large manila envelope—probably containing their love letters—into Elinor's casket before it was burned. Her memorial service took place at the Amherst College chapel on April 20. A faculty wife noted that just before the ceremony some women squabbled audibly about how the flowers should be arranged. While they were arguing, Frost quietly entered the chapel and placed a tiny clump of orchises beside the ashes of his wife.

Elinor wanted her ashes to be scattered in Hyla Brook on their old farm in Derry. Frost went there to ask the owner's permission and was offended by her coldness. He failed to recognize some of their precious spots, which had become overgrown, and decided it would be a desecration to leave her ashes there.[2] The ashes remained in a cupboard in Carol's house in South Shaftsbury for three more years. In September 1941 Frost arranged for them to be buried in the cemetery of the First Congregational Church in Old Bennington, and asked a minister to officiate. When he and his family entered the churchyard they saw him talking to a parishioner, and waited at the grave for his arrival. Frost waited for thirty long minutes, without ever summoning the nearby minister or clarifying the reason for his delay. Finally, he put the ashes in the ground himself. His shocked passivity during the delayed interment of Elinor's ashes recalled his behavior outside her sickroom.

After her death, and their final separation and silence, Frost said he had not been away from Elinor for more than a month in forty years. He told DeVoto that she had always been present to "govern" his loneliness without making him feel less alone, and that he had pretended for her sake that he did not think the world was as bad a place as she did. In November 1917 he had frankly told Untermeyer that Elinor had never given him any practical support. She had even resisted his efforts to make money and increase his reputation. Now that she was dead, he began to idealize her and to feel irrational guilt. He told George Roy Elliott, with great exaggeration, that nearly all his poems, if rightly read, were actually about Elinor. He wrote Lesley that Elinor "was not as original as I in thought, but she dominated my art with the power of her character and nature. . . . She was cumulatively laying up against me the unsuccess of the children I had given her."

In a letter of August 2, 1938 to J. J. Lankes, whose woodcuts had illustrated Frost's books, he blamed himself for their troubles and regretted his selfishness. Alluding to their different response to the deaths of Elliott and of little Elinor, he confessed: "I'm afraid I dragged her through pretty much of a life for one as frail as she was. Too many children, too many habitations, too many vicissitudes. And a faith required that would have exhausted most women. God damn me when he gets around to it. I refused to be bowed down as much as she was by other deaths. . . . [I have] prospered in an outrageously self-indulgent life. I have been given absolutely my own way." Thoughts of Elinor's sacrifice of her own career, her ill health, poverty and household drudgery, the numerous babies, the death of two infants and of Marjorie, the failure of her children in adult life, her loss of religious faith, her desire to keep Frost's poetry private and resentment of his ever-increasing fame now seemed to obliterate all the joys of their marriage. Recognizing the cruel paradox of his life Frost, like a tragic hero, observed: "Evil clings so in all our acts that even when we not only mean but achieve our prettiest, bravest, noblest, best, we are often a scourge even to those we do not hate."

As in Henry James' "The Lesson of the Master" (1888), which portrays the insoluble conflict between family life and the higher pursuit of art, Elinor's life seemed to have been sacrificed for her husband's poetry. James' characters discuss how marriage interferes with the quest for artistic perfection, and how a man endangers his work if he devotes himself to personal rather than to intellectual passion:

"One's children interfere with perfection. One's wife interferes. Marriage interferes."

"You think, then, the artist shouldn't marry?"

"He does so at his peril—he does so at his cost.". . .

"Are there no women who really understand—who can take
part in a sacrifice?"

"How can they take part? They themselves are the sacrifice."

Sixteen years after Elinor's death, Alfred Kazin reported that Frost was
still tormented by guilt and "kept circling around her name, their
difficult family life, his fears that all Frosts were somehow off balance."[3]

II

Seeking consolation in poetry, Frost quoted Alfred Tennyson (as he had
quoted Matthew Arnold after Marjorie's death):

> And I, the last, go forth companionless,
> And the days darken round me.

Three weeks after Elinor's death he told George Roy Elliott that he
planned to wander—Lear-like—among his children until he could calm
his turbulent state of mind and decide about his future. But it was not to
be. Irma blamed her father for her mental instability, fear of sex and
marriage problems, and became permanently estranged from him. Lesley, whom Frost was thinking of when he told Robert Francis that there
had been too much "unexpressed jealousy in his family," quarreled
violently with him. She was not only jealous of Frost's favorite daughter,
Marjorie, but also (according to his daughter-in-law, Lillian) "had a
certain amount of jealousy of her mother, thinking that R. F. thought
more of Elinor than he did of her."

Immediately after Elinor's death both Frost and Lesley were in a state
of shock. Remembering the terrifying episode when Frost had threatened to shoot either Elinor or himself, Lesley paid him back by wounding him at *his* most vulnerable moment. She attacked the "genius" who
had given his wife and children such a miserable existence, and vented
her resentment about their itinerant habits and lack of friends. She
accused him of ruining Elinor's life and even of killing her by forcing her

to climb the two flights of stairs. Ignoring Elinor's influence on the children, she blamed Frost for Marjorie's death, Irma's mental illness and Carol's depression, and screamed that she would never allow him to live in her home and injure her daughters in the same way that he had destroyed his own.

Close to both her parents, Lesley—who looked like Frost and had his brilliant blue eyes—became the sole survivor of the six children in the family. Her attitude toward her father had three distinct, even contradictory phases. She condemned him in 1938, releasing her jealousy and resentment in that ferocious outburst. Later on, she adopted a more balanced but self-aggrandizing point of view, revised her attitude toward him and became her father's alter-ego. She then spent the rest of her life advocating Elinor's political prejudices and living off Frost's name and reputation. After his death, she played the role of the devoted daughter and constructed the myth of the idyllic Derry childhood. She became a professional Frostian, appeared in films about him and published photographs of Frost surrounded by his grandchildren.

By attacking Frost while benefitting from his reputation, Lesley tried to have it both ways. She had accused Frost of being duplicitous—a genial sage in public, a monster at home—and now seemed duplicitous herself. But since there were two sides of Frost (both exaggerated by Lesley, depending on her mood and role), she *could* try to have it both ways. Less forgivable perhaps was her letter of 1970 to the *New York Times Book Review*. While apparently defending him from Thompson's biography, she indulged in superficial psychologizing, declared her father mentally ill and portrayed herself (as she had done in 1938) as his victim: "Robert Frost's chief trouble was his closeness to the razor's edge of insanity—with a persecution complex involved . . . which his family, particularly my mother, saved him from. We may have suffered deep scars in the process."

Recalling his own father's cruel treatment of his mother, Frost was absolutely devastated by Lesley's accusations. Hervey Allen, like Untermeyer, rushed to Gainesville to give him comfort and support. Though Frost had known Elinor's death was imminent and had time to prepare for it, Allen reported that he had completely collapsed and was close to death himself. In a letter of March 24 to his publisher John Farrar, the old soldier described Frost's condition as if it were a war wound:

> I got in yesterday afternoon and found Frost pretty low. . . . It was a combination of shock and "throat trouble" that had Robert laid

out. He looked dreadful. . . . The doctors were worried it might
be bronchial pneumonia. . . . Up until today he hadn't been able
to see life at all without Mrs. Frost, just couldn't imagine it. This
was partly the result of the sheer jolt of her death. . . . Some
people seem to have no idea at all how to cope with a physical
remorse. . . . One of the most complicated and sensitive men of
our time [was] kind of bleeding to death mentally—and I trying
to persuade him it would be worthwhile to stop the wound. . . . I
thought Robert would just elect to go after his wife. He would
have. It would have been easy—too easy. He isn't an easy spirit.

In the fall of 1938 Frost himself admitted that he had been "crazy"
since Elinor's death and had not really known what he was doing. Ted
Morrison, who saw him at Bread Loaf that summer, agreed that he "was
in a state of desolation that all but unhinged his mind and seriously
disrupted his control of himself." During this crisis, the disturbing voices
of Frost's childhood returned to haunt him. Kay Morrison told Thompson about Frost's terrifying trance-like behavior: "When he's in these
strange moods he starts chanting a phrase in a monotone, and that tone
of voice scares Kay. She has tried throwing cold water on him, tried
slapping him across the face, and both methods have brought him out of
his chanting mood which frightens her so."[4]

In this chaotic state, Frost made several decisions that would have a
profound effect on his future life. In December 1937, three months
before Elinor's death, he had expressed chronic dissatisfaction with his
academic ties and told Joseph Blumenthal: "I get awfully cross with
college life sometimes, slight as my contact with it is, and would just as
soon wash my hands of it to hell." Some of his Amherst colleagues felt
that Frost, who had made very few public appearances, had not even
bothered to fulfill the minimum obligations of his contract. In October
1937 Frost had invited Untermeyer to lecture at Amherst. Though Untermeyer was an amusing speaker, who could reach a popular audience
and awaken the students' interest in poetry, the English faculty condemned him as superficial and refused to attend the talk. This pettiness
provoked Frost's outburst in a letter of March 1938 to DeVoto (who had
been having his own troubles at Harvard) about the characteristic malice
of academics. They had to magnify and defend their status, he said, and
were inveterately jealous and hostile to writers who had a reputation in
the real world. Frost was also irritated, he told Lesley, by the fact that he

"never had technical standing [i.e., tenure] as a full professor. I could have been dropped at any time and I never had the least claim to a pension. . . . I was kept on from year to year out of some rich man's pocket."

Frost's position at Amherst reached a crisis when President Stanley King (on vacation in Florida) visited him, just after Elinor's death, when Frost himself was seriously ill. According to accounts he gave to several friends, Frost, touched by King's appearance, apologetically said that sickness had kept him away from Amherst and that he feared he was "more bother than I'm worth." Instead of reassuring him, King shrugged his shoulders and callously remarked: "We won't talk about that *now!*" Frost took "*now*" to mean, "Here's your hat, but don't hurry." He was furious that King seemed to seize the chance to get rid of him and decided to jump ship before he was thrown overboard. After twelve years at Amherst, he resigned in June 1938 and sold his Sunset Avenue house to the college.

King was a wealthy man who had made a million dollars before he was thirty by manufacturing shoes in Boston. He was worried about Frost's cost to the college, did not offer him a pension when he resigned and did not even try to retain him as professor emeritus. King had no literary taste and did not realize—despite the enthusiastic support of Whicher, Elliott and Manthey-Zorn—that Frost was an eminent poet. He failed to see what benefit Amherst could get out of its association with him. In July 1938 Frost told his son-in-law Willard Fraser (who had gone into Democratic politics in Montana) that he had been thinking of leaving for several years. He was willing to sacrifice the income so that he would not have to try to please people and would have more freedom to write his poems. In June 1938, then, Frost came to a major turning point in his life. As Kay Morrison wrote, he "found himself bereft, without a home, with no prospect of living with his children, and with no academic ties."[5]

III

In July 1938 Frost was living alone on his own farm, The Gulley, near Carol in South Shaftsbury, Vermont. Theodore Morrison, director of the Bread Loaf Writers' Conference—the granddaddy of all writers' workshops—invited him to lecture during the August session. With nothing else to do, Frost accepted the invitation and received his normal fee of $200 (later rising to $300). At the Conference (in contrast to the more academic Bread Loaf School of English) professional writers and editors taught aspiring amateurs in a rather carefree bohemian atmosphere. Frost had been associated with Bread Loaf since 1921, the year after its inception, but had not had much contact with it in recent years. He had doubts about the Conference and in his Preface to the *Bread Loaf Anthology* (1939) warned that it had "to be kept from degenerating into a mere summer resort for routine education in English, or worse still for the encouragement of vain ambition in literature." Paraphrasing Oscar Wilde's epigram on fox-hunters, "the unspeakable in full pursuit of the uneatable," Frost told Untermeyer, his frequent crony and tennis partner at Bread Loaf, that it was "a Mecca for the unpublishable in search of a publisher."

Though subject to bronchial attacks Frost, at the age of sixty-four, seemed handsome, strong and vigorous when he appeared at Bread Loaf that summer. He weighed about a hundred and seventy pounds, was neat and well-dressed, wore an open-necked white shirt and had shifted from high black shoes to Keds Casuals, blue canvas shoes with white rubber soles. While gesticulating he would habitually rumple his thick white hair and produce his characteristically uncombed appearance. Peter Davison, who met him a few years later, described the vivid gestures that accompanied his speech: "The old man sat still, talking and talking, a mischievous grin playing over his strangely wrinkled face, his big hands, rough on the backs and smooth on the palms, making rhythmical chops in the air like someone splitting kindling with a hatchet, a gesture at once emphatic and lyrical, as though he were conducting his own music."[6]

Frost's reception in August 1938 set the tone for his future role at Bread Loaf, where he became the presiding deity. His lecture was brilliant and evoked a rapturous response. One participant recalled that "he always demanded to be treated like royalty and generally was; this had the effect of making him virtually unapproachable to younger, less eminent writers. Ted Morrison and his wife hovered over Frost as if he were a prize Easter egg, and discouraged ordinary mortals from contact with him." Pilgrims to this literary Mecca were warned not to bother him with their manuscripts. One woman, however, broke protocol by implying that Frost might die soon and fatuously asked: "Is it safe to buy the *Complete Poems* NOW?" He angrily responded: "I don't give a damn whether you buy the book or not."

But no amount of fawning deference and flattering attention could soothe Frost's emotional turmoil. Distracted by grief and guilt, and profoundly insecure about his powers, he would become sulky and miserable if he did not also perform well on the tennis court and baseball field. Ted Morrison observed that he could be "touchy, spoiled like a child, used to being the center of attention, jealous and capable of paranoid suspicions." Charles Foster, an Amherst graduate and promising poet, also noted that Frost was (most unusually) drinking whiskey, behaving badly and condemning himself. He said he was "a God-damned son of a bitch, Charlie, and don't let anyone tell you different."[7]

Frost's turbulent state led to an absurd and comic confrontation with Archibald MacLeish. An ambitious, popular but depressingly mediocre poet, with all the qualities needed to irritate Frost, MacLeish was born in a wealthy suburb of Chicago in 1892, and had been educated at Yale and Harvard Law School. He had abandoned law for poetry in 1923 and in 1932 had won the Pulitzer Prize for *Conquistador,* which used Mexican history as Frost had in "La Noche Triste." Pound had justly called Mac-Leish's poem "damn bad." In the 1930s—before becoming an establishment figure at the Library of Congress, in the Roosevelt administration and at Harvard—MacLeish worked on Henry Luce's *Fortune* magazine. He borrowed from and vulgarized Yeats, Pound and Eliot, filled his verse with high-sounding banalities, wrote slick journalism, trimmed his political sails to meet the expedient moment, and, later on, gathered undeserved honors with astonishing ease.

Frost disliked MacLeish's poetics as well as his politics. He was annoyed by the attention his rival was receiving at Bread Loaf and could not resist (as with Sandburg) some caustic cracks. He told Untermeyer that it was difficult to discover Archie's "muffled rhymes" in all his archeology, and said his prose belonged to an educated and experienced publicist who was trying hard to think. Just as Frost had resented and competed with the public performances of Amy Lowell and T. S. Eliot, so he disrupted MacLeish's talk on August 28. Wallace Stegner reported:

> About halfway through the reading [Frost] leaned over and said in a carrying whisper, "Archie's poems all have the same *tune.*" As the reading went on, to the obvious pleasure of the audience, he grew restive. The fumbling and rustling of the papers in his hands became disturbing. Finally, MacLeish announced "You, Andrew Marvell" . . . a favorite. Murmurs of approval, intent receptive faces. The poet began. Then an exclamation, a flurry

in the rear of the hall. The reading paused, heads turned. Robert Frost, playing around like an idle, inattentive schoolboy in the classroom, had somehow contrived to strike a match and set fire to his handful of papers and was busy beating them out and waving away the smoke.

When his friend Bernard DeVoto had the nerve to cry out: "For God's sake, Robert, let him read!" Frost *ate* a cigarette to protest the rebuke. The gentlemanly MacLeish later recalled that he "hadn't felt any indignation or anger about it at all." Frost's behavior puzzled and annoyed the audience, who wondered what had provoked him, and sympathized with MacLeish. Though the fire was in bad taste, it was also amusing in a childish way.[8]

IV

With Elinor, Frost had usually lived in a country house surrounded by land. He had been family oriented, and he had taught at Michigan and Amherst. After Elinor's death Frost began to inhabit a different world. He became closely connected with Bread Loaf and the Morrisons. He spent most of the time in Cambridge, with winters in Florida and summers in Vermont. He taught at Harvard and Dartmouth before returning to Amherst in 1949.

In October 1938, with the help of Kay Morrison, who had agreed to become his secretary and manager, Frost rented a small apartment at 88 Mount Vernon Street on Beacon Hill in Boston. While the flat was being prepared, he lived at the St. Botolph Club (where Eliot had lectured). But he became infuriated when Kay, like all women, was not allowed on the premises, and moved into the Ritz Hotel. Walking at night on Beacon Hill in about 1940, Frost was accosted by a drunk and brushed off his incoherent advances. The man then surprised him by referring to the hero of a recent novel by John Marquand and asking: "Who do you think you are—the late George Apley?"

In the spring of 1941 Frost, then teaching at Harvard, bought with Kay's help his last, permanent home, at 35 Brewster Street in Cambridge. The three-story residence had shuttered windows, peaked gables and a steep-pitched roof, with steps leading up to a covered front porch and a double front door. The quiet house was only ten minutes' walk from

Harvard Square. Calling himself a nomad in his own home, Frost told a friend that he had slept in every room but the kitchen. One icy winter, when he was in his eighties, the still sprightly Frost boasted that he had "slipped at the top and shot over all those steps out onto the sidewalk. . . . I think I exceeded my record of last year. I think I shot out a foot and a half farther than I did last year."

In the summer of 1939 he increased his rural holdings, and strengthened his connection to the Morrisons and to Bread Loaf, by purchasing, as his last summer residence, the Homer Noble farm in nearby Ripton, Vermont. Surrounded on three sides by the Green Mountain National Forest, it had a farmhouse, where the Morrisons lived, and just up the hill, a simple three-roomed log cabin, with a fireplace and screened-in porch, where Frost resided. The novel arrangement seemed perfect. In the main town of Middlebury, he could take the train to Boston or New York. At Bread Loaf, a little farther up the mountain, he had tennis, conversation and social life. The Morrison farmhouse screened visitors and provided meals cooked by a housekeeper. His solitary cabin was for work.

Frost took great satisfaction in the daily round of work and pleasure on the farm: feeding the horses, cutting the hay and chopping wood; searching for wildflowers, watching the birds and gazing at the stars; reading and writing in front of the fire and talking into the night. The Western novelist A. B. Guthrie said that farmer Frost was proud of his garden produce: "knotty carrots, tortured corn and barely surviving potatoes." The old pyromaniac, who had accidentally lit a dangerous blaze at the Derry farm in 1906, soon surpassed his little fire at MacLeish's reading. In the fall of 1941 he caused a serious blaze at the Ripton farm by throwing a school exercise book into the incinerator. As the wind whipped the flames through the dry grass, "the cabin was mercifully saved and the fire plunged through the forest, flames crowning the trees with a terrific roar."

In 1940, the year after he bought the new farm, Frost acquired a beloved border collie to provide companionship and fill the emotional void after Elinor's death. He emphasized his ancestry by naming him Gillie, Scots for a sportsman's attendant or guide. Just before America entered World War II, Frost described him to Willard Fraser as a black sheep dog with a white front and white-tipped nose, tail and paws. Extremely intelligent, Gillie was his constant companion during meals, games and hikes. But, Frost explained, the dog was a gentle pacifist, not a fighter. He playfully told one critic that since he and Gillie took walks together after midnight, they made up the only "nightclub" in Ripton. By 1952, when Gillie had grown old and morose, Frost (punning again) told a friend how he spoiled his pet: "my big dog, the famous talking dog Gillie from Beacon Hill, ex-speaker of the house and yard, is now alas fallen on silence with age or pessimism. I have had him twelve years and always take a bedroom in the train so he can travel with me in it and not be separated into the baggage car."[9]

When Gillie died, Frost paid him loving tribute in "One More Brevity." The poem begins with the poet going out to look at Sirius, the bright dog star, before going to sleep. As he does so a stray dog, whom he calls Gustie, seeks asylum from the speed of modern life by running into the house. He is royally received and "talks dog" to the master. Next morning, when Gustie wants to leave and rushes off, the speaker imagines that he may have been an avatar, or canine embodiment, of Sirius. Having depended on Gillie for so long, he now celebrates him in a poem. The visit of the dog and the glimpse of the star suggest the connection between earthly love and spiritual aspirations.

14

Kay Morrison

1938–1942

I

The events that took place at the beginning of Frost's love affair with Kay Morrison were tragic and turbulent. Elinor's death in March 1938 changed the course of his life and the development of his poetry. His fierce quarrel with Lesley alienated him from the closest member of his family. He was also debilitated by illness and depression. He began to drink heavily and to use foul language, and by his own admission was "crazy" for the next six months. In June he abruptly resigned from Amherst and sold his house. No longer a husband, rejected as a father, he turned to Kay Morrison, when she reappeared in his life in July, and became her lover. In August he resumed his long-term association with Bread Loaf, where Ted Morrison was director. Scarcely recovered from the assault of grief and guilt, he proposed marriage to Kay. She refused, but remained his manager, mistress and muse for the last twenty-five years of his life.

After forty years of a passionately monogamous marriage, Frost now had to endure the uncertainty of a love affair with a woman who could not always put him first. In the winter of 1938–39, on a tempestuous vacation in Florida with the Morrisons, Frost became bitterly jealous. In July 1939 Newdick suddenly died and Thompson, who would also become sexually involved with Kay, became his official biographer. Frost entered the hospital for a hemorrhoid operation in January 1940, and in March went berserk and broke up the furniture in his flat. In October Carol Frost killed himself. These deaths and his own emotional upheavals both challenged and strengthened Frost's character. His poetry was recharged and given new direction in the passionate love poems to Kay that he published in *A Witness Tree* (1942).

Kathleen Florence Johnston, the daughter of a Scottish Episcopal clergyman, was born on November 18, 1898, in Parrsboro, Nova Scotia, where her father had exchanged pulpits for a year. Soon after her birth Robert Johnston accepted a church in Stirling, then in Edinburgh, and Kay, a British citizen, was raised in Scotland. The oldest of five children, she had two brothers and two sisters, and had to put up with the white mice they kept in the bathroom. Precocious and intellectual as a child, she accompanied her father when he visited parishioners in the slums of the city.

In 1910, when Kay was eleven, Robert was offered an attractive church in Philadelphia, where they lived in fashionable Chestnut Street and she attended Miss Hill's School. Their elegant house, which she helped to run, had fine antiques, old silver and oriental rugs as well as several servants. Her father's private income enabled them to live in grand style and to take summer holidays in Nova Scotia. Robert was liberal in church policy and in his Sunday sermons, but went in for costly hare-brained schemes. He suffered from "hysterical complaints" and would suddenly lose his power of speech. According to Kay's daughter, Robert had abnormally close relations with Kay and may have sexually molested her. This experience forced her, at an early age, to keep secrets and deal with conflicting emotions. In the 1930s, while driving with his sister, Robert was killed in an automobile accident.

The attractive, capable and commonsensical Kay was a member of the literary society and editor of the *College News* at Bryn Mawr. She first met Frost at a lecture during her senior year. After graduating from college in 1921, she studied English at Oxford for a year. Kay wanted to come out as a debutante and blamed her mother for not offering her a glamorous social life. She met Theodore Morrison, a young lecturer at Harvard, while they were both working on the *Atlantic Monthly* and married him on October 22, 1927. Their son Robert was born in December 1930, their daughter Anne in January 1937.[1]

Frost's "devoted, astringent, and affectionate amanuensis" had a slight build and bright auburn hair. Well dressed, elegant and *soignée*, she often mumbled her words and squinted her eyes. Wade Van Dore said she was self-possessed in moments of crisis and that "outward calmness seemed to be hers by birthright." Daniel Aaron, her husband's colleague at Harvard, found her cold, distant and officious. He thought she avoided intimacy with polite, wintry smiles and was amiable but not sexy. She was eager to maintain her husband's precarious dignity and was clearly more than a solicitous handmaiden to Frost.

Her daughter remarked that Kay was both proper and unconventional. She insisted on keeping up appearances and was content as long as things seemed all right on the surface. At the Vermont farmhouse the laundry, hung on the line with the intimate garments huddled in the middle, was snatched out of sight as soon as visitors appeared. Anne was allowed to smoke when she was ten, but no lady could ever smoke in the street. Frost, who contrasted Kay to Elinor, was bothered by her "society manners" and her academic approach to poetry. The poet Adrienne Rich, Ted's student at Harvard, noticed Kay's "repressed anger and bitterness."[2] Her daughter believed this came from her frustrated social ambitions, her disappointment in Robert Johnston's failure to achieve eminence and become a bishop in the church, and her uneasiness about Ted's modest and ambiguous position at Harvard.

Theodore Morrison (three years younger than Kay) was born in Concord, Massachusetts, in 1901, the youngest of four brothers. His father, an engineer, was head of the Lynn Gas and Electric Company. Two of his brothers, a pitcher-catcher team who had major league baseball offers, went to M.I.T. and also became engineers. Ted, the literary member of the family, graduated from Harvard in 1923. He had been an editor at the *Atlantic Monthly* before joining the Harvard English department. Since he had no doctorate, Ted could not be a professor; but as the effective and generous head of English A (which taught expository rather than creative writing) he eventually became a tenured lecturer. Kay, acutely aware that Ted's position was lower than his academic colleagues', resented the fact that her husband, like her father, had not fulfilled his promise and advanced his career.

The handsome, tweedy, pipe-smoking Ted was a Roman Stoic and stiff-upper-lip New Englander who rarely revealed his feelings. He was also a kind and sensitive man who knew how to deal with Frost's moody and volatile temperament. Writing in September 1938 to Bernard DeVoto, his close friend as well as Frost's, just after Frost had appeared at Bread Loaf, Ted criticized his public persona: "The colloquialism of Frost, his continually putting on the rustic tone and writing under his subjects and wearing homespun is also a limitation." Ted unfavorably compared Frost to Robinson, completely missing the allusion to Robinson's "The Sheaves" in "Nothing Gold Can Stay": "I doubt, honestly, whether Frost has ever had it in him to record the sudden vanishing from perception of the stacked-up corn sheaves in the autumn in an image as gorgeous" as Robinson's.

Ted had a puritan temperament and at Bread Loaf, despite his wife's liaisons, strongly disapproved of illicit sex (an outstanding feature of most writers' conferences). He spoke of such behavior with horror, and seductive poets were not invited back. (Untermeyer, a great fornicator between and during his marriages, was protected by Frost and given special dispensation.) In September 1934, when DeVoto sent his latest novel, *We Accept with Pleasure,* Ted (writing from Nova Scotia) minimized the importance of sexual relations, both illicit and marital. He opposed DeVoto's idea that "some mystical and romantic value is to be attributed to illegal cohabitation" and declared: "The impression left by the book is that cohabitation out of wedlock is, if not the clue, at least a necessary ingredient in arriving at personal integrity. It ain't; not even in wedlock."[3]

II

In the spring of 1936, when Elinor was ill and Frost gave the Norton lectures at Harvard, the Morrisons had a series of receptions for him at their Cambridge house. Kay, who loved literature, sought him out at South Shaftsbury in July 1938. Realizing his desolation and loneliness, she invited him to join her family and friends at a nearby summer house. According to her daughter, Kay was a very unhappy woman who wanted a career rather than a family. "Incredibly romantic and passionate," she also craved more wildness in her life and more brilliance than Ted could offer. She wanted to help and rescue Frost, who was out of control after Elinor's death and desperately needed both a new secretary and a new source of poetic inspiration. Frost—the same age and with the same first name as her recently deceased father—gave her what she had long been seeking. For the first time in her life Kay could realize her ambition to achieve status, exert social and literary influence, and share the fame of a great man.

In the summer of 1938 Frost was a white-haired but handsome and vigorous man of sixty-four, Kay a refined and stylish woman of thirty-nine. Frost took a keen interest in the sexual life of his friends, but had never slept with any woman but Elinor. Though her dowdy dress and chronic illness had made her seem much older than Frost, she had been his high school sweetheart and he had remained faithful (despite many temptations) until her death. Just as Kay associated Frost with her father, so he was drawn to Kay by her similarity to his delicate, auburn-haired mother. Like Belle, Kay had grown up in Scotland and come to America at the age of eleven. To Frost, who had discussed the significance of personal names in "Maple," her name had positive associations. Cathleen was the Celtic heroine of the Yeats play Frost had put on at Pinkerton; Morrison was the New Hampshire Superintendent of Public Instruction who had praised Frost's teaching and advanced his career.

A. B. Guthrie, who was loyal to Ted Morrison and observed Frost that summer at Bread Loaf, said he was "the captive of fierce and aberrant passions." John Ciardi also noted his powerful inner conflict: "Frost was intensely puritanical. I think he had also a very strong sexual impulse, and these two things set up a contest of forces"—in which passion won. His sexual urge, though always strong, had been restrained with Elinor, but he once admitted: "If I had a beautiful studio, I'd never paint. I'd have ladies visiting. . . . Might as well be candid." He dreaded the thought of trouble and a public scandal, and hated the dishonesty of Kay's double life, but frankly told Thompson: "I'm a perfectly normal animal; I can't always behave." He seemed to define his emotional and moral ambiguity in a prophetic letter of June 1937 when he said: "All our ingenuity is lavished on getting into danger legitimately so that we may be genuinely rescued."[4] As Oscar Wilde remarked in *De Profundis*, illicit sex "was like feasting with panthers. The danger was half the excitement."

Frost openly discussed Kay with his close friends as well as with his biographers. He told the ponderous Newdick that for the first time in his life he felt unconstrained, and Newdick wrote that he "needs, wants feminine companionship and friendship, and will have it. Is fearful of arrangement with K. Morrison—for her and Ted, rather than for himself. If he were Ted, he wouldn't permit it." But Kay aroused the old Adam in Frost and tempted him to fall. He was astonished that a woman who behaved so conventionally could be so wild sexually. When she suddenly, almost magically reappeared in his life, he felt: "Here's a lady who's willing, why not let go?" She would be good for him—and for his poetry.

In late July 1938 Frost accepted Kay's invitation, while Ted was away at Bread Loaf, to visit her in central Vermont. Troubled and excited by their long walks in the woods, he took along condoms (which he had been reluctant to use with Elinor). Kay had revered him as a poet for seventeen years, and now realized how much he needed and wanted her. He talked brilliantly, describing his family tragedies, and he loved her that she did pity them. One day they came to a place Frost thought sufficiently secluded "for either rape or murder." They sat on the warm earth and talked some more. "Then Frost began making passionate love to her and found that she was willing. . . . All he had to do was to take off her drawers and consummate an urge that seemed mutual." Frost (to use one of his own favorite metaphors) rode on her own melting. The contrast between Elinor's virginal rejection of his first sexual overtures, which had made him feel bestial, and Kay's eager response, which revived and inspired him, was reflected in the placement of "The Subverted Flower" just after "Never Again Would Birds' Song Be the Same" in *A Witness Tree*. Their first, mutually gratifying encounter also provoked a comic quatrain on in- and outdoor fooling. Frost wrote that no one could object to being legally wed when the marriage was consummated naked in bed. But it is an entirely different matter when you have sex out of doors with no clothes off but drawers.[5]

Just after they became lovers, Frost proposed marriage and pressed Kay to divorce her husband. She firmly rejected this idea and told him that even if they were both twenty years younger and both free she would never agree to marry him. (Ted later wrote in his essay on the poet: "To marry Robert Frost was no light undertaking for any woman.") Kay felt that divorce was impossible: it would cause scandal and harm the children. She pleaded that their affair be kept secret. During the next few years Frost strained their relations by forcefully pressing her to marry him. Though he agreed to behave with discretion, he distressed her by telling several close friends about the affair, hinting about it to others and instructing his biographers to reveal the full story.

Frost confessed to Thompson that his love for Kay contained an element of sadism: "he punished her, and she (according to Frost) permitted him the somewhat brutal pleasure of having sexual intercourse with her. . . . Frost says that his initial love-making was motivated by resentments but that he suddenly found himself in love with Kay, and dependent on his love for her."[6] Frost said he resented Kay for trying to help him, for making him depend on her and for "mothering" him—as Belle and Elinor had done. For many years he continued to punish her—quite irrationally—for sleeping with him, for taking Elinor's place, for refusing to marry him and for the guilt *he* felt about betraying Ted.

Frost was alternately invigorated, disturbed, grateful, jealous, vindictive and loving. At first, his love for her revealed new and rather surprising aspects of his character, which seemed very different from his role as faithful husband and genial lecturer. Like Yeats after his late Steinach operation, Frost was passionate, wild, even mad. Margaret Bartlett (who did not yet know about Kay) saw a rejuvenated man and thought his liberation from Elinor explained his new energy and vigor. In letters to his friends (as in his poems), he struggled between concealment and revelation. Kay had agreed to handle his correspondence and arrange his readings. In early 1939 he jubilantly told Cox: "My secretary has taken me in hand to keep me lecturing and talking as of old. But I am very wild at heart sometimes. Not at all confused. Just wild—wild."

Just after the August session at Bread Loaf, Frost expressed his gratitude to Kay and contrasted her solicitude and Ted's with the callous behavior of President Stanley King: "You two rescued me from a very dangerous self when you had the idea of keeping me for the whole season at Bread Loaf. I am still infinitely restless, but I came away from you as good as saved. . . . Stanley King's charge against me was ingratitude. It will be a sensitive subject with me the rest of my life. . . . Tears in my heart when I left you people." Tears in the writer would soon produce tears in the reader. Keenly aware of the difference between Lesley's cruelty and Kay's kindness, he tried to reassure his possessive and censorious daughter about the woman who had eased his loneliness. "You must be grateful to her for having helped me through my bad time," he wrote in November 1938. "I am best as I am, though the hours alone are sometimes pretty desolate."

In a revealing letter to Untermeyer that same month, Frost connected Kay's soothing voice to the music of his verse, explained that she had relieved his guilt about the treatment of his family and provided the absolution that Elinor had failed to give him. Though Kay was not an innocent girl, he idealized and saw her that way. She seemed perfect for him, and he called on the sympathetic Untermeyer to tell Kay how much he loved her:

> My secretary has soothed my spirit like music in her attendance
> on me and my affairs. . . . I was thrust out into the desolateness of
> wondering about my past whether it had not been too cruel to
> those I had dragged with me and almost to cry out to heaven for
> a word of reassurance that was not given me in time. Then came
> this girl stepping innocently into my days to give me something
> to think of besides dark regrets. . . . You can figure it out for
> yourself how my status with a girl like her might be the perfect
> thing for me at my age in my position. I wish in some indirect way
> she could come to know how I feel toward her.[7]

Frost told one friend that "there have been just two women in my life." But by May 1939, when he saw Raymond Holden in Boston, Kay seemed to have supplanted Elinor. Unlike Kay, who adored Frost, was eager to please him and was attracted by his fame, Elinor had rejected his sexual overtures, disapproved of his public persona, criticized his self-promoting readings, did nothing to advance his career, condemned his egotism, complained of her sacrifice and resented his success. Though Frost considered women "sources of male gratification," he revealed that he was afraid of his powerful passion for Kay. He told Holden, "in his lightest, aphoristic manner that he had had many troublesome feelings about different women, but had loved only one. I do not know why I felt that he was meaning to imply that the one was not Elinor. . . . He once told me that he didn't dare let his emotions be aroused for fear that they would ruin him, so strong were they potentially."

Frost also poured out his heart to Mertins, linking Kay to Belle and stressing her maternal role, crediting her for both saving and inspiring him, and revealing how profoundly his existence was now bound up with hers: "I owe everything in the world to her. She found me in the gutter, hopeless, sick, run down. She bundled me up and carted me to her home and cared for me like a child, sick child. Without her I would today be in my grave. If I have done anything since I came out of the hospital [in January 1940], it is all due to her."[8]

When traveling and separated from Kay, Frost wrote about five hundred letters to her, but she destroyed most of them, cut and tore parts of many others, and only nineteen fragments have survived. He addressed her as Dearest and Milady (a dig at her social pretensions) as well as the classical Venusta, Augusta, Egeria (a woman counselor) and consulatrix (a pun on consoler). The letters expressed his sentimental and romantic as well as his passionate and idealistic feelings. In one undated note he told Kay that the clock in his room had stopped ticking at the very moment she was boarding the train. Since she was the last one to wind it, he would let it remain silent as a token of their love. In a letter written at midnight in mid-October 1938, Frost includes a *double-entendre* on lecturing and sex that sounds like Hemingway, a grateful acknowledgment of her inspiration, and a fervent but unfulfilled hope that she will keep his letters and eventually reveal their love:

> Egeria, You told me to do it well and so it is no brag. . . . I have a
> weakness *for* you but a strength *from* you. . . . Surely no one could
> object to love that courses in the inflection of my sentences like

impassioned blood in the veins. You must find a place to keep
the most earnest [love] words I ever wrote. They can only do you
honor when the time comes to divulge them; and meanwhile
they could in no way compromise you if discovered by chance.
All this says I am yours in a very noble sense.

Four months later, while Frost was writing his love poems to Kay, he
again assured her that her inspiration was vital to his work: "The poetry
into which my heart would go for you aches at the threat of being denied
birth." Ten years later he confirmed that he was still her faithful trouba-
dour: "Ninety-nine percent of the time I am yours and the Muses' only."
Frost also expressed his love by buying rare and expensive first editions
of his earliest books as presents for Kay, and by writing an amusing (and
punning) poem, which contrasted her conventional wedding ring with
the more exotic jewelry (of the sort pupils had noticed on his mother)
that he had given her to symbolize their wildness and "sin." Her husband
had given her a wedding ring to keep her virtuous. But Frost surpassed
him by giving her an earring for erring and a necklace for being wickedly
reckless.[9]

But their honeymoon did not last very long, and during the early years
of the affair they lurched from crisis to crisis. From December 1938 to
January 1939 the Morrisons accompanied Frost on his annual trip to
Florida. They spent a week at the Casa Marina Hotel in Key West and a
week as guests of Hervey Allen near Miami. Their close proximity, the
need to share Kay with Ted and even defer to her husband, caused
constant anxiety and tension. Frost got into petty disputes with Ted, and
Kay had trouble separating the antagonists. In February 1939 Frost told
Untermeyer that "my chief signs of life are shown in any debate *with my
rival.*" Writing from Florida that same month he suggested, in a letter to
Lesley, that they had come close to an explosion and that he was, as
always, terribly lonely whenever Kay left him: "I came through the two
weeks with the Morrisons pretty well considering all there was on all sides
to dissemble. I am alone now in a rather desolated house. . . . My entan-
glement has had critical moments when it looked near openly declared
trouble." After this anguished holiday, Frost would never allow Ted to
come to Florida. He would remain at home while Kay traveled south with
Frost.[10]

In early February 1939, to distract him from Kay, Frost went to Cuba
for five days with the poet Paul Engle. He told Lesley that he admired the
tropical scenery and was thrilled by his first flight in an airplane, which

"made a high sky" in one leap. Suddenly he found himself exiled on a strange island among loud but unintelligible speakers: "We went down to Camaguey, saw several cities besides Havana and plenty of sugar cane and royal palms. The land is rich; the people miserably poor. Everywhere beggars and beggar-vendors. We saw one great beach to beat the world . . . [with] the most transparent ocean water I have ever looked into. . . . I am not much on foreign parts. I favor that beach for you to resort to someday though. To me the best of the excursion was the flight both ways in the big Pan American plane and especially the swoop and mighty splash into the bays on arrival."

A second and more serious crisis erupted in the spring of 1939 when Frost and the Morrisons spent the night at Untermeyer's farm in Eliza-bethtown, New York. Frost had told Untermeyer that jealousy alone gave him the sense of being physically and emotionally held. Whenever he was locked into a triangle with Kay and Ted, he found it very difficult to maintain the pretense of innocence. At Untermeyer's house Ted as-sumed the role of husband and slept with Kay in the only double guest bed. Frost felt rejected, became deranged and almost dared to force the moment to its crisis.

Frost continued to put pressure on Kay and thought she would even-tually agree to marry him. When she remained loyal (after her fashion) to Ted and her children, the jealous Frost, driven to emotional extremes by the confrontations in Florida and Elizabethtown, went dangerously out of control. Thompson, accepting Lesley's view of her father and certainly exaggerating his condition (for Frost never lost touch with reality), recorded: "During the summer of 1939, in Ripton, and then during February 1940 in Key West, I saw Frost come very close to the verge of insanity. He was a wild man, he was frantic; he was deeply upset, he was just plain 'crazy' in some of his actions."

The situation became more tangled by Frost's illness in early 1940. "I have been very sick," he told Cox, "largely we now think from some very drastic medicine that doctors tried on me for cystitis. I went crazy with it one night alone and broke chairs ad lib till a friend [Dr. Merrill Moore] happened in to save me." Moore thought Frost's voice sounded strange on the telephone, rushed over to his apartment, found him almost unconscious and took him to the hospital.

Frost had had hemorrhoids for years, but refused to see a doctor until his kidneys became inflamed and he was overcome by pain. The opera-tion for "asteroids" took place in Boston on January 10. On February 1

Kay took him down to Key West and nursed him back to health. While there, she shrewdly wrote Thompson that whenever Frost was in a crisis he either bought land or took to his bed. In Florida he had used Kay "as a kind of safety valve" to release his frustration, anger and pain, and she had just been through the hardest two weeks of her life. Thompson suggested that Lesley visit Frost. But Kay, knowing the terrible effect the daughter had on the father, said that Lesley "would defeat anything the doctors could do" to help him. Thompson, rather than Lesley, finally took over as servant and nurse-companion. He told Kay that Frost was pathetically dependent on her letters and used his illness to exert power over his friends. In Florida he "ate his heart out . . . watching, between your many letters, for *more* letters. . . . He said, 'If I don't hear from her tomorrow, you're going to have your patient back in bed,' and he tried to smile while his eyes filled with tears and his lips quivered."[11]

III

Despite frequent crises—when Frost became a possessive, jealous and demanding lover, and the unpleasant truth threatened to burst out—he and the Morrisons tried hard to preserve appearances. After a few years of distressing emotional upheavals, they eventually contrived a service-able mode of existence and settled on a formula of transparent lies that seemed acceptable to all parties. In order to protect herself and preserve the status quo, Kay tried to placate and control Frost by telling him that she no longer had sexual relations with Ted. At the same time she assured Ted that her relations with Frost were purely secretarial. But Kay's insistent denials, to friends as well as to her husband, seemed to call Frost's manliness into question and he responded by indiscreetly boast-ing about his conquest. "Trying to prove himself 'a bad, bad man,' " Kay wrote, while trying to conceal the truth, "he laced his conversations with innuendoes of sexual exploits that were utterly foreign to his nature." But Frost's innuendoes were also a form of flirtation and seduction, and tried to suggest, to Kay and to others, "what a devil I am!"

Torn between a wish to preserve secrecy and a desire to achieve eventual recognition for her crucial role in Frost's life, Kay boldly retali-ated by declaring that he was merely a vain, boastful old man. In a characteristic letter to the wealthy businessman and Frost-collector Earle

Bernheimer, Kay tried to quell the gossip by insisting that she was devoted to her family and was merely trying to be kind to Frost, who liked to indulge in sexual fantasies:

> My friends know what I am doing for Robert and have backed me in my wish not to make him too unhappy and to give him care and affection while he lives. I am well settled with my husband and children and they know they are my first care. What I do for Robert is something different. He is devoted to me and sometimes is carried away in his talk beyond fact because he is emotionally upset and lonely and because he would have things different.

Kay gave the same story to Richard Wilbur, who accepted her account and later wrote: "No doubt Frost was enamored and possessive of her, and tried her good husband's patience; but she told me once that there had never been an 'affair' between her and Robert, and I believed her. When Frost 'let on' to the contrary, as he sometimes did, I think it was an old man's vanity talking."[12]

According to Thompson (who knew the truth), Ted forced himself to believe everything Kay told him in order to preserve his sanity. But Frost found it more difficult to accept her transparent but necessary falsehoods. He "accused Kay of betraying their love, through the act of denying their love, and of pretending that it never was [sexual love]. It's lucky for her that Frost has been willing to deceive himself by accepting as truths so many of Kay's deceptions."

In order to convince himself that Kay was telling the truth about Ted (for he never really knew), Frost seized on what he took to be convincing evidence in Ted's poem in the *Atlantic Monthly* of September 1939—just after what Thompson called Frost's first "crazy" crisis at Ripton. Ted's "The Schism" portrays the puritanical split between body and soul, and between wife and husband in marriage. The unhappy couple go

> From holy to unhallowed scene
>   (Such alteration is our lot)
> From cleanly straightway to unclean
>   A tincture never quite forgot.
> From duty well or badly kept
>   Straightway to bed; but should a trace

> Hint that we loved before we slept
> We quickly turn aside the face.

Frost interpreted the poem as an autobiographical confession that confirmed Kay's lack of sexual relations with Ted and justified his own role as her lover. Thompson thought Frost's analysis was far-fetched and even absurd. But Ted's letter to DeVoto about the insignificance of sexual relations, both in and out of marriage, suggests that Frost was right in believing that Ted—who was, in fact, still sleeping with Kay—found sex somewhat repellent. Thompson wrote:

> The poem made it perfectly clear [to Frost] that Ted was a prude in sexual matters. . . . Kay had turned her back on Ted in bed and the reason was clear: Ted had a puritanical revulsion for love-making and Kay had confessed as much to Frost. What did that leave for Ted? The kind of love that leaves stains on the sheets: masturbation. And here in his reading of the poem Frost found all he wanted to find, to justify his own position, as the lover of another man's wife. Here, said Frost, was Ted's public confession that his own marriage was a marriage only in name.

Frost clung to this interpretation of Ted's character till the end of his life. In 1961, after reading a review of Ted's third novel, *The Whole Creation,* Frost told Kay: "Just what I said to you years ago. The man has *no feeling*—never had. Read it yourself! Even a person who's never set eyes on him sees what's missing." Frost's unpublished poem, "On the Question of an Old Man's Feeling" (1953), though ostensibly a riposte to Robert Francis, contains an unmistakable satiric passage on the lack of feelings in the poet and critic Ted Morrison. The poem expresses Frost's loathing for the critic who wears poet's clothing, and calls him a gelding who had never slept with his wife and a neurotic case who never had real feelings. Frost also describes having sex with the man's wife, who responded actively and eagerly as he penetrated her. She felt his member hard as bronze and matched his passion with her Mons to press him in her "crack."[13]

Frost's relations with Kay were complicated by her contemporaneous involvement with at least three other men. Stafford Dragon (the name itself was irresistible) was Frost's lively and handsome hired man on the Vermont farm. Visiting writers familiar with the sexual situation at Bread

Loaf (where Stafford's father sang ballads) joked about her social pretensions and knowingly referred to "Stafford-the-man-Kay-hires as 'Lady
Chatterley's Lover.' " When Thompson urged Dragon to behave more
discreetly, Dragon told him that he knew Thompson was also Kay's lover.

Kay had been sleeping with Ted's "best friend," the married writer
Bernard DeVoto. The short, porcine "Bennyvenuto" (as Frost called
him) had thick glasses, thick lips and a broad flat Babe Ruth nose with
tunnel-like nostrils. Born in Ogden, Utah, of Catholic-Mormon parents,
a year before Kay, DeVoto had graduated from Harvard in 1920 and
returned to his home state to begin his career as a novelist. He came back
to Harvard in 1930 but, not eligible for tenure without a doctorate,
taught for six years on a temporary appointment. When he failed to get a
permanent job, the embittered DeVoto consulted Frost and then resigned to become editor of the *Saturday Review of Literature*. He had met
Frost in Florida in 1936 and thought of writing his biography. He looked
after Frost when he gave the Norton lectures and supported him when
Left-wing critics attacked *A Further Range*. In a vituperative but critically
weak defense, DeVoto exclaimed that Blackmur's "piece in the *Nation*
may not quite be the most idiotic review our generation has produced,
but in twenty years of reading criticism—oh, the hell with scholarly
reservations, Mr. Blackmur's is the most idiotic of our time."[14]

Thompson, an on-the-spot observer, noted the mutual recrimination
and entangled moral issues: "Kay had described [DeVoto's] innocence
as impotence. Kay had been involved in his harem by Benny, very early.
So when Frost moved into the picture, with Kay, Benny had become
jealous. He had accused Frost of breaking up—not Benny's harem but
the Morrison marriage." DeVoto's frequently quoted but little understood condemnation of Frost at the Bread Loaf Conference in August
1938 — "You're a good poet, Robert, but you're a bad man"—referred
to Frost's relations with Kay. DeVoto thought it was morally acceptable to
sleep with Kay as long as he did not try to take her away from Ted. But
when Frost proposed marriage to Kay, DeVoto got on his moral high
horse and expressed disapproval of Frost's attempt to break up Ted's
marriage.

The third member of Kay's sexual *ménage* was the ubiquitous and
"incredibly attractive" Lawrance Thompson. Eight years younger than
Kay, he also maintained the necessary façade and helped her to look
after Frost. Thompson's intimacy with Kay allowed him to participate in
and even change the course of the life he was writing. During the Florida
crisis of February–March 1940, which followed Frost's hemorrhoid oper-

ation, he secretly advised Kay to reject Frost's persistent proposals and even suggested a way to escape from his clutches. In another letter of March 3, he told Kay to protect herself from Frost's emotional on-slaughts by being tough with him and by using (Elinor-like) silences to express her anger:

> (1) He has thrown the whole weight of his life on you, and has no freedom apart from you; (2) if, for his own sake, a substitution were made, the only substitute must be some woman whose unrestricted freedom to devote herself to him would or could attract him. . . .
>
> It takes your kind of commonsense plus a little ruthlessness (which you might borrow from Robert himself) to deal with Robert almost harshly. . . . Don't you worry too much about his *nerves;* worry more about your own. He has 'em plenty, but he isn't in danger of being killed by them—unless this present conflict becomes a "war of attrition." And don't let him bully or threaten; you bully and threaten with your silences instead.

Kay, who feared he knew too much, remained friendly to Thompson, but he finally became exasperated with her. Their relations became tense in January 1945 when he summoned her to New York. The eight-year-old Anne, who was also fond of Thompson, thought he might be getting married. Kay frowned at her suggestion, got upset and said, very stiffly, "No, it couldn't be!" When she discovered the truth she became jealous of his wife. In his "Notes" Thompson complained that Kay treated his family (who also spent the summers near Frost's cabin in Vermont) like "poor relations." She never concealed her dislike and was "bitchy" to his wife, Janet, his children and himself.

Thompson often replaced Kay (both before and after his marriage) as Frost's companion, keeper and body servant, and knew what she had to endure when he was in a bad mood. In September 1945 he criticized Frost's behavior, praised her forbearance and praised her for the way she handled him: "I admire you deeply for the longsuffering patience with which you've accepted his self-indulgence when it comes to asking more of your time and strength and life than he has a right to ask. . . . You've done a superb job under the most exasperating conditions, and I respect all your decisions and actions in all the difficult task of walking a tight-rope during all these emotional hurricanes and thunderstorms of his."[15]

These dangerous, even treacherous, letters strengthened the bond between Thompson and Kay (since there was no one else she could turn to in this way), but they also gave her considerable power over him. If she had shown them to Frost, Thompson would have been cast into the outer darkness and his biography instantly terminated. The handsome Thompson also had an emotional hold over Kay, who was in love with him and helped him because they were lovers. He had to remain on good terms with her through all the *Sturm und Drang*. If she became Frost's literary executor, and disliked what Thompson wrote (and wrote about her) in his biography, she could withhold permission to quote from Frost's works. If Thompson wanted Kay to remain a vital ally, he would not only have to take her side, rather than Frost's, during the recurrent emotional crises, but would also have to conceal her relations with Frost.

Frost agreed to maintain the deception during his lifetime, but created another tense conflict by insisting the truth be told after his death. He believed the full story of his relations with Kay was essential to an understanding of his life and work, and hated to have his passion for her belittled or demeaned. He believed, as he had written in "Birches," that "Earth's the right place for love," and warned Thompson: "Don't let it be confused with anything so pale as platonic." Frost realized that Kay would be opposed to any revelations about their affair (and for this reason did not appoint her his literary executor). But he believed that she should not be allowed to conceal the importance of their sexual relationship—even if the revelation hurt her: "He thought there were certain penalties which Kay had to pay for intimacy, and one of them was to have the story told." When he asked how widely the story was known, Thompson replied that many of the writers at Bread Loaf (Ted, DeVoto, Guthrie and Ciardi) suspected they were having an affair and others (Untermeyer, Hervey Allen, Bernheimer and Thompson) knew because Frost had told them about it. Frost felt so strongly about this matter that he threatened to leave the beloved farm at Ripton to Lesley if Kay did not permit Thompson to tell the whole story.

But Thompson (unlike most biographers, who struggle with the family to reveal rather than conceal the truth) did not agree, and was bound by Kay's rather than by Frost's wishes after his death. He twisted Frost's desire for revelation into a supposed wish "to glamorize and dramatize the story, so that he and Kay Morrison as lovers would somehow seem noble and dignified in their ways of pretending that Ted Morrison blocked them off from fulfilling their romance."[16] Thompson died in

1973, and when the third volume was completed and published by R. H. Winnick three years later, Kay and Ted (who still were very much alive) gutted the book before publication by excising all traces of her intimacy with Frost.

Kay and her four lovers followed their instincts and their passions, pursuing their own interests and behaving in a selfish but understandable manner. Ted's situation was more difficult, his response more enigmatic. He could not get away from Frost, either in Cambridge or Vermont, and visitors sometimes confused him with Frost—even in his own house. During meals at the Ripton farm, Thompson noted, "Kay always sits farthest from the kitchen, which means that Ted, nearest the kitchen, always does the hopping and fetching." Though Ted *seemed* to accept the situation, several close friends—DeVoto, Ciardi and Guthrie—expressed anger on his behalf and intensified his pain.

Friends never saw the tight-lipped, courtly Ted show any rage or resentment. He found it hard to reach his own emotions and tried to deny the reality of the situation. He did not express physical affection, even with his children, but he too had human feelings and was furious underneath. His daughter Anne still remembers terrible fights at home when she was a little girl. Ted, who was usually so gentle, terrified Anne by radiating anger, storming out of the house and slamming the door. After drinking a great deal at a party, Ted once admitted to Richard Wilbur: "I hate the position I'm in. I never want Robert to be in my house." The year after Frost's death Ted, almost apologetically, told Thompson: "Well, let's face it: I didn't like him."[17]

Ted's volatile mixture of resignation and rage about Frost seemed to block his academic and poetic life in the same way that Ernest Weekley's career had been thwarted by his wife's scandalous liaison with D. H. Lawrence. Like Weekley, Ted lacked ambition and made an almost deliberate choice to be second-rate. But he was, according to the poet William Jay Smith, a decidedly minor writer and would not have achieved a great deal even if he had not been overshadowed by Frost.

Ted was willing to put up with anything as long as his marriage *seemed* to be happy. Despite Kay's affair with Frost, Ted still loved her, continued to sleep with her and felt he was achieving a higher good by his personal sacrifice. A somewhat bloodless character, he had a low sex drive, was used to his wife's infidelities and would have done anything to avoid publicly accusing Kay of adultery and going through a scandalous divorce. Though his acceptance of Kay's lovers was personally humiliating,

Ted thought it was worth the sacrifice not only to preserve his marriage, but also to sustain Frost and enable *Frost* (if not himself) to write great poems. Ted also endured the situation and went to great lengths to protect Kay. His tolerance allowed him to be the "better" person and do the noble thing.

All these New England puritans had been brought up to maintain superficial propriety—no matter what passions thrashed beneath the surface. The suppression of emotions, the preservation of decorum, the denial of intolerable reality, were all intensely Jamesian. The lies hurt everyone concerned, but all the players gained something valuable by accepting them. Family, friends and lovers all learned the Lesson of the Master and realized that they had to be sacrificed for Art.[18]

A close friend of the Morrisons, Sylvia Berkman, wrote a rather Jamesian story about them. She taught at Wellesley, was a good friend of Nabokov and had published a perceptive study of Katherine Mansfield. In her story "Blackberry Wilderness" (1959), in which the characters are more important than the plot, Kay and Ted appear as Julia and Harold Ransome, Anne as their daughter Beatrice and Frost as Wilbur Crane. Julia, a bright and elegant woman, is both daring and conventional:

> Julia Ransome . . . stood apart, brilliant, critical, and cold. . . . She kept up her appearance in a remarkable way, disciplined and taut, always sheathed in some bright lustrous garment, with her flashing necklaces and rings. . . .
>
> Julia Ransome hadn't conducted herself in a seemly way, according to what was said. The matter was on the verge of open scandal, just when Wilbur Crane died. Underneath she was a conventional woman, for all her independent show; she didn't want that kind of divorce.

Her husband (in contrast to the real-life Ted) has an unpleasant personality and is intensely jealous. Harold Ransome "was surly and rancorous. . . . He was a difficult man, taciturn, touchy, always feeding on a secret poison that kept him lean and pinched his features with the acrid aftertaste." Beatrice, the real focus of this *What Maisie Knew* story, had "some general foreboding that whatever her life might hold that sensitive pure instrument must record the mark of pain."

Frost's, Thompson's and Anne Morrison Smyth's view of the poet's relations with Kay were inevitably quite different. Frost thought his love was paramount and that he and Kay had made the greatest sacrifice by not marrying. He felt Kay was torn apart and suffered greatly, believed they were "caught in an awkward situation, and acted as honorably and as nobly as love would permit them to act. . . . The cost to both of them had been heavy, [and] had even been injurious to Kay's emotional and spiritual and physical health." Thompson disliked Frost intensely and saw the affair in a negative light. Though in no position to judge others, he declared: "The more evidence I find on the story, the more unpleasant and shameful the 'romance' becomes."

Anne, remembering all the quarrels and lies, did not think that Kay had made a noble choice. By attracting men and forming several attachments, she used marriage for her own convenience, and was both disloyal to Frost and "rotten about Ted." The great irony, according to Anne, was that Kay told her she had never experienced sexual satisfaction with anyone. Her troubled relations with her father may have caused her frigidity and her frustrating quest for a satisfying lover. Sexually unfulfilled, she lived vicariously through Frost (Anne thought) and caused great pain to everyone connected to her.[19] Entering middle age but filled with romantic longing, Kay, I believe, felt great power by manipulating a number of distinguished men while assuring her place in literary history.

IV

Kay became Frost's secretary and manager in September 1938. He paid her an annual salary (which reached $2,000 in 1954 and rose to $3,000 in the early 1960s) and she was supposed to work at his home—first in Beacon Hill and then in Cambridge—from 9:30 to 4:00 on weekdays. Kay typed, edited, read proofs, answered the mail, kept files, scheduled the readings, made the travel arrangements, managed the money, paid the bills, furnished his flats and houses, drove him around, advised him about family problems, entertained guests, protected him from unannounced visitors and often from himself. She fussed over Frost, was solicitous about his food and made sure he did not get too tired. She even cleaned up when his puppy soiled the rug. But he demanded even more from her and she had to be entirely at his disposal. "I could be summoned after hours," Kay wrote, "on Saturdays and Sundays, on holidays, sometimes finding real problems but more often emotional upsets." This, of course, put an additional strain on her family. As Kay told Thompson in February 1940: "He cannot be alone any more and it is impossible to promise steady companionship."[20]

Frost soon became completely dependent on Kay and resented the power she exerted. Their intimacy allowed Kay to nag him and Frost to vent his anger. She could be as stern and exasperated as a schoolmarm, and many friends were irritated by the way she guarded him. Though he admitted that women—like his mother and Elinor—had always run his life, he called Kay a very severe disciplinarian. She would ask, "What's wrong with you?" whenever she wanted to bring him "out into the open for a hunt." Since she took dictation, he called himself her "Easy Dictator," but he could also be a temperamental and difficult tyrant. Kay complained to Thompson about Frost's unremitting demands and his desire to dictate every aspect of her life. Frost wants "complete control of a person," she wrote in 1940. "More and more he tells me what to think and say."

For emotional and practical reasons the lonely and jealous Frost wanted to be with her all the time. When she left him after their annual trip to Florida, he called her his "chronic deserter" and (in a passage deleted from the published letter) hinted to Earle Bernheimer of his conquest and desire to pursue her. After three weeks of the most perfect bliss, he said, Kay had deserted him to return to Cambridge. The weather (though not his emotional life) was still perfect, and he had great difficulty controlling his impulse to follow her north. When Frost could not have his way, he sometimes regressed to infantile behavior. In December 1946, when Kay made plans to spend New Year's Eve with friends, Frost retaliated by pretending he had invited some cronies for a party of his own. He upset the furniture, filled the room with cigar smoke, spilled whiskey on the table, broke glasses on the carpet, and scattered the remains of crackers and cheese. After discovering the mess the next morning, Kay immediately saw through his ruse, but could not summon up much pity for the lonely celebrator.

Frost's possessiveness lasted until the very end of his life. In 1962 Kay again complained to Thompson that "Frost had been so jealous, during the past year, that he had made it impossible for her to go on any trips with Ted" during his sabbatical.[21] The only way she could ever escape from Frost was by refusing, despite his urgent pleas, to accompany him on foreign journeys. She desperately needed a rest from him, did not want to assume an even greater burden by becoming his traveling companion and let the eager Thompson take her place. Daily proximity had cooled their passion and led to frequent quarrels. She once got so exasperated that she threw a bucket of cold water over Frost. When the strain became too great she would explode, resign her job and take to her bed. But there would always be a tender reconciliation.

The ferocious Lesley, whose very appearance was enough to send Frost straight to bed, and who was as jealous of Kay as she had been of her mother and sisters, intensified the turmoil. Of the two, Lesley (a year younger) was more lively and attractive, Kay more intelligent and sophisticated. Each had two children. But Kay had graduated from Bryn Mawr and was married to a teacher at Harvard while Lesley had dropped out of college and was divorced.

Lesley's hatred of Kay was fueled by her profound resentment of her father. She was grateful that she did not have to do Kay's job and take care of Frost, but she also looked for things "to get Kay on." Lesley saw Kay as an "intruder" who had taken her place in Frost's life and was severely moralistic about her sexual infidelity. She feared that Kay might get her share of Frost's increasingly valuable estate and condemned her, Thompson wrote, as "a scheming, money-grubbing crook." Lesley was especially enraged by Frost's love poem to Kay, "The Silken Tent." Though it was written in August–September 1938, soon after Frost met Kay, Lesley insisted he had composed it "way back in her mother's day" and wanted to engrave the opening line, "She is as in a field a silken tent," on Elinor's gravestone. Frost tried to mollify Lesley in December 1938 by gently encouraging her "to be grateful to Kathleen for her ministrations. The closest criticism will discover no flaw in her kindness to me." But Lesley remained adamantly bitter and even referred to Kay as "the whore."[22]

Donald Hall, Frost's friend and protégé, took (like most others) a benign view of Kay and admired her devotion as well as her defiance: "Kay Morrison was devoted and worked hard and was tolerant although I think she had much reason for impatience. Robert came first. She was concerned for Frost: to protect him, to please him. One did not feel that anybody else in the room had the importance that Frost did, and certainly Frost wanted it that way. . . . Many people were frightened of him. Day in, day out, Kay may have done more standing up to him than anybody else." Thompson saw only base, even mercenary motives. Ignoring her devotion, he emphasized her high salary, gifts of money and property, and the Morgan horses Frost bought for Kay and her daughter. Though he himself had greatly benefitted from his association with Frost, Thompson also declared that Frost "satisfied Kay's grotesque fondness for lion-hunting and for name-dropping." John Ciardi, who disapproved of Frost's liaison with Kay, resented both Kay's power over Frost and her malign influence on Frost's friendships:

> It was almost impossible to spend time with Frost apart from the Morrisons. . . . Kay had a mind that naturally spun intricate webs. It is quite possible that I came to see Frost in considerable part through her machinations. They were more intricate than evil . . . but they may have influenced me more than I know in my views of Robert.
>
> I was already aware that he was a literary politician in ways I found personally distasteful. . . . If I have been swayed to look for something like evil in Robert, it may have been Kay's hissing that I heard. I do believe he was self-centered—enough so, I believe, to have been a disastrous father. . . . I believe she might have stewed [my innocent remark] in witches' brew for a year before letting me know she had taken the hex off it.

As Kay's children grew older Frost became an avuncular figure in their household. Since Kay was, in any case, "not a very maternal type," the children did not mind all the attention she paid to him and came to adore the benign old gentleman. Frost, for his part, was fond of Bobby and Anne, who were the same age as his grandchildren. He wrote them charming letters, taught them to memorize poems, gave them money and presents, encouraged them to be rebellious and took a keen interest in their school work. (A strong believer in progressive education, he caused the fire at Ripton by contemptuously throwing Anne's pointless class exercises into the incinerator.) When Anne's horse got sick and she had to inject it every four hours throughout the night, she told Frost that she had to get some sleep between the treatments and could not stay up to talk to him. Nevertheless, he appeared at the farmhouse at ten at night and talked away, as usual, until two in the morning. Still fearing the dark in old age, he thought Anne would also be afraid to walk to the barn alone in the middle of the night. His impulse was both selfish and kind: he would not let her sleep, but stayed up to accompany her to the barn.

Tragedy struck the Morrisons in December 1954 when the twenty-four-year-old, recently married Bobby, like his grandfather before him, was killed in an automobile accident. During a skiing trip at Stowe, while taking chains off a tire at the edge of the road, he was hit by a car driven by a sixteen-year-old French-Canadian boy. Since the weather was exceptionally beautiful, Frost said, in a Hemingway-like phrase: "It's a bad day to be dead." But he was so upset that Kay had to calm *him* down. Anne, the first to hear the tragic news, had to break it to her parents and always felt she had "not done it properly." To comfort her, Frost talked about the deaths in his family and assured her that one somehow survives every tragedy. Though his therapeutic comfort helped Anne while she was still in a state of shock, she also—like Kay—felt overwhelmed by *his* grief.

Anne, who grew up idolizing Ted and hating Kay, saw enough affectionate gestures between Frost and Kay (there was no public display between Ted and Kay) to know the truth. When Ted drove them up to Vermont, she would ride in the back with Gillie and watch Frost, seated next to Kay, with his arm around her. Anne knew what was happening but, unwilling to choose between Frost and Ted, or hurt either of them, she followed the repressive Jamesian rules and "crafted denial." They never talked about the real situation or expressed their true feelings.

When Kay's book was published in 1974 she and Ted were apprehensive that reviewers might allude to Kay's real relationship with Frost. They sat down with the thirty-seven-year-old Anne and assured her that Kay and Frost had never had a love affair. She knew they were lying. They wanted to protect her, but they also wanted her to continue to keep the secret. Frost's oft-quoted but little understood couplet in *A Witness Tree* opposes speculation against knowledge and suggests how the truth remained hidden: "We dance round in a ring and suppose, / But the Secret sits in the middle and knows."

Anne, still bitter about some aspects of her childhood, feels Kay hurt other people because she had been hurt by her father. She hurt Ted by her affairs with Frost and other men; she hurt Frost by refusing to leave Ted and by making him jealous of his rivals; she hurt her children (Bobby even more than Anne, for he was older and "saw the craziness more clearly") by her betrayal and her lies.[23] But Kay's behavior also had some positive aspects. She rescued Frost from emotional chaos, enabled him to write and inspired some of his finest poems. She greatly enhanced the children's lives by making Frost a member of their household. Ted cooperated in her effort to keep the family together. They preserved appearances and convinced almost everyone that they had a happy life. Kay managed, somehow, to hold things together when they constantly threatened to break apart.

V

The full story of Frost's relations with Kay finally reveals—as he intended—the real meaning of *A Witness Tree*. The book, published on April 23, 1942 (four months after America entered the war), was dedicated, not to Kay and Ted, but: "To K.M. for her part in it." Though rejected by the Literary Guild and the Book-of-the-Month Club, it sold 10,000 copies in the first eight weeks and won Frost's fourth Pulitzer Prize. (When a clerk in the Bennington drugstore read about Frost's award, he remarked: "Guess you didn't have much competition, eh?") Since few readers knew about Kay or expected to find sexual passion in Frost's poetry, the revelation of his love went unnoticed. In typically obtuse reviews, the *Booklist* spoke of "characteristically quiet poems with little emotional stress" and the innocent *Catholic World* exclaimed: "Here again are honestly beautiful nature poems."

Though the sexual imagery in these love poems is as powerful as Dylan Thomas' "force that through the green fuse drives the flower," the poetry gains in strength by its more subtle expression of emotion. With characteristic elusiveness, Frost declared that metaphor is the divinely appointed way of writing one thing when you mean another, instead of clearly stating what you mean. As the poet James Dickey observed: "He's able to say the most amazing things without seeming to raise his voice."

In May 1943 Frost acknowledged Kay's inspiration in a letter to his editor William Sloane: "you can find internal evidence in the book itself that but for her there would have been no seventh book. . . . [I] couldn't have been induced to do anything except with something far better than tact. . . . The dedication of the book is no ordinary acknowledgment."[24] A witness tree, which is called "deeply wounded" in the opening poem, "Beech," is a tree trunk and iron stake that mark the boundary of a piece of country property. The signature at the bottom of "Beech," "The Moodie Forester," refers to Frost's temperament as well as to his mother's maiden name. It links Kay to both mother and son, and testifies (or witnesses) that he will respect the boundaries of their love. The first section of the book, "One or Two," takes up the question of whether Frost will be alone or joined with Kay. It includes the fourteen best poems in the book—from "The Silken Tent" to "The Discovery of the Madeiras"—all of which express, directly or indirectly, his love for Kay. Frost also makes several affectionate but subtle allusions to Kay in *A Masque of Reason* (1945), the book that followed *A Witness Tree*. In this work the enchanting Kay appears as Job's wife, Thyatira, and is named for a city famous for its witches. Thyatira is beautiful, she does not try to be Platonic and she has a past that won't bear looking into. She also, like Kay with Frost, falls asleep whenever Job tries to read to her and always claims she hasn't been asleep.

"The Silken Tent," which opens the love sequence in *A Witness Tree,* is a perfect example of Plato's concept of the horse and charioteer, of passion restrained by art. The original title of this intensely personal poem was "In Praise of Your Poise." Brower points out that "as the first poem of his eightieth birthday selection, *Aforesaid,* Frost printed 'The Silken Tent,' where it takes the place of 'The Pasture,' the dedicatory poem [to Elinor] of several earlier volumes." This sonnet, written in a single sentence and dominated by a single metaphor, was inspired by the sensual imagery of the Song of Solomon—"I am . . . comely . . . as the tents of Kedar" (1:5)—an exotic contrast to the stony harshness of rural New England, and by the seductive invitation in John Donne's "The Baite":

> Come live with mee and bee my love,
> And we will some new pleasures prove
> Of golden sands, and christall brookes,
> With *silken lines,* and silver hookes.

In Frost's poem the beloved woman is compared to a silken tent in a field when the summer breeze—an allusion to the "correspondent breeze" of the Romantic poets, which represents inspiration and creative power—has dried the dew on its ropes so that it sways gently in "guys" (a triple pun on ropes, mockery and men). Its masculine cedar pole (a hint of the aromatic cedars of Lebanon) shoots upward toward heaven, symbolizing the sureness of the soul. Though not strictly held by any single cord, the feminine tent, supported by the masculine pole, is loosely bound by countless silken ties of love. Only when the ropes become taut as the summer air becomes capricious (another pun on the lady's whimsy and the man's goatish lust) is the tent made aware of the slightest bondage.

This love poem describes, with the greatest possible delicacy, the conflict between Kay's bondage and freedom as she is pulled, loosely by Ted in marriage or tightly by Frost in love, but remains "strictly held by none." The "silken ties" refer to her love-making, not to her marriage, and suggest (as Frost wrote in "Not Quite Social"): "You have me there, but loosely, as I would be held." Her daughter said Kay was "ecstatic" about this tribute, and agreed that the poem described the two men and two ties of love that pulled Kay in different directions.[25]

"All Revelation," which follows "The Silken Tent," refers back to "the agitated heart" in Frost's early poem "Revelation." "All Revelation" describes sexual intercourse and the revelation or insight that comes from that experience. The first stanza invokes Cybele, the sensual earth goddess, as the male force "thrusts in" (or "into") three times and makes the woman "come." This act is repeated metaphorically (and rather awkwardly) in the third stanza as the male cathode ray enters the concave geode. Eyes gazing at eyes, as the man and woman make love, seem to bring out the stars and the flowers, concentrate the earth and the sky, and make them feel, through their union, a part of both earthly nature and the heavenly cosmos.

"The Most of It," in "One or Two," which describes Frost's longing for and response to Kay, harks back to "Two Look at Two," in which the tame buck and doe encounter the lovers (based on Frost and Elinor). In the later poem the man seems alone and finds nothing but a mocking echo in answer to his call for companionship. When he calls out to life, he wants an "original" (that is: a novel and also elemental, primitive and even godlike) response. His cry is answered by an embodiment of sexual power, when a great buck suddenly appears on the opposite cliff and swims across the lake. He walks with horny tread, penetrates the brush and creates an orgasmic waterfall so that his mate can make The Most of It. Frost had identified with a buck as early as July 1921 when he told Raymond Holden that he would soon be crashing through the woods in his direction.

"Never Again Would Birds' Song Be the Same," which appears between "The Most of It" and "The Subverted Flower," is (Frost said) an "Old-fashioned praise poem about a lady's voice" that his audience would "have to like whether you like it or not." In this sonnet the birds in Eden recognize Eve's sound of sense and grasp her tone of meaning without understanding her actual words. Her soft eloquence influences the birds so profoundly that their song permanently changes and will never again be the same: "And to do that to birds was why she came." Emphasizing the bold sexual pun on the final word, Frost suggests that just as the lady's voice intensified the birds' song, so Kay's sexual passion inspired the words that made this poem.

The long narrative poem in couplets that concludes this section, partly based on a story in Richard Hakluyt's *Voyages* (1600), is so puzzling and uncharacteristic that Brower, Richard Poirier and William Pritchard do not even mention it. The narrative describes two contrasting women. One is a weak, silent and unresponsive lady, stolen and brought aboard ship by her lover, and then left with him on the Atlantic island of Madeira, where she dies of a weak heart. The other is a passionate black slave, who kisses her lover, "drinks" his breath and is overwhelmed by sexual desire. When she becomes infected by her lover's dangerous fever, they are bound naked, face to face, and thrown overboard in a funereal wedding. One woman shrinks from life; the other sacrifices herself for love.

In February 1938, the month before Elinor died, Frost alluded to the metaphysical image in "Two Tramps in Mudtime" and took a characteristically anti-Platonic stance. He told a poet-friend that he was philosophically opposed to having one "Iseult" for his vocation (poetry) and another for his avocation (sexual love). His aim was to write—as he did with Kay—about the real and the ideal in one woman. In "The Discovery of the Madeiras" the "stolen lady" symbolizes Tristan's theft of Iseult; the feverish bound slave girl represents Iseult's fatal passion. The pale, thoughtful lady was based on Elinor; the dark lady was based on Kay.[26] In this poem Frost revealed how Kay had supplanted Elinor.

15

Harvard and
Dartmouth
1940–1949

I

Frost had re-established ties with Harvard, where he had studied in the late 1890s, when in 1935 he agreed to write an ode for the 300th anniversary celebrations, to be the Phi Beta Kappa poet at graduation and to deliver the prestigious Charles Eliot Norton lectures on literature. But he was never able to write a verse to order. He compared pulling a poem out of him to tearing a swallowed hook out of a fish and, claiming sickness, failed to compose the two ceremonial poems. Invited by the Coleridge scholar John Livingston Lowes, he did, however, deliver the six Norton lectures in the spring of 1936.

Frost approached Harvard with a certain wariness. He did not read his darker poems in public and was content to hide the real meaning of his work. Though he had won two Pulitzer Prizes and would soon win two more, his popularity, rustic persona and apparent simplicity led most academics to condemn him as a popular ladies' club poet. He felt the English department was dominated by F. O. Matthiessen and his Left-wing followers, who (at the outbreak of the Spanish Civil War) disapproved of his politics as well as his poetry.

The titles of his Norton lectures were deliberately vague ("The Old Way to the New," "Does Wisdom Signify?," "After the End of a Poem"), the ideas familiar, the delivery—without a text or even notes—spontaneous and rambling. But his personality was engaging, and the brilliant performance by the genial, grey-thatched Vermont villager, speaking as if his friends were gathered around the stove, filled the largest theater to overflowing. More than a thousand enthusiastic people from both the city and the university poured in to hear him. John Holmes wrote that Frost "says things that sound famous on the instant: epigrammatic;

sound; wise. . . . He had such an ovation as one dreams of in the ideal state, where poets and prophets are properly honored by the people." Though a stenographer took down Frost's extemporaneous lectures, he never delivered the final text (as he had promised) to Harvard University Press. He was not good at logical exposition and knew that his lively, witty, playful talks would lose their effectiveness if written up and presented in a formal fashion. "Some lectures," he told a friend, "would be better off if no one ever recorded them."

Since his resignation from Amherst in June 1938 Frost had had a lonely and emotionally difficult year in Boston and Florida. The tremendous success of the Norton lectures enabled his Harvard friends Ted Morrison and Robert Hillyer to arrange an offer from President James Conant that brought him back to the university in the fall of 1939. This academic connection structured his life and provided more social contact. The Ralph Waldo Emerson Fellowship in Poetry, a two-year appointment at an annual salary of $1,500, left Frost free to make whatever contribution he wished. He had often carried a Latin edition of Lucretius on his travels, and at first offered to teach a course on his favorite Latin works. But he soon realized that the Latin department had doubts about his scholarship and wanted to plant a faculty member to monitor his classes. He told Hillyer that the chairman, "though writing warmly to welcome my idea, yet winds up with the suggestion that I might like John Finley as a watcher in my classes. Don't I know those boyos of old? They are too humanistic to be human."[1] Frost finally decided to offer a poetry seminar for forty students, which met one night a week in Adams House.

The Harvard of his youth had taken him "away from the question of whether [he] could write or not," but in his mid-sixties Frost warmed to the university and told Kay that he liked it more than he thought he would. In 1941 he became Harvard Fellow in American Civilization at a doubled salary of $3,000. Two years later he was appointed "seer" on the Harvard governing Board of Overseers. During the wartime constraints of 1942–45, when Harvard's first priority was to train officers for military service, Frost retained his title but became an honorary faculty member —without pay. Though Conant had brought him to Harvard, he showed little interest in Frost's poetry. Used to royal treatment, Frost did not get on well with him. After a sharp exchange of words about Roosevelt's New Deal, Conant criticized his "bitter tongue." Frost also resented his rigid personality and his Meiklejohnian tendency to dominate his colleagues. "With all his science," Frost told Mertins, "with all his learning, which nobody begrudges or denies him, Conant was always a very 'proper' individual, a Puritan and a prude if not a prig. He tried to regulate the lives of all the faculty."[2]

During his four years at Harvard Frost's friendship with Bernard DeVoto deepened and then reached a crisis. DeVoto, whose attitude was "close to worship," called Frost "the greatest living American" and confessed: "I go tearful whenever I talk about him. . . . He is the quintessence of everything I respect and even love in the American heritage." His adoration, like Thompson's, was bound to lead to disillusionment. According to his biographer, DeVoto "felt endangered, feared being devoured . . . [and] *couldn't* stand association with a father figure so potent as Frost." Well acquainted with his own family's psychological disorders, Frost had found a way of dealing with mental suffering. Though he sometimes succumbed to spells of self-pity, he despised people who sought help from psychiatry. When he discovered that DeVoto had been treated by Dr. Laurence Kubie, who specialized in helping writers and later published *Neurotic Distortion of the Creative Process* (1961), Frost could not resist exaggerating his power over his disciple. In 1943 he told mutual friends that DeVoto "has been under the care of a psychiatrist, who has told him that I am not good for him, that if he is ever to succeed, he must not cultivate my company: I am too strong for him and have a bad effect on him." When DeVoto heard about this he felt betrayed and sent Frost a furious letter. He vehemently denied Frost's assertions, asked "what satisfaction you get from circulating a false and damaging statement about me" and warned him that he would no longer tolerate such slander.

As with Joseph Warren Beach in 1922, Frost first spread malicious rumors and, when confronted with them, apologetically withdrew. Shocked by DeVoto's violent response and unwilling to lose a valued ally, Frost, in a letter to DeVoto of June 10, said that Kay had given him Hell for gossiping about his friend's private life. He insisted that he had always praised DeVoto, mentioned him for membership in the American Academy and predicted he would be summoned back to Harvard. He blamed the "disappointed novelist" in himself for claiming that DeVoto's doctor had advised him to stay away from Frost. He accepted DeVoto's assertion that the story was untrue—though could not resist saying that his behavior made it seem plausible—solemnly promised never to repeat it and humbly begged DeVoto to forgive their differences.

The real but unspoken source of the quarrel was DeVoto's sometime lover Kay Morrison. Only a year older than Kay and angry at being supplanted by a much older man, DeVoto had once directly challenged

Frost by asking: "Are you sleeping with her?" Sensing the truth at Bread Loaf, he had called Frost a "bad man." Kay, who told Frost about DeVoto's psychological problems, roused Frost's jealousy and made him want to dominate his rival. According to Thompson, DeVoto had forced Frost to write that conciliatory letter by threatening to expose his relations with Kay. Though they remained on frosty terms for the next four years, they finally became reconciled at Bread Loaf in 1947 when DeVoto suddenly said: "Robert, you've been a damn fool and I've been a damn fool. Let's forget it and be friends."[3]

While Frost was teaching at Harvard, America entered World War II. Frost had always thought war—a trial by existence—came naturally to men; it tested their courage and decided which nations were superior. Though he could not participate, he was fascinated by the violent spectacle and counted on the war to improve America's position with both allies and enemies. Of those close to him, only Carol's son, Prescott (who was invalided out of the army in 1943), and Thompson (who was in the Navy in San Diego) were serving in the armed forces. Before the attack on Pearl Harbor and the declaration of war, Frost had doubts about whether America should fight to defend England. But once America entered the war, he remembered his first publications in London, became a fervent supporter of Britain and told Lesley (who was even more fanatically Right-wing than Elinor) that "it ill becomes a Frost not to sympathize with a nation that has done so much for our family." Touched by Jonathan Cape's interest in publishing his work during the war, he reminded a friend that both his mother's family and Kay's were Scottish, and that he would never forget his obligations to these people. He had always respected the imperial greatness of Britain and disliked the liberals' easy talk about the postwar dissolution of the Empire, which he considered a stable and generally benign system of government. Later on, he told a Russian friend that America's *Declaration of Independence* set a bad example. Look at what happens in Africa: every vacant lot declares independence." He did not believe that American democracy was the ideal system for all countries.

Frost was sceptical of the alliance with totalitarian Russia, which had first signed a peace treaty with Nazi Germany and then joined the Allies when Hitler invaded that country in 1941. He considered Lenin a sinister figure and Stalin a dangerous maniac. Speaking ironically, he told Thompson that he was fascinated by the Russians' spectacle of ruthlessness for its own sake and their willingness to stick at nothing to accomplish nothing. He imagined the eastern barbarians breaking through the German lines and coming right through France to the English Channel—bringing their typhus with them. He accepted them but did not rejoice in them as allies, and counted on the Russians to prevent Germany from conquering the world.

Untermeyer, a passionate opponent of Fascism, was working for the Office of War Information in New York. He invited Frost to join the cause and was bitterly hurt by his refusal to help the Allied effort by writing war propaganda. In May 1943 Frost tried to justify his refusal in an illogical and unconvincing letter to his editor. No effort in war, he said, counts for very much if it doesn't involve risk and danger. It would simply be too easy, while living in America, to write propaganda essays against Hitler, and it would not take much courage to do so.[4] His odd mixture of selfishness and scepticism was much stronger than his patriotism, and kept him out of the war.

When his relations with Conant deteriorated and the money ran out at Harvard, Frost accepted a position, beginning in September 1943, as George Ticknor Fellow of the Humanities at Dartmouth, where he had been an undergraduate for less than a term in 1892. He was still eager to compensate for his failure to graduate, and his old friend Sidney Cox, then teaching in the English department, would smooth his path. Frost earned $3,000 a year (equal to his highest salary at Harvard) and met students from Friday to Sunday in the fall and spring. On Thursdays from October to January Kay would put him on the train from Boston to Hanover, where he would remain until Sunday night. Idiosyncratic as always, he graded his students on their reading, conversation and listening as well as on their writing. The topics of his own brilliant conversation, one pupil remembered, ranged from war, politics, poetry, education, democracy, social changes, personality, biography, autobiography, industrial developments in Vermont and the advantages of a non-farming farm to apples and the best way to make a log fire.

The unusual arrangement with Dartmouth allowed Frost to spend winters in Florida—part of the time with Kay, while Ted remained in Cambridge with the children. He had acquired a new property, Pencil Pines, near Hervey Allen's estate in South Miami. Following Allen's example, he had assembled two prefabricated Hodgson houses, surfaced with coral stone cut from the ancient reef beneath the land. The simply furnished house had a screened-in porch and cushioned wicker furniture, but no heating or air conditioning.

In 1949, after six years at Dartmouth, the academic voyager was eased into his final berth at Amherst, where he had started his teaching career in 1917. Just as he had returned to Amherst in 1923 after President Meiklejohn was replaced by George Olds, so he now returned once again, after President King was replaced by Frost's former student Charles Cole. Amherst made the seventy-five-year-old Frost an offer he could not refuse. As Simpson Lecturer in Literature he received $3,500 a year, but had only minimum obligations: one public lecture, some class visits and a few informal conferences. Best of all, at the end of his five-year contract in 1954 he would receive (for the first time in his career) an annual pension of $2,500. Old friends like Whicher, Elliott and Manthey-Zorn were still on the faculty and welcomed him back. In a gracious letter to President John Dickey of Dartmouth, Frost explained that he had been asked back to Amherst on terms so extravagantly generous that he could never expect any other college to equal them. The greatest appeal, the author of "Provide, Provide" admitted, was that he would finally be well provided for during his remaining years in and out of education.

II

While Frost was teaching and barding around, Carol, his only surviving son, was trying without much success to run the farm in South Shaftsbury. Silent, withdrawn and "queer," Carol had been difficult since childhood. He disliked his "feminine" name, resented the fact that his parents had not called him Charles or Carl (or even Robert), and when he was nineteen changed the spelling to the more manly Carroll. A tall, thin, handsome man, he was good with his hands and could fix or make anything. But "he was one of the most unsocial of beings," Frost told Mertins. In contrast to the sociable, voluble Frost, Carol "just wouldn't make friends, just wouldn't talk, couldn't talk. He would close right up the minute somebody started to make himself friendly." His wife, Lillian, like Willard Fraser, blamed his parents for isolating all the children from their contemporaries: "Elinor's big fault, both hers and R.F.'s, was not insisting on the children going to school. My husband had not more than a couple of months at most of formal schooling. . . . He had no playmates but his sisters and never did make friends."

Sealed off from the world and locked into the rather stifling atmosphere of his family, Carol became abnormally close to his mother and unusually dependent on his father. After Elinor's death Kay tried to advise Frost about how to deal with his troubled son. Remembering how insistently Frost had pressured her to marry him, Kay gently criticized him for interfering with Carol instead of allowing him to lead his own life. In her view "his presence was not good for Carol, whose own problems were only intensified by Robert's consistent conviction that he knew how to direct other people's lives. . . . In his efforts to guide Carol he sometimes seemed unaware that his son had become a grown man and could not be treated as though he were still a minor. . . . He often seemed oblivious to the humiliations he caused Carol, who was still in part financially dependent on him."

A characteristic confrontation took place in Ann Arbor in October 1921, when Carol changed the spelling of his name. According to one of Frost's students, "Carol proposed to pay twenty-five dollars for a champion rooster to improve his poultry. When his father harshly put down the idea, son Carol disappeared from Ann Arbor and made his way back to [Vermont]. His presence there was traced through frantic telephone calls to Marjorie, still in high school in North Bennington. He was to make the rooster part of the flock, defying his father, as he often did."[5] Reginald Cook noticed Frost's well-meaning but tactless domination during their visit to Carol's house in September 1935: "What interested me was how quickly the poet took charge. The hospitable Carol was a bit daunted (I felt) by his father. The poet, quite as much as Mrs. Frost, arranged tea, sandwiches, and ice cream. It was he who reprimanded the inattentive Prescott, and it was he who fanned the conversation." Carol responded with self-protective withdrawal, and seemed to feel more enmity than affection for his father. Despite their common interest in sports, Frost told Newdick that "Carol is very shy, talks little, and I feel a gulf between us."

Frost tried to bridge the gulf in various ways. He paid the rugged and capable Wade Van Dore, who was three years older than Carol, to work on the South Shaftsbury farm and provide some companionship for his gloomy, solitary son. Van Dore said that "Carol and I got along well, mainly, I think, because I approached nature as a workman. . . . He was also beguiled by my wilderness experiences and was always asking about adventures I had with animals there. Frost was happy about this." Frost also tried to help Carol with his small sweet pea business. In July 1939, when Carol got an order from the Catamount Inn in Bennington, Frost delivered the flowers himself. As he approached the lobby of the hotel, a guest, yelling out of the window, ordered him to use the service entrance.

Van Dore described an incident that revealed Carol's obsessive work habits and rather hopeless attempt to deal with his officious father: "Frost told me about his once coming upon Carol lying down in his garden, painstakingly sifting the loose soil through his fingers in order to eliminate quack grass roots. . . . Shocked, Frost had exclaimed: 'Don't you know you can't make a success of farming that way?' 'But isn't this the way you write your poetry?' returned Carol in dark desperation. . . . Carol's star was just too humiliatingly small beside his father's light of the first magnitude."[6]

Frost realized that Carol's life was too closely bound up with his own. But since Carol could not support his family, he remained pathetically dependent. Taking up Van Dore's point in 1935, Frost explained to his Michigan friend Morris Tilley that "Carol has never really been well and strong. His unhappiness is mine—and the more mine that my own personal affairs prosper almost too much." Carol felt he was a failure as parent, as farmer and—since he also had artistic aspirations—as poet. Father and son poets are extremely rare (Edward and Peter Davison, Louis and Allen Ginsberg, Roy and John Fuller have been exceptional) and Carol was unwise to enter the arena with his father. In several letters of the 1930s Frost gave Carol considerable advice and encouragement about his poetry ("'Songs' is fine, deep and effective"), but judging from the feeble example printed in *Family Letters,* Carol had very little talent. Frost, more realistically, told Untermeyer that Carol *was* a failure as a farmer and poet, and that he had been unable to convince him that he was the least bit successful in anything. Recalling his own long years of financial dependence on his grandfather, Frost told his poet-friend Wilbert Snow that all his attempts to help Carol seemed to backfire. Snow recalled: "The boy had failed in several business ventures; was also lamentable, the father told me, in his attempt to be a poet. . . . Robert said, 'I had just settled a monthly income on him. Perhaps that was the last straw. His pride couldn't take it.'"[7]

Carol's marriage in 1923 to Marjorie's close school friend Lillian LaBatt (one of the few girls he knew) was a promising event. But it also increased his responsibilities and caused new problems. The soft-spoken, frizzy-haired Lillian had taken care of Dorothy Canfield Fisher's children in Vermont, and was (Frost said) uncommonly pretty, quiet and impractical. She was also deaf, wore a hearing aid with wires dangling down and often had the eager but puzzled expression of someone who had not quite caught the conversation. Her deafness, Frost thought, tended to intensify Carol's isolation. Lillian said that she "wouldn't describe Carol as irritable or sullen, but he had times of being very depressed. These times got worse and oftener as he got older." Marjorie's little daughter, Robin, who sometimes lived with Lillian and Carol, found him sad, frightening and severe. Like the ten-year-old Rob Frost, when he first came east to his grandfather's house in Lawrence, Robin was punished for not finishing her dinner and for wiping dirty hands on a clean towel. She got the only spankings of her life from Carol.

Carol seemed to inherit his grandfather's sullen manner. He was dark, smoldering and resentful, and felt beaten by the world. Like his grandfather, he also despised "frail careful people." Even when he had dangerous symptoms, he would not admit that he was sick. Carol's paranoia made him suspicious of everyone. He felt that potential friends were trying to take advantage of him and that strangers were spying on him and persecuting him. Frost told Kay that Carol was overcome both by paranoid fears of persecution and by more rational fears that he was going mad. Lillian, he said, "had to get up at two or three in the morning sometimes and go down in the cellar with Carol to look for dictaphone wiring." (His obsession may have been connected to her hearing aid.) "By daybreak he got over such fears or exchanged them for the fear that there were signs of insanity."[8]

The thirty-eight-year-old Carol reached his final crisis in September–October 1940, when Lillian entered the hospital in Pittsfield, Massachusetts and was told she needed an operation. Her latent tuberculosis and weak heart made this a dangerous undertaking—and her doctor made a great mistake by telling Carol that he was not sure he could save her. The operation led to another irrational fear. As Kay wrote nervously to Thompson in October, Carol "has been beside himself since September 17 or so when he learned that Lillian needed a complete hysterectomy. The shock of no more children (after 16 years) sent him off his balance. Robert has been ready for insanity, but this was quite a blow even though he had been dreading it, fearing it. Carol has been calling once or twice a day for a week." His mind clouded by suspicion, Carol became uncharacteristically talkative and hysterical, and pitifully lamented that no one (by which he meant his father) loved him. His lack of a job and money as well as his dangerously sick wife intensified his "inferiority complex." As Lillian later observed: "If I hadn't been so ill so much of the time Carol would have made more of a success of his life." Lillian was his "grounding" and he was scared to death of living without her.

Lillian said that on their wedding night in November 1923 Carol, in a bizarre death wish, had "announced to her that now his experience was complete, his life fulfilled, so he might as well kill himself." Always obsessed by a desire to commit suicide, he once again turned his thoughts to self-destruction and every threat made the possibility of suicide more real. He had always been, Van Dore noted, "a gun-conscious, gun-polishing, gun-displaying person."[9] During his manic conversations he had even threatened to kill his father, and Frost feared that Carol might also threaten Lillian and Prescott.

In a desperate effort to save Carol, who refused to see a psychiatrist, Frost went from Cambridge to South Shaftsbury on about October 1. He tried, with all his formidable powers of persuasion, to restore Carol's mental balance and convince him that he still had something to live for. Untermeyer, whose own son had committed suicide, explained that Carol "succumbed to a sense of persecution; rejected and despondent, he turned against the world. He had hallucinations; he suspected the men who worked around the place and felt that passing cars were spying on him. . . . After listening to Robert speaking all night against frustration, Carol said grimly, 'You always have the last word.'" In this case, however, Carol did. Frost called it "suicide for spite against the argufier."

On the night of October 9, 1940, with Elinor's ashes still in his house two years after her death, Carol—in a last, desperate plea for help —woke up his son "to tell Prescott he was going to kill himself. Prescott had heard this before, and went back to sleep." While Prescott was sleeping upstairs, Carol burned all his poetry in the kitchen and shot himself with his deer rifle. Awakened by the shot, Prescott ran downstairs and discovered his father's bloody corpse. Instead of rushing off for help, he called the police and Frost, and waited near his dead father till they arrived. Three days later, pleased that Prescott at least had shown the right spirit, Frost praised his cool behavior: "Disaster brought out the heroic in you. You now know you have the courage and nerve for anything you may want or need to be. . . . You would have had plenty of excuse if you had gone to pieces and run out of that house crying for help."[10] Frost then had to break the news to Lillian, who had been close to death in the hospital for several weeks. Frost was not surprised by Carol's suicide and thought death was better for him than life in a mental institution. He told Untermeyer that Carol was splendid with animals and, remembering the misanthropic and half-demented Gulliver among the Houyhnhnms, sadly said that he should have lived with horses.

Frost's mistakes as a parent, his ridiculing the purchase of a rooster, dominating Carol's household and criticizing his farming habits did not begin to account for Carol's suicide. But like any father, Frost was devastated, felt terribly guilty and attempted to find an explanation for what had happened. He had tried to help Carol in many different ways, but it now seemed that every one of them was wrong. Frost learned, he later told a friend, "how little influence a father has with his own son" and how little a father can do "for such a son." Still searching for a reason, he explained to Lillian, just after the suicide, that Carol had always been peculiar and that Frost had never been able to alleviate his destructive obsessions: "I was up there trying to clear his conscience of guilt and his mind of worry . . . his returning again and again to your not being able to have any more children. . . . His mind had in it a strange twist from childhood that no wrench we could give it could seem to straighten out. . . . I failed with him. Do my best with money or advice it was always the wrong thing."

The reasons for Carol's suicide extended far beyond his alienation from his father and included the history of insanity in the family, the recent death of his mother, his isolation, his lack of employment and income, his sense of failure, his desire to escape from a futile existence, his persecution mania, his wife's inability to have more children, his fear that Lillian would die, his overwhelming depression, his fascination with guns, his obsession with death, and his need to threaten, defy and punish Frost. Just as Frost could not bear to see the wrecked car lot on the site of the Derry farm, so from now on he always avoided the southwest corner of Vermont, where Carol had killed himself.[11] During the past six years Frost had suffered three devasting deaths in his immediate family: Marjorie in 1934, Elinor in 1938 and Carol in 1940. But with the help of Kay Morrison he continued to teach, lecture and write. In the next few years he would realize, with King Lear, "The worst is not, / So long as we can say, 'This is the worst.' "

III

Frost's blank-verse closet-dramas, *A Masque of Reason* (March 1945) and its complement *A Masque of Mercy* (October 1947), appeared when he was teaching at Dartmouth. They are—like "New Hampshire" and "Build Soil"—his most conspicuous failures and add nothing to his poetic reputation. Frost had always been interested in the theater and had put on plays at Pinkerton and Amherst. The narrative poems in *North of Boston* had intensely dramatic characters and dialogue. In February 1919 his little drama on the theme of the double, *A Way Out* (1917), had been produced in Northampton. Referring to *The Guardeen* (1943), Untermeyer wrote that "besides his masques and a burlesque playlet ['The Cow's in the Corn," 1941] Robert wrote a serious full-length play, which, in spite of his hopes, was never produced. According to a number of readers it was unplayable."

Inspired perhaps by Eliot's poetic dramas—*Murder in the Cathedral* (1935), about the death of Thomas à Becket, and *The Family Reunion* (1939), based on the *Oresteia* of Aeschylus, and by the three Auden-Isherwood plays of the late 1930s—Frost naively tried for a Broadway production of his leaden *Masques*. Reuben Brower pointed out that Frost's works, despite their titles, had nothing in common with the elaborate, mythological and musical court masques by Jonson and Milton in seventeenth-century England. In spirit they were "closer to the anti-masque, the mocking entertainment that served as a foil to the main action of the masque proper, a kind of satyr play to the more serious moral and ceremonial drama."

Raymond Holden wrote that the emotionally battered Frost identified with the suffering of the biblical Job. He believed "he's a kind of latter-day Job and that unlike Job he has proved, in not being bowed by grief [during his struggle with the Deity], that he is a better man than God." Taking his title and text from Job 13:3: "Surely I would speak to the Almighty, and I desire to reason with God," Frost said his analysis of the archetypal sufferer's relation to God had added a 43rd chapter to the 42nd and last chapter of the Book of Job. Frost's masque is intensely allusive, but in this work the literary references are heavy-handed and pedantic, rather than subtle and suggestive, and add very little to the meaning.[12] Only Kay's cameo appearance as Thyatira (which nobody recognized) provides the slightest interest.

Like Milton, Frost made God argue. But his masque, in which God sits on a collapsible plywood throne and speaks with ponderous jocularity, is closer to the biblical and satanic tomfoolery of Shaw's *Back to Methuselah* (1921) than to the exalted solemnity of *Paradise Lost*. Ostensibly Frost, like Milton, tries to show that man must accept the divinely ordained evil and suffering in the world. But when Job questions God about the reason for his suffering, His explanation—"I was just showing off to the Devil" —is deliberately trifling and undermines the potentially grave content of the poem.

A Masque of Reason attracted serious critical attention—most of it quite negative. In the *Atlantic Monthly,* where Frost had published many of his best poems, Mark Schorer tried to justify Frost's tone by explaining that "he is at least as intent on writing an entertaining poem as he is on writing a philosophical one." Robert Lowell, in the *Sewanee Review,* also began sympathetically before lapsing into a truthful judgment: "The masque proceeds for twenty-three pages of engaging and idiomatic banter. . . . At one point the dialogue rises to a pitch of considerable intensity. . . . [But it] is too long, random, and willful." Lowell's friend Randall Jarrell, noting Frost's radical decline, called it "a frivolous, trivial, and bewilderingly corny affair, full of jokes inexplicable except as the contemptuous patter of an old magician certain that *he* can get away with anything in the world."[13]

Zeroing in on Frost's weakest poem, the more hostile critics, who had ignored his greatest work, rejoiced in the opportunity to deflate the old man's popular reputation. In the *New Republic* the poet Conrad Aiken called his blank verse "unrewardingly blank" and said "the cracker-barrel wisecrack grates a little, and the texture and text alike become too thin." F. W. Dupee, writing in the *Nation,* also condemned Frost's manner: "it is too often not a laugh but a smirk—the reflex of an incorrigible complacency." Yvor Winters, in his damaging critical assault on Frost in the *Sewanee Review,* noted with some irritation that the trivial "details are irrelevant to any discernible theme" and that "the poem as a whole is at loose ends; no single part of it is intelligent or even tries to be intelligent." The poet Louise Bogan, writing in the *New Yorker* in April 1945, after six years of worldwide slaughter and atrocity, expressed the fundamental criticism of the work: "Frost, bringing us up against the problem of Pain and Evil, adds nothing to our insight on the subject."[14] He could not sustain an argument in his self-indulgent longer poems, and was too self-absorbed and sceptical to deal with the serious implications of his subject.

The bitter failure of *A Masque of Reason* was compounded thirteen years later by Archibald MacLeish's enormously successful play on the same subject, *J.B.* (1958). Frost called MacLeish "a great lifter" and remarked: "Too bad he never read the Book of Job." Their modern settings and interpretations of Job were very different. In the final lines of MacLeish's verse play, J.B. extols man's capacity for suffering and his strength to live. "Our labor always, like Job's," MacLeish wrote in an explanatory essay, "is to learn through suffering to love—to love even that which lets us suffer." Frost's privately expressed beliefs were much less uplifting. "Archie has always been derivative," he told Mertins. "Did you catch the end of *J.B.*? People think everything is solved by love. Maybe just as many things are solved by hate."[15]

Despite the severe attacks on his first masque, Frost boldly brought out *A Masque of Mercy*, a similar, much longer and even more lifeless work on the Book of Jonah. The poem takes place in a modern New York bookstore and has four characters: Jonah, in flight from God; Keeper, the socialistic bookstore owner; Jesse Bel, his neurotic wife; and her doctor, Paul, who speaks for the biblical St. Paul. Frost called himself an "Old Testament Christian" who praised strict justice and denounced the softening effects of New Testament mercy. In the central conflict of the masque the former takes precedence. As he wrote in "Poverty and Poetry" (1938), "we're in danger, in our way of thinking that mercy comes first in the world. It comes in, but it comes in second. The thing you are most interested in is justice." He expresses his theme through the plea for courage in the final speech and in the double negative of the last line: "Nothing can make injustice just but mercy."

Reviewing the masque in *Poetry* and trying to be kind, William Carlos Williams spoke of Frost's "well sustained philosophical lyrics full of spicy rhetoric." But more severe critics focused on its weaknesses. Rolfe Humphries, who had written a harsh notice of *A Further Range*, condemned "the arch gerontic garrulities and mock sapience of the two masques." In the *Partisan Review* Leslie Fiedler, echoing Jarrell's unerring judgment, compounded Frost's personal and poetic faults, and called it "a bad book, shallow, corny, and unmercifully cute. . . . [Frost's role] cannot be played on past seventy without penalty: the platform charm, the public face, the sly hatred of the young, the foreigner, the failure—the otiose revenges of success on the unaccepted. To seem at last somewhat stupid is a just reward. Frost's humor has always appeared a little dull, a little cruel."[16]

IV

In 1946, between the publication of the two masques, William Sloane left Holt to start his own publishing firm and was replaced by Frost's sixth editor. Alfred Edwards, "who had recently joined Holt as financial man-

ager and who had neither publishing experience nor literary pretensions, offered the septuagenarian poet the admiration and advice which
he now needed even more than editorial guidance." Under Edwards'
direction Frost's works continued to sell. He had earned $3,000 to
$4,000 a year from book royalties during the early years of the Depression, was paid $7,000 in 1936 when the Book-of-the-Month Club took
A Further Range and earned more than $10,000 for *Collected Poems* in
1949. His total income for 1954 was nearly $13,000. Frost's work also did
well in England. In 1944 *Come In,* an anthology of his poems edited by
Untermeyer, sold 5,600 in wartime Britain and the *Complete Poems* of
1951 sold 9,500 in seven impressions.[17]

Frost's eighth volume of poetry, *Steeple Bush,* was published on May 28,
1947 and dedicated to his six grandchildren. The title, mentioned in
"Something for Hope," refers to a weed, crowded out by trees, which
takes its name from its steeple-like blossom shoots and suggests some sort
of spiritual aspiration. After the love poems inspired by Kay in *A Witness
Tree,* this book was distinctly flat and disappointing. Apart from the
(previously mentioned) short, bitter and satiric "The Night Light," "Beyond Words" and "An Importer," there were two interesting poems and
one masterpiece.

"One Step Backward Taken" (1946) is related to the cataclysm of
nature in "Once by the Pacific." In the later poem (which borrows the
"ices . . . crisis" rhyme from Eliot's "Prufrock") a tremendous avalanche
hurls great boulders down a gully and tears off massive capes of earth.
Though the speaker's standpoint—and viewpoint—are shaken by this
universal crisis, he manages to save himself by stepping backward just in
time as the world rushes by him to destruction. The poem sounds like a
justification of Frost's self-protective aloofness from the war—or from
domestic tragedy.

The cunning, punning "Iota Subscript" is a marvelous example of
Frost's light, comic-erotic vein. Since its meaning depends on a point in
ancient Greek grammar, most readers failed to realize that it describes
Frost's relations with Kay. When the iota is appended beneath a letter
like a small tail, it lengthens the sound from a short to a long vowel. In
the poem the speaker-lover modestly says that he is neither the capital I
nor minuscule letter i, but rather the tiny iota subscript. Punning on a
Greek letter, he claims that he is actually inferior to or underneath the
upsilon, or Greek "u." Claiming attention, though he is small, Frost
suggests that "I" is not only dominated by "You," but is also under "You"
when they make love.

"Directive" is one of Frost's most difficult and important poems. The poignant opening describes an escape from the distracting world of the present (as in Wordsworth's "The World Is Too Much With Us") and a regression in time to a nearly obliterated but still meaningful place in the past where children grew up and where their relics remain. This description strongly suggests Frost's disillusioned return to the Derry farm, after an absence of thirty years, when he decided not to scatter Elinor's ashes in the sacred source of Hyla Brook. The "brook to none but who remember long" in "Hyla Brook" and the "backward motion toward the source" in "West-Running Brook" are clearly related to the brook that is the source of truth and meaning in "Directive." Apart from "source" the key words in this poem are "loss"-"lost" and "children's playhouse" (both repeated four times), in which he finds the broken drinking goblet like the Holy Grail. With four of Frost's own children dead and one going mad, the line about the lost children— "Weep for what little things could make them glad"—is heart-rending.

The Grail, identified with the cup used at the Last Supper and subject of many a knightly quest in medieval literature, is an ironic allusion to Eliot's use of this symbol in *The Waste Land*. But it also represents redemptive purity in Frost's poem. The passage alluded to in St. Mark (4:11-12) says that Christ speaks in parables so that the wrong ones —those outside the faith and unworthy of salvation—may see but not perceive the real meaning of his teaching. It is extraordinary, after all the critical attention this poem has received, that no one has seen Frost's allusion to Communion during the Last Supper, which links the Grail to its sacred source, the redemptive blood of Christ. "Directive" concludes: "Here are your waters and your watering place. / Drink and be whole again beyond confusion." Matthew 26:27-28 says: "And he took the cup, and gave thanks, and gave it to them, saying, Drink ye all of it; For this is my blood."

"Directive" instructs you to go back to your inner source, to whatever enables you to understand and be worthy of the spiritual, sacramental and regenerative aspects of poetry—which once again in Frost takes the place of religion. Though Frost kept the deeply personal side of the poem hidden, he did reveal the meaning by telling a friend: "It is the same [for religion] as for poetry; only those who approach it in the right way can understand it. And not everyone can understand no matter what they do because it just isn't in them. They cannot 'be saved.'. . . You can't be saved unless you understand poetry—you can't be saved unless you have some poetry in you."

In 1947 Randall Jarrell published a respectful but disappointed review of *Steeple Bush* in June, when he observed that Frost's poems were "full of complacent wisdom and cast-iron whimsy . . . productions of somebody who once, and somewhere else, was a great poet." But, looking at Frost's entire work, he also called him "one of the subtlest and saddest of poets." In November Jarrell published "The Other Frost," the most important essay ever written about him. Thirty-four years after the publication of *A Boy's Will,* Jarrell saw, for the first time, both out far and in deep. After his revelations, never again would Frost's song be the same. He identified the dark Frost, perceived his real meaning and suggested an entirely new way to read his work. "The extraordinarily subtle and strange poems," Jarrell wrote, "express an attitude that, at its most extreme, makes pessimism seem a hopeful evasion; they begin with a flat and terrible reproduction of the evil in the world and end by saying: It's so; and there's nothing you can do about it."

In a letter to Robert Lowell, another great admirer of Frost, Jarrell expressed his reverence, described him as a natural force and mentioned Frost's charitable acceptance of Jarrell's criticism:

> I always treated him, when we talked, as Gorki did Tolstoy—as a unique natural phenomenon beyond good and evil. I asked and listened, we never had an argumentative sentence. (I *loved* to listen to him, really was fond of him, and knew I was, so to speak, getting to see a waterspout inside a rainbow.) He never saw me without expressing his gratitude to me, oddly enough; he didn't hold any of the unfavorable things I'd said against me, said that I'd made people see the black half of his poetry, which had hardly existed for them.[18]

Despite Jarrell's incisive essays Frost continued to be misunderstood by professional critics. Liberals like Leslie Fiedler used his public persona and political views to condemn his work while conservatives like Yvor Winters blasted him for having no moral point of view. The idiosyncratic, moralistic Winters launched a misguided but damaging attack on Frost in 1948. He called him "a spiritual drifter," who had taken the easy way with the various currents of his time, and was "unlikely to have either the intelligence or the energy to become a major poet." Winters criticized Frost for a "commonplace Romantic distrust of reason and trust in instinct," claimed he mistook "whimsical impulse for moral choice" and concluded that "he has willfully refrained from careful thinking." By concentrating on Frost's weakest and most didactic poems, in which he offers opinions rather than ideas, Winters missed his playfulness and willingness to consider both sides of moral questions. He also failed to realize that Frost, far from being indecisive, was writing about the quintessential modern problem of indecision.

During the 1940s, as his poetic reputation fluctuated wildly, Frost bolstered his academic salary, lecture fees and book royalties by selling his manuscripts to collectors. His most ardent fan was the wealthy Los Angeles businessman Earle Bernheimer, who had become a Frost collector under the guidance of the New York book dealer Louis Cohn. Bernheimer had been sending Frost items to sign since 1936 and now expressed interest in buying his most precious work: the sole surviving copy, which Frost had presented to Elinor in 1894, of *Twilight*. This booklet always had extremely unpleasant associations for Frost, and in November 1939 (when he was teaching at Harvard) he told Bernheimer that he might not be able to refuse a serious offer. Two months later he sold it to Bernheimer for $4,000—nearly three times more than his annual salary.

In June 1941 Frost offered to sell two of his "most valuable manuscripts"—his unpublished play *The Guardeen* and his Introduction to Edwin Arlington Robinson's *King Jasper*—for the inflated price of $2,000. Bernheimer did not jump at this bargain, but counteroffered with a loan of $1,000, to be applied to future purchases, and a monthly stipend of $150. For the next two years Frost took these payments (as he had done with his grandfather's annuity) pretty much for granted, but supplied very little material in return. In March 1943 Bernheimer's bank suddenly stopped his monthly check, which made Frost realize that he had not been fulfilling his rather vague obligations. Bernheimer explained, with considerable embarrassment, that he had been forced to close his bank account because of a domestic crisis and continued to send the checks (now raised to $250 a month) until May 1945.

In March 1947 Frost went out to Berkeley, California, to collect an honorary degree and gave some readings at $350 each. He visited his mother's best friend, Blanche Rankin Eastman, who was nearly a hundred years old and was having mystical visions about the atomic bomb. He saw the streets and haunts of his childhood, and complained that the new prison on the island of Alcatraz, built in 1933, was spoiling the best bay in the world. In Los Angeles he was assiduously courted by both Bernheimer and his rival collector, Louis Mertins, a Kansas City–born Baptist minister. Eleven years younger than Frost, Mertins taught at Redlands University and was about to publish a critical bibliography of the poet.

As Bernheimer's collection, enhanced by many letters from his subject, became the best in the world, Frost frequently expressed the hope that his Maecenas would donate it to a university library and preserve their names in the Bernheimer Frost Collection. In March 1950 Bernheimer disappointed (and, Frost thought, punished) him by announcing that "financial conditions and other important reasons have precluded the possibility" of giving his Frost materials to a worthy institution. He offered to pay Frost a handsome commission if he could help Bernheimer *sell* the collection. The domestic crisis that had stopped Frost's check was followed by an expensive custody case and high alimony payments for his second divorce, and Bernheimer had to give up his luxurious home in Beverly Hills. Unable to sell his collection for $18,000, he auctioned the 230 items separately at the Parke-Bernet Galleries in New York on December 11 and 12, 1950.

The collection included, in addition to *Twilight* and Frost's letters to Bernheimer, the *Independent* of November 8, 1894 with Frost's first poem, "My Butterfly," an inscribed first edition of *A Boy's Will,* a first of *North of Boston* with "The Pasture" copied in by Frost, manuscripts of *A Witness Tree, The Guardeen, A Masque of Reason, Steeple Bush* and many individual poems, and most of the printed works by and about Frost. In a bearish market *Twilight,* for which Bernheimer had paid $4,000, was bought by Louis Cohn for $3,500. The manuscripts, for which Bernheimer had paid $9,950, brought in (after commission) only $8,266. The entire sale made $15,000. Bitter about the division of the spoils, Frost told the acquisitive Mertins: "Collecting is the lowest form of literary appreciation. Very low."[19]

V

In 1947 Frost's second daughter, Irma, suffered the same sort of agonizing mental breakdown that his sister, Jeanie, had experienced in 1920. Like Carol, Irma had always been peculiar. Like Jeanie, she was obsessed with the idea that the sexual act was bestial. In 1917, when Irma was fourteen, she told Frost that his Amherst student Walter Hendricks had tried to molest her. He believed Irma and quarreled furiously with Hendricks. This incident made him suspicious, shortly afterwards, of Raymond Holden's friendly overtures to Lesley. Only later, when Irma's affliction became worse and she imagined that all men were trying to violate her, did Frost realize that Hendricks had been falsely accused. When she later told Frost, for the hundredth time, that she was about to be captured for the White Slave Trade, he lost patience and angered her by declaring that they would offer her "only twenty cents a throw."

Despite her emotional and sexual problems, Irma married John Cone in 1926, went to live on his family's farm in Kansas and had her first son, John Jr., the following year. She hated Kansas, felt her fiendish mother-in-law was persecuting her and in 1928 ran away from her husband. She was eventually reconciled with John; and when they came east from Kansas, Frost bought them a poultry farm in Bennington and paid for John's architecture school at Yale. When he finished his training, John practiced architecture in Hanover, New Hampshire. Despite Frost's generosity, Irma blamed him for her problems, felt an irrational but deep-rooted resentment toward him and did not go down to Gainesville after Elinor's death in 1938. In February 1939 Irma had a successful operation to remove a large tumor. The following year she gave birth to a second son, Harold.

But her mental and marital crises continued, and in March 1942 Frost wrote Lesley: "I have nothing but sorrow for Irma—and John too—yes and Jack and Harold. But for some reason they seem not to want my sympathy. At least they give me no chance to show it." Two years later Irma separated from her husband. In 1946, after an unsuccessful fight against her divorce, she became even more embittered and unbalanced. Frost, who always quarreled with Irma when they met, tried to avoid her. When he asked Lillian, who had a weak heart, to look after Irma, she was appalled by the idea and told Kay: "I wish there would be some way to keep Irma away from Ripton this summer," that "it would be hellish" to have her to stay.[20] During 1946–47 Frost arranged for Irma to live in many different houses outside Boston, but she constantly quarreled with everyone, made wild threats and accusations, and had to move. When Frost went to visit her in Acton in May 1947, he could not bring himself to enter the house. From the street he could see, exhibited in the window and in public view, Irma's monstrously sculpted heads with horribly ugly mouths.

In August 1947 Irma, terrified that she would be kidnapped and raped, went out of control on a visit to Cambridge. Fearing for the safety of the seven-year-old Harold, Frost followed the advice of his psychiatrist friend Merrill Moore and agreed to commit her to the State Hospital in Concord, New Hampshire. Dr. Moore forced Irma to get her clothes on by threatening to dress her himself. He put her in the front seat of the car between himself and his wife while Frost, Kay and his lawyer sat in the back. When they reached the hospital, shortly before dawn, and Moore said he hoped she had managed to sleep, Irma (who knew where they were taking her) bitterly exclaimed: "How *very* kind of you." Irma's commitment as a hopeless case to a hospital for the insane, Frost told Bernheimer, was a horrible end to see one's child come to. Lesley did not offer to take care of Irma but, always looking for a scapegoat, blamed Frost for putting her in an asylum.

Frost thought that John Cone's Christian Science family had not given Irma proper help during the birth of her first son. He also felt Cone had let him down by not being a good husband and by not taking care of his wife. When Frost telegraphed her former husband after her breakdown, which had been triggered by the divorce, John replied that he would not take part in her commitment. He withdrew from the crisis and left all responsibility (as he had done since 1944) to Frost. Irma was eventually moved to a home in Vermont, where she lived, supported by Frost and then by his legacy, until 1981. Driving past a Vermont farm with a friend, Frost explained that "he owned it and that he had a daughter living on it. 'She won't let me visit, though.' . . . He hoped that some day she would get over her bitterness towards him." Recalling his domestic tragedies, he also said that "he did not care if he ever saw any of his children again as they had never been anything but a curse to him." Irma's younger son, Harold, had no contact with Frost after his mother's divorce and break-down in 1947. He wrote to his grandfather but never received a reply, and felt all the anger and bitterness was on *Frost's* part. Harold always thought it was a burden to be Frost's grandson and has kept their relationship secret.[21]

Tormented by his Job-like misfortunes, Frost was torn between blaming himself and cursing his fate. "Cast your eye back over my family luck," he told Untermeyer, "and perhaps you will wonder if I haven't had pretty near enough." Robert Lowell's poem on Frost recorded some important personal revelations about his family. When Lowell meets him after one of his stunning performances, Frost reveals that when he told Carol that

Merrill Moore was coming to treat him, his son exclaimed: "I'll kill him first." Irma, Frost says, thought every man she met wanted to make her, but "the way she dresses, she couldn't make a whorehouse." Lowell tries to cheer him up by expressing exhilaration at Frost's "great act." But the old poet bitterly replies: "When I am too full of joy, I think / how little good my health did anyone near me."[22]

16

An Abundance
of Honors

1950–1957

I

As Frost passed his seventy-fifth birthday, his popular acclaim increased while his poetry inevitably declined. His critical reputation had peaked, in fact, with *West-Running Brook* in 1928. After years of praise, the critics attacked *A Further Range* for political reasons, ignored the love poems in *A Witness Tree,* dismissed *Steeple Bush* and condemned the two masques. He published very few poems in the 1950s and did not bring out a new book between 1947 and 1962.

Frost's career epitomized the fate of the artist in America. Extravagantly praised when he finally made his mark with *North of Boston,* he was savagely criticized when his work diverged from its early perfection and deeply resented when he achieved great worldly success. Both critics and readers cherished the same benign image of Frost, which he encouraged—despite the tragic content of his poetry—in his public performances. During the last decade of his life, he became the apotheosis of the public poet (a kind of Japanese "living treasure"), and assumed the privileges and burdens of his role by becoming a roving cultural ambassador.

In 1931, seven years after Frost's first Pulitzer Prize, James Southall Wilson wrote that he had already become "the subject of essays [and books], the guest of complimentary dinners, the starred performer of the lecture agency." Three years later in *Recognition of Robert Frost,* his editor Richard Thornton made the grandiose but generally accepted claim that "No one now disputes his place as America's greatest living poet." In 1944, nearly twenty years before the end of his abundantly rewarded life, Malcolm Cowley disapprovingly noted that "Frost has been heaped with more official and academic honors than any other American poet, living or dead."[1] Frost appeared on the cover of *Time* on October 9, 1950 and of *Life* on March 30, 1962, and the television program "Meet the Press" on December 23, 1956. Toward the end of his life he was celebrated by the celebrated, and actually came to enjoy hobnobbing with the boring but munificent breed of college presidents.

As early as November 1917, when he won a $100 prize from *Poetry* magazine for "Snow," Frost felt the need to disguise his pleasure by sending the editor, Harriet Monroe, a witty and self-deprecating account of his random awards: a few dollars for winning a boys' race at the Caledonia Club picnic in San Francisco, part interest in a set of gold earrings and a gold-headed cane for impersonations at a masquerade, a gold medal for "sheer goodness" at Lawrence High School and a book prize for scholarship at Harvard. Not much, perhaps, but a start.

Frost wrote Lesley that "prizes are more or less accidents." But his small army of faithful supporters, led by Dorothy Canfield Fisher at the Book-of-the-Month Club and Louis Untermeyer on the Pulitzer Prize committee, made certain that he was always well rewarded. Speaking more frankly, he told Harriet Monroe that he did not care what people thought of his poetry as long as they gave him prizes. Though Frost sometimes had doubts about whether he deserved all these rewards, he confided to a friend, with some irony, that "we take it like men and we keep our doubts to ourselves."

Constantly distracted by demands on his time, Frost clearly needed more solitude to compose his poetry. He sometimes tired of all the public attention, and declared: "I'm pretty me-sick." While angling in January 1957 for his greatest honors, he told an Amherst trustee that his ambition was pretty well sated. Yet during his late years of glory his need for praise and honors was insatiable. He had once told his teaching colleague Ernest Silver that he could bear too much praise better than too little praise; and during one of his birthday celebrations, he used a favorite rustic expression and admitted: "I like to be made of, you know. I like to be made of."[2] Though his ambition had been slow-burning and patient, he had always secretly hoped for even greater recognition than he had received.

Frost craved honors because he came from a humble background and thought it was "mighty fine to get them." He had been poor for a long time, had no recognition for the first forty years of his life, and remained personally insecure and emotionally needy. But even "the countless honors that came later," Untermeyer wrote, "could never compensate for the long, lonely times when he had to suffer the humiliation of being a failure." His public honors not only assuaged his long neglect, but also compensated for his disastrous personal life. They made Frost seem more attractive in Kay's eyes and more worthy of the sacrifices she made for him. Though all the adulation exhausted him, he believed it transcended the personal and enhanced the cause of poetry.

Frost shared T. S. Eliot's attitude to honors. In 1956, toward the end of his life, Eliot suffered severe coughing and choking from an attack of bronchitis that induced an excessively rapid heartbeat and put him in the hospital for five weeks. As soon as he was released, he risked his health and dragged himself across the ocean to America to lecture before 14,000 people (the largest crowd ever to hear a poet) at the University of Minnesota. Though he had won the Nobel Prize and the Order of Merit, Eliot craved still more adulation and needed the cheers and applause of the Midwestern multitudes. Both Frost and Eliot had a traditional European sense of their dignified role as nationally acclaimed poets.

Edmund Wilson, a contemporary man of letters, had a very different sense of his due. Long-lived, like Frost and Eliot, he did not gather public honors until the end of his life. But he did not set out to win prizes and did not participate in self-promoting activities. He adopted a consistently ironic attitude toward his own awards, and accepted them with a fine discrimination. He defensively said, "these medals make me feel like a stuffed shirt," but took them because he needed the money. Showing off one of his smaller medals, he claimed: "This is for your pajamas." When offered a minor award by a library, Wilson rejected it and said: "I feel that I now have all the medals that I'll ever be able to use."[3]

Frost and Eliot never reached that saturation point, and were incapable of such authentic self-deprecation. They were, moreover, willing to gratify the egos of the complacent patrons who endorsed their achievement and provided all the medals and prizes. They had published their best work during and after the Great War, yet lived long enough to receive confirmation that they had written poetry of enduring value. In private, they had many faults and personal tragedies; in public, they were revered cultural icons.

Frost's public honors began, shortly after he returned to America from England, with his election to the National Institute of Arts and Letters in 1916. He was also elected to the American Academy of Arts and Letters in 1930 and to the American Philosophical Society in 1937. By 1950 he had come to be regarded as a national poet whose work brought glory to his country. To mark what was then supposed to be his seventy-fifth birthday, March 26, the United States Senate passed a resolution introduced by Robert Taft of Ohio that offered Frost the pleasant but meaningless "felicitations of the Nation which he has served so well." This event, like several others, was spoiled by some idiocy. The climax came when Senator Charles Tobey of New Hampshire paid tribute to Frost by quoting some doggerel from Henry Van Dyke's "God of the Open Air."

Frost's "fiftieth" birthday dinner had been held at the Hotel Brevoort in New York in 1925. His eightieth birthday dinners were much more elaborate affairs. On March 25, 1954, after a televised press conference, Holt sponsored a banquet at the Waldorf-Astoria Hotel in New York. Each of the eighty guests was presented with a signed copy of *Aforesaid,* a new selection of his verse, published that day in a limited edition of 650. The following day, at the Lord Jeffery Inn at Amherst, another eighty, but more intimate, friends gathered for a second formal dinner. Thornton Wilder, who sat next to Frost, mentioned the difficulty of paying homage to the living and noted in his journals that the poet was "too big for friendship, too small for apotheosis." Wilder impressed the audience during his tribute to Frost by knocking off his glasses while gesticulating with his right hand and then catching them in mid-flight with his left. Untermeyer, MacLeish and Van Doren also said nice things, and Frost was presented with Andrew Wyeth's fine watercolor *Winter Sunset.* Wondering if he deserved all the tributes, Frost exclaimed: "This word 'great' grates on my nerves!"

Just as Marian Anderson was always chosen to sing "The Star-Spangled Banner," so Frost was always present when they were handing out honorary degrees. Since Frost, a college professor, never got close to earning a bachelor's degree at Dartmouth or Harvard, he was amused by these pompous and faintly absurd proceedings. He said he was "educated by degrees" and "would rather get a degree than an education." He always borrowed a cap and gown so he would not have to carry them around with him, and eventually reached 44 "honorary degrees above zero" —receiving two each from Michigan and Dartmouth, and averaging one a year from 1918 to 1962.

Like his public readings, these affairs did not always go smoothly. A bat disrupted his reading at Allegheny College and the president rudely interrupted his lecture at Connecticut College. In June 1932, when he read the Phi Beta Kappa poem and got an honorary degree from Columbia, he had to endure a fatuous luncheon speech from Professor Clayton Hamilton, who dropped a brick by comparing Frost to his illustrious predecessors: "even our distinguished guest, Mr. Robert Frost, whom we rejoice in honoring today, must be the first to concede that the sum of his achievements, noteworthy as they are, falls short of the eminence of these heroic masters." Infuriated, Frost turned to his host and exclaimed: "Get me out of here as soon as possible. To come here to be insulted! I knew it was a mistake almost as soon as I'd accepted."[4]

Unlike Edith Sitwell, Frost did not use the honorific title and never called himself *Dr.* Frost. But he had more hoods than a Mafia Don and in June 1955 he took revenge on the burdensome paraphernalia by having all the colored silks cut up and sewn into a patchwork quilt. Howard Schmitt—the "cymbalist" from Buffalo who arranged to have his aunts perform the surgery—was annoyed, after the job was completed, when Frost picked up a few more colored hoods.

II

Until Frost began his officially sponsored trips during the last decade of his life, he had spent very little time in non–English-speaking countries: a few weeks in France in August 1928, a few days in Cuba in January 1939. Like Philip Larkin, who said "I wouldn't mind seeing China if I could come back the same day," Frost hated being abroad. "I'm no traveller and don't like travelogues," he told the cosmopolitan Lesley, who was always dashing around the world. "The only country I can have any interest in is the one I have lived in." But when Lesley, who had lectured extensively in South America, heard that São Paulo was holding an international writers' conference to celebrate the city's 400th anniversary, and that if she acted as his interpreter the State Department and Brazilian government would pay all expenses for both of them, she persuaded her eighty-year-old father to go to Brazil for two weeks in August 1954.

The other American representative was William Faulkner, who had won the Nobel Prize in 1950. His latest biographer followed the official diplomatic line and piously stated: "Reports from Brazil indicated that

Faulkner's and Frost's visits 'had established a new level of distinction in inter-American cultural relations; and are immensely valuable . . . in counteracting international communist propaganda attempts to depict the United States as not only lacking in culture but inimical to it.' " Faulkner's earlier biographer, while more realistic about Faulkner's inability to reach *any* "level of distinction" in cultural relations, gave a wildly distorted view of Frost's attitude toward his fellow representative. He stated that Faulkner arrived drunk from Lima and remained that way most of the time. After collapsing, he partly recovered and departed early. The biographer then added that Frost had told Lesley, who served up a diplomatic version of the truth: "I looked forward so much to meeting Faulkner, and I was so disappointed because I never saw him. . . . I think he'd been doing something naughty."[5]

Far from being eager to meet Faulkner, Frost loathed all his writings and had never been able to finish any of them. He found Faulkner's bombastic Nobel acceptance speech insincere, full of cant and as repugnant as his drinking habits. In an angry letter to Kay he described Faulkner's irresponsible behavior and hopeless condition in Brazil: "It was as I feared with Faulkner. He has stolen the show by doing nothing for it but to lie up dead drunk like a genius. The consul . . . has been caring for Faulkner day and night, bathing him in the tub and feeding him in bed. . . . He looked very sick and ashamed to me."

At a Bread Loaf talk the following summer, Frost said that he had found Brazil as unimpressive as Faulkner. The poor sections of the cities were appalling, the political violence frightening, the scenery tediously familiar and the cities just like those in America:

> There are slums down there, I've heard. . . . I didn't have time to go slumming. . . . I saw a little bit of a revolution. I saw a few cars tipped over the street, burned, you know, and the night I spoke down there everybody was warned on my part—burned, you know—to keep off the street. . . .
>
> Saw a little—didn't need to see Rio. I'd seen so many pictures of Rio in my life, it looked really stale to me—mountains sticking right up out of the water like that. And I felt I didn't get anything out of that, but I got a good deal out of São Paulo. They were both cities of about three million. Big cities. And São Paulo is just like Chicago or Dallas; it's a huge humming city, tall buildings over it all.

Frost kept himself amused by thinking about whether the deer had broken into his garden in Vermont and got back to the farm just as fast as he could.

His official duties—poetry readings, press conferences, receptions —kept him busy most of the time. He was pleased that Brazilians honored poetry and poets. At the height of the Cold War, he tried to assuage their fears about the dangers of American materialism. He later told his Amherst students that Brazilians "think we lead them astray with our movies, automobiles, our chewing gum, and Coca-Cola. . . . I reassured them. If they don't trust us, they shouldn't buy our things. They shouldn't be so willing to be seduced." In his brief official speech Frost made some appropriately patriotic remarks about Washington, John Adams and Tom Paine.[6]

The distinguished American poet Elizabeth Bishop, then living in Brazil, attended Frost's reading at the American Embassy in Rio. Influenced by gossip before she met him, she had called him a "malicious old bore" and (later on) "the Bad Gray Poet." But writing to poet-friends after she had seen Frost, she praised his performance, which transcended the barriers of language, and suggested the kind of philistinism he encountered from his own countrymen: "Frost did marvelously, of course—the Brazilians got his every joke. . . . He gave a reading at the Embassy. . . . He is amazing for a man eighty years old, and the audience—mostly Brazilian—liked it very much. But I was so appalled at our ambassador here [James Scott Kemper] and his behavior (he sat with a large unlit cigar in his mouth, between Frost and Frost's daughter) that I haven't got over it yet."

The best part of the trip for Frost was the journey home. Just as he had been thrilled by his first plane ride to Cuba, so he loved crossing the Amazon, the Andes and Lake Titicaca by air on the way to lecture in Lima, Peru. "I saw the wild parts of Brazil," he said, "that I'd never dreamed of seeing. You see unbroken wilderness." As he flew over the mountains and looked down on Arequipa, Peru, he remembered that Harriet Monroe had died there in 1936 on the way back from a writers' conference in Buenos Aires. His stop in Lima allowed Frost to indulge his interest in archeology. He visited an Inca site in the mountains outside the capital and spent the afternoon "in an ancient city that probably had half a million inhabitants and all in adobe, and the graves all around." When he returned to Washington, he was debriefed by the Secretary of State, John Foster Dulles. Frost put in a good word for the diplomats who handled the arts and took the opportunity of telling

Dulles "to be nicer to the cultural relations people in those places. They haven't diplomatic standing. They can't go through red lights."[7]

III

As Frost got older and more famous, younger poets looked to him for encouragement, recognition and help. Though he spoke of wreaking vengeance on his literary "enemies," he was not entirely serious. Apart from making witty and caustic cracks about their faults, he almost never did anything to harm his fellow poets. His competitive spirit did not prevent him from giving significant help to Edward Thomas, Ransom and Van Doren, and he maintained a friendly rivalry with his older contemporaries. He was also generous to younger writers and adored by many poets of the next generation. Richard Wilbur explained the two sides of Frost's character when he said: "There was paranoia in him, and a savage competitiveness. But that was not what you felt when you were with him. Personally, he was extremely warm." Frost's reputation as a mean and jealous old man disguised his fundamental kindness.

W. H. Auden, relying on gossip in poetic circles, believed Frost was "ungenerous towards others, especially the young and the vulnerable." Frost did not write reviews or blurbs, and was hostile to some younger poets, like Dylan Thomas and Allen Ginsberg, whose poems seemed obscure and emotions out of control. Thomas retaliated, when reproached for obscurity, by disdainfully replying: "Read Frost." When asked if he would be hard on "the beatniks and chanting poetry to jazz," Frost (perhaps remembering Sandburg and his "geetar") rose to the bait and responded with mock-serious exaggeration: "Yes, absolutely. Death! Hang 'em all!" He told literary friends that he had "read only Ginsberg's *Howl*. . . . It's not very good—just a pouring out. Anyone can do it. . . . *Howl* is not real: one can't howl on for so many pages."[8] But if Frost had *heard* the sound of sense and seen *Howl* come alive when Ginsberg recited it, he might have perceived an entirely new dimension in that work.

Frost was often asked to name the contemporaries he most admired and the younger poets who seemed most promising. His composite answer (from memoirs, interviews, letters and conversations) showed shrewd judgment. He believed the poets most likely to last were Jeffers, Stevens and Millay; Auden, Roethke, Bishop and Karl Shapiro; and his special favorites, whom he called "my children" and said he had "helped bring up": Lowell, Meredith, Wilbur and Donald Hall. As Frost told a friend in 1922: "No one gets away from me who ever really belonged to me."[9]

Frost sometimes lost his temper with importunate writers. When an unknown novelist mailed her inscribed book, he angrily asked "why this stupid lady had sent him her stupid novel" and then made quite a scene to impress his British visitor: "He carried it outside and ceremoniously deposited it (open face downward) on a midden-heap in his backyard. Then he jumped on it." Most of the time, however, as his unpublished correspondence reveals, Frost offered sound, practical advice to many unknown, would-be poets. He gave his books, inscribed with holograph poems, to people he scarcely knew, and invited many acquaintances to visit him for a good talk. He revised the poems of many young friends, and encouraged poets like William Jay Smith by writing next to Smith's poem about him: "Visa-ed and much approved of, by the subject."

Since Frost has often been described as envious and vindictive by Thompson and other hostile critics, it is essential to note that between 1927 and 1958 he recommended at least forty people (some of them quite obscure) for Guggenheim grants. The ten successful candidates included Edward Davison, John Crowe Ransom, Genevieve Taggard, Louise Bogan, Conrad Aiken, Lawrance Thompson, Paul Engle, Reuben Brower, Elizabeth Sergeant and Philip Booth.[10]

Frost's closest friend among the younger poets was Amy's cousin Robert Lowell. He was introduced by the poet-doctor Merrill Moore, who treated both Frost and Lowell and had a love affair with Lowell's mother. Moore was born in 1903, went to Vanderbilt, became a member of the Fugitive group and eventually turned out 50,000 sonnets. He became a psychiatrist, taught at Harvard Medical School, and specialized in alcoholism and attempted suicide. Untermeyer described him as an enthusiast and yea-sayer, an athlete, walker and gardener. Moore had rescued Frost in March 1940 when he "went crazy" from medication and broke up the furniture, and helped Frost commit Irma to the state asylum in August 1947. In his obituary tribute to Moore in the *Harvard Alumni Bulletin* of 1957, Frost called him a "serious physician and serious artist, [who] had no notion of being taken lightly; still there was something of the rogue there that was part of his great charm."

Though their poetry was very different, Lowell, like Frost, was descended from an old New England family with roots in the Puritan past. He too dropped out of Harvard and then returned to teach there. Born in 1917, he studied under Ransom at Kenyon College and came under the influence of Allen Tate. Lowell married three talented novelists —Jean Stafford, Elizabeth Hardwick and Caroline Blackwood. He was a conscientious objector in World War II. Like Frost, he became a conspicuously public poet and guest at the White House, but during the 1960s he also became an influential political figure and effectively opposed the war in Vietnam. Lowell's sophisticated and urbane, learned and allusive mind was clouded by a long history of mental illness and by a series of tragic breakdowns.

In the spring of 1936, when Frost was delivering the Norton lectures at Harvard and Lowell was still an undergraduate, Lowell had sought him out, asked his opinion about a long poem he was writing and received the kind of excellent advice that an experienced teacher can give a novice. Lowell later remembered:

> I'd gone to call on Frost with a huge epic poem on the First Crusade, all written out in clumsy longhand on lined paper. He read a page of that and said, "You have no compression." Then he read me a very short poem of Collins, "How Sleep the Brave," and he said, "That's not a great poem, but it's not too long." He was very kindly about it. . . . [He then read] the opening of [*The Fall of*] *Hyperion;* the line about the Naiad, something about her pressing a cold finger to her cold lips, which wouldn't seem like a voice passage at all. And he said, "Now Keats comes alive here." That was a revelation to me.[11]

Frost had perceived Lowell's talent, despite his clumsy effort. Soon after Lowell won the Pulitzer Prize for *Lord Weary's Castle* (1946), Frost expressed great pleasure in his protégé's success: "Isn't it fine that the young promise I began to entertain hopes of when it visited me on Fayerweather Street Cambridge in 1936, should have come to so much and to so much promise for the future?"

Most friends were terrified by Lowell's mental breakdowns. But Frost, who had a great deal of experience with mental illness, was able to help Lowell on a number of occasions. He was distressed that so many of the younger poets were troubled by insanity, and when Lowell and Roethke walked up the path to the Ripton farm in the dark, heard them shouting to each other, "C'mon, manic," "C'mon, manic." But he visited Lowell in a mental hospital near Boston in 1949 and in 1957 calmed him down when he entered his manic state. Lowell's friend William Alfred recalled the scene in Lowell's house in Boston: "I realized that there was something the matter with [Lowell]. Mr. Frost went up into [Lowell's] study, you know it was on the top floor, and tried to engage him in conversation, but then Lowell would come down every once in a while. He tried to calm him down. That's what I mean about Mr. Frost. He was just a very good man."

Lowell later asked Frost's advice about whether to publish the savage portrait of Lowell's late father in "91 Revere Street," a prose section of his confessional *Life Studies* (1959). Frost urged Lowell to think carefully about this matter. Though he did not approve of the portrait, he realized that there might be a psychological necessity to bring it out: "Give you time you're sure to be your own best critic of your own things. . . . I wish you wouldn't publish the piece against your father unless you find you must to relieve pressure."[12]

Immensely grateful for Frost's tuition, sympathy and friendship, Lowell recognized his intellectual powers and (in a letter to Elizabeth Bishop) saw through his transparent faults to the deeper aspects of his character: "He had a more electric and energetic mind than any poet I've known. . . . Walking by his house in Cambridge last Thanksgiving, I thought with some shame about how wrong I was to be bothered by his notoriety and showing off," for in truth the man's life had been "bounded and simple." Borrowing a comparison from Randall Jarrell, Lowell reverentially compared both Frost's art and his character to the great Russian masters:

> I've gathered from talking to him that most of the *North of Boston* poems came from actual people he knew, shuffled and put together. But then it's all-important that Frost's plots are so extraordinary, so carefully worked-out, though it almost seems they're not there. Like some things in Chekhov, the art is very well hidden. . . .
>
> Frost was infinitely civilized and possible to talk intimacy with. . . . He had that sort of quality that Gorky describes in Tolstoy. He was beyond the good and evil of the druidic rock that stood there.[13]

IV

Frost, like Lowell, became increasingly involved in public affairs toward the end of his career. The State Department had been well pleased by his performance (especially when compared to Faulkner's) in Brazil. Sherman Adams, who was Assistant to President Eisenhower and interested in poetry, had met Frost at the St. Botolph Club when Adams was governor of New Hampshire. In 1956 Adams suggested that the State Department arrange an exhibition of Frost's works at the American Embassy in London and lure him to England as cultural ambassador. Frost, seeking much higher stakes, told a friend that he might accept an official invitation to England if the terms were right and the command on a high enough level. What he really wanted was honorary degrees from both Oxford and Cambridge (with a couple of others thrown in for good measure) so that he could equal the achievement of Longfellow in 1868 and James Russell Lowell in 1873, the only Americans who had ever been accorded that rare double honor. The appropriate signals were sent and strings pulled at the highest level. Jack Sweeney, curator of the Poetry Collection at Harvard, wrote to I. A. Richards at Cambridge and to his brother-in-law Michael Tierney, president of University College, Dublin, and Frost got exactly what he wanted. "Sneak up on things," he cunningly told an interviewer. "And never be caught looking as if you wanted them."

Though Frost was in good health for his age, he compared himself (when writing to Harold Howland of the State Department) to the eighty-three-year-old Voltaire, who had died (Frost thought) on his last journey. Frost was ready to serve, but wanted a full and active rather than a purely decorative schedule: "if my country believes I can be of any use, even at my age, in reminding the British people of our own warm affection and strong friendship, why, of course, I'll go. I don't want to be an unguided missile, however; don't spare me. Tell me where you want me to go and when. I'll be ready." Frost was obviously too old to travel alone, so when Kay (who needed a break from her duties) refused to accompany him, Thompson stepped in and volunteered to go in her place.

In November 1956 England had lost face during the Suez crisis, largely because of American opposition to the disastrous Anglo-French invasion of Egypt. America's relations with England had to be strengthened; and Frost's personal charm, stunning lectures and connections with the leading English literary figures would help repair the damage. On May 17, 1957 Frost flew to London, and stayed at the Connaught Hotel. Just before his departure, he wrote to the president of Amherst and explained why he could not attend the trustees' meeting by alluding to "To Lucasta, Going to the Wars": "I may well say to my college after Lovelace: 'I could not love thee, dear, so much / Loved I not Honors more.'"[14]

During his rigorous month's trip to England and Ireland, his first since 1928, Frost received honorary degrees from Durham, Oxford, Cambridge and Dublin, and also spoke and read at the universities of Manchester and London. He saw many of his old friends and made a nostalgic visit to Gloucestershire. He was constantly feted—at the Athenaeum, the Garrick and the Savile Clubs—by editors, publishers and poets. Most important of all, he saw Eliot four times, enhanced their friendship and received a handsome tribute from his rival.

After readings in London and Cambridge Frost, fortified by ginger beer and a box of chocolates, went north to Durham for the weekend to collect an honorary degree that had been awarded in absentia in 1952. Thompson infuriated him by trying to direct as well as record his life. He had to be excluded from his lectures, Frost told Kay, "because he began to criticize me and tell me what I ought to do next." When Thompson fell asleep on the train up to Durham, the old woodchuck took evasive action and planned to let him sleep on to Edinburgh—or even to the Orkneys. Lodged in episcopal splendor in the Castle of University College, Frost also told Kay: "My bed is a great canopied four-poster I sleep in like a Lord Bishop. All the streets are one-way streets. You may wonder how anyone returns."

Frost was invited to Manchester University by Geoffrey Moore, a specialist in American literature, who had first met him at Bread Loaf in the summer of 1948. Moore introduced him to an enormous audience, using Randall Jarrell's description of his work, and Frost spoke of his friendship with Edward Thomas. Moore was fond of Frost, who stayed in his home, but felt he "laid on the charm a bit thick."

The Chaucer scholar Nevill Coghill, lecturer in English and fellow of Exeter College, heard from the American Embassy that Frost would be in England in 1957 and would be willing to lecture at Oxford. He then wrote to the University Registrar, Sir Douglas Veale, that Frost was the "doyen of American men of letters and a man of real impressiveness in every dimension," and that the honorary degree "would be a great honour to English literature and to Oxford, as well as to Frost." The proposal was formally made in Hebdomadal Council by Maurice Bowra, the warden of Wadham College, who looked after Frost in Oxford. During the degree ceremony, the elegant Latin oration mentioned that Frost's face reflected the characteristics of his work, emphasized his connection to the pastoral tradition of classical poetry and said the tranquillity of his art brought comfort in an age of war:

In truth he has for so long now devoted himself to the arts of the poet and the husbandman that his work has passed into his character, nay, into his features which reflect the genius of the poet, the sturdiness of the farmer, and the peace of old age. . . . How often, reading his poetry, one seems to catch the tones of a Roman voice: the voice of one who, as a poet, venerates "the rustic deities at hand to aid" and watches with gentle humour the small beasts of the field, and yet as a farmer never forgets the curst labour of the farm, or the pinch of want when times are hard. . . . Amid the clash of arms and the mounting terror of our new instruments of war, his poetry, with its echoes of Virgilian serenity, has brought, and will continue to bring, unfailing consolation to a suffering world.[15]

As in 1914, England made Frost "Yankier and Yankier." In a Cambridge restaurant he rejected a stodgy dish that had been recommended by the waiter and testily exclaimed: "This is nothing more than a boiled dinner with corned beef and cabbage. Waiter! I can't eat this. I'll pay for it, but bring me a steak." Matters improved the next day when the Chancellor of the University, Air Marshal Lord Tedder, conferred honorary degrees on Frost along with Arthur Ramsey, Archbishop of York; Baron Ismay, Churchill's wartime Chief of Staff; Sir Lewis Namier, the Oxford historian; Mario Praz, the learned literary critic; and three eminent scientists. During the formal procession Frost, wearing an academic robe and a soft velvet Renaissance hat, looked well pleased. He was invited to lunch by the Vice-Chancellor and Master of Christ's College; and the University Orator and Professor of Ancient Philosophy made the speech of presentation in Latin. The citation alluded to Hesiod and Horace, and also translated one of Frost's most famous lines, "Good fences make good neighbors" into "*Ubi boni limites, ibi boni vicini.*" It criticized the obscurity of contemporary verse and, as at Oxford, appropriately emphasized the purity of Frost's style and the relation of his pastoral poetry to the classical tradition:

He speaks to us informally, avoiding all turgid language as if it led to a precipice. He writes the works he has given to us in an ordinary style; he favors a subtle manner of speaking that contains wit and a certain sense of irony and the words of a homespun philosopher. . . . His work is as pleasing to learned readers on account of the keen insight of his genius as it is, on account of its simplicity, to unschooled readers who become mired in the labyrinthine ambiguities of modern poets.

Frost had tea with Lascelles Abercrombie in London, saw the botanizing barrister John Haines in Cheltenham and returned, as he had in 1928, to his old haunts near Dymock. He visited his charming cottage at Little Iddens and Gibson's Old Nailshop, skimmed stones and walked through a knee-high field of wildflowers as his stately Bentley limousine waited on the country lane. Frost also called on the former editor of the *London Mercury*, J. C. Squire, whom he had invited to speak at Michigan in 1921 and met in London seven years later. The contrast between the two men of letters could not have been greater. Though Squire had been knighted in 1933, he was now in pathetic condition: bald, bearded, rheumy-eyed, wearing dirty clothes and sneakers with no socks, living in a squalid Sussex cottage with an equally decrepit secretary, and clearly drunk.

Frost fared better with the three British poets who had contributed introductory essays to the English edition of his *Selected Poems* in 1936: Edwin Muir, Cecil Day Lewis and W. H. Auden. After meeting Frost in America in 1956, Muir wrote to the poet Kathleen Raine: "I am very much impressed by him; he is really a great man and a very wise man." Frost got on best with Day Lewis, who had expanded his essay of 1936 for his Introduction to the Penguin edition of Frost's poems in 1955, and interviewed Frost, while he was in England, for the BBC. He later wrote Frost's obituary for the *Listener* and cited examples of his poetry in his Norton lectures, *The Lyric Impulse* (1965). Day Lewis attended two of the parties for Frost and had him to dinner at home. Knowing that Frost's Gillie was bred to herd sheep, Day Lewis took Frost—as a relief from honorary degrees—to see the sheep-dog trials in Hyde Park (one of the most pleasant moments of the trip) and wrote a charming Frostian poem about it.[16]

Day Lewis' friend Auden "had developed a passion [for Frost's poems] while still at school" and imitated Frost's 1921 "Dust of Snow" ("The way a crow / Shook down on me / The dust of snow / From a hemlock tree") in "The Robin" (1923):

> Yes, always now
> He follows me
> About the lawn
> From tree to tree.

We have seen that the conclusion of "'Out, Out—'" influenced the end of Auden's "Musée des Beaux Arts." Auden borrowed the famous phrase from the conclusion of "Stopping by Woods" in "Their Lonely Betters":

> We, too, make noises when we laugh or weep:
> Words are for those with promises to keep.

He also lifted the title of his late book, *About the House* (1965), from "The Census-Taker." Auden lectured on Frost in May 1957, when he was Professor of Poetry at Oxford. In a photograph taken that June, Frost, dressed in a smart suit under a colored academic robe, chats with Auden, wearing a remarkably dirty jacket, in the well-tended gardens of Wadham College. In a perceptive essay, published in *The Dyer's Hand* (1962), Auden praised Frost's "auditory chastity."[17]

At a dinner in the Savile Club, sponsored by *Encounter* magazine, Frost met Graham Greene and had a contretemps with E. M. Forster. In 1952, five years before their meeting, Frost had alluded to Greene's idiosyncratic theology in *The Heart of the Matter* (1948) and told Thompson: "Graham Greene's formula for an entertaining salvation is to have sinned deeply and repented greatly. Always lots of nonsense abroad. He must be thinking of St. Augustine more than St. Thomas Aquinas." When they met at the Savile the Left-wing Greene—who had recently published *The Quiet American* (1955) and attacked the United States' involvement in Vietnam—questioned what he took to be Frost's nationalism and said: "The most difficult thing I find in recent literature is your saying that 'good fences make good neighbors.'" Realizing that Greene had perhaps deliberately misinterpreted the poem (since Frost did not "love a wall"), which was published in 1914 and had nothing to do with American foreign policy, he refused to be baited. Instead, he diplomatically replied: "'I wish you knew more about it, without my helping you.' We laughed," Frost wrote, "and I left it that way."

Isaiah Berlin—who attended the dinner, along with Day Lewis, Arthur Waley and Laurie Lee—explained how Frost inadvertently gave offense to E. M. Forster:

> An absurd event occurred: Frost was sitting between [the critic and editor] Dwight Macdonald and E. M. Forster; he talked in a lively way to Dwight, who plied him with questions, laughed loudly at his answers, said things like "Oh, did you really . . . ?" "Oh, no! did you . . . ?" which Frost evidently took very well. He

turned to Forster, and asked him what he did. Forster, no doubt a little taken aback, said something like "I used to write a bit, I don't do much now, in fact I don't really do much at all," whereupon Frost turned away. Immediately the dinner was over Forster left, obviously offended. Frost then at some point asked Macdonald who it was who had been sitting next to him on the right. Macdonald told him. Frost said, "The man who wrote *A Passage to India?* Oh, my God, I put my foot right in it, up to the hip."

When Forster, through the host, Stephen Spender, asked Frost to apologize for his rudeness, Frost gladly did so, and later visited Forster at his rooms in Cambridge.

Frost had had rather stiff encounters with Eliot in London in 1928 and in Boston in 1932, when he pretended to compose a poem on the spot. He had been pleased and flattered in May 1947 when Eliot, lecturing in America, unexpectedly turned up at his house on Brewster Street and explained: "I was in town and I couldn't leave without coming to pay my respects." On that occasion Eliot seemed to have lost his stiffness and affectation, and they had a lively talk about London in the days before the Great War. Two weeks before he left for England Frost—who now recognized Eliot's achievement and could afford to be more generous—wrote to announce his imminent arrival. He said he hoped to give Eliot "the highest sign of my regard" and called him a "great poet."[18] Though their temperaments and poetry were very different, they shared a New England Puritan background, had studied at Harvard, spent formative years in England and had a significant friendship with Pound. Since their last meeting Eliot had won the Nobel Prize. But he never achieved anything like Frost's popular success until, sixteen years after his death, his humorous verse inspired the musical *Cats.*

Responding to his overture, Eliot came to the London University reception for Frost and attended his lecture on May 21. Despite his vast experience, Frost was as frightened about his first talk in England in 1957 as he had been when he gave his first performance in America in 1915. He could no longer remember when he "began to be less than mortally scared." He was therefore especially grateful, he told Kay, that "Eliot honored me by sitting out the lecture. I was too gossipy but he seemed amused. I could see him with his young wife"—the thirty-year-old Valerie Fletcher, whom Eliot had married the previous January. A week later, wearing formal dress en route to another occasion, Eliot stopped in at a party given by the publisher Jonathan Cape. He invited Frost, along with the novelist Rosamond Lehmann, to lunch at his home on June 9.

Their last and most important meeting took place two days later when Eliot made a gracious speech at a formal dinner given for Frost by the English-Speaking Union. When Eliot proposed a toast Frost, who could not hear well and did not know if the toast was for him, looked toward his young American friend Edward Lathem (who was studying at Oxford that year). Lathem signaled that it was for the Queen by drawing a little crown over his head. Eliot then asked Frost to sit next to him so he could hear his remarks during the toast. He said that Frost had been praised in both Latin and English ever since he arrived in England. Since he could not praise Frost in Latin, he would have to speak in English. He called Frost (as Frost had called Ransom at Kenyon in 1956) "perhaps *the* most eminent, the most distinguished, I must call it, Anglo-American poet now living." Lathem and Thompson thought Eliot was not merely being polite but really meant what he said. Frost was certainly more sincere than Eliot when he declared: "There's nobody living in either country I'd rather hear that from." Frost had once said that he played Euchre and Eliot played Eucharist. But in 1962 he told his Russian translator: "Eliot is my friend. . . . Our friends always try to make us enemies, to no avail. He is more churchly than I, I am more religious than he."[19]

On June 15 Frost and Thompson flew to Ireland and met Constantine Curren, who had been Frost's host in Dublin in 1928, Michael Tierney of University College, Dublin, and William Howard Taft III, the American ambassador to Ireland. At one reception, Thompson wrote, "an Irish poet named Patrick Kavanaugh got in his cups and tried hard to insult Frost. Instead of being offended, Frost carried it off very gracefully." The young critic Denis Donoghue, then teaching in Dublin, heard Frost repeat a remark about Thompson that he had made a few days earlier in England: "He's a charming man, but charm is not enough, is it?" Donoghue spent some time with Thompson while Frost was entertained by higher officials and found him an elegant, well-dressed and charming ladies' man. Thompson made no attempt to hide his hostility to Frost. He praised Donoghue's negative essay, "The Limitations of Robert Frost," which repeated Yvor Winters' charge of "intellectual slackness" and would appear in the *Twentieth Century* in 1959. He also blamed Frost for his son's suicide and condemned him as a moral monster.

The seventy-five-year-old Eamon de Valera, Prime Minister of Ireland and Chancellor of the National University of Ireland, presided over the honorary degree ceremony. In the formal address, Professor Jeremiah Hogan described the character and themes of Frost's verse, and compared him to a seventeenth-century Metaphysical poet:

> [Frost is a] man who knows but has not been absorbed by the academic world. . . . The scene is the country, trees, the apple and the birch being specially loved, houses and their interiors seen from without, the stars, in rendering which last he is preeminent; some of the effects are strange to us, though the universal language of poetry brings them home—ice and monstrous snow, and the terror of loneliness in dark and storm. . . . I see in him some of the traits of a much earlier poet, George Herbert, more serene in temper . . . with whom he shares an exact observation of things, a frequent parabolic tendency, and a conspicuous rightness in the use of plain diction.[20]

The poetic career that began in London in 1913 came to brilliant fruition with the honorary degrees in 1957 and provided, Frost said, "a rounding out that we seldom get except in story books." Having equalled Longfellow's achievement of two honorary degrees, Frost (distorting the facts) told Lathem: "They say the only thing he beats me at is being buried in Poets' Corner [in Westminster Abbey]. So if somebody will knock me over the head while I'm in England I may come even with him." The poet John Masefield expressed the English admiration of Frost when he thanked him, in a letter of May 1957, for "so fair an output of verse, deeply felt and nobly uttered." Flying home on June 20, Frost was ecstatic and called the trip to England "A great experience—one of my greatest—more than that. Probably, all things considered, it *was* the greatest experience of my whole life."[21]

17

Pound and the
Terrifying Frost
1958–1959

I

Frost's brief friendship with Pound had ended acrimoniously in 1913 when he became angry at Pound's patronizing attitude, misguided reviews and interference in his affairs. But they kept a wary eye on each other's work, and had some intermittent and mostly hostile contact between the wars. Pound's opinion of Frost seemed to go down as Frost became more famous and Pound more unbalanced. Imitating what he took to be the New England tone of Frost's poetry, he sent a typically ill-informed Ezraic letter to MacLeish in November 1926: "Mr. Frost . . . hzas prebebly gawt the gnasty gnoyse of gnu inglend in his bloody dull meritoria. I dont know, I haven't read enny fer a glong time." Six years later, after Frost had published *West-Running Brook,* Pound echoed the criticism he had made of Frost's boring, mindless characters ("I don't much want to meet them, but I know that they exist") in his 1914 review of *North of Boston:* "Sincere, very dull, without tragedy, without emotion, without metrical interest, a faithful record of life without intellectual interest or any desire for anything not in it . . . inferior to Crabbe, but infinitely better than fake. A great deal of New England life is presumably as Frost records it. It is difficult to see how such life differs greatly from that of horses and sheep."

Having achieved eminence, Frost could now afford to be more generous to the perennial outsider. In a letter of December 1932 to an acquaintance, he praised Pound as the great teacher of two Nobel laureates, Yeats and Eliot, and expressed gratitude for Pound's sympathetic understanding of his work:

Pound has been a great influence. I speak of him and praise him more than does anyone else except in his own immediate gang. He taught Eliot, J. Gould Fletcher and Amy Lowell; he converted Yeats from writing his old way to writing his new way and he treated me as a friend. He is still my friend and I am his, though we seldom [i.e., never] see each other. I had already two and a half books written (*A Boy's Will, North of Boston,* and half *Mountain Interval*) when first we met, so there was not much he could do for me except back me. He did that most generously in spite of the difference in our schools. I lost patience with him when I saw him backing just as enthusiastically [the expatriate American writer] Skipworth Cannell.[1]

In April 1935 when Frost, who had two Pulitzers and an armful of honorary degrees, was giving the Norton lectures at Harvard, Pound, wounded by reports of what Frost had said about him, unleashed a violent and vitriolic letter that was much worse than DeVoto's angry threat:

> Once having known you, and not done you dirt, I am surprised at hearing from Harvard the following: Frost stated that Pound believed only in visual images and denied tone. Also that you let off a lot of cheap senile witticisms. Which I don't mind, but a deliberate damned lie, or filling up the young on misinformation to relieve your inferiority complex puts you in the swine class. When you don't know, keep your trap shut, and when you do know, don't lie to the young. You always were dominated by envy, but you shouldn't let it get the better of you on the edge of the grave. I recognized your limitations as a writer, but had hitherto considered you a man, not a shit. Candidly yours, Ezra Pound.

Four years later, oblivious of what he had recently written, Pound sent Frost an inscribed copy of *Cantos LII–LXXI,* urging him to read it appreciatively: "For R.F., who w'd like it—if he w'd like it—E.P." Frost perceived the magnificent bankruptcy of *The Cantos,* not at all his sort of poem, and later remarked of "those lengthy things": "I don't say I'm not up to them, I say they're not up to me. Nobody ought to like them, but some do; and I let them. That's my tolerance."[2]

Pound had moved to Rapallo in 1925 and become a fanatical follower of Mussolini. During World War II, before and after Pearl Harbor, he had written and delivered three hundred seven-minute propaganda broadcasts from Rome. Arthur Miller, describing Pound's manner and content, stated that "in his wildest moments of human vilification Hitler never approached our Ezra for sheer obscenity." As millions of Jews were being gassed in Auschwitz and Buchenwald, Pound urged a pogrom at the top, a new style of killing important Jews, and called Hitler "a saint and martyr." He was charged with treason in July 1943 and gave a reasoned, if unconvincing, defense of his actions. Arrested by Italian partisans in May 1945, he was handed over to the American Army and confined for twenty-five days in a six-by-six-by-ten-foot cage in Pisa. In July he was examined by three Army doctors, who found him "psychiatrically normal." Nevertheless, he was declared insane and unfit to stand trial by a panel of psychiatrists who wanted to protect him from punishment, and in December 1945 was confined in St. Elizabeths Hospital for the criminally insane in Washington, D.C.

Frost's attitude toward Pound wavered between sympathy and severity. During the war Frost, who had always disapproved of him, was unwilling to express his animosity in public and hoped that Pound would (like the Nazi war criminals) find asylum in Argentina and continue to write his "scolding cantos." After the war he adopted a more severe attitude to Pound. He told Richard Wilbur: "To hell with him, he's where he belongs," and in an interview of 1949 (after Pound won the Bollingen Prize for *The Pisan Cantos*) said that he "deserved to be hung as a traitor to his country—and got off easily." By 1953 Frost felt that Pound ought to stand trial like an "honest traitor." But if Pound was still insane and a trial was impossible, he did not want him to be martyred. He disliked Pound as a poet and a person but, remembering his visits to insane asylums and the sad fate of poets from Tasso through John Clare to Ivor Gurney, "just couldn't stand the thought of any poet dying among a lot of drooling, obscene idiots."[3]

Frost's rapprochement with Eliot in London in June 1957, when they discussed Pound's predicament, softened Frost's attitude and made him more responsive to the idea of his release. MacLeish—a Harvard-trained lawyer who knew his way around government bureaucracy—also spoke to Frost in London, and pressure to free Pound intensified that year. On June 24, just after he returned to America, Frost wrote MacLeish that he would not want to take Pound into his family or even his neighborhood, but agreed to be guided by MacLeish's judgment. On July 8 Eliot, ignoring the fact that other radio traitors (like William Joyce) had been executed for treason, suggested in a letter to Frost a line of argument that had been recommended by MacLeish: "If the government of the United States could see its way to dropping the indictment by *nolle prosequi* [unwilling to prosecute] I am sure that this act of clemency, as a recognition of the fact that any crime or error of Pound had been sufficiently punished, would be received with gratification and applause by poets and lovers of poetry the world over."

Like Frost and Eliot, Hemingway had also been helped by Pound at the beginning of his career. He was one of the few literary friends who had never quarreled with Pound, and had been attempting to defend and assist him since his arrest in 1945. He had read the transcripts of Pound's wartime broadcasts, decided they could be used to prove that Ezra was crazy and had invented the insanity plea. He condemned Pound's pathological behavior and ideas, and stated that he was guilty of treason and ought to be punished. But he also insisted that the crackpot broadcasts were ineffectual and agreed with Frost that Pound should not be martyred.

Having won the Nobel Prize in 1954, Hemingway was brought in to strengthen the argument, as he said, to "get him the hell out of St Elizabeths." Hemingway feared that Pound's close friendship with the fanatical neo-Nazi segregationist John Kasper might make it dangerous to release him. But in a letter to Frost of June 1957 he defended Pound on personal and artistic rather than on moral and political grounds. He mentioned the paradoxical aspects of Pound's character and career, the potential danger he presented inside (as well as outside) the hospital and his belief that Pound—as a major poet—should continue to receive special treatment:

> [I could never] believe he would have committed [his crimes] if he were sound in the head. I have never regarded him however as a dangerous traitor, and his influence was no more than that of a crack pot. . . . The problem is that Pound, while incompetent on various subjects, is still one of our greatest poets and one of the greatest poets of the world. . . . If Pound were to die in confinement after eleven years in St. Elizabeths, it would make an impression in all of the civilized world that cultural missions and programs would not undo. . . . Great poets are very rare and they should be extended a measure of understanding and mercy. . . . I detest Pound's politics, his anti-semitism and his

race-ism. But I truly feel it would do more harm to our country for Pound to die in confinement, than for him to be freed and sent to live with his daughter in Italy.[4]

All the elements required for Pound's release fell into place in the first few months of 1958. MacLeish had sent a lawyerly letter to the attorney general, which Frost, Eliot and Hemingway had signed. Pound had been persuaded to detach himself from John Kasper. James Laughlin, Pound's publisher, agreed to pay him a monthly stipend (similar to the one Frost received from Holt) of $300 and Hemingway generously sent a check for $1,000. Dr. Winfred Overholser, the head of St. Elizabeths, maintained (as always) that Pound was too crazy to stand trial, but said he was not dangerous and agreed to release him if the criminal charges were dropped. Since MacLeish was closely connected to the New Deal Democrats, and Eliot and Hemingway were expatriates in England and Cuba, Frost, with strong ties to the Republican administration, became the essential intermediary between the White House and the mad house.

MacLeish's initiative gave him the chance to put frosting on the pound cake. Frost had mentioned Pound to his old friend Sherman Adams during his first dinner at the White House in 1953. On February 12, 1958 he urged Adams to use his position as Assistant to the President to help the cause of the arts. Four days later, while Frost was on Captiva Island, west of Fort Myers in the Gulf of Mexico, he was summoned by walkie-talkie to a stag dinner at the White House with President Eisenhower. To I. A. Richards, the Harvard critic and professor who saw Frost in Florida at the time and was unaware of his shrewd powers of persuasion, his former colleague seemed a "nice, acrid, savage, pathetic old chap."

Adams, at Frost's suggestion, invited Attorney General William Rogers to a White House lunch just before the dinner with Eisenhower on February 27. Warning Rogers that the seventy-two-year-old Pound might embarrass the government by dying in St. Elizabeths, Frost said: "There may not be much time left, you know." Frost's fellow guests at the stag dinner that night were the president of General Motors, the head of Doubleday (Eisenhower's publisher), his wartime colleague General Walter Bedell Smith, his brother Milton and his son John. Frost admired Eisenhower and called him "a very, very fine man, even if he doesn't read too many books." Eisenhower returned the compliment with a hand-

some tribute in *At Ease* (1967): "During the White House years I found
support from a distinguished American poet who had had more years
than most of us to appraise life and had used them well and wisely. At a
time when I was being criticized by many people who thought I was
moving too slowly about matters close to their hearts, Robert Frost visited
my office one day. He gave me a book of his poetry. On the flyleaf, at the
end of the inscription, he wrote: 'The strong are saying nothing till they
see.' "[5]

Frost made three trips to Washington (in addition to the White House
luncheon) for formal meetings with Rogers at the Justice Department.
On July 19, 1957 he came down from Vermont to the sweltering Washington summer. Rogers greeted him with the polite opening: "I'm so
glad to meet you again. My daughters are great admirers of your poetry,"
to which Frost bluntly replied: "Why aren't you?" Frost saw Rogers again
on October 23, but matters were delayed, during the Civil Rights crisis,
because of Pound's involvement with John Kasper. The breakthrough
finally came during their third meeting, on April 14, 1958, when Frost
came right to the point: " 'I come down here to see what your mood is
about Ezra Pound.' . . . 'Our mood's your mood; let's get him out.' Just
like that, that's all. And I said, 'This week?'. . . 'This week if you say so.
You go get a lawyer, and we'll raise no objection.' "

Frost—whose last connection with the law was in 1896 when he was
fined in Lawrence for punching Herbert Parker—engaged the well-
known liberal Thurman Arnold and wrote an effective legal statement,
which Arnold read in court four days later to secure Pound's release.
Frost's efforts on Pound's behalf—coming after Pound's hate-filled letter of 1936 and his treasonable activities during the war—were truly
magnanimous. His statement praised the administration for responding
to Pound's case and preventing his disgraceful death in a government
mental institution. He condemned Pound's crazy behavior and quoted
the cunningly devised medical opinion that justified his liberation:

> I am here to register my admiration for a government that can
> rouse in conscience to a case like this. . . . I feel authorized to
> speak very specially for my friends, Archibald MacLeish, Ernest
> Hemingway and T. S. Eliot. None of us can bear the disgrace of
> our letting Ezra Pound come to his end where he is. It would
> leave too woeful a story in American literature. He went very
> wrongheaded in his egotism, but he insists it was from patriotism
> —love of America. He has never admitted that he went over to

the enemy any more than the writers at home who have despaired of the Republic. I hate such nonsense and can only listen
to it as evidence of mental disorder. But mental disorder is what
we are considering. I rest the case on Dr. Overholser's pro-
nouncement that Ezra Pound is not too dangerous to go free in
his wife's care, and too insane ever to be tried—a very nice
discrimination.

Thurman Arnold later provided an acute analysis of the reasons why
the government chose to release Pound. The hospital was fed up with
their star patient (who played tennis and entertained his mistress on the
premises) and wanted to get rid of him: "He was permitted to hold court
for his admirers from all over the world. At such sessions people with a
reputation for hating Jews were particularly welcome." The government
did not want a great poet (who had won a major American prize) to serve
a life sentence because he was too insane to be tried, nor did they want
him to die in confinement. Arnold also gave Frost full credit for liberat-
ing Pound: "He was probably the only American poet who could have
accomplished what he did. He was universally admired. He was a rock-
ribbed conservative. . . . His espousal of Pound's cause gave it a dignity
sufficient to protect the government if it permitted him to be freed. . . .
Instead of circulating another petition, he went directly to Sherman
Adams, who had been his close friend for many years and who was at the
time the most powerful figure in government next to the President."[6]
MacLeish agreed that "there is no question whatever that it was [Frost's]
intervention which persuaded the Eisenhower administration to take
action." In a letter to Hemingway, he revealed how forceful and vigorous
Frost was in his mid-eighties: "Frost gets a large part of the credit. The old
boy despises Ez for personal reasons but once he got started nothing
could stop him and I think Rogers finally gave up out of sheer exhaustion."

Pound's response showed the two sides of his bizarre character. Asked
about Frost's arduous efforts on his behalf, Pound replied: "He ain't
been in much of a hurry"—and gave the Fascist salute when he boarded
the Italian liner bound for Genoa. But when a friend read him an
editorial that said after forty years Frost had repaid Pound for his help in
London, Pound smiled and remarked: "Frost's debt was paid when he
published *North of Boston*."[7]

Though Frost and Hemingway never met, Frost visited his house in
Key West and played tennis with his second wife, Pauline. But they had a

good deal in common and respected each other's work. Like Eliot and Lowell, Frost and Hemingway came from old New England families. Both were disillusioned with their fathers, feared the dark in adult life and portrayed that fear in "The Night Light" and in "A Clean, Well-Lighted Place." They did not graduate from college, were strongly anti-academic and believed in educating themselves by experience in the real world. They were good athletes and liked to compare writing to sports. They were intensely competitive and tended to resent people who had helped them early in their careers. They had a sharp sense of weather and a magnificent ability to evoke the natural setting, and wrote in a colloquial and compressed literary style, based on the sound of ordinary speech. Beginning with *New Hampshire* (1923) and *Death in the Afternoon* (1932), both developed a self-conscious, fake and ultimately harmful public persona. Both became, in the course of their careers, the two most famous literary icons in modern American literature.

We have already noted some striking similarities in their work: the direct, monosyllabic diction in "The Black Cottage" and in Hemingway's *In Our Time;* the convincing portrayal of the woman's point of view in "Home Burial" and "Hills Like White Elephants"; the woman's dramatic repetition of "please" in "Snow" and "Hills Like White Elephants"; the death wish expressed in "Stopping by Woods on a Snowy Evening" and "Big Two-Hearted River" as well as the description of death by massive hemorrhage after a violent wound: the buzz-saw accident in "'Out, Out—'" and the goring of a bullfighter in *In Our Time,* when "Maera felt everything getting larger and larger and then smaller and smaller. . . . Then he was dead." Since Frost's work appeared first, we can now see that his influence on Hemingway's early stories was as great as Pound's. Frost thought Hemingway was "the best American novelist" and called him a "great" writer.

When Hemingway shot himself in July 1961, his fourth wife, Mary, claimed it was an accident. Frost (thinking of his son Carol) intuitively knew what had really happened and understood the dark impulses that had driven Hemingway to suicide. He felt great sympathy for Hemingway, would not let any of the Bread Loaf writers condemn him and insisted that he had shown great courage in killing himself when convinced that he had lost the ability to write. When asked to make a statement to the *New York Times,* Frost (to preserve decorum) pretended that Hemingway had died by accident. He praised his strength of character and admired the pure style of his work: "He was rough and unsparing with life. He was rough and unsparing with himself. It is like his brave free ways that he should die by accident with a weapon. Fortunately for us, if it is a time to speak of fortune, he gave himself time to make his greatness. His style dominated our story-telling long and short. I remember the fascination that made me want to read aloud 'The Killers' to everybody that came along. He was a friend I shall miss. The country is in mourning." The following month, when interviewed by Mark Harris, he called Hemingway "a brave man gone where we all must go."[8]

II

In October 1958, six months after Pound's release, Frost succeeded Randall Jarrell as Poetry Consultant at the Library of Congress. He agreed to spend four separate weeks in Washington during the fall and spring, and to give two formal talks. His duties also included answering letters of students and professors, meeting scholars who were working at the Library of Congress, building the poetry collection and inviting poets to record their works. But Frost had far greater ambitions as "Poet-in-Waiting." He wanted to be consulted about everything—politics, religion and science as well as poetry, to make the rather philistine politicians more concerned with their cultural responsibility and to establish a Cabinet position, like a European Minister of Culture, for the Arts. After two months in office Frost complained that he had been consulted only three times—by the White House, the Supreme Court and the Senate. But Sherman Adams' departure from office in September 1958, after a minor bribery scandal, had weakened Frost's position and power in Washington.

The Library was well pleased with his work, however, and prolonged his tenure for three more years (and into the Kennedy administration) by naming him Honorary Consultant in the Humanities. Roy Basler, chief of the Library's manuscript division, gave a useful summary of Frost's cultural achievements: "His presence on the Washington scene from 1958 through 1962 lent considerable impetus to the movement culminating in the establishment of the Kennedy Center and the National Foundation of the Arts and the Humanities, helped bring about the continuing series of Cabinet-and-White House-sponsored literary and performing arts presentations in the State Department Auditorium, and the White House receptions, dinners, presentations of awards, and festivals honoring prominent figures in the arts and humanities." In recognition of his poetry, as well as of his cultural work, in June 1960 Frost was awarded a Congressional Gold Medal, which brought a cash award of $2,500 and was finally presented by President Kennedy two years later.

Holt invited a hundred guests to a formal dinner at the Waldorf-Astoria to celebrate Frost's eighty-fifth birthday on March 26, 1959. Holt's president, Edgar Rigg, originally wanted to ask Richard Nixon, then Vice-President of the United States, to be the speaker at the banquet, but Stanley Burnshaw, one of his editors, managed to talk him out of it. Instead Burnshaw invited Lionel Trilling, Professor of English at Columbia, and expected a speech that would praise the poet with elegance and discernment. Trilling, a Left-wing critic and subtle novelist, could not possibly endorse the popular and generally conservative view of Frost as a benign pastoral poet who enshrined traditional American values. While acknowledging the extent of Frost's fame, he used the occasion to reveal that Frost's popularity was largely based on a misreading of his work.

Trilling began and ended his talk with a flattering comparison to Sophocles, who worked until he was ninety: "Like you, Sophocles lived to a great age, writing well; and like you, Sophocles was the poet his people loved most." Trilling admitted that as a city-dweller he had been "alienated from Mr. Frost's great canon of work" and that there was probably "no one here tonight who has not admired Mr. Frost's poetry for a longer time than I have." He quoted at length from D. H. Lawrence's *Studies in Classic American Literature,* and then got to the main point of his talk. Frost's radical work, Trilling observed, "is not carried out by reassurance, nor by the affirmation of old virtues and pieties. It is carried out by the representation of the terrible actualities of life in a new way. I think of Robert Frost as a terrifying poet. Call him, if it makes things any easier, a tragic poet." He cited the example of "Design" and of "Neither Out Far Nor In Deep" (which he misread) to substantiate his theme, and rightly declared that "a great many of your admirers have not understood clearly what you have been doing in your life in poetry."

Randall Jarrell had recognized the terrifying Frost as early as 1947, when he wrote that Frost's poems "begin with a flat and terrible reproduction of the evil in the world and end by saying: It's so; and there's nothing you can do about it." Jarrell later added that "Frost's obsessive themes [were] those of isolation, of extinction, and of the final limitations of man."[9] Only critics and academics had paid attention to Jarrell. But when the more eminent and influential Trilling repeated Jarrell's ideas and even used his specific examples (without mentioning Jarrell's essay), his remarks were attacked in the *New York Times Book Review,* provoked a flow of letters and stirred up considerable controversy. People took notice because Trilling's speech was made on a public and ceremonial occasion. He had refused to repeat the traditional tributes and banalities about Frost that were considered appropriate for the banquet, and presented what his listeners considered to be a startling and upsetting interpretation of the poems.

The audience felt embarrassed and ill at ease. Frost, who had trouble hearing what Trilling had said but was sensitive to the atmosphere, was obviously shaken and had unusual difficulty in reciting his own poetry. He was puzzled by Trilling's quotation of Lawrence's provocative statement that "the old American artists were hopeless liars" and by the perceptive analysis of his work: "I have enjoyed being looked into more penetratingly than ever before," Frost said, "but am I terrifying? . . . It's all new to me—to approach by D. H. Lawrence. . . . I'm nervous tonight, I'm very nervous. . . . Am I simply telling lies as Mr. Trilling says? . . . Oh, dear, I haven't been given to think about myself so much in my whole life." In an interview the following year, Frost said that the speech "didn't hurt me, but I thought at first he was attacking me. Then when he began comparing me to Sophocles and D. H. Lawrence I was completely at sea. . . . [In my poetry] there's plenty to be dark about, you know. It's full of darkness."

Trilling's lecture took place at the end of a conservative, self-righteous decade that tended to see the Cold War and most other events in terms of black and white. The old-fashioned critics clung desperately to the cherished image of the genial, homespun Frost and opposed Trilling's truths, which challenged their limited but comforting understanding of his work. J. Donald Adams, a quintessential middle-brow writing in the *New York Times Book Review,* responded to Trilling's concept of the "terrifying poet" by calling him a Freudian symbol hunter, by comparing Frost's to Margaret Fuller's acceptance of the universe and by using down-home diction and a baseball metaphor: "Holy mackerel! Frost simply sees the universe as it is and accepts it. He isn't terrified by what he sees, and neither should we be. He takes it in his stride, which is one reason why he is in there pitching at 85."

The letters that poured in to the *Book Review* during the next few weeks divided the popular from the serious readers of Frost's work and were overwhelmingly pro-Adams and anti-Trilling. Edward Weeks, the editor of the middle-brow *Atlantic Monthly,* under the impression that

Trilling had attacked Frost by revealing the depth and complexity of his work, declared that his remarks were "ill-judged and condescending for an occasion which was intended to be appreciative." Others were sneering and vituperative: "I hope Robert Frost was having a nice plate of buckwheat cakes and Vermont maple syrup as he read Mr. Adams' remarks. He couldn't have done better unless he had taken the so-called professor out to the woodshed. . . . This Trilling fella had it coming to him for some time. . . . Frost might have had the Nobel Prize if so many New York critics hadn't gone whoring after European gods."[10]

Trilling optimistically told his wife (who had not been present) that "Frost himself seemed a bit confused in his response but predominantly pleased." A month after the speech Trilling wrote apologetically to Frost: "I seem to have made Donald Adams angry. I suppose I meant to do just that—what is criticism if it is not contentious? And I hope it gives you some wry pleasure that your admirers quarrel over you." In June Frost tried to comfort Trilling by writing that he had not been distressed but merely taken aback by being so closely examined in public and then added: "No sweeter music can come to my ears than the clash of arms over my dead body when I am down." In July Frost told Thompson that Trilling at least seemed to see that his poems were as strong on badness as on goodness.

In August 1959 Edmund Wilson, who disliked Frost, moved—in a reassuring letter to Trilling—from an attack on Frost's public image, through an ironic allusion to one of the fatuous letters, to an acute perception of the essence of his work: "Frost is partly a dreadful old fraud and one of the most relentless self-promoters in the history of American literature. The general acceptance of him as 'a symbol of America'—a dear old sturdy simple New Englander—has become absolutely revolting. . . . Certainly the effect of his work is chilling, and whatever is authentic there is not buckwheat cakes and maple syrup."[11]

18

Kennedy
and Israel

1960–1962

I

Frost's last years were like the explosion of a star before it dies. By 1960 ten books (three of which were published that year) had been written about him and he had appeared in numerous recordings, television programs and films. He had been endlessly honored with degrees, banquets, prizes, medals, awards and citations. He had secured Pound's release from St. Elizabeths, had a successful extended tenure at the Library of Congress and had made valuable government-sponsored trips to Brazil, Peru, England and Ireland. Now, in his late eighties, he read his poetry at Kennedy's Inauguration and carried out triumphal cultural missions to Israel, Greece and Russia—where he managed to meet Khrushchev.

Frost's public career revived the nineteenth-century tradition of American literary ambassadors. He surpassed the diplomatic achievements in Europe of Nathaniel Hawthorne, James Russell Lowell and William Dean Howells, and matched the political power that MacLeish had attained during Roosevelt's administration. Frost had been snubbed in the mid-1920s by President Calvin Coolidge, a member of the Amherst Board of Trustees, who had dismissed him with a joke when asked by common friends to invite him to the White House. Frost had frequently referred to his boyhood campaign for Grover Cleveland. His friendship with two presidents and his influence in Washington and abroad helped to compensate for his father's crushing political failures in San Francisco.

Hostile to Roosevelt and indifferent to Truman, Frost was on good terms with Eisenhower and quite close to Kennedy. He admired Kennedy's *Profiles in Courage,* which won the Pulitzer Prize in 1956, and thought "it was a pretty lofty book." In Russia he told Andrei Sergeev: "You can't imagine how gifted the lad is." At his eighty-fifth birthday press conference in March 1959 Frost was asked "Is New England in decay?" He boldly prophesied before Kennedy had entered the presidential race: "The successor to Mr. Dulles will be from Boston: Mr. [Christian] Herter. And the next President of the United States will be from Boston. Does that sound as if New England is decaying? . . . He's a Puritan named Kennedy. The only Puritans left these days are Roman Catholics." Grateful for the boost, Kennedy wrote Frost: "I don't know how you said that, but thanks just the same." Frost was quite sincere, and thought the country should "repent" after failing to elect Al Smith, the Catholic governor of New York, who had been defeated by Hoover in 1928.[1]

Stewart Udall, a congressman from Arizona who became Secretary of the Interior in the Kennedy administration, was the intermediary between Frost and Kennedy just as Sherman Adams had been between Frost and Eisenhower. In May 1959—when Frost, at the Library of Congress, complained that he was not being consulted by the government—Udall invited him to dinner and they soon became friends. By seeking out Frost, Udall seemed more cultured than the common run of philistine politicians and (as his many photographs with Frost reveal) gained some valuable publicity. Frost slyly told a friend: "Udall is moved by the fact that he knows a man who writes poetry." But in May 1961, when Udall was accused of asking a wealthy friend to solicit contributions to a Democratic fundraiser, Frost (wanting to avoid another Sherman Adams scandal and resignation) staunchly supported him at a press conference and helped Udall survive the crisis.

When Udall, who was intimate with Kennedy, suggested that Frost read his poems at the Inauguration, Kennedy's first reaction was fear of being upstaged: "Oh, no. You know that Robert Frost always steals any show he is part of." But he soon saw the obvious advantages and changed his mind. Carl Sandburg had spoken at Adlai Stevenson's Inauguration as governor of Illinois in 1949. Frost's appearance—as Virgil in the court of a modern Augustus—would enhance the prestige of the ceremony, pay tribute to the New England tradition shared by the poet and the president, and emphasize Kennedy's interest in the arts, which he sustained throughout his presidency.

Frost was still composing "For John F. Kennedy His Inauguration" on January 20, 1961, the day of the ceremony. Having relied on his memory as his vision deteriorated, he would have had great difficulty reading his typescript even in ideal circumstances. But the cold and the glare of the sun on the snow were intense that day. He was tired after sitting through speeches for an hour, and the wind whipped his papers as he stood at the podium. The bare-headed, white-haired Frost began by mistakenly dedicating his poem "to the President-elect Mr. John Finley," a professor, associated with Boston, who was supposed to supervise his proposed Latin classes at Harvard and whose name (John F inley) was fairly close to John F. ennedy. After stumbling through the first few lines of the poem, Frost hopelessly exclaimed: "I'm not having a good light here at all. I can't see in this light." Lyndon Johnson tried to shield Frost's papers from the bright sun with his tall silk hat. But Frost complained that he had shut out all the light, grabbed the hat, and provoked laughter and applause with an audible: "Here, let me help you."

Frost saved the day by reciting an earlier poem, "The Gift Outright," which he had planned to read after the new poem to Kennedy. He later declared: "I came through that almost miraculously. I went home thinking I'd made a mess of it, very depressed . . . I was feeling kind of sick at heart. Then everybody began to say I did wonders. Some said, 'I bet you did all that on purpose,' it was a show I put on. I hadn't thought of that. The wind and the sun and the cold—I just couldn't read, that's all —nothing was right. Somebody said Mrs. Kennedy looked worried about me." Photographs confirm the expressions of anxiety and concern on the faces of Jacqueline Kennedy, Lady Bird Johnson and other dignitaries on the platform. Though the glare emphasized Frost's old age and poor vision, his quick wit and sound memory transformed a troubled moment into a national triumph. Observed on television by more than sixty million Americans, Frost thought of a favorite poem by Kipling, "M.I." [Mounted Infantry], which begins: "I wish my mother could see me now."[2]

Modern authors have expressed conflicting views about the political effect of poetry. Yeats asked of a work that had incited the Irish to rebel against oppression: "Did that play of mine send out / Certain men the English shot?" But Auden, in his elegy to Yeats, insisted: "Poetry makes nothing happen." In 1935—four years before Yeats' death and Auden's poem—Frost told Untermeyer that poetry leads to nothing on the lower plane of politics. But as he became increasingly influential, he wanted a "division of spoils" between poetry and power, and his dedicatory poem to Kennedy gloriously announced: "A golden age of poetry and power

/ Of which this noonday's the beginning hour." Since Frost hastily wrote this work for the occasion and did not have time to revise it, Untermeyer told Udall: "It was a good thing he couldn't read the dedicatory poem—it was the worst thing he ever wrote."

Frost called "The Gift Outright" (1942), which he recited from memory, "a history of the United States in a dozen [i.e., sixteen] lines of blank verse." In this patriotic poem he expresses a nation's spiritual and physical union with the land and its manifest destiny to complete the conquest of the continent. He declares that the American people owned the land before they were its people—for one hundred and fifty years, between the arrival of the *Mayflower* and the Declaration of Independence. He plays on the sexual connotations of "possessed," and balances the legal "deed of gift" with the martial "deeds of war" as the people realize their westward progress from New England to the Pacific coast. Despite its limitations, this nationalistic verse seemed appropriate for the occasion and made a magnificent impression.

Right after the Inaugural the President invited Frost to the White House for a personal talk. The poet Richard Eberhart "asked what Kennedy had to say. He turned and without hesitation said 'I did most of the talking.' He was in fine shape; at the Ball we encountered him talking animatedly to all comers at 2 A.M."[3] During his presidential campaign, Kennedy had often alluded to Frost by concluding his speeches with the idealistic couplet: "But I have promises to keep, / And miles to go before I sleep."

II

Always interested in archeology, Frost had met and been impressed by Professor E. L. Sukenik, who was the first to realize the importance of the Dead Sea Scrolls and had purchased some of them for Israel. When Hebrew University in Jerusalem invited him to be the first Samuel Paley Lecturer in American Culture and Civilization in March 1961, and the State Department also asked him to visit Greece, Frost was delighted to bring glory to himself while serving his country. He seized the opportunity to observe the two cradles of Western culture, which Matthew Arnold had described in the "Hebraism and Hellenism" chapter of *Culture and Anarchy* (1869).

President Kennedy's wire wishing Frost a safe journey made the front pages of each of Israel's twenty-four dailies, and all the weekend newspapers published translations of his poems and long articles about him. His ten-day visit in March 1961 coincided with the closing of *West Side Story* and the opening of the Hotel Sheraton Tel Aviv. The trial of Adolf Eichmann began in late March, just after Frost left. "I'm glad I'm not going to be here during the Eichmann trial," Frost said. "After the record of his crimes, what can justice do to him? . . . When the trial ends, death is too good and easy for Eichmann"—who was convicted and hanged in May 1962.

Just before leaving New York Frost unintentionally offended some Israelis by referring to their country as an "American colony." He soon assuaged their feelings by explaining that Israel's relation to America "has more to do with spiritual affinity than political control," and added that he wanted "to ruffle their brains as one ruffles the hair—affectionately." On the flight with Thompson to Israel, Sandburg's friend and biographer Harry Golden picked up this metaphor and compared both Sandburg's poetry and his hair to Frost's. Predictably enraged by the fatuous analogy, Frost exclaimed: "What's he always talking about Sandburg for? And how dare he say I have the same kind of hair as Carl? My hair's my own, and I don't copy anybody else's haircut."

Once in Israel, Frost seemed fatigued and lost interest in archeology; he was "bored stiff" by sightseeing and by the tedious factual background supplied by his guides. Surrounded by animated street-vendors and staring children, he sampled a banana in the ultra-Orthodox quarter of Jerusalem, and then crossed into Jordan to see the Old City. He took a short trip to Ashkelon, on the coast south of Tel Aviv, and drove right in and out of a kibbutz. "He met a lot of Israelis," one reporter wrote, "but instead of asking them questions, he told them things."

In his speeches and readings Frost, with a professional twinkle in his eye, said that Israel and Vermont were about the same size and equally rocky, and that he would just as soon tell an obscure joke as write an obscure poem. Just as Thomas Mann, while in exile, had said: "Where I am, that is Germany," so Frost publicly announced that he did not intend to talk *about* American civilization because "*I* am American civilization."[4] When Frost became exhausted toward the end of the arduous trip, Thompson took over and recited "The Death of the Hired Man" while Frost dozed and "looked as if he were acting out the part." Like Denis Donoghue in Ireland, H. M. Daleski, a professor at Hebrew University, met Thompson in "his role as general factotum" and was "bowled over by the venom of his description of Frost."[5]

In Athens РОМПЕРТ ФРОΣТ met his Amherst colleague Armour Craig, who was on sabbatical there. Frost had once passed an examination in the geography of Athens and now, on the balcony of Craig's flat, was able to point out all the ancient sites. He visited the Acropolis with Craig, but did not want to see any other sites and could not even be lured to the Archeology Museum. Frost also impressed the Greeks with his knowledge of ancient history and literature, and did exceptionally well during his three public performances in Athens. He ended his stay with a bit of panache by being driven in the American ambassador's chauffeured limousine right on to the airfield and up to the plane for England.[6]

Frost was homesick, tired and ill by the time he reached the Connaught Hotel in London. He attended a party in his honor given by the American ambassador, David Bruce. He went to high tea with Sir Charles Tennyson, who, according to Frost, led a society designed "for the prevention of forgetting Tennyson." But he canceled plans to spend his eighty-seventh birthday with E. M. Forster at King's College, Cambridge, and flew home toward the end of March.

III

As Frost got older and his health became more precarious, his formal birthday celebrations—which had begun when he was fifty—took place more frequently. There were two formal banquets on his eighty-fifth birthday and on March 26, 1962 (in case he did not make it to ninety) Holt sponsored an eighty-eighth birthday dinner for two hundred people at the Pan American Union in Washington. The fifteen principal guests were extended along a vast table, with a mass of flags hanging behind them and Greek columns rising to the high ceiling. Louise Bogan—who felt, like most people, that Frost had been over-honored —gave a witty and satiric account of Frost's effective but somewhat self-indulgent response to the impressive occasion:

> It was all as grand as you please. The high table included R. P. Warren (looking v. red in the face); Sec. and Mrs. Udall (he is a dark visaged gent, with a rather *low* forehead; she is pretty); Adlai

Stevenson, looking like his photographs; and M. Van Doren, looking striking, as usual. *Also,* the Poet, the Poet's publisher and a sprinkling of anons. The Poet disappeared, for most of the feast. Then he came back, and the eulogies began: Udall, Publisher, Warren (far too long and rather rambling), Felix Frankfurter (looking v. brisk and noble), Stevenson (good!) and Van Doren (really excellent!). *Then,* the Poet arose, and, I regret to say, rather maundered on. He let out one or two vulgar truths (such as that he had made himself and his publisher *rich*) and struggled with a few immensities ("matter is transformed into spirit"). Then he began to *recite* his own poems, which was fine. That mother of his certainly trained her boy well, in those gloomy evenings beside the oil-lamp and the nice warm kitchen stove, in S. F. and Methuen, Mass.—But I thought it went on too long, even this *good* period of platform appearance. A touch of senile vanity and a touch of vulgar exploitation.

Kay, who was not at the main table, got drunk in the course of the long evening and was reproached by Frost for her unseemly behavior.[7]

Eight months later, on November 8, Bogan (the poetry critic of the *New Yorker*) was again on the scene, at Hunter College in New York, when Frost received the Edward MacDowell Medal for his outstanding contribution to literature. Though she tried to be catty at Frost's expense, she was (like Elizabeth Bishop in Brazil) deeply moved by his performance on this stuffy occasion:

I went to the do for Frost, given by the MacDowell Colony: an invited audience, *black tie.* Aaron Copland . . . introduced the old Fox, and presented him with yet another *medal,* and we all got up and sat down and got up and sat down. (No *kneeling,* but that may come when the old F. hits 90. . . .) HE was in full control, this time, and put on an excellent act. He insisted that "Stopping by Woods" was NOT concerned with Death, and gave a little scratch to John Ciardi: as a *new critic!* It's the *tune* that counts, he kept saying. He really is remarkable, when he recites a long poem (such as "Birches") by heart. Everyone (and the large auditorium at Hunter was *packed*) loved him.

At the birthday dinner Bogan cast a cold eye on Lesley Frost, who had changed from a stunning young girl into a harsh and sinewy old harridan, "done up like Mrs. Astor's pet: low green dress (showing pushed up rather *freckled* bosoms) and all sorts of Indian silver and turquoise jewelry. Our eyes met once: a chill." Frost continued to give Lesley a stipend of $600 a year, even after she married the retired diplomat Joseph Ballantine in 1952, but tried to keep a safe distance between them. Thompson recorded that Frost got "cross because he thinks I did not turn Lesley off him. I tried, but if you have seen Lesley in action there is no turning off."

In 1955, when Lesley was running a school near Madrid, Frost told a friend that he was anxious about her fanatical hatred of the Spanish Left: "Her adventure gives me a strange uneasiness. The [Civil] War isn't over in that part of the world. . . . She'll have to wear a muzzle to keep from talking herself into trouble with one party or the other in Spain." Myfanwy Thomas, Edward's daughter, met Lesley in England shortly after Frost's death in the early 1960s, when she was feted by the American Embassy in London. Myfanwy found her extremely arrogant. With some difficulty she managed to secure tickets for the Russian Ballet, but Lesley—a passionate supporter of Senator Joe McCarthy—disapproved of their performance and claimed they all were spies.[8] In October 1963 Lesley quarreled bitterly with the president of Amherst, who she felt had not properly invited her to the dedication of the Robert Frost Library and punished him by giving thousands of her father's books to New York University.

Frost—an indulgent grandfather—was especially fond of Carol's son, Prescott, who became a naval architect, and also kept closely in touch with Marjorie's daughter, Robin. In the mid-1950s, when Robin was an undergraduate at Smith, Frost invited her to dinner at the Lord Jeffery Inn at Amherst. The waitresses, who knew Frost was a prominent guest, gave them the best table and finest service. Robin began with a jellied consommé and realized, halfway through the dish, that a fly was embedded in it. She did not want to upset the attentive waitresses or have to eat another first course. So when Frost pointedly asked, "Aren't you going to finish it?," she avoided trouble by swallowing the jellied fly. Just after graduation Frost told Robin, who hoped to become an artist, that she would have to put her creative work before everything else. When she asked: "But, don't you believe it's important to do good?" Frost replied that it was more important to do well and Robin trumped him by saying: "All right, I'll try to do good well."[9]

IV

On his eighty-eighth birthday Frost received the Congressional Gold Medal, originally awarded by President Eisenhower, from President Kennedy and published his ninth volume of poetry, *In the Clearing*. In his writing career—which began in Lawrence High School in 1890 and lasted until 1962—Frost surpassed Robert Bridges, who had published his last volume of poems at the age of eighty-five, and Thomas Hardy, who had brought out his last volume when he was eighty-seven, and almost equalled Walter Savage Landor, who had continued to write lyrics till he was nearly ninety. Frost once warned Bartlett that "too many writers bury themselves in the rubbish of their old age." But he reversed the normal poetic pattern of inspiration in youth, followed by a sharp decline in early middle age. Instead—like Picasso and Henry Moore, but unlike any other modern poet (even Yeats)—Frost's creative energy lasted until his late eighties. His final volume contained, in addition to the long work "Kitty Hawk," three very fine poems: "Questioning Faces," "Away!" and "In Winter in the Woods," and two masterpieces: "Pod of the Milkweed" and "The Draft Horse." Frost's "claim to distinction," wrote W. W. Robson, echoing Geoffrey Grigson's observation in 1931, "is the impressive level maintained in a large body of work."[10]

The title *In the Clearing* comes from "The Pasture," which originally appeared in *North of Boston* and after 1930 was used to introduce his collected editions. "And wait to watch the water clear" suggests the deeper, clearer vision that comes with the wisdom of old age and enables Frost to pronounce on political and philosophical as well as on poetic questions. In this volume he moves from short to unusually long, gnomic and rather awkward titles: "Lines Written in Dejection on the Eve of Great Success," "Does No One at All Ever Feel This Way in the Least?" and "How Hard It Is to Keep from Being King When It's in You and in the Situation." The last of these poems, "the story of the king who could not successfully abdicate but was continually thrown back into leadership," was inspired by Sir Richard Burton's Supplemental Nights to the *Book of a Thousand Nights and a Night*.[11]

"Kitty Hawk" is a rambling and generally unsuccessful poem. The first part—which equates Frost's flight to the Dismal Swamp and the coast of North Carolina in November 1894 with the Wright Brothers' first biplane flight from the same place in December 1903—has (we have seen) considerable biographical interest. Frost, deeply impressed by his first airplane journey to Cuba and his ride over the Amazon to Peru, compares the flight of his Muse to the Wright Brothers' ability to implement their idea and put "the soul's ethereal / Into the material." In 1959 Frost warned that "in taking us deeper and deeper into matter, science has left all of us with this great misgiving, this fear that we won't be able to substantiate the spirit," as God did when He descended into flesh. But their inspiring invention *had* achieved this end and launched men through the heavens toward the moon and stars.

In the magnificent six-line "Questioning Faces" a winter owl banks (like a plane) just in time to avoid crashing into a window. The glassed-in children, watching the bird from inside the house, see the underside of its straining wings, which reflect the color of the sunset instead of the blood from broken glass, and realize how close beauty has come to disaster. "Away!" belongs with Frost's recurrent farewells in verse that began with "Into My Own" in *A Boy's Will.* The speaker walks out into the empty world, leaving his friends behind, but not (he assures us) for hell or the outer dark—"Like Adam and Eve / Put out of the Park." He has made his peace and is bound away, as in the song "Shenandoah." But he threatens to return, like Christ, if dissatisfied "With what I learn / From having died." In this poem, with great wit and skill, Frost comes to terms with his own impending death. "In Winter in the Woods," the last poem in the book, develops the theme of "Away!" Walking alone through the trees, he marks a maple and cuts it down. At sunset, he shoulders his ax and follows his tracks back across the snow. Just as Nature has not been defeated by the loss of one tree, so he himself achieves a small triumph by retreating to strike another blow—or write another book.

"Pod of the Milkweed" describes a chromatic catastrophe as thousands of butterflies, drunk on the bitter milk of the weed, beat each other to death in a frantic but hopeless struggle for survival. The vivid battle leaves only a single butterfly hanging with talon feet from the fatal plant. The violent diction—war, tumult, bitter, wound, intemperate, struggle, beaten—describes the meaningless destruction in nature. The crucial words—waste and lust—allude to Shakespeare's Sonnet 129, "The expense of spirit in a waste of shame / Is lust in action," to express "the theme of wanton waste in peace and war."

"The Draft Horse" is Frost's "Stopping by Woods on a Bloody Evening." The negatives in the first quatrain—the lantern that would not light, the frail buggy, the too heavy horse, the hellish wood—all prepare for a terrible tragedy, as a couple ride through the darkness and violent death erupts in a peaceful rural scene. Suddenly, a strange man comes out of the trees, takes the strong but slow horse by the head and mysteriously but deliberately stabs it—not the people—to death. The ponderous animal collapses, breaking the shaft of the weak buggy as a hateful draft of wind (a pun on the title) blows through the pitch-dark trees. The unquestioning passengers do not struggle with the executioner, who slips away, but passively accept their fate, as they know they must. They assume that the murderer is the agent (rather than the initiating force) of a hellish power and acknowledge the sacrifice to inexplicable, motiveless evil.

Frost had sold several poems from this volume to the *Atlantic Monthly,* which paid $200 to $300 for the shorter pieces and $750 for the 471-line "Kitty Hawk." Seven of the poems appeared in *Life* on March 30. His book royalties in 1960—mainly for *You Come Too,* a collection for young readers—were $24,500 and he soon surpassed this substantial figure. Readers who had seen Frost stumble and recover at Kennedy's Inauguration were eager for his first new book in fifteen years. *In the Clearing* went briskly and eventually sold more than 100,000 copies. At the time of Frost's death, according to an obituary in *Newsweek,* "more than a million copies of his books had been sold."[12]

19

Frost at Midnight

1962–1963

"Forever are the windows boarded up.
What's out there—frost or thunder?"
Boris Pasternak

I

In May 1962, while Frost was in Washington as Consultant at the Library of Congress, Stewart Udall, who was going to Russia to inspect hydroelectric power stations, invited him to dinner with the Soviet ambassador, Anatoly Dobrynin. When Udall suggested a cultural exchange with a Russian writer and Dobrynin supported the idea, Frost agreed to accompany Udall in order to promote what he called the highest kind of intellectual, creative and athletic rivalry with Russia. Sandburg had been on a government-sponsored trip to Russia in 1959, and Frost thought he could do something more significant than wandering around and playing his guitar.

During the 1920s and 1930s many idealistic and often naive American writers (Eastman, Dreiser, Dewey, Steffens, Waldo Frank, Cummings, Dos Passos and Edmund Wilson) had traveled to Russia to see the Communist experiment and report on economic conditions. They went with a distinctly Socialist perspective, conscious of the hardships of the Depression, hopeful that they would find a superior social system and fascinated by the relatively unknown Soviet culture.

Frost, who claimed his main qualification was having been born near Russian Hill in San Francisco, was quite different. He had been hostile to the Soviets since the Revolution and, as Malcolm Cowley wrote in 1944, was "continually declaiming against the Russians of all categories: the pessimistic Russians, the revolutionary Russians, the collectivistic Russians, the five-year-planning Russians: he seems to embrace them all in a global and historical dislike that extended from Dostoyevsky to Dnieper-stroy."

Frost was not interested in or sympathetic to Russia, which had been the enemy of America since 1945. He had no curiosity about the language, culture or scientific achievements. A world-renowned figure, he was sent by the U.S. government to represent American civilization and was treated magnificently. His one aspiration, at the height of the Cold War, was to meet Nikita Khrushchev and help create better relations between Kennedy and the Russian dictator. Frost wanted to temper the leader's hostility and encourage a magnanimous gesture that would reduce the chance of a nuclear disaster, lead to peace and perhaps even change the course of modern history. Though he was desperately eager to meet Khrushchev, there was no promise before he left that he would be able to do so.

In Russia, during the decade before the Great War, an outstanding concentration of creative genius had coincided with the final stages of political collapse. But the Russian writers who began so brilliantly before the Revolution were mercilessly suppressed, persecuted and murdered after the Bolsheviks seized power in 1917. Yesenin and Tsvetaeva hanged themselves, Mayakovsky shot himself and Mandelstam died in a Siberian prison camp. One Russian writer, thinking of Frost, sadly observed: "our poets don't live so long." Boris Pasternak, who had won the Nobel Prize in 1958 but was forced by the Soviet government to decline it, died in 1960. Udall wrote that "In 1959, when some students asked [Frost] about Boris Pasternak's troubles with the Soviet hierarchy, he replied sharply, 'Pasternak is a brave man. He wants to be a Russian and we're going to get him killed if we keep trying to use him against Russia.' "

Conditions in Russia had radically changed in October 1961, when Khrushchev denounced Stalin as a murderer who had violated Lenin's principles. Yevtushenko's description of anti-Semitism in Russia, "Babi Yar," had caused a sensation in 1960 and his politically electrifying "Stalin's Heirs" would appear six weeks after Frost's visit. At the end of 1962 Khrushchev personally approved the publication of Solzhenitsyn's searing novel of life in a Gulag prison camp, the first such account to appear in Russia, *One Day in the Life of Ivan Denisovich.*

Though the literary climate had improved before Frost's visit to Russia from August 29 to September 9, 1962, Khrushchev was also preparing the sudden military build-up in Cuba that led to the missile crisis in October. Udall wrote that "in late spring or early summer of 1962 the Soviet Union began preparing to install about 60 offensive intermediate-range ballistic missiles in Cuba. . . . The beginnings of the nuclear showdown—the first in history—were taking shape. . . . Even as we arrived in the U.S.S.R. Soviet technicians were preparing the launching sites in Cuba, and the missiles were being crated for shipment by sea."[1]

After Kay's refusal to travel abroad, Frost had to find other companions. Thompson had infuriated him in England by trying to control his life. According to Kay's daughter, the handsome libertine aroused Frost's anger yet again by having a brief affair on their official trip to Israel. For these reasons, and many others, Thompson was excluded from the journey to Russia. As Frost, eager to escape his scrutiny, explained to the furious biographer in August 1962: "I want a variety in the followers on my trail and I want some of them to be not too critically intent on who and what I am." Frederick Adams, who accompanied Frost to Russia, explained that "Larry Thompson's second volume distorted Frost damnably—partly in revenge for being excluded from the Russian trip. There was no soothing him."[2]

Adams—born in 1910, a graduate of St. Paul's and Yale, director of the Morgan Library and trustee of many institutions—had taken part in a film about Frost earlier that year and become a close friend. Wealthy, aristocratic, connected to the Roosevelts and to New York society, Adams was helpful in complex situations and effective on a diplomatic mission. The poet William Meredith suggested, as Frost's translator, Franklin Reeve, who taught Russian at Wesleyan and knew many of the writers they would meet in Russia. The eighty-eight-year-old Frost, who had nearly died of pneumonia the previous winter, told Reeve that the trip was "crazy. At my age going all the way over there just to show off." When Frost got bored on the visit and felt he was wasting his time, he would impatiently ask what the hell he was doing in Russia. Before he left, Dr. Jack Hagstrom, a former Amherst student, sent Kay a list of eminent urologists in Moscow, Warsaw, Stockholm, Paris and London. During a farewell dinner, Frost told a friend who had doubts about the journey: "You just don't want me to go out and get lost, do you?"[3]

РОБЕРТ ФРОСТ knew little and cared less about contemporary Russian writers and their work. But they certainly knew who Frost was, and published several new translations of his poems in the literary magazines to celebrate his visit. He was housed in the luxurious, chandelier-filled Sovietskaya Hotel (which before 1917 had been the Jahr restaurant, famous for its Gypsy singing) and found the furniture, like the people, overstuffed. The newly appointed American ambassador, Foy Kohler, had not yet arrived in Moscow, so John McSweeney was temporarily in charge and Frost was looked after by the cultural attaché Jack Matlock.

Frost's increasing deafness and tendency to speak in monologues without listening to what others had to say helped transcend the language barrier, and he made as great a hit with the Russians as he had with the Brazilians and Israelis. Dragged around to the various tourist sites, he was obviously bored by Peter the Great's palace outside Leningrad. When he disdainfully remarked, "I suppose it's all very grand," his hosts, instead of being offended, admired him as a man of the people. Adams was afraid he would also be bored by the Bolshoi Ballet and made arrangements for an early exit, but Frost loved it—partly because "for several hours he didn't have to listen to Russian being spoken."

Russia was tremendously proud of its recent scientific achievements. The Sputnik had been successfully launched in 1957 and four years later Yuri Gagarin became the first man to travel in space. But in a *Denver Post* interview in 1959, Frost had found the whole business rather tedious and said: "I'd rather go to the Adirondacks than take a trip in space." When he asked a class of Russian schoolchildren if they wanted to be cosmonauts, they all responded with an eager "Yes!" Frost then quipped: "You want to get away from here any way you can," a remark the translators did not bother to explain. Andrei Sergeev, who translated Frost's work, saw a good deal of the poet on this visit. He wryly reported that Alexey Surkov, boss of the Writers' Union, and E. Romanova, head of the Foreign Committee (KGB branch), "were ordered to organize a reception and were at a loss what agricultural object to demonstrate. We usually drove visitors to Gorky (an estate where Lenin died, near Moscow, an exemplary farm for the Kremlin), said Surkov. But Frost was a farmer and he will understand. So agriculture was skipped" because Frost knew too much about it.[4]

The Russians responded warmly to Frost's poetry, but they could not understand his playful puns and missed a good deal of his subtle meaning. Borrowing a simile from Mark Twain, Frost compared their mutual readings and experiments in translation to duelling with battle-axes at a hundred yards in fog. He continued, nevertheless, to frost his wintry poems with rime and intrigued the Russians with "Good-By and Keep Cold." Following the Party line, they offered a Marxist interpretation of "Two Tramps in Mud Time," in which proletarian Robert was made to sympathize with the unemployed workers. Since many writers and intellectuals saw a negative reference to the Berlin Wall, which had been thrown up by the East Germans in 1961, in "Something there is that doesn't love a wall," the Russian officials jump-started "Mending Wall" by translating it without the first line.

Reeve said that Frost was the "personification of a [democratic] tradition and embodiment of the young Russians' dreams of their future." The main purpose of his "cultural exchange" (though his Russian counterpart was never sent to America) was to meet the officially sponsored writers. These included the Lithuanian poet Eduard Mezhelaitis, who had just published in *Pravda* a long free-verse poem, "The Blue-Eyed Rock," about his visit to Frost in Vermont ("a piece of hollow rhetoric," according to Sergeev, "which Frost loathed"); Hemingway's friend and translator, Ivan Kashkin (whose name was given to a character in *For Whom the Bell Tolls*); the popular children's writer Kornei Chukovsky, whose book of Russian folk tales had sold an impressive sixty million copies; the leading poets of the younger generation, Andrei Voznesensky and Yevgeny Yevtushenko; and the grande dame of Russian letters, Anna Akhmatova. Joseph Brodsky, a friend of Akhmatova and admirer of Frost, wrote: "I did not meet Frost on his visit to Russia. At the time of his sojourn in my home town I was behind bars."

Yevtushenko, who had recently sold 100,000 copies of his latest volume of poetry, gave Frost the unwelcome news that Hemingway was the most popular American writer in Russia. He took Frost, Adams and Reeve to a famous jazz café where they drank Georgian wine and recited poetry. When Frost ordered red wine, Yevtushenko teasingly asked if he had been infected by Red propaganda. Frost read "Stopping by Woods on a Snowy Evening" and Yevtushenko celebrated the occasion with a dramatic rendition of his tribute, "Robert Frost in the Café Aelita":

> with farmerish cunning
> Robert Frost . . .
> [is] at the Café Aelita
> reading us poems.
> Gray-headed
> he's speaking
> not from a position of strength
> but from a position of blue
> above the green earth.[5]

Yevtushenko closed his account of the visit by reporting that Frost "read poetry of American snow while Russian snow was falling out of doors"—though there was no snow in Moscow in September. Frost was fond of the handsome twenty-nine-year-old Siberian poet, who was passionate about Castro's Cuba: "the best one of them all is the liveliest one of them all. . . . He was a lively, youngish man, and I got quite an impression of him, quite bohemian, and quite stirred up to heroic feelings about Cuba, and all that, for some more revolution. His revolution was more than 40 years old and they need some new ones for refreshment. . . . He's a regular Byron in his life, kind of reckless boy, had a high old time, very popular, coming here to be popular."

The regal, seventy-three-year-old Akhmatova, to whom Pasternak had once proposed marriage, had suffered fierce persecution and suppression of her work under Stalin's regime. Her quarters were so disgracefully shabby that the authorities had to move her into a luxurious dacha, which they told Frost was her own. She had translated Shakespeare and spoke to Frost in English about Greek, Latin and American literature, but they scarcely understood each other. Though Frost had read Pushkin in Babette Deutsch's translation and discussed his poetry with Sergeev, Akhmatova was under the impression that he had never heard of Russia's greatest writer and caustically remarked: "Grandfather Frost now looks like a grandmother. It's not good to live that long." In 1962, when both poets were candidates for the Nobel Prize, Akhmatova commented: "Let him have the Nobel recognition and money; that will make him happy. The doctor has forbidden me to go to Sweden." After the toasts and the seven-course banquet were over, Akhmatova reflected bitterly on the terrible difference in their countries and careers. She nevertheless felt kinship with the aged poet as she faced the prospect of her own death:

> I kept thinking: "Here you are, my dear, a national poet. Every year your books are published. . . . They praise you in all the newspapers and journals, they teach you in the schools, the President receives you as an honored guest. And all they've done is slander me! Into what dirt they've trampled me! I've had everything—poverty, prison lines, fear, poems remembered only by heart, and burned poems. And humiliation and grief. And you don't know anything about this and wouldn't be able to understand if I told you. . . . But now let's sit together, two old people, in wicker chairs. A single end awaits us. And perhaps the real difference is not actually so great?"[6]

The government newspapers and literary journals were deeply impressed by Frost's rugged appearance, astonishing vitality and ingratiating humanity, and treated him like a hero of the Soviet Union. They said he had arrived at the airport with "a luggage tag attached to the button of his overcoat, and with his tie somewhat on one side, as if it were a hindrance. [He had] a kind, lively, even mischievous face. . . . Time had whitened the poet's hair and marked deep grooves in his face, but it had not touched the youthfulness of his heart nor quenched his thirst for living. . . . We all felt . . . the breadth and firmness of his judgments on life and literature, his efforts to understand and sense the spirit of our people."

Frost responded with some appropriately diplomatic statements. He maintained that "he had long wanted to broaden his conception of socialism"—though he loathed their oppressive system of government. Noting the recent cultural thaw, he said that "Soviet society was making its austere ideal still more and more humane." He praised the "fresh spirit of Soviet poetry," which he did not understand, and was genuinely "amazed . . . at the great number of copies in which poetry was published in the U.S.S.R."[7] Deeply moved and grateful, his Russian hosts presented him with a huge and quite hideous ceramic pig.

All this palaver was trivial and meaningless compared to his real purpose, which seemed to elude Frost as he approached the end of his visit. On September 5 an American reporter told Adams that Udall was leaving Moscow the next morning to meet Khrushchev on the Black Sea. It was too late to call Udall that evening, and when Matlock tried to intercept him at the airport and ask him to arrange Frost's meeting with Khrushchev, Udall had already left on an earlier flight. Adams broke the news to Frost next morning, just before he appeared on television in front of seven million people, and the poet felt deserted and betrayed.

Later that day Matlock brought the long-awaited news that Khrushchev would indeed see Frost the next day in the Crimea. Khrushchev agreed to meet Frost, six weeks before the Cuban missile crisis, because he considered him to be Kennedy's envoy and hoped, through Frost, to convey the impression that he was a decent and capable leader. According to Udall, "Khrushchev needed to send tidings of his sanity, to prove that he was still in charge. Our visits would give Kennedy a window into his mind."

Frost became so nervously ill at the good news that he was not sure he would be able to travel to the Black Sea. But after a sleepless night he pulled himself together and flew south with Reeve to Sochi. They were then escorted to a guest house in Gagra, Georgia, which was only twenty minutes' drive from Khrushchev's dacha. After the exhausting trip, Frost had severe stomach pains and felt ghastly. A lady doctor was summoned and discovered that he had a fever of 101.5°. Faulkner had died in July of that year, Cummings had died on September 3 while Frost was in Leningrad and Frost "frightened the hell out of Freddy Adams by almost dying in Russia." He declared that he was too sick to go any farther and precipitated a diplomatic crisis. Khrushchev saved the day by sending his personal physician and then coming to talk to Frost in his bedroom.

Reeve recorded that "Frost wore shirt and trousers. Khrushchev wore a natty summer suit, olive-tan in color, over a pale beige Ukrainian blouse. He was sun-tanned and healthy-looking, full of vigor and extremely courteous. He asked about Frost's health, chided him for not taking care of himself, expressed admiration at Frost's traveling so far, said how pleased he was to see him, reminded him to be sure to follow doctor's orders if he was going to live to be a hundred." They discussed the political problems of Berlin, the dangers of nuclear war, the economic competition between their countries, and the cultural traditions of Russia and America. Thinking of Shakespeare's "They that have power to hurt and will do none," Frost advocated a noble rivalry, with magnanimous leadership on both sides. When he suggested that Berlin could be reunited if both countries made significant concessions, "the Premier castigated the military organization of NATO, the recrudescence of Nazi power in West Germany, and the irresponsible politics of the Western Allies in allowing Germany to become a threat to peace." The tough-minded Khrushchev, who thought Frost was innocent and idealistic, politely suggested that he was out of his depth by observing: "You have the soul of a poet."

The two men had expressed good will and achieved a certain heart-to-heart understanding, and the ninety-minute talk seemed to have gone very well. Frost was profoundly impressed by Khrushchev's homely proverbs, sense of humor and charming peasant's smile. Frost admired his humane reforms, realized he had to confront dangerous enemies both at home and abroad, and considered him a courageous leader. But, influenced by his personal impressions, Frost was rather naive about the brutal and ruthless side of Khrushchev's character, which had enabled him to seize and maintain power. While Khrushchev was preparing to destroy the world by bringing nuclear missiles into Cuba, Frost—with some reservations—observed: "We were charmed with each other. I'm very fond of him. He's a lovable man. I could talk out to him and he could talk out to me. . . . He is very good-natured, hearty, jolly, rough in a

way, you'd call it: coarse . . . probably a good deal deeper than I fathomed. . . . We were both so affable that we may both have been self-
deceived."[8]

Yeats once wrote of poets: "We have no gift to set a statesman right."
Frost undoubtedly had a successful meeting with Khrushchev, but then
failed to follow his own advice before leaving for Russia: "I can be a little
political but I mustn't be too political." His first *faux pas* occurred at a
Moscow press conference on September 8 when he called Khrushchev a
"ruffian. A big fellow. All ready for a fight. He's not a coward. He's not
afraid of us." When a Russian reporter protested and asked if Frost
meant "rough and ready" but not "ruffian," Frost, who did not hear well,
disregarded her and went on to state: "He was a little severe about my
country. He said the dollar was not as strong as it used to be. He said they
were beating us in some ways. He mentioned hydroelectric power and
said they learned it from [American engineers]."[9]

During a memorial service for Marion Burton of the University of
Michigan in February 1925, Frost had attributed many of his own ideas
about education to the late president and hoped none of his listeners
would notice. But when he tried the same tactic with Khrushchev, after
meeting reporters in America on September 9, he created an international furor. "By the time he got back to New York" after an eighteen-
hour plane trip, Adams wrote, "he was very tired and he hadn't been
expected to be *bombarded* by journalists. What he reported was in part his
own wishful thinking." Udall, who also arrived in New York with Frost,
recalled: "He was exhausted—and threw out one of his old chestnuts he
used to put down Harvard professors (i.e., 'the trouble is you are too
liberal to fight'). It was a ghastly mistake. I should have helped him avoid
an encounter with the press."

In 1915, while trying to keep America out of World War I, Woodrow
Wilson had angered Frost by pronouncing: "There is such a thing as a
man being too proud to fight." When he got off the plane from Moscow,
Frost adopted Wilson's phrase and misleadingly told reporters that
Khrushchev had said "Americans were too liberal to fight." By attributing
his own ideas to Khrushchev and emphasizing America's weakness, Frost
embarrassed and infuriated Kennedy at the most dangerous moment of
the Cold War. "Kennedy was upset, and rightly so," Udall wrote. "He said,
'Why did Frost say that?' My explanation did not alleviate his dismay."
Though Frost maintained that he had a special message from Khrushchev to Kennedy, he was never summoned to the White House for a
conference. The State Department, eager to learn if "Khrushchev had

made any revelations of international policy," debriefed Reeve, who had translated throughout the fateful interview.[10]

Despite his terrible mistake, Frost—like Pound with Mussolini in 1933—thought his meeting with Khrushchev was one of the most significant events of his life. Though Frost's every move had been reported by the Soviet and American press, the State Department kept asking him for his lost air ticket stubs, as proof that he had actually been in Russia, before they would reimburse him for expenses. The FBI, suspicious of his visit to a Communist country, kept a file on Frost (including an article about him in Russian) but did not mention that he had been sponsored by the State Department.

The Cuban missile crisis peaked with Kennedy's adamant speech on October 22, 1962. He announced that the United States Navy would impose a blockade on Cuba and followed this up by formally requesting the removal of all offensive missiles from the island. There seemed a grave risk of nuclear war. But on October 28 Khrushchev agreed to withdraw the missiles under United Nations supervision. Many people felt that Frost's remark, strangely enough, had influenced the President's strong stand.

On October 23, in the midst of this crisis, Frost gave a talk at the National Poetry Festival in Washington. He generously praised old friends who had supported him in the early phase of his career: Susan Hayes Ward and the Maine editor Thomas Mosher, Abercrombie and Edward Thomas, Pound and Harriet Monroe, Gordon Chalmers, Ransom and Van Doren. The prominent Socialist Norman Thomas had asked Frost to clarify Khrushchev's contentious comment and on September 28 Frost recanted the statement he had made at the airport. He wrote that *he* had been more threatening than Khrushchev and could not understand how the Premier's remark had got turned into the idea that Americans were not men enough to fight. At the National Poetry Festival he categorically withdrew his assertion and stated: "Nothing like that did I hear."

W. D. Snodgrass, who attended the Festival, remembered Frost's obvious enjoyment of this grave situation, and his own shocked response to it:

> The crisis was mounting, Jackie Kennedy had cancelled our lunch with her (she was reportedly hidden in a cave somewhere) and we all expected to be blown to bits within hours. . . .
>
> Frost, within months of his death, not only read a poem of

Robinson Jeffers, "Shine, Perishing Republic," but also made an improvised addition to one of his own—referring to the current crisis with a clean air of triumph. . . . A generous interpretation might say that he was exhilarated by the air of confrontation and that he saw the crisis as a refutation of his liberal critics, a proof that the direct assertion and/or threat of nuclear war WAS the right way to handle international conflict. But some of the remarks he made suggested that he was also glad that he would not have to die alone—and that, moreover, we would die without having the full career he'd had. He ad libbed at one point, "Well, you didn't want just to fade out, did you? Why not go out in a blaze of glory?" Truly cold-blooded mockery.

Udall took a more positive view of Frost's achievement. He believed that the talk with Frost "served Khrushchev's purpose by sending Kennedy a message that he was sane and still had his hands on the levers of power. . . . Cold warriors on both sides of the Iron Curtain regarded Robert Frost's appeal to Nikita Khrushchev as a naive cry in the wilderness. But it led, during the following decade, to Nixon's détente with Brezhnev."[11]

II

The American Academy of Arts and Letters had nominated Frost for the Nobel Prize as early as 1950, and he had been a leading contender when Faulkner won the prize that year and when Hemingway won it four years later. Though Frost's poems had been rendered into twelve languages —including Estonian, Greek, Korean and Persian—his puns and allusions, colloquial diction and deceptive simplicity made him very difficult to translate. He believed poets should be defended against translation and "was glad he didn't know the foreign languages into which his poems had been translated because it saved him the pain of hearing them mutilated." The apparent weakness of his verse in other tongues and his adamantly conservative politics hurt his chances for getting the prize.

In 1957 Ahmed Bokhari, an official of the United Nations, visited Frost at Ripton and tried to sell him on the idea of "Togetherness." He said, Frost recalled, that the King of Sweden "had sent over a chunk of iron as a symbol of the strength of unity, and, before it was put in one of the walls [of the Meditation Room], representatives of the U.N. thought it would be a nice idea if I would write them a poem to be engraved on it. I told him that iron was fine for a weapon of war, but it was a pretty curious emblem of peace." Instead of offering some bland verse on the unity of mankind, which was required for the occasion, Frost sent a savage couplet (on the same theme as "The Objection to Being Stepped On"), which suggested that men, following their natural instinct, were always driven to oppose each other, and deliberately undermined the "Federation of Mankind" theme of the United Nations. In "From Iron: Tools and Weapons," Frost wrote: "Nature within her inmost self divides/To trouble men with having to take sides." The idealistic and influential Dag Hammarskjöld, the Secretary-General, "loved the hunk of Swedish iron" and was deeply offended by Frost's ironic couplet. When asked to name a Nobel candidate, he nominated Saint-John Perse, who won it in 1960. In October 1962, when the aged Frost still hoped to win the only award that had eluded him, the Nobel Prize was given to John Steinbeck, whose Left-wing views were more congenial to the Swedes.

Though disappointed, Frost remained strong, vigorous and active till the end of his life. Despite increasing deafness, he continued his late-night conversations and his exhausting schedule of travel and lectures. After a long day and night in Cambridge, MacLeish stood up at 10:30 to end the evening. Frost said: "Archie, if you are tired, why don't you go to bed?"—and talked on until well past midnight.[12] In November 1962, Frost read to his largest ever audience, 8,500 at the University of Detroit, and showed astonishing resilience and energy. He spoke for ninety minutes without sipping water or missing a line, and answered all the questions with clarity, liveliness and wit. When he finished the stunning performance and came off stage, Kay was waiting for him in the wings. His final appearance took place at the Ford Hall Forum in Boston the night before he entered the hospital for his last illness. At the end of his life, like the 120-year-old Moses in Deuteronomy, "his eye was not dim, nor his natural force abated."

III

Frost, a sickly child and delicate young man who had suffered frequent bouts of bronchial illness, had been remarkably healthy in later life. He had minor surgery for hemorrhoids in January 1940 and for skin cancer in the summer of 1951 and in December 1953. During the second operation, "Scarface" wrote that the surgeon had "sculpted" him with a scalpel and left a horizontal scar on the right side of his lip. He had been hospitalized for pneumonia in Hanover in December 1943 and again in Miami in February 1962. During the second crisis he telephoned Kay: "If you want to see me again, alive, you'd better get down here fast. And tell Al Edwards the same." But he was not afraid and when he felt near death he thought: "All right, good-by. . . . I went up to the edge and I looked over, and instead of going I came back"—as he had predicted he would do in "Away!"

Frost had often said he would like to die on the trail in Vermont. But in December 1962—when his chronic cystitis, or inflammation of the urinary bladder, was complicated by prostate problems—he agreed to enter the Peter Bent Brigham Hospital in Boston to determine if he had a malignant growth. On December 3, as Kay and a doctor were ready to take him to hospital, he sensed the mortal danger and declared: "If I ever go into that place, I'll never come out alive." He then went upstairs to his bedroom and dramatically threatened: "This is when I walk out of your lives—all of you." The doctor followed him upstairs and told Kay that Frost, lying on the bed, would not respond. She asked: "Was he lying face down or face up?" He said: "Face down," and she replied: "In that case, it will be three hours before I can get him to the hospital. I wish it had been the other way." When she left him in the hospital room, before he was moved to the suite that had been occupied by King Saud of Saudi Arabia, Frost assured her: "I will do this on the highest plane—don't fear."

After inserting a catheter to alleviate stoppage in the bladder, the surgeon found Frost had cancer of the prostate and operated successfully on December 10. Frost did well during the next two weeks, but on December 23 he barely survived a pulmonary embolism and a heart attack. He was given anticoagulants, but blood got into his urine. He suffered another pulmonary embolism on January 7, and the next day had a second operation, which tied the veins in his legs in order to prevent the large blood clots from reaching his lungs. His mood fluctuated according to his state of health, but he kept busy by writing

letters, composing poems, seeing visitors, discussing the favorable response to *In the Clearing*, worrying about President Kennedy's displeasure
and talking about the possibility of death.[13]

Frost was cheered, in between medical crises, when on January 5 Allen
Tate called to announce that he had won the $2,500 Bollingen Prize for
In the Clearing. The other members of the committee were Robert Lowell,
Louise Bogan, Richard Eberhart and John Hall Wheelock. When asked
what else he wanted while in hospital, Frost extravagantly replied: "Tell
'em I like orchids." As they poured in and he was surrounded by masses
of the precious flowers, he said: "I deserve 'em." His spirits were also
lifted by a telegram from his Russian favorite, Yevtushenko, who wrote: "I
have read your poems again and again today, and I am glad you live on
earth."

On January 22, three months after the Cuban missile crisis and a week
before his death, a Russian delegation—including the humorist Valentin Kataev, the poet Konstantin Simonov, the film director Victor Rozov
and two translators—visited Frost in the hospital. Champagne was
brought in, a nurse hoisted Frost to a sitting position and he offered a
short toast. Kataev gave a detailed description of the scene and added
that, unable to find the proper words for the occasion, he had lapsed
into solemn silence:

> In a silent multi-storey hospital, surrounded day and night by
> news photographers, reporters and TV cameramen, ninety-year
> [i.e., 88]-old Robert Frost, the famous American poet, lay dying
> on a high bed in a private ward. Propped up by large fresh
> pillows, he was surrounded by flowers and gold-topped bottles of
> French champagne in ice-buckets and he was holding forth
> without pause. He kept rolling his red eyes, which were awesome
> like a prophet's, and naive like a child's. They were set in the
> parchment of his rigid, blotched face, a face already covered by
> the brown finger-marks of eternity. . . . [He was] trying not to
> spill the Veuve Clicquot onto his snow-white gown, which ex-
> posed his parchment neck, mottled with the brown marks of old
> age. . . . What could I say to him during that last minute of our
> earthly meeting? I could only do one thing—loudly proclaim
> the name of that Californian evergreen which is covered with
> bright red flowers in mid-winter, but I had forgotten the word,
> the one word that could save the world and us all. Feeling
> downcast, I remained silent.

Frost had asked Elena Levin, the Russian-born wife of a Harvard professor, to serve as translator. She recalled that he seemed happy to see her and held her hand. She noted that when the delegation arrived, its two translators arrogantly pushed their way in and insisted they *had* to be there. Frost talked animatedly, though he did not fully understand who the Russians were, while one translator angrily corrected the other's mistakes. Kataev tried to calm them by saying: "Girls, girls, it doesn't really matter." Although the visit lasted for only ten minutes, a full five minutes were taken up by Kataev's propagandistic speech about his beloved Soviet homeland, which was intended for publication in *Pravda*. Though Frost smiled benignly and did not take it all in, Elena Levin was both shocked and bitterly angry that Kataev would make such a crude speech in the presence of a dying man. She felt Kataev knew he had done something wrong, but was forced to speak by the political conditions that dominated his existence. In his book, however, he thinks of a poetic image, remains tactfully silent and presents an ideal vision of the way he would have *liked* to behave.[14]

Though Frost knew he was mortally ill, he fought hard to stay alive and still hoped to return to the long trial by existence. During his last interview, just before entering the hospital, he stoically said: "I don't take life very seriously. It's hard to get into this world and hard to get out of it. And what's in between doesn't make much sense. If that sounds pessimistic, let it stand." On January 12, after surviving his second operation, he told George Roy Elliott, in his last letter, that Kay and Anne were helping him "through these hard days in a grand and very powerful hospital. If only I get well, with their help, I'll go deeper into my life with you than I ever have before." Though naturally anxious about his recurring blood clots, "his mind was sharp and clear always," Anne wrote, "and his wit never deserted him and he knew no pain or fear." His final words, shortly before the end of his life, were: "I feel as though I were in my last hours."[15]

Frost was ready for death because he was confident that he had put the "truth of feeling" into his poetry and had achieved universal recognition. At his mortal hour, he *knew* he was immortal. There was no need to carry out his threat to return if dissatisfied with what he learned from having died. He had already become his admirers, and had never been completely engulfed by "The universal cataract of death / That spends to nothingness."

Though Frost had cancer of the prostate, he was killed by infected blood clots in the veins of his left leg and by recurrent pulmonary embolisms. On January 29, 1963, two months before his eighty-ninth birthday, Frost died after complaining of shortness of breath and severe chest pains. The "Discharge Summary" or death report at the Brigham Hospital said that Frost, a "somewhat feeble elderly white male, was alert and cooperative." He entered the hospital because of dysuria (difficult or painful urination); and had recurrent cystitis for twenty-five years, a hypertrophied prostate that caused retention of urine, arthritis of the spine and left knee, carcinoma on the face and tremor of the hand. After he went into shock at 1:30 A.M., "an attempted resuscitation was unsuccessful and the patient was discharged to Ward X."

Anne Morrison stayed with Frost quite late that night, then went home and was called back to clean out his room. The reporters would not leave her alone and intruded on her grief. One of them forced his way into the room, took a few personal objects, grabbed Frost's false teeth and tried to steal "even worse things." When he heard Frost had died, Khrushchev immediately sent Lesley a telegram that recalled their momentous meeting: "Deeply grieved about the death of your father. . . . The name of Frost and his poems, full of love for the simple man, are widely known in our country, and we were glad to greet him here last year as a messenger of good will, as a continued advocate of friendship between our nations. Please accept the expression of my sincerest sympathy on this big [i.e., great] loss."[16]

Frost was cremated at Mount Auburn Cemetery on January 30 and the following day a private service was held at Harvard.[17] The family then went back to Brewster Street for a reading of the will, which had been drawn up on May 5, 1951, and named Alfred Edwards executor. The house and contents in Cambridge and part of the land in South Miami were left to Lesley; the Holt stock, the farm in Ripton, the house and the rest of the land in Miami, all manuscripts and unpublished work, and the Wyeth watercolor (now at Dartmouth) to Kay; the gold and silver medals to Prescott; the rest of the personal property to Lesley, Kay and Prescott; and one-quarter each of the royalties to Lesley, Kay, Irma Cone and Lillian Frost. Thompson said Frost "willed Kay more property and cash than all the others put together," estimating her legacy as worth $198,000 and $8,000 a year royalties.[18] Kay, like her father and son, had a serious car accident on June 13, 1964 and needed two operations to restore her face. She became an alcoholic toward the end of her life and lived until 1989. Several other poets died soon after Frost: Sylvia Plath in

February 1963, William Carlos Williams in March, Theodore Roethke in August and Louis MacNeice in September. John F. Kennedy was assassinated in November.

IV

Frost had become a cultural icon during his lifetime, but had also entered the popular imagination. In "The Dangling Conversation" of 1966, Simon and Garfunkel sang: "You read your Emily Dickinson, and I my Robert Frost"; and Charles Schulz's syndicated "Peanuts" cartoon of January 7, 1975 portrayed a snowman who is very fond of poetry and reads Robert Frost. More significantly, most of the English and American poets of the century had written about Frost. Like Jonson's "Sons of Ben," he had spawned a great many "Sons of Bob," who were influenced by the "sound of sense" theory, colloquial diction, formal structure, dazzling technique and innovative ideas of his poetry. The leading poets in this tradition were Edward Thomas, Robert Graves and W. H. Auden; James Dickey, Donald Hall, Peter Davison, William Meredith, Richard Wilbur, Theodore Roethke and Seamus Heaney.[19]

Frost's influence on Thomas, Auden and Hemingway has already been discussed. His influence on Graves, a lifelong admirer, who called Frost "the first American who could be honestly reckoned a master-poet by world standards," can be seen (for example) in his variation of the last line of "Directive"— "Drink and be whole again beyond confusion"—in "Instructions to the Orphic Adept": "You shall drink deep of that refreshing draught." As an English critic wrote when reviewing *In the Clearing,* "Many of the qualities Mr. Graves praises in Mr. Frost, such as his readiness to accept the unexpected, his unwillingness to place a poem in advance, and his respect for metre, his sense of the life of the poem coming partly from 'the strain of rhythm upon metre,' are qualities which critics would also praise in Mr. Graves." Despite the passionate advocacy of Edward Thomas, Graves, Auden and Day Lewis, the English still tend to see Frost the way Americans see Thomas—as a minor pastoral poet who lived in England during the Great War. As Stephen Spender observed: "I should say that Frost has a good reputation in England though not many people know about him. Many of those who do probably associate him with Edward Thomas and the Georgian poets."[20]

Frost's influence was naturally more extensive in America. But, as the Vermont poet James Hayford remarked, his massive work could be overwhelming: "He had in effect put all New England under his copy-right, for poetic purposes, and anyone who rashly undertook to grow in his immense shadow was bound to have a thin time of it." Frost's impact was personal as well as poetic, and he made a profound impression on everyone who came to know him. Robert Lowell, the leading American poet after World War II, had received, as an undergraduate at Harvard, valuable instruction from Frost. He also adopted Frost's competitive habit of ranking poets to see who was number one. In a letter to Roethke, six months after Frost's death, Lowell declared: "I remember Edwin Muir arguing with me that there is no rivalry in poetry. Well, there is. No matter what one has done or hasn't done . . . one feels each blow, each turning of the wind, each up and down grading of the critics." When Frost died in 1963 John Berryman (a leading contender for the title) nervously looked around at his rivals and asked a friend the overwhelming question: "It's *scary.* Who's number one? Who's number one? Cal [Lowell] is number one, isn't he?"[21]

In "Lines to Mr. Frost" and in two of his Dream Songs, Berryman recalled some of his late conversations with Frost, "the quirky medium of so many truths." In the former Berryman described Frost's charming egoism and tendency to exaggerate his own wickedness:

> you squandered afternoon of your great age
> on my good gravid wife & me, with tales
> gay of your cunning & colossal fame
> & awful character.

In the latter, he noted the important difference between Frost's public persona and real self, and his willingness to apologize to Berryman for actual and imagined slights:

> His malice was a pimple down his good
> big face, with its sly eyes. . . .
> He had fine stories and was another man
> in private; difficult, always. Courteous,
> on the whole, in private.
> He apologize to Henry, off & on,
> for two blue slanders; which was good of him.

In April 1958 Berryman echoed John Masefield's praise when Frost had left England the previous year. In a letter to Frost he delineated the qualities that made him a great poet: "Let me add my thanks too for half a lifetime's delight in your work. It has been clear to me for almost a quarter of a century that you are one of the most nearly perfect poets —for pathos, for insight, for beauty, and for risk—who has ever written, not in this language only but in any literature I know."[22]

William Meredith, who had traveled to California with Frost in November 1960 and was struck by his still keen powers of observation, spoke of Frost's strength as a teacher, his fundamental kindness and his influence on Meredith's work: "I feel that he was one of the great instructors of my life, just to hang around and watch how he took things, his absolute solidity in the face of the twentieth century that he never made. . . . He demanded absolute loyalty from his friends, and if you met that condition, I don't think he was any harder on you than anybody else. . . . I think he has [influenced me] in making me . . . strive for the kind of colloquial language that distinguishes his poems."

Richard Wilbur, nourished but not overshadowed by Frost, agreed with Jarrell, Lowell and Meredith about the essence of Frost's character: "My relations with Frost were both filial (on my part) and friendly; I had many talks with him; he was generous toward me and my poems; his influence on my work was considerable." Wilbur's superb poem "Seed Leaves," written in "Homage to R.F." and partly modeled on "Putting in the Seed," shows how a younger poet can express his own originality within the Frostian tradition. Writing of Wilbur's "The Death of a Toad," the poet Robert Fitzgerald observed that his "immaculate verbal choice, his freshening of the sense of life within a rigid metrical frame and not only within it but by means of it, recall Frost's writing at its best."[23]

Theodore Roethke was older, more aggressive, more insecure and unstable, less personally familiar with Frost than Meredith and Wilbur. He was more critical of Frost's complacent and controlled public personality, which he felt was very different from his own wild recklessness. In his unpublished Notebooks, Roethke wrote: "Many of Frost's poems are implicit with self-congratulation. . . . What bothers me is the psychic stance: he is a mighty cozy character, tough and pleased with himself —his life and self-control." Roethke's nature poetry is most obviously indebted to Frost's. The influence of "The Bear" on "I Knew a Woman" has already been noted. The relation of Frost's title "An Old Man's Winter Night" to Roethke's "Old Lady's Winter Words" is clear. The rhythm of Frost's "I smell the earth, I smell the bruisèd plant, / I look into the crater of the ant" reappears in Roethke's "I am my father's son, I am John Donne / Whenever I see her with nothing on." Roethke also uses the rhyme and meter of Frost's "To Earthward"—"I had the swirl and ache / From sprays of honeysuckle / That when they're gathered shake / Dew on the knuckle"—in "My Papa's Waltz":

> The hand that held my wrist
> Was battered on one knuckle;
> At every step you missed
> My right ear scraped a buckle.

Roethke's "The Voice," as one critic remarked, "takes the ingredients of 'The Oven Bird'—bird, wood, tree, summer, diminishment, and song —and re-orders them to emphasize a wholly different perspective." Yet Frost's conclusion, "The question that he frames in all but words / Is what to make of a diminished thing," strongly marked Roethke's

> And yet I roamed out where
> Those notes went, like the bird
> Whose thin song hung in air,
> Diminished, yet still heard.[24]

The Irish-born Seamus Heaney, the greatest living poet in English, has (unlike Roethke) freely acknowledged his enormous debt to Frost. He said "the first poet who ever spoke to him was Robert Frost," and Heaney's "The Wife's Tale" "emulates those poems of Frost's which dramatize the division between a man and wife." In the best critical appreciation of Frost, Heaney mentioned Frost's denigration by Thompson and expressed the joy he has felt in Frost's poetry: "Among major poets of the English language in this century, Robert Frost is the one who takes the most punishment . . . [as a] calculating self-publicist, reprehensible egotist, oppressive parent." Heaney has had "a lifetime of pleasure in Frost's poems as events in language, flaunts and vaunts full of projective force and deliquescent backwash, the crestings of a tide that lifts all spirits." In a revealing interview, Heaney defined Frost's importance by explaining which of Frost's poems moved him most deeply. He called Frost (as Yevtushenko and Berryman had done) psychologically and artistically "cunning," and favorably compared him to Heaney's countryman and hero, W. B. Yeats:

I read a lot of Frost early on. There are two or three poems which for some reason keep close to me . . . from *North of Boston.* "Home Burial" is extraordinary, its bareness and tremendous understanding. . . . And it has tremendous opening and closing words. At the same time, Frost too has that surrender, the entranced thing, in "After Apple-Picking" which, even though it's an old chestnut, is delightful. He has two things: the capacity-to-surrender-to-a-gift poem, and he has the cunning (in the Elizabethan sense) to handle a poem and make it move in a public kind of way. I would love to write a poem like "The Most of It," which may be in some ways—and this is a bit heretical—a better poem than "The Second Coming." . . . The Frost poem is a revelation. . . . I think it's one of the high points, a poem housing power of some kind. It's not discourse, analysis, judgment, display; it moves by instinct, moves itself, moves the reader; a sense of connection and perhaps not much deliberation. Yet Frost always preserved a strong sense of the art itself; he always believed that poetry should be beautiful.[25]

The most popular, famous and influential American poet since Emerson, Longfellow and Whitman, Frost held the same esteemed position in his own country as Wordsworth and Tennyson did in nineteenth-century England. Just as Dwight Eisenhower paid tribute to Frost's insight and wisdom, so Nehru kept a copy of "Stopping by Woods on a Snowy Evening" (Kennedy's favorite Frost poem) with him during the last days of his life to symbolize responsibility and steadfastness. On October 26, 1963, a month before his assassination, President Kennedy made amends for his anger and silence by speaking at the dedication of the Robert Frost Library at Amherst. At the ceremony, he apologetically told Kay: "We didn't know he was so ill," and then paid tribute to the poet who had helped him become president. Emphasizing the tragic, terrifying Frost, Kennedy also spoke eloquently of the "tide that lifts all spirits" in Frost's poetry:

Today this college and country honor a man whose contribution was not to our size but to our spirit; not to our political beliefs but to our insight; not to our self-esteem, but to our self-comprehension. . . . If Robert Frost was much honored during his lifetime, it was because a good many preferred to ignore his darker truths. . . . He brought an unsparing instinct for reality to bear on the platitudes and pieties of society. His sense of the human tragedy fortified him against self-deception and easy consolation. . . . When power leads a man toward arrogance, poetry reminds him of his limitations. When power narrows the areas of man's concern, poetry reminds him of the richness and diversity of his existence. When power corrupts, poetry cleanses.[26]

APPENDIXES

NOTES

BIBLIOGRAPHY

INDEX

APPENDIX I

Literary Allusions

BIBLE

Genesis 1:3– "And God said, Let there be light" — "Once by the Pacific" (p. 250: line 14)

Genesis 4:9– "Am I my brother's keeper?" — *Masque of Mercy* (494:36)

Genesis 10:25– "a servant of servants shall he be unto his brethren" — "A Servant to Servants" (62:title)

Exodus 3:2– "the bush burned with fire, and the bush was not consumed" — "Sitting By a Bush" (266:16) & *Masque of Reason* (473:6)

Exodus 3:8– "a land flowing with milk and honey" — "Pod of the Milkweed" (411:16)

Exodus 3:14– "I AM THAT I AM" — "How Hard It Is" (460:218)

Exodus 20:5– "the Lord thy God am a jealous God" — *Masque of Mercy* (504:289)

Exodus 29:26– "thou shalt not take the breast of the ram . . . and wave it for a wave offering" — "Maple" (183:106–7)

Leviticus 19:18– "Thou shalt love thy neighbor as thyself" — "Quandary" (467:12)

Joshua 10:13– "And the sun stood still, and the moon stayed" — "October" (27:15)

II Samuel 1:20– "Tell it not in Gath" — "Gold Hesperidee" (284:58)

II Samuel 1:27– "How are the mighty fallen" — *Masque of Mercy* (504:291)

Job 1:7– "From going to and fro in the earth" — "Kitty Hawk" (428:12–13)

Job 1:9–"I only am escaped alone to tell thee"   "Iris by Night" (315:22)

Job 13:3– "I desire to reason with God"   *Masque of Reason* (473:title)

Psalms 19:14– "Let the words of my mouth . . . be acceptable in thy sight"   *Masque of Mercy* (520:725)

Psalms 111:10– "The fear of the Lord is the beginning of wisdom"   *Masque of Mercy* (501:215)

Isaiah 2:4– "they shall beat their swords into ploughshares"   "Objection to Being Stepped On" (450:14–15)

Isaiah 34:7– "their land shall be soaked with blood"   "The Flood" (254:6)

Jeremiah 28:8– "prophesied . . . of war, and of evil, and of pestilence"   "Drumlin Woodchuck" (282:23)

Matthew 5:13– "if the salt have lost his savour, wherewith shall it be salted?"   "Generations of Men" (80:191) & "Does No One At All" (446:24)

Matthew 6:10– "Thy will be done on earth, as it is in heaven"   "Trial by Existence" (19:4) & *Masque of Reason* (484:304)

Matthew 6:13–"deliver us from evil"   *Masque of Reason* (486:373)

Matthew 6:27– "can add one cubit unto his stature"   *Masque of Mercy* (506:339)

Matthew 7:16– "Do men gather grapes of thorns?"   "Wild Grapes" (196:2)

Matthew 10:39– "He that loseth his life for my sake shall find it"   "Directive" (379:62)

Matthew 13:57– "A prophet is not without honour, save in his own country"   *Masque of Reason* (476:90–91)

Matthew 24:2– "There shall not be left here one stone upon another, that shall not be thrown down"   "Mending Wall" (33:1–3)

Matthew 26:27–28– "he took the cup . . . saying, Drink ye all of it; For this is my blood"   "Directive" (379:62)

Matthew 26:38– "tarry ye here, and watch with me"   "Neither Out Far" (301:16)

Matthew 27:24– "[Pilate] took water, and washed his hands before the multitude"   "Self-Seeker" (100:216)

Mark 4:11–12– "all these things are   "Directive" (379:58–59)
done in parables: That seeing
they may see, and not perceive"

Luke 2:49– "I must be about my   *Masque of Reason* (489:431)
father's business"

Luke 19:4– "And he ran before, and   "Sycamore" (331:1–3)
climbed up into a sycamore tree
to see him"

John 1:1– "In the beginning was the   *Masque of Reason* (475:56)
Word"

John 8:32– "ye shall know the truth   "How Hard It Is" (460:191–2)
and the truth shall make you
free"

Acts 2:4– "[They] began to speak   "Snow" (151:248–9)
with other tongues as the Spirit
gave them utterance"

I Corinthians 9:22– "I am made all   *Masque of Mercy* (516:591)
things to all men"

Apostles' Creed– "He descended   "Black Cottage" (58:94)
into Hades"

CLASSICS

Aesop, "The Fox and the Grapes"   "Wild Grapes" (198:63) & *Masque of Mercy* (496:77)

The Greek Anthology–"I lie here, /   "A Question" (362:3–4)
Never having married: and I wish
my father had not"

Virgil, Eclogue I– Tityrus and Meli-   "Build Soil" (316:1–2)
boeus
    "longer shadows fall from the   "The Mountain" (40:1)
lofty mountains"

Horace, Odes 1:3– "Oak and three   "Triple Bronze" (349:11)
layers of bronze made his breast-
plate"
    Odes 1:11– "reap today: save no   "Carpe Diem" (335:10)
hopes for tomorrow"
    Odes 3: 4– "Come down from   "Auspex" (443:2)
the sky, Calliope, goddess"

Tibullus, Elegies 2.6.21–*"spes alit*   "Something for Hope" (376:24)
agricolas"

Villon, "Ballad of Women"– "where   "Spring Pools" (245:12)
are the snows of yesteryear?"

*Marlowe, "The Passionate Shep-   "Line-Storm Song" (26:15)
herd"– "Come live with me, and
be my love"

Doctor Faustus, 3:15– "Why, this is   "New Hampshire" (166:242)
hell, nor am I out of it"

SHAKESPEARE

Sonnets: dedication– "To the Onlie   "To a Moth" (356:16)
Begetter"

Sonnet 49– "And scarcely greet me   "Waiting" (15:27)
with that sun, thine eye"

*Sonnet 64– "When I have seen the   "Once by the Pacific" (250:1–4)
hungry ocean gain / Advantage
on the kingdom of the shore"

*Sonnet 71– "From this vile world,   "Lesson for Today" (352:74)
with vilest worms to dwell"

*Sonnet 116– "But bears it out even   "Into My Own" (5:4)
to the edge of doom"

Rich III, 1.4.277– "I'll drown you in   *Masque of Mercy* (510:449)
the malmsey-butt within"

LLL, 5.2.922– "When icicles hang   "Old Man's Winter" (108:22)
by the wall"

R & J, Prologue, 1.6– "A pair of star-   *Masque of Mercy* (510:441)
crossed lovers take their life"

AYLI, 2.7.144– "Mewling and puk-   "New Hampshire" (170:363)
ing in the nurse's arms"

AYLI, 2.7.166– "Sans teeth, sans   "Brown's Descent" (137:7)
eyes, sans taste, sans everything"

AYLI, 4.1.75– "Very good orators,   "Broken Drought" (400:4–5)
when they are out, they will spit"

TN, 1.1.4– "That strain again! It had   *Masque of Reason* (488:418)
a dying fall"

TN, 1.5.296–7–"What is your par-   "Generations of Men" (75:53–54)
entage?" / "Above my fortunes,
yet my state is well"

TN, 5.1.402– "With hey, ho, the   "The Wind and the Rain" (336:
wind and the rain"   title)

Ham, 1.1.165– "So have I heard and   "Never Again Would" (338:1) &
do in part believe it"   "From Plane to Plane" (408:147)

Ham, 1.5.189–190– "The time is out of joint; O cursèd spite / That I was ever born to set it right!"

"Acquainted with Night" (255:13) & "Lesson for Today" (351:32)

Oth, 1.259– "Keep up your bright swords, for the dew will rust them"

"A Soldier" (261:1–2)

Oth, 5.2.7– "Put out the light, and then put out the light"

"Once by the Pacific" (250:14) & "Too Anxious for Rivers" (379:18)

Mac, 1.1.1– "When shall we three meet again"

"Generations of Men" (80:208)

Mac, 3.1.120– "And bid my will avouch it"

Masque of Reason (477:112)

Mac, 4 1.10– "Double, double toil and trouble"

"Pauper Witch of Grafton" (207:7–8)

Mac, 4.1.93– "until / Great Birnam Wood to high Dunsinane Hill / Shall come against him"

"New Hampshire" (170:371)

Mac, 5.5.23– "Out, out brief candle!"

"'Out, Out–'" (136:title)

*Cym, 4.2.258– "Fear no more the heat o' the sun"

"Mowing" (17:4)

Temp, 4.1.156–7– "We are such stuff / As dreams are made on"

"Waiting" (14:1)

Hen VIII, 3.2.440–1– "fling away ambition. / By that sin fell the angels"

Masque of Reason (481:205–6)

OTHER ALLUSIONS

Donne, "A Valediction: Forbidding Mourning"– "'Twere profanation of our joys"

"Good Hours" (102:15)

   "The Baite"– "With silken lines / and silver hookes"

"Silken Tent" (332:10)

*Herrick, "To the Virgins, to Make Much of Time"– "Gather ye rosebuds, while ye may, / Old time is still a-flying"

"Asking for Roses" (uncollected) & "Carpe Diem" (335:13)

"To Daffodils"– "Stay, stay, / Until the hasting day / Has run
/ But to the even-song / And,
having pray'd together, we / Will
go with you along"

Masque of Reason (489:435–7)

*Waller, "Go Lovely Rose"– "Suffer
herself to be desired, / And not
blush so to be admired"

Masque of Reason (474:30)

*Milton, "Lycidas"– "watery bier . . .
watery floor"

"Spring Pools" (245:11)

*   "On the Late Massacre in Pied-
mont"– "Avenge, O Lord, thy
slaughtered saints, whose bones"

"Forgive, O Lord" (428:1)

Comus– "Shall I go on? / Or have
I said enough?"

"Take Something" (408:134)

Paradise Lost, 1:1–2– "and the
fruit / Of that forbidden tree"

"Quandary" (467:15)

Paradise Lost, 3:134– "But mercy
first and last shall brightest
shine"

Masque of Mercy (508:381)

Bunyan, *Pilgrim's Progress*– "Do you
see yonder shining light? He
said, I think I do"

Masque of Mercy (513:530–1)

Thomas D'Urfey– "Over the hills
and far away"

"Line-Storm Song" (26:7)

Pope, "Essay on Criticism"– "To err
is human, to forgive divine"

"White-Tailed Hornet" (279:52)

Johnson, "Vanity of Human
Wishes"– "Survey mankind, from
China to Peru"

"From Plane to Plane" (408:133)

*Gray, "Elegy"– "And leaves the
world to darkness and to me"

"Acceptance" (249:12)

"They kept the noiseless tenor of
their way"

"Wood-Pile" (102:40)

*Smart, "Song to David"– "Where
knock is open wide"

"Lockless Door" (241:9–10)

*Cowper, "To a Young Lady"–
"Pure-bosom'd as that watery
glass, / And Heaven reflected in
her face"

"For Once, Then" (225:3–4)

Jefferson, "Declaration of Independence"– "all men are created
equal"

"Black Cottage" (57:61)

Johann Voss– "wine, women and song"

"How Hard It Is" (455:62)

*Burns, "The Cotter's Saturday Night"

"An Old Man's Winter Night" (108: title)

"To a Mouse"

"The Exposed Nest" (109:theme)

Wordsworth, "To a Butterfly"

"My Butterfly" (28:title)

*"She Dwelt Among the Untrodden Ways"– "But she is in her grave, and, oh, / The difference to me!"

"The Road Not Taken" (105:20)

"Resolution and Independence" –the leech gatherer

"The Gum-Gatherer" (140:title)

* "The World Is Too Much With Us"

"Directive" (377:1)

*Scott, "The Rover"– "He gave the bridle-reins a shake"

"Stopping By Woods" (224:9)

* "Datur Hora Quieti"–"All meet whom day and care divide . . . / And to the thicket wanders slow / The hind beside the hart"

"Two Look at Two" (229:15, 27)

"The Lay of the Last Minstrel"– "Breathes there the man, with soul so dead"

"On Being Chosen Poet" (469:1)

Coleridge, "Christabel"–"When lo! I saw a bright green snake"

"Mowing" (17:12)

Landor, "I Strove With None"– "Nature I loved; and next to Nature, Art"

"Lucretius" (393:epigraph)

Byron, "Isles of Greece"– "And musing there an hour alone / I dream'd that Greece might still be free"

"Greece" (uncollected)

* "She Walks in Beauty"– "She walks in beauty, like the night"

"Mending Wall" (34:41) & "The Lovely Shall Be" (257:33)

Shelley, "Adonais"– "Life, like a dome of many-coloured glass, / Stains the white radiance of Eternity"

"Birches" (121:12–13)

* "Ozymandias"– "I met a traveller from an antique land"

"New Hampshire" (159:1)

"The Witch of Atlas"

"The Witch of Coös" (202:title)

"To Jane: The Recollection"–
"We paused beside the pools that
lie / Under the forest bough,
— / Each seemed as 'twere a
little sky / Gulfed in a world below"

"Spring Pools" (245:1–2)

*"Ode to the West Wind"– "Thou,
from whose unseen presence the
leaves dead / Are driven, like
ghosts from an enchanter
fleeing"

"Leaf-Treader" (297:7–8)

*"To a Skylark"

"Kitty Hawk" (428:epigraph)

*"Stanzas Written in Dejection"

"The Lost Follower" (358:11) &
    "Lines Written in Dejection"
    (462:title)

Clare, "Badger"– "He tries to reach
the woods, an awkward race . . . /
He turns again and drives the
noisy crowd . . . / He drives away
and beats them every one . . . /
He falls as dead and kicked by
boys and men"

"Cow in Apple Time" (125:6–10)

*Keats, "Ode to a Nightingale"– "My
heart aches, and a drowsy numbness pains / My sense, as though
of hemlock I had drunk"

"After Apple-Picking" (68:7–8)

"But being too happy in thine
happiness"

"Prayer in Spring" (12:7)

"With beaded bubbles winking at
the brim"

"Tuft of Flowers" (23:28)

"I cannot see what flowers are at
my feet"

"After Apple-Picking" (68:9)

"To cease upon the midnight
with no pain"

"Oven Bird" (120:11)

"Keen Fitful Gusts"– "The stars
look very cold about the sky /
And I have many miles on foot
to fare"

"Stopping By Woods" (225:15)

"Endymion"– "A thing of beauty
is a joy forever"

"Young Birch" (375:21)

*   "Bright Star"– "Bright star!
Would I were steadfast as thou
art!"

"Take Something Like a Star" (403:
    1,18)

Beddoes, "The Phantom Wooer"– "Our bed is lovely, dark, and sweet"	"Stopping By Woods" (224:13)
Emerson, "The World-Soul"– "He serveth the servant"	"A Servant to Servants" (62:title)
"Ode to Channing"– "The God who made . . . with little men"	"New Hampshire" (166:218–19)
"The Concord Hymn"– "And fired the shot heard round the world"	"A Soldier" (261:4)
"The Rhodora"– "I found the fresh rhodora in the woods"	"Design" (302:1)
"Uriel"– "Unit and universe are round; / In vain produced, all rays return"	*Masque of Reason* (485:342–3)
Longfellow, "My Lost Youth"– "A boy's will is the wind's will / And the thoughts of youth are long, long thoughts"	*A Boy's Will* (title)
Tennyson, "Locksley Hall"– "In the Parliament of Man, the Federation of the World"	"Courage To Be New" (387:8)
"Guinevere"– "Too late, too late! ye cannot enter now"	*Masque of Mercy* (493:9) & (519:669)
"The Passing of Arthur"– "and the moon was full"	"Kitty Hawk" (433:167)
Browning, "The Lost Leader"	"The Lost Follower" (358:title)
"Childe Roland"– "He must be wicked to deserve such pain"	*Masque of Reason* (486:364)
Thoreau, *Walden*– "Extra-vagance!"	"Record Stride" (294:16)
Arnold, "In Harmony with Nature"– "Nature is cruel, man is sick of blood"	"New Hampshire" (170:371)
"Sohrab and Rustum"–"a foil'd circuitous wanderer"	"New Hampshire" (171:383–4)
"The Scholar Gipsy"– "takes dejectedly / His seat upon the intellectual throne"	"New Hampshire" (171:384–5)
Hardy, "An Ancient to Ancients"	"A Servant to Servants" (62:title)
"Bereft"	"Bereft" (251:title)
"The Darkling Thrush"– "The tangled bine-stems scored the sky / Like strings of broken lyres"	"Death of Hired Man" (38:107) & "Lone Striker" (274:29)

"An aged thrush, frail, gaunt, and small, / In blast-beruffled plume, / Had chosen thus to fling his soul / Upon the growing gloom"   "Come In" (334:1–4)

"In Time of 'The Breaking of Nations' "– "Only a man harrowing clods / In a slow silent walk / With an old horse that stumbles and nods / Half asleep as they stalk"   "Strong Are Saying" (299:5–9)

"An August Midnight"–"On this scene enter—winged, horned and spined— / A longlegs, a moth, and a dumbledore; / While 'mid my page there idly stands / A sleepy fly, that rubs its hands"   "Design" (302:1–4)

William James, *The Will to Believe*–"If we take the wrong road we shall be dashed to pieces. We do not certainly know whether there is any right one. What must we do?"   "Road Not Taken" (105:1–2)

Pragmatism– "a tramp and vagrant world, adrift in space, with neither elephant nor tortoise to plant the sole of its foot upon"   "Too Anxious for Rivers" (379: 15–16)

Thompson, "The Hound of Heaven"– "I fled Him, down the nights and down the days; / I fled him, down the arches of the years"   *Masque of Mercy* (494:22–23)

Kipling, *Departmental Ditties*   "Departmental" (287:title)
    "Recessional"– "Lord God of Hosts, be with us yet, / Lest we forget—Lest we forget!"   "Warning" (uncollected) & *Masque of Reason* (479:179)

Yeats, "The Lake Isle of Innisfree"– "I will arise and go now"   "Summering" (uncollected)
    "The Tower"– "Now I shall make my soul"   "Triple Bronze" (348:5)
    "Sailing to Byzantium"– "Of hammered gold and gold enameling"   *Masque of Reason* (473:14, 459)

"Two Songs from a Play"– "The Babylonian starlight brought / A fabulous formless darkness in; / Odour of blood when Christ was slain / Made all Platonic tolerance vain / And vain all Doric discipline"	*Masque of Mercy* (511:465–8)
Robinson, "The Sheaves"– "A thousand golden sheaves were lying there, / Shining and still, but not for long to stay"	"Nothing Gold Can Stay" (223:7–8)
Maugham, *The Razor's Edge*	"Milky Way Is a Cowpath" (465:36)
Stein, "Sacred Emily"– "Rose is a rose is a rose is a rose"	"The Rose Family" (246:1–2)
Joyce, "The Dead"– "Snow falling faintly through the universe and faintly falling"	"Desert Places" (296:1)
Finnegans Wake	*Masque of Mercy* (502:242–3)
Eliot, "The Love Song of J. Alfred Prufrock"– "Should I, after tea and cakes and ices, / Have the strength to force the moment to its crisis?"	"One Step Backward Taken" (377:7–9)
"I have seen them riding seaward on the waves / Combing the white hair of the waves blown back / When the wind blows the water white and black"	"West-Running Brook" (258:19–21)
"Sweeney Among the Nightingales"– "The nightingales are singing near / The convent of the Sacred Heart"	*Masque of Reason* (473:14–15)
Orwell, *Nineteen Eighty-Four*– "Freedom Is Slavery"	"How Hard It Is" (460:190)
Greene, *The Ministry of Fear*	"Why Wait for Science" (395:2)
Gellhorn, *A Stricken Field*	*Masque of Mercy* (507:365)
Kennedy, *Profiles in Courage*	"For John F. Kennedy" (423:58–60)

BALLADS

"Waly, Waly"– "I've locked my heart in a case o' goud / And pinned it wi' a siller pin"	"Love and a Question" (8:23–24)

"Thomas Rymer"– "My tongue is my ain"   *Masque of Mercy* (505:296)

"Shenandoah"– "Oh, Shenandoah, I long to hear you. / Away, I'm bound away"   "Build Soil" (325:278–9), "Away!" (413:title and 20) & *Masque of Mercy* (500:172)

NURSERY RHYMES

"I Will Sing You One-O"   "I Will Sing You One-O" (217:title)

"A Frog He Would A-Wooing Go"   "A-Wishing Well" (451:1)

"Hey diddle diddle, the cat and the fiddle / The cow jumped over the moon"   "Lines Written in Dejection" (462: 1)

"Three Little Kittens"   *Masque of Mercy* (498:118)

"Little Boy Blue"– "Little Boy Blue, come blow up your horn, / The sheep's in the meadow, the cow's in the corn"   "The Cow's in the Corn" (uncollected: title)

"Star light, star bright, / First star I see tonight, / I wish I may, I wish I might"   "A-Wishing Well" (451:28)

---

*In Palgrave

Academic Positions

Jan 1917–May 1920– Amherst, Professor of English (President: Alexander Meiklejohn). $2,000; 2 instead of 3 courses per term.

1920–21– not teaching

1921–22– Michigan, Poet in Residence (Marion Burton). $5,000; one-year appointment, no assigned work.

1922–23– Michigan, Fellow in Creative Arts (Burton). $5,000; one-year appointment, no assigned work.

1923–25– Amherst, Professor of English (George Olds). 2 courses a year, no other duties.

1925–26– Michigan, Fellow in Letters (Clarence Little). $5,000, no teaching hours, permanent appointment.

1926–38– Amherst, Professor of English (Olds; from 1934, Stanley King). $5,000+ for ten weeks a year.

1938–39– not teaching

1939–40– Harvard, Ralph Waldo Emerson Fellow in Poetry (James Conant). $1,500; two year appointment, no assigned work.

1941–42– Harvard, Fellow in American Civilization (Conant). $3,000.

1942–43– Harvard, Fellow in American Civilization (Conant). Honorary, no salary.

1943–49– Dartmouth, George Ticknor Fellow in the Humanities (John Dickey). $3,000; Friday to Sunday only, October to January.

1949–63– Amherst, Simpson Lecturer in Literature (Charles Cole; from 1960, Calvin Plimpton). $3,500; minimum duties, life appointment, with pension after 1954.

Notes

1. SAN FRANCISCO

1. Lawrance Thompson, *Robert Frost: The Early Years, 1874–1915* (New York, 1966), p. 4; William Frost, in Robert Frost, *Selected Letters,* ed. Lawrance Thompson (New York, 1964), pp. 7, 8.

2. Louis Mertins, *Robert Frost: Life and Talks-Walking* (Norman, Okla., 1965), pp. 19–20; Robert Frost, *Family Letters,* ed. Arnold Grade, Foreword by Lesley Frost (Albany, N.Y., 1972), p. 144; Quoted in Mark Harris' unpublished journal, August 1961, p. 446, courtesy of Mr. Harris.

3. Robert Louis Stevenson, "The Amateur Emigrant," (1879), *From Scotland to Silverado,* ed. James Hart (Cambridge, Mass., 1966), p. 187; Charles Barker, *Henry George* (New York, 1955), pp. 216, 168; Rudyard Kipling, *From Sea to Sea* (1899; London, 1919), I: 494, 496; Mertins, *Life and Talks-Walking,* p. 23. For more on Buckley, see William Bullough, *The Blind Boss and His City: Christopher Augustine Buckley and Nineteenth-Century San Francisco* (Berkeley, 1979).

4. Winfield Davis, *A History of Political Conventions in California, 1849–1892* (Sacramento: California State Library, 1893), pp. 422, 435, 437; Quoted in Robert Frost, *Interviews,* ed. Edward Connery Lathem (New York, 1966), p. 178; Lawrance Thompson, "Notes on Robert Frost, 1939–1967," University of Virginia Library.

5. *Robert Frost and Sidney Cox: Forty Years of Friendship,* ed. William Evans, Foreword by James Cox (Hanover, N.H., 1981), p. 209; Robert Frost, *Letters to Louis Untermeyer,* ed. Louis Untermeyer (New York, 1963), p. 342; Robert Frost, *Poetry,* ed. Edward Connery Lathem (New York, 1969), p. 256.

6. William Frost, Jr., to his mother, Judith Frost, November 29, 1874, Virginia; "Night Light," *Poetry,* p. 382.

For a similar fear, see Ernest Hemingway, *Selected Letters, 1917–*

1961, ed. Carlos Baker (New York, 1981), p. 697. Recalling his postwar years, Hemingway wrote that his sister "would sleep with me so I would not be lonely in the night. We always slept with the light on" because he had been wounded in the dark and associated darkness with death. In Hemingway's "A Clean, Well-Lighted Place," *Stories* (New York, 1953), p. 382, the old waiter says: "[I am] with all those who need a light for the night."

7. Mertins, *Life and Talks-Walking*, pp. 8–9; Kathleen Morrison, *Robert Frost: A Pictorial Chronicle* (New York, 1974), p. 77; Mertins, *Life and Talks-Walking*, p. 12.

8. *Interviews*, p. 258; Mertins, *Life and Talks-Walking*, p. 11.

9. When D. H. Lawrence was dying of tuberculosis in 1930, he asked his wife, Frieda, to sleep in his bed. "He was falling away from life and me," she wrote, "and with all my strength I was helpless" (Jeffrey Meyers, *D. H. Lawrence: A Biography*, New York, 1990, p. 380).

10. Quoted in William Sutton, "Robert Frost's Parents," *Ball State University Forum*, 16 (1975), 4. The mortally sick Will Frost misdated this letter, which was written three weeks—rather than fifty-five weeks—before his death; Mertins, *Life and Talks-Walking*, pp. 17, 6.

11. There are two memorials to Frost in San Francisco: a bronze plaque near the Hyatt Regency Hotel on lower Market Street and a stained glass window in Grace Cathedral on Nob Hill.

2. NORTH OF BOSTON

1. *Letters*, p. 18; Elizabeth Shepley Sergeant, *Robert Frost: The Trial by Existence* (New York, 1960), p. 48; Letter from Lesley Frost Francis to Robert Frost, 1939, Dartmouth College Library.

2. Harris, unpublished journal, p. 445; Quoted in David Daiches, "The Many Faces of a Poet," *New York Times Book Review*, September 20, 1964, p. 5; Sergeant, *Trial by Existence*, p. 22; *Robert Frost and the Lawrence, Massachusetts, "High School Bulletin": The Beginning of a Literary Career,* ed. Edward Connery Lathem and Lawrance Thompson (New York: Grolier Club, 1966), pp. 12, 21.

3. Percy Bysshe Shelley, "Love's Philosophy," in *The Golden Treasury*, ed. F. T. Palgrave (London, 1861), p. 213; Richard Poirier, "Robert Frost" (1960), *Writers at Work: The "Paris Review" Interviews*. Second Series, Introduction by Van Wyck Brooks (New York, 1963), p. 26.

4. Joan St. C. Crane, *Robert Frost: A Descriptive Catalogue of Books and Manuscripts in the Clifton Waller Barrett Library, University of Virginia* (Charlottesville, 1974), pp. 238–239; *Letters*, p. 167; *Interviews*, pp. 23–24; *Robert Frost on Writing*, ed. Elaine Barry (New Brunswick, N.J., 1973), p. 117; Edward Connery Lathem, "Freshman Days," *Dartmouth Alumni Magazine*,

51 (March 1959), 22. I am grateful to Edward Lathem for sending me this article as well as the *High School Bulletin*.

5. Sergeant, *Trial by Existence*, pp. 29–30; Lathem, "Freshman Days," p. 18; *History of the Class of 1896 at Dartmouth College During Its Freshman Year* (Hanover, N.H., 1893), p. 12; Lathem, "Freshman Days," pp. 21–22; Philip Gerber, "Remembering Robert Frost: An Interview with William Jewell," *New England Quarterly,* 59 (1986), 6.

6. Sergeant, *Trial by Existence,* p. 30; *Interviews,* p. 14; Thompson, *Early Years,* p. 172; Robert Frost, "The Self-Seeker," *A Boy's Will and North of Boston* (New York: Dover, 1991), p. 79.

7. Interview with Richard and Charlee Wilbur (Susan Ward's great-niece), Cummington, Mass., October 31, 1994; Lathem, "Freshman Days," p. 20; Lesley Lee Francis, "Robert Frost and Susan Hayes Ward," *Massachusetts Review,* 26 (1985), 343.

8. Letter from Elinor White Frost to Mrs. Bromley, December 27, n.d., Virginia. The second line of "An Unhistoric Spot" echoes "I summon up remembrance of things past" from Shakespeare's Sonnet 30; the lonely lover in "Twilight" echoes Sidney's "With how sad steps, O Moon, thou climb'st the skies!" These two poems are quoted in Thompson, *Early Years,* pp. 173–174; Sergeant, *Trial by Existence,* p. 42.

9. Henry Wadsworth Longfellow, "The Slave in the Dismal Swamp," *Complete Poetical Works* (Boston, 1948), pp. 21–22; Edgar Allan Poe, "Dream-Land," *Poems,* ed. Thomas Mabbott (Cambridge, Mass., 1969) p. 344; Thomas Moore, "A Ballad: The Lake of the Dismal Swamp," *Poetical Works,* ed. A. D. Godley (Oxford, 1924), p. 99. Moore and Longfellow use the same meter and ballad form.

10. Joseph Conrad, "Heart of Darkness," *Three Great Tales* (New York, [1960]), pp. 249, 255; Letter from Frost to Jean Gould, December 12, 1962, Dartmouth; "Into My Own," *A Boy's Will and North of Boston,* p.1.

3. MARRIAGE

1. Meyers, *D. H. Lawrence,* p. 42; Stearns Morse, "Lament for a Maker: Reminiscences of Robert Frost," *Southern Review,* 9 (1973), 56; Quoted in Lesley Lee Francis, *The Frost Family's Adventure in Poetry* (Columbia, Mo., 1994), p. 154; William Evans, "Robert Frost and Helen Thomas: Five Revealing Letters, (Part 2)," *Dartmouth College Library Bulletin,* 30 (1990), 38.

2. Elinor Frost, in *Letters,* p. 78; "A Servant to Servants," *A Boy's Will and North of Boston,* pp. 53–54; Helen Thomas, *Under Storm's Wing* (Manchester, 1988), pp. 228–229; Eleanor Farjeon, *Edward Thomas: The Last Four Years* (London, 1958), p. 88.

3. Thompson, "Notes on Frost," pp. 305–306 (on Elinor's abortion; in his

book he calls it a "miscarriage"); Sidney Cox, *A Swinger of Birches: A Portrait of Robert Frost,* Introduction by Robert Frost (1957; New York, 1961), p. 23; Thompson, "Notes on Frost," p. 149.

4. Robert Frost, "The Middletown Murder," *Poetry and Prose,* ed. Edward Connery Lathem and Lawrance Thompson (New York, 1972), pp. 287, 289.

5. John Gould Fletcher, *Life Is My Song* (New York, 1937), p. 204; Helen Thomas, *Under Storm's Wing,* p. 228; Marian Squire, "Robert Frost," *The Stag at Ease* (Caldwell, Idaho, 1938), p. 64.

6. Daniel Smythe, *Robert Frost Speaks* (New York, 1964), p. 89; Sergeant, *Trial by Existence,* p. 26; Peter Stanlis, in *Frost Centennial Essays III,* ed. Jac Tharpe (Jackson, Miss., 1978), pp. 224, 226; Martha Byrd Porter, *Straight Down a Crooked Lane* (Richmond, 1945), p. 191.

7. Reginald Cook, *Robert Frost: A Living Voice* (Amherst, Mass., 1974), p. 5; Robert Frost, "A Time to Talk," *The Road Not Taken and Other Poems (Mountain Interval)* (New York: Dover, 1993), p. 19. For the books devoted to Frost's conversation, see section II of the bibliography.

8. John Lynen, *The Pastoral Art of Robert Frost* (New Haven, 1960), p. 152n; Baird Whitlock, "Conversations with Robert Frost," *Xavier Review* (New Orleans), 3 (1983), 15; Raymond Holden, "Reminiscences of Robert Frost," p. 36, Dartmouth.

9. Holden, "Reminiscences," p. 5; Letter from Frost to Harold Rugg, October 20, 1927, Dartmouth; *Family Letters,* p. 8; Mark Van Doren, *Autobiography* (New York, 1958), pp. 170–171.

10. Mertins, *Life and Talks-Walking,* p. 99; Margaret Bartlett Anderson, *Robert Frost and John Bartlett : The Record of a Friendship* (New York, 1963), pp. 73, 145; Thompson, *Early Years,* p. 264; Frost, *Poetry and Prose,* p. 371.

11. William Sutton, ed., *Newdick's Season of Frost: An Interrupted Biography of Robert Frost* (Albany, N.Y., 1976), p. 233; Theodore Morrison, "Robert Frost and Poetry at the Conference," *Bread Loaf Writers' Conference: The First Thirty Years (1926–1955)* (Middlebury, Vt., 1976), p. 71; "Frost's Aide, Publishing Picture Book, Fondly Recalls His Atrocious Spelling," *New York Times,* March 26, 1974, p. 36; Mark Van Doren, *Selected Letters,* ed. George Hendrick (Baton Rouge, 1987), p. 265.

12. In Thompson's book the "whore-housekeeper's daughter" ("Notes," p. 134) is bowdlerized into "considered socially disqualified for membership in the Parker family" (*Early Years,* p. 225) and the point of the fight—to preserve the respectability of the down-and-out Frost family—is completely lost; Sutton, *Newdick's Season of Frost,* p. 48; Arthur Harris, "Conversation with Robert Frost," pp. 22–23, Amherst College Library.

13. Sergeant, *Trial by Existence,* p. 54; A. E. Housman, *Letters,* ed. Henry Maas (London, 1971), p. 65; Theodore Ziolkowski, *Virgil and the Moderns*

(Princeton, 1993), pp. 163, 159; *Poems from the Greek Anthology,* trans. Dudley Fitts (New York, 1956), p. 70. See also Robert Newdick, "Robert Frost and the Classics," *Classical Journal,* 35 (1940), 403–417; Helen Bacon, "'In- and Outdoor Schooling': Robert Frost and the Classics," *Robert Frost: Lectures on the Centenary of His Birth* (Washington, D.C.: Library of Congress, 1975), pp. 3–25; Helen Bacon, "Dialogue of Poets: *Mens Animi* and the Renewal of Words," *Massachusetts Review,* 19 (1978), 319–334; L. R. Lind, "Robert Frost, Classicist," *Classical and Modern Literature,* 1 (1980), 7–23; and Thomas Rosenmeyer, *The Green Cabinet: Theocritus and the European Pastoral Lyric* (Berkeley, 1969).

14. Letter from Lillian LaBatt Frost to Sandra Katz, October 11, 1982, courtesy of Professor Katz; Thompson, *Early Years,* p. 258; John Meisner, "Frost Four Years After," *Southern Review,* 2 (1966), 869; Robert Frost, "Notebook: After England," ed. Margot Feldman, *Antaeus,* 61 (1988), 155; *Frost and Cox,* p. 76.

15. In the "Death and Love" chapter of D. H. Lawrence's *Women in Love* (1920), Gerald Crich reveals the morbid side of his character and foreshadows his destruction by entering Gudrun Brangwen's bedroom with mud on his boots from his father's grave.

4. A HAMPSHIRE LAD

1. Perry Westbrook, "Robert Frost's New England," *Frost Centennial Essays,* ed. Jac Tharpe (Jackson, Miss., 1974), p. 240; Henry James, "New England," *The American Scene,* ed. Leon Edel (1908; Bloomington, Ind., 1968), pp. 14, 23; Lawrance Thompson, *Robert Frost: The Years of Triumph, 1915–1938* (New York, 1970), p. 470.

2. Mertins, *Life and Talks-Walking,* p. 88; Letter to Ernest Jewell, September 15, 1914, Boston University Library; John Kemp, *Robert Frost and New England: The Poet as Regionalist* (Princeton, 1979), p. 66; Robert Lowell, "Robert Frost," *Selected Prose,* ed. Robert Giroux (New York, 1987), p. 9.

3. Smythe, *Robert Frost Speaks,* p. 82; *Robert Frost: Farm-Poultryman,* ed. Edward Connery Lathem and Lawrance Thompson (Hanover, N.H., 1963), pp. 36, 67, 56, 95, 62–63.

4. *Farm-Poultryman,* pp. 83, 18.

5. G. Armour Craig, "Robert Frost at Amherst," *Amherst Alumni News,* 16 (1963), 11; Massachusetts Library Association, *Books We Like* (Boston, 1936), pp. 140–142; Robert Frost, "Thoreau's *Walden,*" *Listener,* 52 (August 26, 1954), 319; Robert Frost, "My Favorite Books," *Chicago Sunday Tribune,* November 30, 1958, 4: 28.

6. Wilbert Snow, "The Robert Frost I Knew," *Texas Quarterly,* 11 (1968), 14–15.

7. Sutton, *Newdick's Season of Frost,* p. 304; Charles Lamb, "On an Infant Dying as Soon as Born," in Palgrave, *The Golden Treasury,* p. 269; Letter from Donald Hall to Jeffrey Meyers, August 30, 1994; Interview with Anne Morrison Smyth, Amherst, Mass., November 3, 1994.

8. Hyde Cox, "Robert Frost Notes," p. 8, Dartmouth. For family reading, see Sergeant, *Trial by Existence,* p. 81, and Lesley Frost, "In Aladdin's Lamp Light," *Centennial Essays III,* p. 315.

9. Letter from Lillian LaBatt Frost to Sandra Katz, October 11, 1983; Letter to Martha White, October 21, 1917, Amherst; Lesley Frost, *New Hampshire's Child: The Derry Journals,* ed. Lawrance Thompson and Arnold Grade (Albany, N.Y., 1969), III. 108; Letter to Richard Thornton, June 1933, Dartmouth. Frost wrote a number of poems for his children and his *Stories for Lesley,* edited by Roger Sell, was published in Charlottesville in 1984.

10. Thompson, *Early Years,* p. 308; Quoted in Sergeant, *Trial by Existence,* pp. 78, 80; Mertins, *Life and Talks-Walking,* p. 91; Lesley Frost, "Robert Frost Remembered," *American Way* (American Airlines magazine), 7 (March, 1974), 13; Thompson, "Notes on Frost," p. 907.

11. Francis, *Frost Family's Adventure,* p. 76; Mertins, *Life and Talks-Walking,* p. 88; Hyde Cox, "Notebook on Frost," p. 3, Dartmouth; F. D. Reeve, *Robert Frost in Russia* (Boston, 1963), p. 95.

5. PINKERTON AND PLYMOUTH

1. *Interviews,* p. 12; Mertins, *Life and Talks-Walking,* p. 89; Letter from William Wolcott, January 29, 1906, Dartmouth; "The Tuft of Flowers," *A Boy's Will and North of Boston,* pp. 18–19.

2. Cook, *A Living Voice,* p. 96; Sutton, *Newdick's Season of Frost,* pp. 287–288; *Frost and Bartlett,* p. 20.

3. John Walsh, *Into My Own: The English Years of Robert Frost* (New York, 1988), p. 46; Robert Frost, Introduction to Cox, *Swinger of Birches,* p. 7; Sidney Cox, *Robert Frost, Original "Ordinary Man"* (New York, 1929), p. 10; Frost, Introduction to Cox, *Swinger of Birches,* pp. 7–8.

4. *Frost and Cox,* p. 169; Sutton, *Newdick's Season of Frost,* p. 221; *Frost and Cox,* pp. 285, 173; Letter to Wilson Follett, n. d., Dartmouth.

5. Sergeant, *Trial by Existence,* p. 406; Smythe, *Robert Frost Speaks,* p. 83; Lesley Frost, *New Hampshire's Child,* Foreword to Book IV; Letter to George Whicher, May 10, 1926, Amherst.

6. Robert Frost, "A Literary Dialogue," *Amherst Writing,* 39 (May 1925), 4; "Robert Frost," *Writers at Work,* p. 32; Robert Frost, *Selected Prose,* ed. Hyde Cox and Edward Connery Lathem (New York, 1966), p. 97; T. S. Eliot, "Tradition and the Individual Talent" (1919), *Selected Essays,*

1917–1932 (New York, 1932), p. 4; Cook, *A Living Voice,* pp. 216–217.

7. Bacon, "Dialogue of Poets," p. 323. Frost has been studied by American critics in relation to Emerson, Thoreau and Dickinson in the same way that Hemingway had been misleadingly studied in relation to Stein, Anderson and Pound. In my 1985 biography, I argued that Hemingway's real masters—Tolstoy, Kipling and T. E. Lawrence—belonged in the European tradition. Frost's best critics noted the *contrast* between his work and Emerson's. Reuben Brower, *The Poetry of Robert Frost: Constellations of Intention* (New York, 1963), p. 57, observed that "any close comparison usually brings out points of difference as much as likeness"; and Robert Fitzgerald, "Patter, Distraction, and Poetry," *New Republic,* 121 (August 8, 1949), 18, agreed that "Frost has a harder edge and eye than Emerson, more humor, and more of the fear of God." Frost stressed their main difference by stating that Emerson "didn't give enough credit to evil" (*Interviews,* p. 118).

8. Penelope Niven, *Carl Sandburg: A Biography* (New York, 1991), p. 445; Robert Frost, Introduction to Helen Flanders and Marguerite Olney, *Ballads Migrant in New England* (New York, 1953), pp. xii–xiii.

9. William Wordsworth, Preface to the *Lyrical Ballads* (1802), *The Oxford Authors: William Wordsworth,* ed. Stephen Gill (Oxford, 1984), pp. 596–597; *Interviews,* p. 7; Richard Wilbur, *Conversations,* ed. William Butts (Jackson, Miss., 1990), p. 91; Robert Frost, "A Tribute to Wordsworth," *Cornell Library Journal,* 11 (1970), 86–87.

10. *Robert Frost 100,* ed. Edward Connery Lathem (Boston, 1974), p. 78; Palgrave, *The Golden Treasury,* p. 3; Frost, "Waiting," *A Boy's Will and North of Boston,* p. 11; John Haines, "England," *Recognition of Robert Frost,* ed. Richard Thornton (New York, 1937), p. 90.

11. Stearns Morse, "The Wholeness of Robert Frost," *Virginia Quarterly Review,* 19 (1943), 413; Robert Lowell, "Digressions from Larkin's *Twentieth-Century Verse,*" *Encounter,* 40 (May 1973), 68; Florence Hardy, *The Life of Thomas Hardy* (1930; London, 1962), p. 444.

12. Robert Langbaum, "Hardy, Frost, and the Question of Modernism," *Virginia Quarterly Review,* 58 (1982), 80; David Perkins, "Thomas Hardy," *A History of Modern Poetry: From the 1890s to the High Modernist Mode* (Cambridge, Mass., 1976), pp. 158, 143; Thompson, "Notes on Frost," pp. 670, 1791.

13. Thomas Hardy, *The Return of the Native,* Introduction by Albert Guerard (1878; New York, 1969), p. 198; Samuel Hynes, *The Pattern of Hardy's Poetry* (Chapel Hill, N.C., 1961), p. 114; Randall Jarrell, *Kipling, Auden & Co.* (New York, 1980), p. 141.

14. Thomas Hardy, *Poems: A New Selection,* revised edition, selected, with an introduction and notes, by T. R. M. Creighton (London, 1977), p. 41. D. H. Lawrence, also profoundly influenced by Hardy, describes the

same scene in the opening chapter of *The Rainbow* (1915) when Tom Brangwen first sees his future wife, Lydia Lensky: " 'That's her,' he said involuntarily. As the cart passed by, splashing through the thin mud, she stood back against the bank. Then, as he walked still beside his britching horse, his eyes met hers. He looked quickly away, pressing back his head, a pain of joy running through him. . . . Then she was gone" (Introduction by Jeffrey Meyers, New York: Bantam, 1991, p. 23).

15. James Joyce, "The Dead," *Dubliners* (1914; London, 1962), p. 220; T. S. Eliot, "The Love Song of J. Alfred Prufrock," *Complete Poems and Plays, 1909–1950* (New York, 1958), pp. 6–7.

16. Letter from Anthony Hecht to Jeffrey Meyers, September 15, 1994; *Frost and Bartlett,* p. 52; Whitlock, "Conversation with Frost," p. 5.

17. *Family Letters,* p. 149; Smythe, *Robert Frost Speaks,* p. 80; Letter to Charles Foster, December 1939, Dartmouth.

18. Quoted in the film *Robert Frost at Amherst* (1959), Amherst College Library; Hyde Cox, "Robert Frost Notes," pp. 17–18; Interview with Peter Davison, Boston, Mass., October 30, 1994.

19. Quoted in the film *Robert Frost at Michigan* (1962), Amherst College Library; Henry David Thoreau, *Journals,* ed. Bradford Torrey and Francis Allen (New York, 1962), 6: 100; Crane, *Descriptive Catalogue,* p. 248.

20. Quoted in the film *Frost at Amherst;* Letter to John Hall Wheelock, December 15, 1933, Princeton University Library; Whitlock, "Conversation with Robert Frost," p. 11; Mark Harris, unpublished journal, p. 442.

21. *Family Letters,* p. 267; Letters to Harriet Monroe, March 8, 1916 and July 21, 1920, University of Chicago Library; Walter Pater, "The School of Giorgione," *The Renaissance* (1893; New York, 1959), p. 98; Lascelles Abercrombie, "A New Voice," *Nation* (London), 15 (June 13, 1914), 423; Smythe, *Robert Frost Speaks,* p. 86.

22. Sergeant, *Trial by Existence,* p. 86; *Frost and Bartlett,* pp. 52; 81, 85; *Frost and Cox,* p. 54; Farjeon, *Edward Thomas,* p. 90; *Interviews,* p. 6.

23. "The Fearless Wisdom of Robert Frost," *Vogue,* 141 (March 15, 1963), 118; Horace, "[*Ars Poetica*]," *The Great Critics,* ed. James Smith and Edd Parks, third edition (New York, 1951), p. 117; *Selected Prose,* p. 19.

24. Mertins, *Life and Talks-Walking,* pp. 101–102; Quoted in the film *Voices and Visions* (1988), Amherst College Library; "Frost Disclaims a 'Literary Life,' " *New York Times,* May 19, 1957, p. 87; Thompson, *Early Life,* p. 390.

6. ENGLAND AND EZRA POUND

1. Elinor, in *Letters,* p. 54; Mertins, *Life and Talks-Walking,* pp. 132–133; Francis, *Frost Family's Adventure,* p. 103; Farjeon, *Edward Thomas,* pp. 88–89.

2. Walsh, *Into My Own,* p. 136; Ezra Pound, "Robert Frost (Two Reviews),"
   Literary Essays, edited with an introduction by T. S. Eliot (1935; New
   York, 1968), 382; B. J. Sokol, "The Publication of Robert Frost's First
   Books," *Book Collector,* 26 (1977), 233; Frank Mumby, *Publishing and
   Bookselling: A History from the Earliest Times to the Present Day,* revised
   edition (London, 1954), p. 291. See also "Nutt, Alfred," *Dictionary of
   National Biography: Supplement, 1901–1911,* ed. Sir Sidney Lee (1912;
   Oxford, 1969), pp. 30–31.
3. Stanley Unwin, *The Truth about a Publisher* (London, 1960), p. 127;
   Walsh, *Into My Own,* p. 81; Francis, *Frost Family's Adventure,* p. 182.
4. Sutton, *Newdick's Season of Frost,* p. 264; "Robert Frost," *Writers at Work,* p.
   12; Fletcher, *Life Is My Song,* pp. 76–77; Reeve, *Frost in Russia,* p. 16.

   Through these figures Frost also became acquainted with Gordon
   Bottomley, Padraic and Mary Colum, John Cournos, Hilda Doolittle,
   John Freeman, Maurice Hewlett, Ralph Hodgson, W. H. Hudson, Henry
   James (who left no record of their encounter), John Masefield, Henry
   Newbolt, Arthur Ransome, Ernest Rhys, George Russell ("A. E."), Sieg-
   fried Sassoon, May Sinclair, J. C. Squire, James Stephens and Hugh
   Walpole. Later in life, Frost formed varying degrees of friendship with
   W. H. Auden, Cecil Day Lewis, Edwin Muir and C. P. Snow (all of whom
   wrote about Frost) as well as E. M. Forster, Graham Greene and I. A.
   Richards.
5. Meyers, *D. H. Lawrence,* p. 58; *Letters,* p. 179; D. H. Lawrence, *Letters.
   Volume III: 1916–1921,* ed. James Boulton and Andrew Robertson (Cambridge, England, 1984), 141; D. H. Lawrence, *Studies in Classic American
   Literature* (1923; London, 1924), p. 9; Quoted in Dorothy Hall Judd,
   Robert Frost: Contours of Belief (Athens, Ohio, 1984), p. 6.
6. *Frost and Cox,* pp. 37–38; 34; Robert Graves, "Critical Limitations,"
   Nation and Athenaeum, 35 (July 6, 1924), 542; Robert Graves, "One of
   the Few," *Listener,* 78 (October 5, 1967), 426. See also Laura Riding
   and Robert Graves, *A Survey of Modernist Poetry* (London, 1927), pp.
   176–177; Robert Graves, Introduction to the reissue of Frost's *In the
   Clearing* (London: Holt, 1962), pp. 7–10, expanded version reprinted as
   Introduction to the paperback edition of Frost's *Selected Poems* (New
   York, 1963), pp. ix–xvi; and Robert Graves' obituary of Frost, "The
   Truest Poet," *Sunday Times,* February 3, 1963, p. 26.
7. *Frost and Cox,* p. 30; Mertins, *Life and Talks-Walking,* p. 301; *Frost and
   Bartlett,* p. 44; *Letters to Untermeyer,* pp. 197–198.
8. R. George Thomas, *Edward Thomas: A Portrait* (Oxford, 1985), p. 127;
   Letter to Franklin Folsom, November 10, 1925, Boston University Li-
   brary; *Frost and Bartlett,* p. 76.
9. Christopher Hassall, *Rupert Brooke: A Biography* (London, 1964), p. 449;
   Christopher Hassall, *A Biography of Edward Marsh* (New York, 1959),

p. 285; Letter to Miss McLuesten, Beaconsfield, n. d., Boston University; D. H. Lawrence, *Letters. Volume II: 1913–1916,* ed. George Zytaruk and James Boulton (Cambridge, England, 1987), pp. 119–120; Wilfrid Gibson, "The Golden Room," *The Golden Room and Other Poems* (London, 1928), p. 172.

10. James Reeves, Introduction to *Georgian Poetry* (London, 1962), p. xv; Lawrence, *Letters,* II: 176; T. S. Eliot, "Verse Pleasant and Unpleasant," *Egoist,* 5 (March 1918), 43; Walsh, *Into My Own,* p. 125. For a history and defense of these poets, see Robert Ross, *The Georgian Revolt: Rise and Fall of a Poetic Ideal* (London, 1967) and Myron Simon, *The Georgian Poetic* (Berkeley, 1975).

11. Letter to the Editor of the *Youth's Companion* (Boston), [fall 1912], Boston University; "Procession of the Muses," *Academy,* 85 (September 20, 1913), 360; Norman Douglas, review of *A Boy's Will, English Review,* 14 (June 1913), 505; F. S. Flint, review of *A Boy's Will, Poetry and Drama,* 1 (June 1913), 250.

12. Patricia Hutchins, *Ezra Pound's Kensington* (London, 1965), p. 70; D. H. Lawrence, *Letters. Volume I: 1901–1913,* ed. James Boulton (Cambridge, England, 1979), p. 145; Jeffrey Meyers, *The Enemy: A Biography of Wyndham Lewis* (London, 1978), p. 32.

13. "Robert Frost," *Writers at Work,* p. 13; Mertins, *Life and Talks-Walking,* p. 301; *Oxford Authors: Wordsworth,* p. 601; Ezra Pound, *Selected Letters, 1907–1941,* ed. D. D. Paige (1950; New York, 1971), p. 48; Sergeant, *Trial by Existence,* p. xix.

14. Sergeant, *Trial by Existence,* pp. 103–104; "Robert Frost," *Writers at Work,* p. 19; Robert Francis, *Frost : A Time to Talk* (Amherst, Mass., 1972), p. 31.

15. Pound, *Selected Letters,* p. 14; Richard Ellmann, *James Joyce,* revised edition (New York, 1982), p. 351; Humphrey Carpenter, *A Serious Character: The Life of Ezra Pound* (Boston, 1988), p. 201; Ralph Waldo Emerson, *Journals and Miscellaneous Notebooks,* ed. A. W. Plumstead and Harrison Hayford (Cambridge, Mass., 1969), 7: 374.

16. Letter to Marie Hodge, October 10, 1913, Boston University; Pound, "Robert Frost," pp. 382–383; John Cournos, *Autobiography* (New York, 1935), p. 272; Ezra Pound, "In Metre," *New Freewoman,* 1 (September 1, 1913), 113.

17. *Frost and Bartlett,* p. 45; Letters to Frank Flint, July 6, 1913, July 1914 and June 26, 1913, Humanities Research Center, University of Texas; *Frost and Cox,* p. 60; Thompson, *Early Years,* pp. 421–422.

18. *Frost and Cox,* p. 58; Selden Rodman, "Robert Frost," *Tongues of Fallen Angels* (New York, 1973), pp. 46–47; B. J. Sokol, "What Went Wrong Between Robert Frost and Ezra Pound?," *New England Quarterly,* 49 (1976), 525.

19. Pound, *Letters,* p. 77; T. S. Eliot, *Letters. Volume I: 1898–1922,* ed. Valerie

Eliot (London, 1988), p. 101; Letter to John Gould Fletcher, June 26, 1920, Texas.

7. GLOUCESTERSHIRE AND EDWARD THOMAS

1. Elinor, in *Letters,* pp. 126–127; Letter to Frank Flint, July 1914, Texas; "A Poet's Pilgrimage," *Life,* 43 (September 23, 1957), 110.
2. Lawrence Lipking, *The Life of the Poet* (Chicago, 1981), p. 10; George Nitchie, in *Centennial Essays,* p. 44; W. Jackson Bate, *Coleridge* (Cambridge, Mass., 1968), p. 42; Louis Untermeyer, *Robert Frost: A Backward Look* (Washington, D.C., 1964), p. 37.
3. *Interviews,* p. 112; Ford Madox Hueffer, "Mr. Robert Frost and *North of Boston,*" *Outlook,* 33 (June 27, 1914), 879–880; Richard Aldington, review of *North of Boston, Egoist,* 1 (July 1, 1914), 248; Abercrombie, "A New Voice," p. 424; Pound, "Robert Frost," pp. 384–385.
4. George Thomas, *Edward Thomas,* pp. 26, 102; Andrew Motion, *The Poetry of Edward Thomas* (1980; London, 1991), p. 21; George Thomas, *Edward Thomas,* p. 229.
5. Edward Thomas, "The Mill-Water," *Works* (Ware, Herts., 1994), p. 111; William Cooke, "Elected Friends: Robert Frost and Edward Thomas," *Poetry Wales,* 13 (1978), 22–23; Telephone interview with Myfanwy Thomas, July 20, 1994; *Frost and Cox,* p. 50.
6. Sergeant, *Trial by Existence,* p. 136; Elinor, in *Letters,* p. 126; Edward Thomas, "This England," *The Last Sheaf* (London, 1928), pp. 216–218; Thomas, "The Sun Used to Shine," *Works,* p. 75; *Letters from Edward Thomas to Gordon Bottomley,* ed. R. George Thomas (London, 1968), p. 238.
7. Edward Thomas, "A New Poet," *Daily News and Leader,* July 22, 1914, p. 7; Edward Thomas, "Poetry," *English Review,* 18 (August 1914), 142–143; Edward Thomas, review of *North of Boston, New Weekly,* August 8, 1914, p. 249.
8. Richard Stonesifer, *W. H. Davies: A Critical Biography* (London, 1963), p. 116; For an excellent discussion of Frost's influence on Thomas, see William Cooke, *Edward Thomas: A Critical Biography* (London, 1970), pp. 194–207; Francis, *Frost Family's Adventure,* pp. 155–156; Helen Thomas, *Under Storm's Eye,* p. 311; Francis, *Frost Family's Adventure,* p. 179.
9. Interview with Myfanwy Thomas; *Letters from Thomas to Bottomley,* pp. 244–245, 258; John Moore, *The Life and Letters of Edward Thomas,* (London, 1939), p. 203.
10. Thompson, *Years of Triumph,* p. 89; Thomas, "This England," p. 221; Thomas, "An Old Song," *Works,* p. 158; George Thomas, *Edward Thomas,* pp. 274, 246.

11. George Thomas, *Edward Thomas*, p. 286 (the words in brackets, deleted in the text, come from Thomas' letter, at Dartmouth); B. H. Liddell Hart, *History of the First World War* (1930; London, 1982), pp. 319–320; Helen Thomas, *Under Storm's Eye*, p. 307.

12. Quoted in the film *Voices and Visions;* Farjeon, *Edward Thomas*, p. 141; Interview with Myfanwy Thomas.

8. THE RETURN OF THE NATIVE

1. Padraic Colum, "A Yankee Sage," *Recognition of Frost*, p. 164; Ellery Sedgwick, in *Letters*, p. 176; Thompson, *Years of Triumph*, p. 38.

   Frost also needed but resented Harriet Monroe, who published "The Code" and "Snow" in *Poetry*, and told the young poet Wade Van Dore "how she had tried to rewrite several of his poems, how she reveled in the power of her position, how she flaunted that power over poets" (Wade Van Dore, *Robert Frost and Wade Van Dore: The Life of the Hired Man*, revised and edited by Thomas Wetmore, Dayton, Ohio, 1986, p. 103).

2. Edwin Arlington Robinson, *Selected Letters* (New York, 1940), p. 99; Letter from Andrei Sergeev to Jeffrey Meyers, November 10, 1994, based on conversations with Frost in Russia in 1962; *Selected Prose*, p. 67.

3. Amy Lowell, "*North of Boston*," *New Republic*, 2 (February 20, 1915), 81–82; Amy Lowell, "Robert Frost," *Tendencies in Modern American Poetry* (New York, 1917), pp. 112, 126, 135; Amy Lowell, "A Critical Fable," in *The Shock of Recognition*, ed. Edmund Wilson (Garden City, New York, 1943), pp. 1098–1099.

4. *Letters to Untermeyer*, pp. 106–107; Thompson, "Notes on Frost," p. 50; Edward Garnett, in *Letters*, p. 170; Edward Garnett, "Robert Frost's *North of Boston*," *Friday Nights* (New York, 1922), p. 222; William Dean Howells, "Editor's Easy Chair," *Harper's*, 131 (September 1915), 635.

5. Alfred Harcourt, in *Letters*, p. 133; Mme. Nutt, in *Letters*, p. 134; Charles Madison, *The Owl Among Colophons: Henry Holt as Publisher and Editor* (New York, 1966), p. 168; Alfred Harcourt, *Some Experiences* (Riverside, Conn.: privately printed, 1951), pp. 20, 22.

6. Francis, *Time to Talk*, p. 26; Madison, *Owl Among Colophons*, p. 170; Dorothy Van Doren, Foreword to Mark Van Doren, *Selected Letters*, p. 4.

7. Smythe, *Robert Frost Speaks*, p. 64; W. H. Auden, "Musée des Beaux Arts," *Collected Shorter Poems, 1927–1957* (London, 1966), p. 124; *Letters*, p. 45; William James, *The Will to Believe* (1897; New York, 1956), p. 31; Letter to Walter Prichard Eaton, May 26, 1915, Dartmouth.

   Frost also explored the theme of the "double" in "A Way Out" (in *Seven Arts*, 1917). In this melodrama, an escaped murderer finds and kills his "twin" in a lonely farmhouse, and deceives the police who pursue him by imitating the man whose corpse he has just hidden.

Frost's memorable phrases soon entered the popular imagination. See, for example, Terry Gruber, *Cat High* (New York, 1984), p. 38:

> Two mice converged in a wood
>   and I
> I ate the fatter one,
> and that has made all the difference.

8. *Frost and Bartlett,* p. 100; Mertins, *Life and Talks-Walking,* p. 251; Whitlock, "Conversations with Frost," p. 11; Robert Frost, *Prose Jottings: Selections from His Notebooks and Miscellaneous Manuscripts,* ed. Edward Connery Lathem and Hyde Cox, Introduction by Kathleen Morrison (Lunenberg, Vt., 1982), p. 103.

   For a similar sentiment, see Leonard Woolf, *Beginning Again* (New York, 1964), p. 205, on Virginia Woolf's response to the death, at the age of thirty-four, of her close friend Katherine Mansfield: "One feels —what? A shock of relief?—a rival the less?"

9. Interview with William Jay Smith, San Francisco, January 10, 1995; Rodman, "Robert Frost," p. 45; Cook, *A Living Voice,* p. 241; Brendan Gill, *Here at the New Yorker* (1975; New York, 1976), p. 59; Lawrance Thompson and R. H. Winnick, *Robert Frost: The Later Years, 1938–1963* (New York, 1976), p. 46.

   See Lillian Ross, *Portrait of Hemingway* (New York, 1961), p. 35: "I started out very quiet and I beat Mr. Turgenev. Then I trained hard and I beat Mr. de Maupassant. I've fought two draws with Mr. Stendhal, and I think I had an edge in the last one. But nobody's going to get me in any ring with Mr. Tolstoy unless I'm crazy or I keep getting better."

10. Thompson, *Later Years,* p. 111; John Ciardi, *Selected Letters,* ed. Edward Cifelli (Fayetteville, Ark., 1991), p. 374; Walsh, *Into My Own,* p. 7.

11. George Whicher, "Sage from North of Boston," *Mornings at 8:50* (Northampton, Mass., 1950), p. 35; H. L. Mencken, "The New Poetry Movement," *Prejudices.* First Series (New York, 1919), p. 90; *Interviews,* p. 185; Stanley Kunitz, *A Kind of Order, A Kind of Folly* (New York, 1975), p. 298.

12. Letter to Frank Flint, August 24, 1916, Texas; Holden, "Reminiscences," p. 7; Thompson, *Years of Triumph,* p. 145; Holden, "Reminiscences," p. 12.

   Holden published poems and novels, became managing editor of the *New Yorker* from 1929 to 1932 (when he did a "Profile" of Frost) and was married to the poet Louise Bogan from 1925 until 1932. Edmund Wilson, who had a brief affair with Bogan after that marriage broke up, called Holden an "amiable mediocrity."

13. Interview with Jack Hagstrom, Water Mill, New York, November 5, 1994; Letter from Lawrance Thompson to Kay Morrison, [June] 1957, Vir-

ginia; Edward Cifelli, "Ciardi on Frost: An Interview," *Centennial Essays,*
p. 479.

14. Louis Untermeyer, *Bygones: Recollections* (New York, 1965), pp. 54, 66;
Letter to Jean Starr Untermeyer, June 29, 1955, Dartmouth; Letter from
Lillian LaBatt Frost to Sandra Katz, November 2, 1982; Interview with
Anne Morrison Smyth; *Letters to Untermeyer,* p. 337.

    Frost's other Jewish friends included the printer Joseph Blumen-
thal, the rabbi Victor Reichert, the bookseller Louis Cohn, the collector
Earle Bernheimer and the editor Stanley Burnshaw.

15. *Letters to Untermeyer,* p. 130; Thompson, "Notes on Frost," p. 429; Crane,
Descriptive Catalogue, p. 213; Arthur Miller, *Timebends* (New York, 1987),
pp. 262–263.

9. TEACHING AT AMHERST

1. *Frost and Cox,* p. 53; "A Tape Recorded Interview between Robert Frost
and Jonas Salk," pp. 15, 9, Amherst; " 'To Otto as of Old': The Letters of
Robert Frost to Otto Manthey-Zorn, Part I," ed. Donald Sheehy, *New
England Quarterly,* 67 (September 1994), 372; *Frost and Bartlett,* p. 158;
Irving Yevish, "Robert Frost: Campus Rebel," *Texas Quarterly,* 11 (1968),
51.

2. Quoted in the film *Robert Frost at Michigan* (1962), Amherst College
Library; Robert Frost, Comment on William Meredith's senior thesis,
Connecticut College Library; Thompson, "Notes on Frost," p. 437; Peter
Stanlis, in *Centennial Essays III,* p. 249.

3. *Interviews,* p. 41; *Letters to Untermeyer,* p. 156; Hyde Cox, "Robert Frost
Notes," p. 9; Thompson, *Years of Triumph,* p. 100.

4. Van Doren, *Autobiography,* p. 170; Smythe, *Robert Frost Speaks,* p. 124;
John Ciardi, "Robert Frost," *Dialogue with an Audience* (Philadelphia,
1963), p. 176.

5. Sergeant, *Trial by Existence,* pp. 262; "Interview between Frost and Salk,"
p. 1; Francis, *Time to Talk,* p. 24; Sergeant, *Trial by Existence,* p. 202.

6. Cook, *A Living Voice,* p. 120; *Family Letters,* p. 66; Letter to Mark De
Wolfe Howe, n. d., Harvard.

7. Letter to Lincoln MacVeagh, September 13, 1923, Jones Library, Amherst, Mass.; Craig, "Robert Frost at Amherst," p. 10; Sergeant, *Trial by
Existence,* pp. 321–322.

8. Letter to Hugh [Walpole], [1932], Texas; James Hayford, Preface to
Star in the Shed Window: Collected Poems, 1933–1988 (Shelburne, Vt.,
1989), p. xiii. See also X. J. Kennedy, "The Least Known Major American Poet," *Harvard Review,* 3 (1993), 103–107.

9. Otto Manthey-Zorn, "Notes on Frost," n. p., Amherst; *Frost and Van Dore,*
p. 176; Thompson, *Years of Triumph,* p. 266; Theresa Whistler, *Imagina-*

tion of the Heart: The Life of Walter de la Mare (London, 1993), p. 271.

10. Henry Ladd, "Memories of Frost," *Touchstone* (Amherst), 4 (February 1939), 13; Sergeant, *Trial by Existence*, p. 263; Thompson, "Notes on Frost," p. 355; Letter to Felix Frankfurter, June 28, 1939, Amherst.

11. Douglas Wilson, "The Story in the Meiklejohn Files," *Amherst*, Fall 1982, pp. 10, 12; Letter to the Boston poet Alice Brown, November 2, 1918, Virginia; *Family Letters*, p. 71; Stark Young, *A Life in the Arts: 1900–1962*, ed. John Pilkington, 2 volumes (Baton Rouge, 1975), pp. 1100–1101; Crane, *Descriptive Catalogue*, p. 227.

12. David Bain and Mary Duffy, *Whose Woods These Are: A History of the Bread Loaf Writers' Conference, 1926–1992* (New York, 1993), p. 29 (the title comes from the first line of Frost's "Stopping by Woods on a Snowy Evening"); Dorothy Canfield Fisher, *Keeping the Fires Night and Day: Selected Letters*, ed. Mark Madigan (Columbia, Mo., 1993), p. 91; Clifford Lyons, "Walks and Talks with Robert Frost," *Robert Frost: The Man and the Poet*, ed. Earl Wilcox (Conway, Ark., 1990), p. 62; Henry Dierkes, *Robert Frost: A Friend to a Younger Poet* (Notasulga, Ala., 1984), pp. 68–69.

13. Sutton, *Newdick's Season of Frost*, p. 194; Thompson, "Notes on Frost," p. 11; Katherine Canfield, "A Footnote on Robert Frost," n. p., April 26, 1978, Jones Library; *Letters to Untermeyer*, pp. 62–63; Sutton, *Newdick's Season of Frost*, p. 337.

14. Interview with Frost's granddaughter, Lesley Lee Francis, Washington, D.C., November 12, 1994; Interview with Peter Davison; Holden, "Reminiscences," p. 4; *Family Letters*, p. 18.

15. Sergeant, *Trial by Existence*, pp. 247–248; Letter to Miss M. Doss, April 30, 1923, Amherst; Hart Crane, *Letters, 1916–1932*, ed. Brom Weber (1952; Berkeley, 1965), p. 17.

16. Thompson, "Notes on Frost," p. 433; *Letters to Untermeyer*, p. 103; "A Servant to Servants," *A Boy's Will and North of Boston*, pp. 54–55; *Family Letters*, p. 92; Jeanie Frost, in *Letters*, pp. 318–319, 321–322.

10. MICHIGAN AND THE LECTURE CIRCUIT

1. "A Hundred Collars," *A Boy's Will and North of Boston*, p. 41; *Frost and Bartlett*, p. 128; Cox, *Swinger of Birches*, p. 44; *Frost and Bartlett*, p. 170.

2. Robert Frost, "The Poetry of Amy Lowell," *Christian Science Monitor*, May 16, 1925, p. 8; *Family Letters*, pp. 112, 114; *Letters to Untermeyer*, p. 149.

3. Wilson, "The Story in the Meiklejohn Files," Fall 1982, p. 11 and Spring 1983, p. 65; *Letters to Untermeyer*, p. 167; Thompson, *Years of Triumph*, p. 270.

4. Bernice Stewart, "Michigan," *Recognition of Frost*, pp. 110–111; *Frost and Bartlett*, p. 138; Gordon Haight, "Robert Frost at Yale," *Yale University Library Gazette*, 40 (July 1965), 14.

5. Letter to Miss Lovell, 1924, Boston University; Sutton, *Newdick's Season of Frost,* p. 369; Letter to George Roy Elliott, fall 1924, Amherst; Rolfe Humphries, *Poets, Poetics and Politics,* ed. Richard Gillman and Michael Novak (Lawrence, Kan., 1992), p. 68.

   Frost's response to Millay's work was similar to Bertrand Russell's reaction to Lawrence's frank poems about his marriage, *Look! We Have Come Through!* "They may have come through," Russell remarked, "but I don't see why I should look" (Meyers, *D. H. Lawrence,* p. 112).

6. Thompson, *Years of Triumph,* p. 353; Mertins, *Life and Talks-Walking,* p. 146; *Letters to Untermeyer,* p. 230.

7. Francis, *Time to Talk,* p. 30; *Frost and Bartlett,* p. 163; William Carlos Williams and James Laughlin, *Selected Letters,* ed. Hugh Witemeyer (New York, 1989), p. 40.

8. Edmund Wilson, *Patriotic Gore* (New York, 1962), p. 115; Niven, *Carl Sandburg,* p. 290; Peter Stanlis, in *Centennial Essays III,* p. 243; Interview with Ann Chalmers Watts, New York, November 6, 1994.

9. "Ciardi on Frost," *Centennial Essays,* p. 489; Reeve, *Frost in Russia,* p. 17; *Letters,* p. 277; William Hunter, "An Evening with Robert Frost and Carl Sandburg," *Forum* (University of Houston), 13 (1976), 52; Roy Basler, "Yankee Vergil—Robert Frost in Washington," *Voyages,* 2 (1964), 16–18.

10. Joseph Brodsky, "On Grief and Reason," *New Yorker,* 70 (September 26, 1994), 74. In a similar fashion, Joseph Conrad completed *Lord Jim* after a heroic effort in July 1900: "The end of *Lord Jim* had been pulled off with a steady drag of 21 hours. . . . Dawn broke, brightened. I put the lamp out and went on, with the morning breeze blowing the sheets of MS all over the room. Sun rose. I wrote the last word and . . . shared a piece of cold chicken with [my dog] Escamillo. . . . Felt very well only sleepy" (Jeffrey Meyers, *Joseph Conrad: A Biography,* London, 1991, p. 196).

11. *Interviews,* p. 19; Quoted in the film *Princeton '55: The Enjoyment of Poetry,* Amherst College Library.

    Even as sophisticated a critic as Allen Tate was led by Frost's deceptive ambiguity into thinking that Bones was killed by his own father rather than by the witch's jealous husband. See Tate, "Robert Frost as Metaphysical Poet," *Robert Frost: Lectures on the Centennial of His Birth,* p. 68.

12. Dante Alighieri, *The Divine Comedy: Hell,* trans. Dorothy Sayers (Baltimore, 1968), pp. 271, 274; John Crowe Ransom, "Thoughts on the Poetic Discontent" (1925), *Selected Essays,* ed. Thomas Daniel Young and John Hindle (Baton Rouge, 1976), 32; Hemingway, "Big Two-Hearted River," *Short Stories,* p. 231; Vladimir Nabokov, *Pale Fire* (1962; New York, 1969), p. 145.

13. Kemp, *Frost and New England,* p. 170; Crane, *Descriptive Catalogue,* p. 226; *Family Letters,* p. 204.

14. Thompson, *Years of Triumph,* p. 72; Interview with Richard and Charlee Wilbur; Thompson, *Later Years,* p. 42; Robert Lowell, "Robert Frost," p. 8; Letter to Kay Morrison, Auburn, Alabama, [late 1930s], Dartmouth.

15. Sutton, *Newdick's Season of Frost,* p. 129; Cook, *A Living Voice,* pp. 33; 30; 152; Wilbur, *Conversations,* p. 84; Letter from W. D. Snodgrass to Jeffrey Meyers, September 24, 1994.

16. Thomas Carpenter, "Robert Frost and Katherine Blunt: A Confrontation," *American Notes and Queries,* 8 (1969), 35–36; *Letters,* p. 369; Interview with William Jay Smith; Leslie Fiedler, "Traitor or Laureate: The Two Trials of the Poet," *New Approaches to Ezra Pound,* ed. Eva Hesse (London, 1969), p. 374.

17. W. H. Auden, *Selected Poems,* ed. Edward Mendelson (New York, 1979), p. 248; Paul Mariani, *Lost Puritan: A Life of Robert Lowell* (New York, 1994), p. 367; Sergeant, *Trial by Existence,* p. 315; Letter to Earle Bernheimer, March 1947, Virginia.

18. Interview with Armour Craig, Amherst, Mass., November 2, 1994; Thompson, *Later Years,* p. 26; Interview with Ann Chalmers Watts; *Family Letters,* p. 26. For his visit to Franconia and ideas on Robert Frost's poetry, see Joseph Warren Beach, "Robert Frost," *Yale Review,* 43 (1953), 204–217.

11. ACQUAINTED WITH THE NIGHT

1. *Family Letters,* pp. 121–122, 117; Walter de la Mare, "The Good Grey Poet" [an allusion to Whitman], *Go!* (London), 2 (June–July 1951), 73; Thompson, *Years of Triumph,* p. 336; Snow, "The Robert Frost I Knew," p. 21.

2. Babette Deutsch, "Poets and Poetasters," *Bookman* (New York), 68 (December 1928), 47. See Theodore Roethke (a bear-like poet, who identified with bears), "I Knew a Woman," *Collected Poems* (Garden City, New York, 1975), p. 122: "Or English poets who grew up on Greek / (I'd have them sing in chorus, cheek to cheek)."

3. Letter to Morris Tilley, [December 1926], University of Michigan Library; Percy Bysshe Shelley, "To Jane: The Recollection," *Complete Poetical Works* (Boston, 1901), p. 413; Ford Madox Ford, Introduction to Ernest Hemingway's *A Farewell to Arms* (1932), in Jeffrey Meyers, *Hemingway: The Critical Heritage* (London, 1982), p. 156; Kemp, *Frost and New England,* p. 203.

4. James Southall Wilson, "Robert Frost: American Poet," *Virginia Quarterly Review,* 7 (April 1931), 320; Granville Hicks, "The World of Robert

Frost," *New Republic,* 65 (December, 1930), 77; Geoffrey Grigson, "Still Waters," *Saturday Review* (London), 151 (April 4, 1931), 505.

5. Letters to Joseph Blumenthal, February 18, 1930 and September 9, 1930, Amherst.

6. Smythe, *Robert Frost Speaks,* p. 74; Sergeant, *Trial by Existence,* p. 314; Mertins, *Life and Talks-Walking,* p. 302.

7. Sutton, *Newdick's Season of Frost,* p. 277; Jeffrey Meyers, *Scott Fitzgerald: A Biography* (New York, 1994), p. 226; Thompson, "Notes on Frost," p. 189.

8. Eliot, "The Metaphysical Poets" (1921), *Selected Essays,* p. 248; Eliot, *Letters,* p. 400; T. S. Eliot, "London Letter," *Dial,* 72 (May 1922), 513.

9. Whitlock, "Conversation with Frost," p. 12; Stanlis, in *Centennial Essays III,* p. 198; *Family Letters,* p. 163; Cook, *A Living Voice,* p. 58; *Interviews,* p. 118.

10. Robert Frost, "Perfect Day—A Day of Prowess," *Sports Illustrated,* July 23, 1956, p. 52; Frost, "'To Otto as of Old,'" p. 390; "The Generations of Men," *A Boy's Will and North of Boston,* p. 65; Eliot, "The Love Song of J. Alfred Prufrock," *Collected Poems,* p. 6; T. S. Eliot, *The Waste Land: Facsimile and Transcript,* ed. Valerie Eliot (London 1971), p. 1.

11. Thompson, "Notes on Frost," p. 326; Interview with Lesley Lee Francis; Interview with Robin Fraser Hudnut and David Hudnut, Tiburon, Calif., November 23, 1994; Robert Francis, *Time to Talk,* pp. 16–17.

12. *Family Letters,* pp. 143–144; Letter from Lesley Frost to her parents, c. 1933, Dartmouth; Crane, *Descriptive Catalogue,* p. 218.

13. *Letters to Untermeyer,* p. 178; Letter from Dr. Lawrence Randall of Mayo Clinic to Willard Fraser, May 3, 1934, Dartmouth; Letter to George Whicher, April 29, 1934, Amherst; *Letters to Untermeyer,* pp. 241–242.

14. Elinor, in *Letters,* pp. 379, 412; Robert Frost, in *National Poetry Festival: Held in the Library of Congress, October 22–24, 1962: Proceedings* (Washington, D.C., 1964), p. 243; Matthew Arnold, "Empedocles on Etna," *Poetry and Criticism,* ed. Dwight Culler (Boston, 1961), p. 61.

12. POETS AND BIOGRAPHERS

1. Sergeant, *Trial by Existence,* p. 337; *Frost and Cox,* p. 212; Smythe, *Robert Frost Speaks,* p. 101; Interview with Richard Allen, Berkeley, Calif., April 27, 1995; Richard Allen, "Robert Frost at Exeter," unpublished memoir, courtesy of the author.

2. Thompson, "Notes on Frost," p. 61; Crane, *Descriptive Catalogue,* p. 255; Joan Richardson, *Wallace Stevens: A Biography: The Later Years, 1923–1955* (New York, 1988), p. 169; Peter Brazeau, *Parts of a World: Wallace Stevens Remembered* (San Francisco, 1985), pp. 246, 181; Letter to Wallace Stevens, July 28, 1935, Dartmouth.

3. Thomas Daniel Young, in *Frost: Centennial Essays II,* ed. Jac Tharpe (Jackson, Miss., 1976), pp. 286, 289; Allen Tate, quoted in Jay Hubbell, *Who Are the Major American Writers?* (Durham, N.C., 1972), p. 191; Ransom, "Thoughts on the Poetic Discontent" (1925), *Selected Essays,* pp. 31–32; John Crowe Ransom, "The Poetry of 1900–1950," *Kenyon Review,* 13 (January 1951), 453.

4. Letter to Kay Morrison, April 25, 1941, Dartmouth; Young, in *Centennial Essays II,* p. 288. Thompson's long biography does not even mention Frost's generous friendship with Ransom.

5. D. H. Lawrence, *The Plumed Serpent* (1926; New York, 1955), p. 26; Letter to Witter Bynner, June 29, 1930, Harvard University Library; Witter Bynner, *Selected Letters,* ed. James Kraft (New York, 1981), pp. 80–81.

6. Mertins, *Life and Talks-Walking,* p. 113; Thompson, "Notes on Frost," p. 55; Interview with William Meredith and Richard Harteis, Uncasville, Conn., November 3, 1994.

7. Horatio Colony, *A Book of Leaves* (Boston, 1935), p. 24; Letter to Witter Bynner, March 7, 1939, Harvard; Kraft, Introduction to Bynner's *Selected Letters,* p. lxv.

8. *Letters,* p. 256; Smythe, *Robert Frost Speaks,* p. 129; Mertins, *Life and Talks-Walking,* p. 189; Ziolkowski, *Virgil and the Moderns,* p. 160; Sergeant, *Trial by Existence,* p. 20.

9. Sutton, *Newdick's Season of Frost,* p. 357; Van Wyck Brooks, *Days of the Phoenix* (1957), in *Autobiography* (New York, 1965), p. 460; Crane, *Descriptive Catalogue,* p. 253.

10. Letter to George Whicher, June 20, 1936, Amherst. This volume also includes the previously discussed "A Lone Striker," "A Blue Ribbon at Amesbury," "At Woodward's Gardens," "A Record Stride" and "Iris by Night."

11. Robert Frost, *National Poetry Festival,* pp. 240; 242; Quoted in the film *Two Robert Frost Interviews,* Amherst College Library; Franz Kafka, "The Burrow," *Short Stories,* trans. Willa and Edwin Muir (New York, 1952), p. 256; Letter from Andrei Sergeev to Jeffrey Meyers, November 10, 1994.

12. Lionel Trilling, *The Experience of Literature* (New York, 1967), p. 945; William James, *Pragmatism* (1907; New York, 1963), p. 50; Randall Jarrell, "To the Laodiceans," *Poetry and the Age* (1953; New York, 1955), p. 42.

13. James Dickey, in *Centennial Essays,* p. 59; Granville Hicks, "A Letter to Robert Hillyer" (who had defended Frost in a verse epistle), *New Republic,* 92 (October 20, 1937), 308; Ellen Gilbert, *The House of Holt, 1866–1946: An Editorial History* (Metuchen, N.J., 1993), p. 196.

14. Horace Gregory, "Robert Frost's New Poems," *New Republic*, 87 (June 24, 1936), 214; Granville Hicks, "The World of Robert Frost," *New Republic*, 65 (December 3, 1930), 78; Malcolm Cowley, "The Case Against Mr. Frost," *New Republic*, 111 (September 18, 1944), 345; Morton Zabel, "Poets of Five Decades," *Southern Review*, 2 (1936–37), 171–173.

15. Dudley Fitts, "Robert Frost," *New England Quarterly*, 9 (September 1936), 519–520; R. P. Blackmur, "The Instincts of a Bard," *Nation*, 142 (June 24, 1936), 817–819; Newton Arvin, "A Minor Strain," *Partisan Review*, 3 (June 1936), 27–28.

16. Rolfe Humphries, "A Further Shrinking," *New Masses*, 20 (August 11, 1936), 41–42; Humphries, *Poets, Poetics and Politics*, pp. 179, 181n; James Stephens, "Mr. Frost's New Poems," *Sunday Times* (London), April 4, 1937, p. 9.

17. Sutton, *Newdick's Season of Frost*, pp. 154, 97; 152; 112; Crane, *Descriptive Catalogue*, p. 246.

18. Sutton, *Newdick's Season of Frost*, pp. 230; 165; 250–251.

19. *Frost and Cox*, pp. 204; 262; Letter to Alice Cox, August 21, 1956, Dartmouth.

20. Lawrance Thompson, "Robert Frost Rediscovers Job," *New York Times Book Review*, March 25, 1945, p. 3; Archibald MacLeish, *Reflections* (Amherst, Mass., 1986), p. 240.

21. Thompson, "Notes on Frost," pp. 1614, 532y; 598f; Thompson, Introduction to *Letters*, p. ix; Stanley Burnshaw, *Robert Frost Himself* (New York, 1986), p. 116; Thompson, "Notes on Frost," p. 654e.

22. Reginald Cook, "Robert Frost," *Sixteen Modern American Authors*, ed. Jackson Bryer (Durham, N.C., 1974), p. 358; Pritchard, *Frost: A Literary Life Reconsidered*, p. xii; Leon Edel, *Writing Lives: Principia Biographica* (New York, 1984), pp. 74–75; Lowell, "Robert Frost," p. 207.

23. Though hatred of Frost is Thompson's most egregious fault, it is certainly not his only one. His day-to-day chronology has no principle of selection and, at nearly 2,000 pages, is far too long. He simply puts in *everything* he found (apart from Frost's love affair with Kay Morrison), without interpreting the significance of his massive accumulation of material. He portrays Frost's life as an endless series of trivial facts and meaningless episodes, interspersed with long chunks of vague quotation. The tone, when not malicious, is genteel; the moral judgments tedious; the style ponderous and inert. Thompson misses Frost's constant playfulness and is devoid of humor. He exaggerates Frost's religious beliefs, and has no serious discussion or evaluation of his poetry. Surveying the field in 1988, John Walsh concluded that "Frost biography, despite all that has been written about him, is still in its primitive stages" (*Into My Own*, p. 10).

13. DEATH AND CHAOS

1. *Family Letters,* p. 210. Thompson attributes Lesley's feelings to her father and unconvincingly asserts that Frost, "remembering that his own passionate demands had brought six children, felt that in a sense he had killed her" (*Years of Triumph,* p. 494). But Elinor's "passionate demands" may have been as strong as his own. She may have wanted children as much as he did and took no measures to prevent their conception. Though childbearing probably weakened Elinor, she died thirty-one years after her last child was born.

2. Katherine Canfield, "A Footnote on Robert Frost," Jones Library. Later on, the Derry farm was turned into an automobile scrapyard. When Frost drove by the old house, en route from Hanover to Boston, he would put his hands over his eyes and say: "Tell me when we've passed by" (Interview with Edward Connery Lathem, Hanover, N.H., October 26, 1994). The farm is now preserved as a State Historic Site.

3. *Family Letters,* p. 210; Thompson, *Years of Triumph,* pp. 511–512; Walsh, *Into My Own,* p. 8; Henry James, "The Lesson of the Master," *Stories of Writers and Artists,* ed. F. O. Matthiessen (New York, [1965]), pp. 135, 138; Alfred Kazin, *New York Jew* (New York, 1978), p. 231.

4. Alfred, Lord Tennyson, "The Passing of Arthur," *Poems,* ed. Jerome Buckley (Boston, 1958), p. 469; Letter from Lillian LaBatt Frost to Sandra Katz, October 11, 1983; Lesley Frost, letter to the *New York Times Book Review,* September 27, 1970, VII: 40; Richard Allen, "Robert Frost at Exeter," pp. 19–20; Theodore Morrison, *Bread Loaf Writers' Conference,* p. 67; Thompson, "Notes on Frost," p. 312.

5. Letter to Joseph Blumenthal, December 30, 1937, Amherst; *Family Letters,* p. 226. For Frost's resignation from Amherst, see Mertins, *Life and Talks-Walking,* p. 281, Francis, *Time to Talk,* p. 34, Sutton, *Newdick's Season of Frost,* p. 185, and Thompson, "Notes on Frost," p. xxxii; Kathleen Morrison, *Pictorial Chronicle,* p. 10.

6. Robert Frost, "The Doctrine of Excursions: A Preface," *Bread Loaf Anthology* (Middlebury, Vt., 1939), p. xix; *Letters to Untermeyer,* p. 317n; Peter Davison, "Robert Frost," *One of the Dangerous Trades* (Ann Arbor, 1991), p. 81.

7. Bain and Duffy, *Whose Woods These Are,* pp. 233; 78; Theodore Morrison, *Bread Loaf Writers' Conference,* p. 69; Thompson, *Later Years,* p. 8.

8. Wallace Stegner, *The Uneasy Chair: A Biography of Bernard DeVoto* (Garden City, N.Y., 1974), p. 206–207; MacLeish, *Reflections,* p. 100; Interview with Richard Eberhart, Hanover, N.H., October 25, 1994.

9. Kathleen Morrison, *Pictorial Chronicle,* p. 21; Hyde Cox, "Robert Frost Notes," p. 20, Dartmouth; A. B. Guthrie, *The Blue Hen's Chick: A Life in*

Context (New York, 1965), p. 193; Kathleen Morrison, *Pictorial Chronicle,* p. 38; Letter to Mrs. Lamont, March 2, 1952, Boston University.

14. KAY MORRISON

1. The factual information about Kay's early life comes from the Bryn Mawr College Archives; the details about her family from a telephone conversation with her sister Mary Johnston Colfelt, October 22, 1994 and from an extensive interview with her daughter, Anne Morrison Smyth.

2. Peter Davison, *The Fading Smile: Poets in Boston* (New York, 1994), p. 15; Interview with Peter Davison; *Frost and Van Dore,* p. 275; Telephone interview with Daniel Aaron, October 30, 1994; Interview with Adrienne Rich, Toronto, October 16, 1994.

3. Unsigned obituary of Theodore Morrison, *Daily Hampshire Gazette* (Northampton, Mass.), November 29, 1988, p. 4; Interview with Anne Morrison Smyth; Letters from Ted Morrison to Bernard DeVoto, September 14, 1938 and September 11, 1934, Stanford. Ted published *The Stones of the House* (1953) and three other novels, but none of them are as revealing as his letters.

4. Guthrie, *Blue Hen's Chick,* p. 191; Ciardi, in *Centennial Essays,* p. 474; *Interviews,* p. 183; Thompson, "Notes on Frost," p. 40; Frank Lentricchia, *Robert Frost: Modern Poetics and the Landscapes of Self* (Durham, N.C., 1975), p. 101.

5. Sutton, *Newdick's Season of Frost,* p. 358; Thompson, "Notes on Frost," pp. 12; 187k; 650.

6. Theodore Morrison, "The Agitated Heart," p. 76; Thompson, "Notes on Frost," p. xxxiii.

7. *Frost and Cox,* p. 228 (William Evans misdates this letter "[c. 18 May 1938]"—two months before Frost met Kay that summer. It was actually written *after* their unpleasant trip to Florida in the winter of 1938–1939); Thompson, *Later Years,* pp. 13–14; *Family Letters,* p. 200; *Letters to Untermeyer,* p. 314.

8. Hyde Cox, "Robert Frost Notes," p. 15, Dartmouth; Holden, "Reminiscences of Frost," p. 19, Dartmouth; Mertins, *Life and Talks-Walking,* p. 233.

9. Letter to Kay Morrison, no date, Dartmouth; Donald Sheehy, "Refiguring Love: Robert Frost in Crisis, 1938–1942," *New England Quarterly,* 63 (1990), 193–194; 211; 229; Thompson, "Notes on Frost," p. 674n.

10. *Letters to Untermeyer,* p. 316 (the italicized words were silently omitted

from the published text); *Family Letters,* pp. 203–204; Interview with Stanley Burnshaw, New York, November 6, 1994.

11. *Family Letters,* p. 208; Thompson, "Notes on Frost," p. xxxi; *Frost and Cox,* p. 234; Letter from Kay Morrison to Lawrance Thompson, February 23, 1940, Virginia; Letter from Lawrance Thompson to Kay Morrison, [February 1940], Dartmouth.

12. Kathleen Morrison, *Pictorial Chronicle,* p. 7; Letter from Kay Morrison to Earle Bernheimer, May 26, 1943, Dartmouth; Letter from Richard Wilbur to Jeffrey Meyers, September 15, 1994.

    Apart from Kay's daughter, who was courageously frank, none of the two dozen people I spoke to about her (including her sister) realized that Kay had had an affair with Frost. They were deceived by the Jamesian surface and seemed quite surprised when I told them about it.

13. Thompson, "Notes on Frost," pp. 704, 187n; Theodore Morrison, "The Schism," *Atlantic Monthly,* 164 (September 1939), 386; Thompson, "Notes on Frost," p. xxx; Kay Morrison on Frost, quoted in Burnshaw, *Robert Frost Himself,* p. 173; Thompson, "Notes on Frost," pp. 924–925.

    As the page numbers indicate, Thompson's "Notes" obsessively return, throughout the 2,000 pages, to the fascinating love story of Frost and Kay.

14. Thompson, "Notes on Frost," pp. 689, 606 (Kay includes two photographs of Dragon in her *Pictorial Chronicle,* pp. 28 and 43); Bernard DeVoto, "The Critics and Robert Frost," *Saturday Review of Literature,* 17 (January 1, 1938), 3. F. O. Matthiessen defended Blackmur in a letter of February 5, 1938 to the *Saturday Review of Literature.*

15. Thompson, "Notes on Frost," p. 648; Stegner, *The Uneasy Chair,* p. 209 (Stegner's biography, like Thompson's, does not mention DeVoto's relations with Kay); Interview with Anne Morrison Smyth; Letters from Lawrance Thompson to Kay Morrison [February–March 1940], March 3, 1940 and September 2, 1945, Dartmouth.

16. Quoted in letter from Louis Untermeyer to Lawrance Thompson, June 5, 1964, Virginia; Thompson, "Notes on Frost," p. 647; Thompson, "Frost to Untermeyer," p. 1, in "Notes on Frost."

17. Thompson, "Notes on Frost," p. 572; Interview with Anne Morrison Smyth; Interview with Richard and Charlee Wilbur; Thompson, "Notes on Frost," p. 1498.

18. When I suggested this Jamesian interpretation to Anne Morrison Smyth, she said that she had spent years immersed in his novels, but had never quite understood, until that moment, why she had been so strongly attracted to Henry James.

19. Sylvia Berkman, "Blackberry Wilderness," *Blackberry Wilderness* (Garden City, N.Y., 1959), pp. 135, 130; 136, 130; 131; Thompson, "Notes on

Frost," pp. 652, 587; Thompson, "Frost to Untermeyer," p. 1, in "Notes on Frost"; Interview with Anne Morrison Smyth.

20. Telephone interview with Mary Johnston Colfelt; Kathleen Morrison, *Pictorial Chronicle,* p. 20; Letter from Kay Morrison to Lawrance Thompson, February 10, 1940, Virginia.

21. Letter to Kay Morrison, [August 1954], Dartmouth; Letter from Kay Morrison to Lawrance Thompson, in "Notes on Frost," p. 674; Letter to Earle Bernheimer, March 7, 1944, Virginia; Thompson, "Notes on Frost," p. 687yy.

22. Thompson, "Notes on Frost," p. 1424d; Letter from Kay Morrison to Lawrance Thompson, March 29, 1965, Virginia; *Family Letters,* p. 202; Interview with Stanley Burnshaw.

23. Letter from Donald Hall to Jeffrey Meyers, August 30, 1994; Thompson, "Notes on Frost," p. 674m; Ciardi, *Letters,* p. 413; Interview with Edward Connery Lathem; Interview with Anne Morrison Smyth. After we had finished our long, emotionally charged interview, Anne exclaimed: "I knew this would all come out some day!"

24. *Frost and Van Dore,* p. 164; *Booklist,* 38 (May 15, 1942), 344; Katherine Brégy, "*A Witness Tree,*" *Catholic World,* 155 (August 1942), 626; Letter to Witter Bynner, June 29, 1930, Harvard; James Dickey, in *Centennial Essays,* p. 54; Letter to William Sloane, May 21, 1943, Princeton.

25. Brower, *Poetry of Robert Frost,* p. 184; John Donne, "The Baite," *Poems,* ed. Sir Herbert Grierson (London, 1957), p. 41; Interview with Anne Morrison Smyth.

26. Quoted in the film *Robert Frost at Michigan,* Amherst College Library. For the source of the poem, see Richard Hakluyt, *The Principal Navigations, Voyages, Traffiques and Discoveries,* Introduction by John Masefield (London, 1927), II: 455.

When Thompson accompanied the eighty-three-year-old Frost on a trip in 1957, Kay told him that "if Frost should die in England, I must pounce on his little satchel, because he carried his manuscripts in that, and I would find in them certain poems which should be destroyed pronto" ("Notes on Frost," p. 651). These poems, some of which were inspired by Kay, had to be destroyed because they were obscene. Thompson prints Frost's only limerick, "Preparations Bordering on Copulation" (the last word of the title explains the last word of the second line), which mocks the use of a contraceptive pill to reduce the population:

> Says our Harvard Neo Malthushian
> "We can't keep the poor from futution;
> But by up to date feeding

We can keep them from breeding."
Which seems a licentious conclusion!
(*Later Years,* p. 198)

Another poem contrasts the Immaculate Conception to Zeus-Frost's love of mortal women. God had sex once with the Virgin Mary, but did it only for sacred use. He didn't like "cunts" nearly as much as Zeus ("Notes on Frost," p. 650).

15. HARVARD AND DARTMOUTH

1. John Holmes, in *Recognition of Frost,* pp. 117, 115; Smythe, *Robert Frost Speaks,* p. 92; Letter to Robert Hillyer, August 12, 1938, Virginia.
    Frost was fond of the word "watcher," which he found in Keats' "On First Looking into Chapman's Homer" ("Then felt I like some watcher of the skies") and used it in " 'Out, Out—' " (watcher at his pulse) and in "On Making Certain Anything Has Happened" (watcher of the void).
2. Louise Bogan, "Robert Frost," *A Poet's Alphabet,* ed. Robert Phelps and Ruth Limmer (New York, 1970), p. 167; Mertins, *Life and Talks-Walking,* p. 241.
3. Stegner, *The Uneasy Chair,* pp. 166; 251; DeVoto, in *Letters,* pp. 508–509; Thompson, "Notes on Frost," pp. 415yy; 415z; 627; Thompson, *Later Years,* pp. 165–166.
4. *Family Letters,* p. 232; Letter from Andrei Sergeev to Jeffrey Meyers; Letter to William Sloane, May 21, 1943, Princeton.
5. Mertins, *Life and Talks-Walking,* p. 230; Letter from Lillian LaBatt Frost to Sandra Katz, October 11, 1983; Kathleen Morrison, *Pictorial Chronicle,* pp. 9, 68; Dorothy Tyler, in *Centennial Essays III,* pp. 12–13.
6. Cook, *A Living Voice,* p. 10; Sutton, *Newdick's Season of Frost,* p. 193; *Frost and Van Dore,* pp. 111–112.
7. Letter to Morris Tilley, [1935], University of Michigan Library; *Family Letters,* p. 151 and n1; Snow, "The Robert Frost I Knew," pp. 35–36.
8. Letter from Lillian LaBatt Frost to Sandra Katz, October 11, 1983; Interview with Robin and David Hudnut; Letter to Kay Morrison from São Paulo, [August 1954], Dartmouth.
9. Letter from Kay Morrison to Lawrance Thompson, October 1940, Virginia; Letter from Lillian LaBatt Frost to Sandra Katz, November 2, 1982; Interview with Lillian LaBatt Frost, Ashland, Oregon, August 4, 1995; Thompson, "Notes on Frost," p. 906; *Frost and Van Dore,* p. 111.
10. Untermeyer, in *Letters to Untermeyer,* p. 322; Frost, "Notebook: After England," p. 150; Thompson, "Notes on Frost," p. 907; *Family Letters,* p. 218.

11. Charles Miller, *Auden: An American Friendship* (New York, 1983), p. 90; *Family Letters,* p. 221; Interview with William Jay Smith.

12. Untermeyer, in *Letters to Untermeyer,* p. 328n. See Robert Frost, "Two Unpublished Plays: *In an Art Factory* and *The Guardeen,*" Introduction by Roger Sell, *Massachusetts Review,* 26 (1985), 265–340; Brower, *Poetry of Robert Frost,* p. 212; Holden, "Reminiscences of Frost," p. 32. See Laurence Perrine, "A Set of Notes for Frost's Two Masques," *Resources for American Literary Study,* 7 (1977), 125–133.

13. Mark Schorer, "*A Masque of Reason,*" *Atlantic Monthly,* 175 (March 1945), 133; Robert Lowell, "Current Poetry," *Sewanee Review,* 54 (1946), 151; Jarrell, *Poetry and the Age,* p. 32.

14. Conrad Aiken, "Whole Meaning or Doodle?" *New Republic,* 112 (April 16, 1945), 514; F. W. Dupee, "Frost and Tate," *Nation,* 160 (April 21, 1945), 466; Yvor Winters, "Robert Frost, or the Spiritual Drifter as Poet" (1948), *On Modern Poets* (New York, 1959), pp. 205, 208; Louise Bogan, "Robert Frost," *A Poet's Alphabet,* p. 162.

15. Interview with Peter Davison; Interview with Jack Hagstrom; Archibald MacLeish, "The Men Behind *J.B.,*" *Theatre Arts,* 43 (April 1959), 61–62; Mertins, *Life and Talks-Walking,* p. 385. Frost expressed the same belief to Untermeyer as early as 1918; see *Letters to Untermeyer,* p. 75.

16. Frost, *Poetry and Prose,* p. 369; William Carlos Williams, "The Steeple's Eye," *Poetry,* 72 (April 1948), 41; Rolfe Humphries, "Verse Chronicle," *Nation,* 169 (July 23, 1949), 92; Leslie Fiedler, "Poetry Chronicle," *Partisan Review,* 3(1948), 381.

17. Madison, *Owl Among Colophons,* pp. 181–182. It is worth noting that from *New Hampshire* to *Steeple Bush* Frost used playful variants of proverbs and clichés as titles of his poems: "Good-By and Keep Cold" (warm); "A Peck of Gold" (dirt); "The Lovely Shall Be Choosers" (beggars can't be choosers); "On Taking from the Top to Broaden the Base" (taking from Peter to pay Paul); "Neither Out Far Nor In Deep" (close); "Happiness Makes Up in Height [Depth] for What It Lacks in Length"; (Make) "The Most of It"; "A Serious Step Lightly [Carefully] Taken" and "On Making Certain Anything [Something] Has Happened."

18. For a grammatical explanation (which does not discuss Frost's relation to Kay), see Ward Allen, "Robert Frost's 'Iota Subscript,'" *English Language Notes,* 6 (1969), 285–287; Theodore Morrison, "The Agitated Heart," pp. 78–79; Jarrell, *Kipling, Auden & Co.,* pp. 141–142; Jarrell, *Poetry and the Age,* pp. 27–28; Randall Jarrell, *Letters,* ed. Mary Jarrell (Boston, 1985), p. 482.

19. Winters, "Robert Frost, or the Spiritual Drifter as Poet," pp. 194–199; Earle Bernheimer, in *Letters,* p. 542; Mertins, *Life and Talks-Walking,* p. 293.

See *The Earle Bernheimer Collection of First Editions of American Authors, Featuring a Remarkable Collection of the Writings of Robert Frost* (New York: Parke-Bernet, December 11–12, 1950), pp. 10–65. Cohn sold *Twilight* to Clifton Barrett, who donated it to the University of Virginia Library. Mertins' collection is at the Bancroft Library, University of California, Berkeley.

20. Thompson, "Notes on Frost," p. 415tt; *Family Letters,* p. 232; Letter from Lillian LaBatt Frost to Kay Morrison, May 11, 1946, Dartmouth.

21. Thompson, "Notes on Frost," p. 532xviii; Interview with Robin and David Hudnut (for first two sentences on John Cone); Whitlock, "Conversation with Robert Frost," p. 13; Thompson, *Later Years,* p. 159; Telephone interview with Harold Cone, October 8, 1994.

22. *Letters to Untermeyer,* p. 346; Robert Lowell, "Robert Frost," *Notebook,* revised and expanded edition (New York, 1970), p. 122.

16. AN ABUNDANCE OF HONORS

1. Wilson, "Robert Frost: American Poet," p. 316; Thornton, *Recognition of Frost,* p. viii; Cowley, "The Case Against Mr. Frost," p. 312.

2. *Family Letters,* p. 57; Hyde Cox, "Robert Frost Notes," p. 14, Dartmouth; Interview with Edward Connery Lathem; Thompson, *Later Years,* p. 265.

3. Interview with Richard Eberhart; Untermeyer, *Bygones,* p. 49; Jeffrey Meyers, *Edmund Wilson: A Biography* (Boston, 1995), p. 463.

4. *Congressional Record,* 96: 3 (March 24, 1950), 3997–3998; Thornton Wilder, *Journals, 1939–1961,* ed. Donald Gallup (New Haven, 1985), p. 214; "Amherst Honors Robert Frost," *Alumni News,* April 1954, p. 3; Melville Cane, "Robert Frost: An Intermittent Intimacy," *American Scholar,* 40 (1970–1971), 160.

   Though Frost never fought in a war, by the end of his life he had acquired more medals than the most heroic veteran. For a list of degrees, honors and awards, see *Letters,* pp. 623–624.

5. Philip Larkin, *Required Writing* (London, 1983), p. 55; *Family Letters,* p. 264; Frederick Karl, *William Faulkner: American Writer* (New York, 1989), p. 891; Joseph Blotner, *Faulkner: A Biography* (New York, 1974), pp. 589–590.

6. Letter to Kay Morrison, São Paulo, [August 1954], Dartmouth; Cook, *A Living Voice,* pp. 105, 102–103; *Interviews,* p. 121. For Frost's speech, see Sociedad Paulista de Escritores, *Congresso Internacional de Escritores e Encontros Intelectuales* (São Paulo: Editora Anhembi, 1957), pp. 459–461; for the response to Frost, see George Monteiro, "The Brazilian Academy's Tribute to Frost," *South Carolina Review,* 21 (1988), 3–4.

7. Elizabeth Bishop, *One Art: Letters,* ed. Robert Giroux (New York, 1994), pp. 276; 365; 370; 297; Cook, *A Living Voice,* pp. 103–104. Four years

later, Frost also tried to help education and culture by urging the Mellon Foundation "to endow a permanent chair for outstanding teachers of literature in high school" (*A Living Voice,* p. 117 n5).

8. Wilbur, *Conversations,* p. 182; Humphrey Carpenter, *W. H. Auden: A Biography* (Boston, 1981), p. 425; Cook, *A Living Voice,* p. 255; *Interviews,* p. 202; Smythe, *Robert Frost Speaks,* p. 139; Letter from Andrei Sergeev to Jeffrey Meyers, November 10, 1994.

    Ginsberg, unaware of (but not surprised by) Frost's hostility, had nothing but good will toward the older poet and wrote: "I liked some of his poetry, familiar via my father and Untermeyer's anthologies, since the 1930s" (letter to Jeffrey Meyers, October 12, 1994).

9. Quoted in the film *Frost at Michigan,* Amherst College Library; *Letters,* p. 274. Frost also praised several minor, unthreatening poets who were his friends: Ridgely Torrence, Wilbert Snow, Leonard Bacon, Robert Francis, John Ciardi and John Holmes.

10. Daiches, "The Many Faces of a Poet," p. 5; Interview with William Jay Smith; Letter from Thomas Tanselle, of the Guggenheim Foundation, to Jeffrey Meyers, March 24, 1995.

11. Quoted in *Letters to Untermeyer,* p. 370; Jeffrey Meyers, *Robert Lowell: Interviews and Memoirs* (Ann Arbor, 1988), p. 64. The lines (317–318) from Keats were: "the Naiad 'mid her reeds / Pressed her cold finger closer to her lips."

    Frost's rhetoric lesson was as brilliantly effective as the one Ford gave Pound in Germany in 1911. Pound wrote that when he showed Ford his early book *Canzoni* (which he had rejected by the time he met Frost), Ford "felt the errors . . . to the point of rolling (physically, and if you look at it as mere superficial snob, ridiculously) on the floor of his temporary quarters in Giessen, when my third volume displayed me trapped . . . [in] the stilted language that then passed for 'good English.'. . . And that roll saved me at least two years, perhaps more" (*Pound/Ford: The Story of a Literary Friendship,* ed. Brita Lindberg-Seyersted, New York, 1982, p. 172).

12. Mariani, *Lost Puritan: A Life of Robert Lowell,* p. 152; Interview with Peter Davison; Davison, *Fading Smile,* p. 274; Letter to Robert Lowell, [c. 1959], Harvard.

13. Lowell, "Robert Frost," p. 207; Mariani, *Lost Puritan,* p. 313; Meyers, *Lowell: Interviews and Memoirs,* pp. 72, 158, 146.

14. *Interviews,* p. 197; Letter to Harold Howland, [early 1957], Dartmouth (Voltaire actually died *after* completing the journey from Ferney to Paris to attend the first performance of his tragedy *Irène*); Letter to Charles Cole, April 25, 1947, Dartmouth.

15. Letters to Kay Morrison, May 1957, Dartmouth; Telephone interview with Geoffrey Moore, December 22, 1994; Letter from Geoffrey Moore

to Jeffrey Meyers, March 21, 1995; Letter from Nevill Coghill to Sir Douglas Veale, February 25, 1957, Oxford University Archives; Letter from Simon Bailey, Oxford University Archivist, to Jeffrey Meyers, October 11, 1994; Translation of the Oxford Latin oration, Oxford University Archives.

16. Thompson, *Later Years*, p. 225; Cambridge University Archives, translation by Barbara Hill; Edwin Muir, *Selected Letters*, ed. Peter Butter (London, 1974), pp. 179–180. See Cecil Day Lewis, "Sheepdog Trials in Hyde Park" (dedicated to Frost), from *The Gate* (1962), in *Complete Poems* (London, 1992), pp. 542–543.

17. W. H. Auden, "A Letter of Introduction" to Geoffrey Handley Taylor and Timothy D'Arch Smith, *C. Day Lewis: A Bibliography* (London, 1968), p. vi; Carpenter, *W. H. Auden*, p. 34; Auden, "Their Lonely Betters," *Collected Shorter Poems*, p. 280; W. H. Auden, "Robert Frost," *The Dyer's Hand* (1962; New York, 1968), p. 343.

18. Letter to Lawrance Thompson, May 9, 1952, Virginia; Robert Frost, *National Poetry Festival*, p. 258; Letter from Sir Isaiah Berlin to Jeffrey Meyers, September 28, 1994; Thompson, *Later Years*, pp. 152–153; *Letters*, p. 567.

19. Robert Frost, "Notes," England, May 1957, Dartmouth; Letter to Kay Morrison, May 23, 1957, Dartmouth. (Frost wanted Kay to know that though he was twenty-four years older than her, Eliot was thirty-eight years older than his former secretary); Interview with Edward Connery Lathem; Thompson, *Later Years*, p. 244; Letter from Andrei Sergeev to Jeffrey Meyers.

20. Thompson, "Notes on Frost," p. 598; Interview with Denis Donoghue, New York, November 6, 1994 (Donoghue has now changed his opinion of Frost); National University of Ireland Archives.

21. *Letters*, p. 565; Thompson, *Later Years*, p. 237 (Longfellow died and was buried in Cambridge, Mass., and was honored with a bust in Poets' Corner); Letter from John Masefield to Frost, May 16, 1957, Dartmouth; Mertins, *Life and Talks-Walking*, p. 345.

17. POUND AND THE TERRIFYING FROST

1. Carpenter, *A Serious Character: Pound*, p. 201; Ezra Pound, *Profile: An Anthology* (Milan, 1932), p. 46; Letter to Albert Bobrowsky, December 14, 1932, Amherst.

2. Letter from Ezra Pound to Frost, April 10, [1936], Dartmouth; Barry, *Frost on Writing*, p. 39; *Interviews*, p. 183.

3. E. Fuller Torrey, *The Roots of Treason: Ezra Pound and the Secrets of St. Elizabeths* (London, 1984), p. 200; Hugh Kenner, *The Pound Era* (Lon-

don, 1972), p. 535; Rodman, "Robert Frost," p. 48; Untermeyer, in *Letters to Untermeyer*, p. 373.

4. Letter from T. S. Eliot to Robert Frost, July 8, 1957, Dartmouth; Ernest Hemingway, quoted in appendix to Frost's statement to the U. S. District Court for the District of Columbia, April 13, 1958; Hemingway, *Letters*, pp. 878–879.

5. I. A. Richards, *Selected Letters*, ed. John Constable (Oxford, 1990), p. 146; Sherman Adams, *Firsthand Report: The Story of the Eisenhower Administration* (New York, 1961), p. 428; *Interviews*, p. 181; Dwight Eisenhower, *At Ease: Stories I Tell to Friends* (Garden City, New York, 1967), p. 168. Frost's line comes from "The Strong Are Saying Nothing" in *A Further Range*.

6. Scott Donaldson, *Archibald MacLeish: An American Life* (Boston, 1992), p. 447; "Robert Frost," *Writers at Work*, p. 21; Thurman Arnold, *Fair Fights and Foul* (New York, 1965), pp. 240–241; 238–239.

   Frost's legal statement was supported by comments from John Dos Passos, Van Wyck Brooks, Marianne Moore, Hemingway, Sandburg, Auden, Eliot, MacLeish, Robert Fitzgerald, Allen Tate, Dag Hammarskjöld and Richard Rovere. See Julian Cornell, *The Trial of Ezra Pound* (London, 1966), pp. 131–134.

7. Donaldson, *Archibald MacLeish*, p. 449; Archibald MacLeish, *Letters, 1907–1982*, ed. R. H. Winnick (Boston, 1983), p. 411; Harry Meacham, *The Caged Panther: Ezra Pound at St. Elizabeths* (New York, 1967), p. 132.

8. Hemingway, *Short Stories*, p. 207; Peter Stanlis, in *Centennial Essays III*, p. 264; Frost, quoted in "Authors and Critics Appraise [Hemingway's] Works," *New York Times*, July 3, 1961, p. 6; Mark Harris, unpublished journal, p. 444.

9. Basler, "Yankee Vergil," p. 22; Lionel Trilling, "A Speech on Robert Frost: A Cultural Episode," *Partisan Review*, 26 (1959), 449–452; Jarrell, *Poetry and the Age*, pp. 27–28, 46.

10. Lewis Nichols, "In and Out of Books," *New York Times Book Review*, April 12, 1959, p. 8; "Robert Frost," *Writers at Work*, pp. 26–27; J. Donald Adams, "Speaking of Books," *New York Times Book Review*, April 12, 1959, p. 2; Letters to the *New York Times Book Review*, May 3, 1959, p. 24.

11. Letter from Diana Trilling to Jeffrey Meyers, October 14, 1994; Lathem, ed., *Robert Frost 100*, p. 92; *Letters*, p. 583; Meyers, *Edmund Wilson*, p. 453.

18. KENNEDY AND ISRAEL

1. Mark Harris, unpublished journal, p. 444; Letter from Andrei Sergeev to Jeffrey Meyers; *Interviews*, pp. 197–198; Quoted in the film *Frost at Michigan*, Amherst College Library.

2. Harris, unpublished journal, p. 442; Thompson, *Later Years,* p. 277; Arthur Schlesinger, Jr., *A Thousand Days: John F. Kennedy in the White House* (Boston, 1965), p. 3; Harris, unpublished journal, p. 443; Rudyard Kipling, "M.I.," *Verse.* Definitive edition (Garden City, New York, 1940), p. 461.

3. Yeats, "The Man and the Echo," *Collected Poems,* p. 337; Auden, "In Memory of W. B. Yeats," *Collected Shorter Poems,* p. 142; Stewart Udall, "Robert Frost, Kennedy, and Khrushchev," *Shenandoah,* 26 (1975), 55; *Poetry and Prose,* p. 411; Joel Roache, *Richard Eberhart: The Progress of an American Poet* (New York, 1971), p. 217.

4. Thompson, "Notes on Frost," p. 687mmm; Samuel Margoshes, "An Hour with Robert Frost," *Jewish Day and Morning Journal* (New York), March 1961; Thompson, *Later Years,* p. 286; Rinna Samuel, "Robert Frost in Israel," *New York Times Book Review,* April 23, 1961, pp. 42–43.

5. Thompson, "Notes on Frost," p. 687ggg; Letter from H. M. Daleski to Jeffrey Meyers, November 27, 1994. For Frost in Israel, see "Robert Frost at the University," *Scopus: Hebrew University of Jerusalem,* 15 (May 1961), 19 and Harold Howland, "Visit to the Land of the Bible," *Foreign Service Journal,* July 1961, pp. 24–25.

6. Interview with Armour Craig. For Frost in Greece, see M. Munro, "U. S. Nationalist Sounds Off, Covers Waterfront," *Athens News,* March 22, 1961; Fr. Germanos, "Robert Frost—Sa Foi et Ses Idées, *Messager d'Athens,* March 23, 1961; and John Mavrogenis, "Meet Robert Frost," *Athens College Bulletin,* November 1961, pp. 18–20.

7. Louise Bogan, *What the Woman Lived: Selected Letters, 1920–1970,* ed. Ruth Limmer (New York, 1973), pp. 341–342; Thompson, "Notes on Frost," pp. 808–809. For two of the speeches, see Adlai Stevenson, "Robert Frost at Eighty-Eight," *New Republic,* 146 (April 9, 1962), 20–22 and Felix Frankfurter, "Robert Frost, 1962," *Of Law and Life: Papers and Addresses,* ed. Philip Kirkland (Cambridge, Mass., 1965), pp. 232–234.

8. Bogan, *What the Woman Lived,* pp. 349, 342; Thompson, "Notes on Frost," p. 674l; Letter to Hyde Cox, October 20, 1955, Dartmouth; Telephone interview with Myfanwy Thomas.

9. Interview with Robin and David Hudnut; Quoted in *Letters to Untermeyer,* pp. 372–373.

10. *Frost and Bartlett,* p. 167; W. W. Robson, "The Achievement of Robert Frost," *Southern Review,* 2 (1966), 750.

   We have already discussed, from this volume, "Auspex," "Kitty Hawk" (Part I), "Forgive, O Lord," "One More Brevity" and "For John F. Kennedy His Inauguration."

11. Whitlock, "Conversation with Frost," p. 2. For the source in Burton

(London, 1903), 2: 322, see Sister Mary Finnegan, *Centennial Essays*, pp. 389–397.

12. John Ciardi, "Robert Frost: Master Conversationalist at Work," *Saturday Review*, 42 (March 21, 1959), 17; "Frost: 'Courage is the Virtue That Counts Most,'" *Newsweek*, 61 (February 11, 1963), 90.

19. FROST AT MIDNIGHT

1. Cowley, "The Case Against Mr. Frost," p. 345; Stewart Udall, "Robert Frost's Last Adventure," *New York Times Magazine*, June 11, 1972, pp. 11; 10–11 (the page numbers refer to the "Compact Edition").

2. Interview with Anne Morrison Smyth; *Letters*, p. 590; Letter from Frederick Adams to Jeffrey Meyers, November 18, 1994.

3. Interview with Edward Connery Lathem; Reeve, *Robert Frost in Russia*, pp. 14, 78; Thompson, *Later Years*, p. 309.

4. Frederick Adams, *To Russia with Frost* (Boston: Club of Odd Volumes, 1963), pp. 23, 21; "Conquest of Space Bores Robert Frost," *Denver Post*, April 22, 1959, p. 6; Reeve, *Robert Frost in Russia*, p. 55; Letter from Andrei Sergeev to Jeffrey Meyers.

5. Reeve, *Robert Frost in Russia*, p. 59; Letter from Joseph Brodsky to Jeffrey Meyers, February 11, 1995 (according to reference books, Brodsky was jailed, after Frost's visit, during 1964–65); Reeve, *Robert Frost in Russia*, pp. 60–61.

6. Letter from Andrei Sergeev to Jeffrey Meyers; Robert Frost, *National Poetry Festival*, p. 239; Jerome Irving, "A Parting Visit with Robert Frost," *Hudson Review*, 16 (1963), 58; Letter from Andrei Sergeev to Jeffrey Meyers; Roberta Reeder, *Anna Akhmatova: Poet and Prophet* (New York, 1994), pp. 374–375.

7. Igor Popov, "The Last Toast of Robert Frost," *Soviet Literature*, 7 (1984), 137; Valentin Kotkin, "Robert Frost in the Soviet Union," *USSR*, 1: 76 (1963), 52; Alexei Surkov, "A Poet's Youthful Heart," *Pravda*, September 10, 1962, p. 4; Mikhail Khitrov, "Interview with 'The Blue-Eyed Rock,'" *Izvestia*, September 3, 1962.

   See also M. Tugushcva, *Literaturnaia Gazeta*, September 1, 1962; A. Sharimov, "Arrival of Robert Frost," *Leningradskaya Pravda*, September 4, 1962; "Robert Frost's Press Conference," *Pravda*, September 9, 1962; Alexei Surkov, "Robert Frost's Visit to the Soviet Union," *Soviet Review*, 3 (1962), 59–61; A. D. Siniavskii, "Come Walk with Us," *For Freedom of Imagination*, trans. L. Tikos and M. Peppard (New York, 1971), pp. 63–71.

8. Udall, "Robert Frost's Last Adventure," p. 23; Letter from Richard Zeisler to Newton McKeon of Amherst College, August 21, 1969, Am-

herst; Reeve, *Robert Frost in Russia,* pp. 110; 113; 115; W. J. McCarthy, in the *Boston Herald,* January 23, 1963; Irving, "A Parting Visit with Robert Frost," p. 59.

9. Yeats, "On Being Asked for a War Poem," *Collected Poems,* p. 153; *Family Letters,* p. 269; Seymour Topping, "Frost Gives Picture of Soviet Premier as Big and Unafraid," *New York Times,* September 8, 1962, p. 1; David Miller, *New York Herald Tribune,* September 9, 1962.

10. Letter from Frederick Adams to Jeffrey Meyers; Letter from Stewart Udall to Jeffrey Meyers, November 30, 1994; Thompson, *Years of Triumph,* p. 330; Letter from Udall to Meyers; Letter from F. D. Reeve to Frost, October 3, 1962, Dartmouth.

11. Robert Frost, *National Poetry Festival,* p. 242; Letter from W. D. Snodgrass to Jeffrey Meyers, September 24, 1994; Stewart Udall, *The Myths of August: A Personal Exploration of Our Tragic Cold War Affair with the Atom* (New York, 1994), pp. 12–13.

12. Peter Stanlis, in *Centennial Essays III,* p. 294; Quoted in *Letters to Untermeyer,* p. 372; Thompson, "Notes on Frost," p. 756; MacLeish, *Reflections,* p. 190.

13. Thompson, *Later Years,* p. 298; *Interviews,* pp. 272, 278; Morrison, *Pictorial Chronicle,* p. 123; Interview with Anne Morrison Smyth.

14. Interview with Richard and Charlee Wilbur; Udall, "Robert Frost's Last Adventure," p. 25; Valentin Kataev, *The Holy Well,* trans. Max Hayward and Harold Shukman (New York, 1967), pp. 153–155; Telephone interview with Elena Levin, October 30, 1994.

15. *Interviews,* p. 295; *Letters,* p. 596; Letter from Anne Morrison to Frost's Russian translator Frida Lurie, February 26, 1963, Dartmouth; Thompson, "Notes on Frost," p. 875.

16. Discharge Summary, Peter Bent Brigham Hospital, Dartmouth; Interview with Anne Morrison Smyth; Telegram from Nikita Khrushchev to Lesley Frost, January 29, 1963, Dartmouth.

17. The service was attended by Lesley and her family, Willard Fraser and his family, Prescott Frost, Frost's niece Vera Harvey and the Frosts from Kittery, Maine, as well as by the Morrisons, Untermeyer, Thompson, Alfred Edwards of Holt, I. A. Richards and David McCord of Harvard, John Dickey of Dartmouth, Frost's lawyer Erastus Hewitt and Hyde Cox. Irma remained in confinement and her sons, John and Harold Cone, were not present at the service nor mentioned in the will. Frost's ashes were buried in the family plot next to the First Congregational Church in Old Bennington, Vermont.

18. Will of Robert Frost, May 5, 1951, Bancroft Library, University of California, Berkeley; Thompson, "Notes on Frost," p. 940. Thompson's figures were:

Manuscripts	$100,000
Pencil Pines, Florida	40,000
Ripton farm	30,000
Holt Stock	27,000
books	1,000
	$198,000

19. The minor "Sons of Bob," whose birth dates ranged from 1884 to 1926, included: Wilbert Snow, Leonard Bacon, R. P. T. Coffin, Raymond Holden, Robert Hillyer, Merrill Root, David McCord, Vrest Orton, Wade Van Dore, Joseph March, Robert Francis, Merrill Moore, Daniel Smythe, Henry Dierkes, Kimball Flaccus, James Hayford, Charles Foster, John Ciardi and John Holmes. Many of these poets dedicated books to Frost and wrote poems about him.

    His "Incalculable" Influence on Others: Essays on Robert Frost in Our Time, ed. Earl Wilcox (Victoria, B.C., 1994), offers a very tentative discussion of Frost's influence on Mark Van Doren, Randall Jarrell, William Jay Smith, James Wright, Galway Kinnell and Wendell Berry. The *Beloit Poetry Journal Chapbook Number Five* (Summer 1957), 1–48, includes some fine poems on Frost by Witter Bynner, Babette Deutsch, James Dickey, Richard Eberhart, Galway Kinnell, Howard Nemerov, Adrienne Rich, Carl Sandburg and William Carlos Williams.

20. Robert Graves, Introduction to *Selected Poems of Robert Frost* (New York, 1963), p. ix; Robert Graves, "Instructions to the Orphic Adept," *Collected Poems* (Garden City, New York, 1961), p. 255; "The Old Masters," *Times Literary Supplement,* December 21, 1962, p. 987; Letter from Sir Stephen Spender to Jeffrey Meyers, September 16, 1994.

21. Hayford, Preface to *Star in the Shed Window* p. xiv; Ian Hamilton, *Robert Lowell: A Biography* (New York, 1982), p. 336; John Haffenden, *The Life of John Berryman* (London, 1982), p. 319.

22. John Berryman, "Lines for Mr. Frost," *Delusions* (New York, 1972), p. 39; John Berryman, "Three around the Old Gentleman," *Dream Songs* (1974; New York, 1982), pp. 41–43 (the Morrisons are mentioned in the second Dream Song); Letter from John Berryman, April 25, 1958, Dartmouth.

23. Gregory Fitzgerald and Paul Ferguson, "The Frost Tradition: An Interview with William Meredith," *Southwest Review,* 57 (1972), 114–115. See Meredith's "In Memory of Robert Frost," *Earth Walk* (New York, 1970), pp. 18–19; Letter from Richard Wilbur to Jeffrey Meyers, September 15, 1994; Robert Fitzgerald, "Patter, Distraction, and Poetry," p. 19. See Wilbur's "The Death of a Toad," *Poems* (New York, 1963), p. 152, and "Seed Leaves," *Walking to Sleep* (New York, 1969), pp. 16–18.

24. Pamela Davis, "Teacher-Poets: Robert Frost's Influence on Theodore Roethke," *His "Incalculable" Influence*, p. 40; *A Boy's Will and North of Boston*, p. 13, and Roethke, "The Swan," *Collected Poems*, p. 135; Frost, "To Earthward," *Poetry*, p. 227, and Roethke, "My Papa's Waltz," *Collected Poems*, p. 43; Davis, "Teacher-Poets," p. 44; Frost, "The Oven Bird," *The Road Not Taken*, p. 14, and Roethke, "The Voice," *Collected Poems*, p. 123.

25. Robert Buttel, *Seamus Heaney* (Lewisburg, Pa., 1975), pp. 29, 57; Seamus Heaney, "Above the Brim: On Robert Frost," *Salmagundi*, 88–89 (1990–1991), 275, 278; John Haffenden, *Poets in Conversation* (London, 1981), pp. 70–71.

26. See M. J. Akbar, *Nehru: The Making of India* (New York, 1988), pp. 563–564; Udall, "Robert Frost's Last Adventure," p. 25; John F. Kennedy, "Poetry and Power," *Atlantic Monthly*, 213 (February 1964), 53–54.

Bibliography

I. WORKS BY FROST

The Poetry of Robert Frost. Ed. Edward Connery Lathem. New York, 1969.

Letters of Robert Frost to Louis Untermeyer. Ed. Louis Untermeyer. New York, 1963.

Selected Letters. Ed. Lawrance Thompson. New York, 1964.

Family Letters. Ed. Arnold Grade. Foreword by Lesley Frost. Albany, N.Y., 1972.

Robert Frost and Sidney Cox: Forty Years of Friendship. Ed. William Evans. Foreword by James Cox. Hanover, N.H., 1981.

Robert Frost: Farm-Poultryman. Ed. Edward Connery Lathem and Lawrance Thompson. Hanover, N.H., 1963.

Selected Prose. Ed. Hyde Cox and Edward Connery Lathem. New York, 1972.

Poetry and Prose. Ed. Edward Connery Lathem and Lawrance Thompson. New York, 1972.

Early Frost: The First Three Books. Ed. Jeffrey Meyers. Hopewell, N. J.: Ecco Press, 1996.

II. TALKS

Richard Poirier. "Robert Frost" (1960). *Writers at Work: The "Paris Review" Interviews.* Second Series. Introduction by Van Wyck Brooks. New York, 1963. Pp. 7–34.

Daniel Smythe. *Robert Frost Speaks.* New York, 1964.

Louis Mertins. *Robert Frost: Life and Talks-Walking.* Norman, Okla., 1965.

Interviews. Ed. Edward Connery Lathem. New York, 1966.

Robert Francis. *Frost: A Time to Talk.* Amherst, Mass., 1972.

Reginald Cook. *Robert Frost: A Living Voice.* Amherst, Mass., 1974.

William Sutton, ed. *Newdick's Season of Frost: An Interrupted Biography of Robert Frost.* Albany, N.Y., 1976.

III. BIOGRAPHY

Sidney Cox. *A Swinger of Birches: A Portrait of Robert Frost.* Introduction by
Robert Frost. 1957; New York, 1961.

Elizabeth Shepley Sergeant. *Robert Frost: The Trial by Existence.* New York,
1960.

Margaret Bartlett Anderson. *Robert Frost and John Bartlett: The Record of a
Friendship.* New York, 1963.

F. D. Reeve. *Robert Frost in Russia.* Boston, 1964.

Lawrance Thompson. *Robert Frost: The Early Years, 1874–1915.* New York,
1966.

———. *Robert Frost: The Years of Triumph, 1915–1938.* New York, 1970.

——— and R. H. Winnick. *Robert Frost: The Later Years, 1938–1963.* New
York, 1976.

Kathleen Morrison. *Robert Frost: A Pictorial Chronicle.* New York, 1974.

Stanley Burnshaw. *Robert Frost Himself.* New York, 1986.

Wade Van Dore. *Robert Frost and Wade Van Dore: The Life of a Hired Man.*
Revised and edited by Thomas Wetmore. Dayton, Ohio, 1987.

John Walsh. *Into My Own: The English Years of Robert Frost.* New York, 1988.

Lesley Lee Francis. *The Frost Family's Adventure in Poetry.* Columbia, Mo.,
1994.

IV. CRITICISM

Richard Thornton, ed. *Recognition of Robert Frost.* New York, 1937.

Randall Jarrell. "The Other Frost" and "To the Laodiceans." *Poetry and the
Age.* 1953; New York, 1955. Pp. 26–62.

John Lynen. *The Pastoral Art of Robert Frost.* New Haven, 1960.

Reuben Brower. *The Poetry of Robert Frost: Constellations of Intention.* 1963; New
York, 1968.

Theodore Morrison. "The Agitated Heart." *Atlantic Monthly,* 220 (July
1967), 72–79.

Jac Tharpe, ed. *Frost: Centennial Essays.* Jackson, Miss., 1974.

———. *Frost: Centennial Essays II.* Jackson, Miss., 1976.

———. *Frost: Centennial Essays III.* Jackson, Miss., 1978.

Frank Lentricchia. *Robert Frost: Modern Poetics and the Landscapes of Self.*
Durham, N.C., 1975.

Richard Poirier. *Robert Frost: The Work of Knowing.* New York, 1977.

John Kemp. *Robert Frost and New England: The Poet as Regionalist.* Princeton,
1979.

William Pritchard. *Frost: A Literary Life Reconsidered.* New York, 1984.

Seamus Heaney. "Above the Brim: On Robert Frost." *Salmagundi,* 88–89
(1990–1991), 275–294.

Index

compiled by Valerie Meyers